797,885 Books
are available to read at

Forgotten Books

www.ForgottenBooks.com

Forgotten Books' App
Available for mobile, tablet & eReader

ISBN 978-1-330-33738-7
PIBN 10032165

This book is a reproduction of an important historical work. Forgotten Books uses state-of-the-art technology to digitally reconstruct the work, preserving the original format whilst repairing imperfections present in the aged copy. In rare cases, an imperfection in the original, such as a blemish or missing page, may be replicated in our edition. We do, however, repair the vast majority of imperfections successfully; any imperfections that remain are intentionally left to preserve the state of such historical works.

Forgotten Books is a registered trademark of FB &c Ltd.
Copyright © 2015 FB &c Ltd.
FB &c Ltd, Dalton House, 60 Windsor Avenue, London, SW19 2RR.
Company number 08720141. Registered in England and Wales.

For support please visit www.forgottenbooks.com

1 MONTH OF FREE READING

at

www.ForgottenBooks.com

By purchasing this book you are eligible for one month membership to ForgottenBooks.com, giving you unlimited access to our entire collection of over 700,000 titles via our web site and mobile apps.

To claim your free month visit: www.forgottenbooks.com/free32165

* Offer is valid for 45 days from date of purchase. Terms and conditions apply.

English
Français
Deutsche
Italiano
Español
Português

www.forgottenbooks.com

Mythology Photography **Fiction** Fishing Christianity **Art** Cooking Essays Buddhism Freemasonry Medicine **Biology** Music **Ancient Egypt** Evolution Carpentry Physics Dance Geology **Mathematics** Fitness Shakespeare **Folklore** Yoga Marketing **Confidence** Immortality Biographies Poetry **Psychology** Witchcraft Electronics Chemistry History **Law** Accounting **Philosophy** Anthropology Alchemy Drama Quantum Mechanics Atheism Sexual Health **Ancient History Entrepreneurship** Languages Sport Paleontology Needlework Islam **Metaphysics** Investment Archaeology Parenting Statistics Criminology **Motivational**

THE
RUSSIAN TURMOIL

Memoirs : Military, Social, and Political

. BY .

General A. I. Denikin

WITH 27 ILLUSTRATIONS, DIAGRAMS AND MAPS

LONDON: HUTCHINSON & CO.
PATERNOSTER ROW

CONTENTS

	PAGE
FOREWORD	11

CHAPTER I.
THE FOUNDATIONS OF THE OLD POWER: FAITH, THE CZAR, AND THE MOTHER COUNTRY — 13

CHAPTER II.
THE ARMY — 23

CHAPTER III.
THE OLD ARMY AND THE EMPEROR — 33

CHAPTER IV.
THE REVOLUTION IN PETROGRAD — 40

CHAPTER V.
THE REVOLUTION AND THE IMPERIAL FAMILY — 48

CHAPTER VI.
THE REVOLUTION AND THE ARMY — 57

CHAPTER VII.
IMPRESSIONS OF PETROGRAD AT THE END OF MARCH, 1917 — 66

CHAPTER VIII.
THE STAVKA: ITS RÔLE AND POSITION — 72

CHAPTER IX.
GENERAL MARKOV — 79

CHAPTER X.
THE POWER—THE DUMA—THE PROVISIONAL GOVERNMENT—THE HIGH COMMAND—THE SOVIET OF WORKMEN'S AND SOLDIERS' DELEGATES — 84

CHAPTER XI.
THE BOLSHEVIK STRUGGLE FOR POWER—THE POWER OF THE ARMY AND THE IDEA OF A DICTATORSHIP — 96

CHAPTER XII.
THE ACTIVITIES OF THE PROVISIONAL GOVERNMENT—INTERNAL POLITICS, CIVIL ADMINISTRATION—THE TOWN, THE VILLAGE, AND THE AGRARIAN PROBLEM — 106

CHAPTER XIII.
The Activities of the Provisional Government: Food Supplies, Industry, Transport, and Finance - - - - - - 116

CHAPTER XIV.
The Strategical Position of the Russian Front - 127

CHAPTER XV.
The Question of the Advance of the Russian Army 138

CHAPTER XVI.
Military Reforms—The Generals—The Dismissal from the High Command - - - - - - - - - - - 146

CHAPTER XVII.
"Democratisation of the Army"—Administration, Service and Routine - - - - - - - - - - - 153

CHAPTER XVIII.
The Declaration of the Rights of the Soldier and Committees - 159

CHAPTER XIX.
The Democratisation of the Army: The Commissars 168

CHAPTER XX.
The Democratisation of the Army—The Story of "The Declaration of the Rights of the Soldier" - - - - - - - 174

CHAPTER XXI.
The Press and Propaganda - - - - - - - - 189

CHAPTER XXII.
The Condition of the Army at the July Advance - - - - 209

CHAPTER XXIII.
Officers' Organisations - - - - - - - - - 229

CHAPTER XXIV.
The Revolution and the Cossacks - - - - - 239

CHAPTER XXV.
National Units - - - - - - - - - - 248

CHAPTER XXVI.
May and the Beginning of June in the Sphere of Military Administration—The Resignation of Gutchkov and General Alexeiev—My Departure from the Stavka—The Administration of Kerensky and General Brussilov - - - - - 255

CHAPTER XXVII.
My Term as Commander-in-Chief on the Western Russian Front 264

CHAPTER XXVIII.
The Russian Advance in the Summer of 1917—The Débâcle - 271

CHAPTER XXIX.
The Conference at the Stavka of Ministers and Commanders-in-Chief on July 16th - 281

CHAPTER XXX.
General Kornilov - 297

CHAPTER XXXI.
My Service as Commander-in-Chief of the South-Western Front—The Moscow Conference—The Fall of Riga - 308

CHAPTER XXXII.
General Kornilov's Movement and its Repercussion on the South-West Front - 318

CHAPTER XXXIII.
In Berdichev Gaol—The Transfer of the "Berdichev Group" of Prisoners to Bykhov - 329

CHAPTER XXXIV.
Some Conclusions as to the First Period of the Revolution - 338

And the new.

The old banner

LIST OF ILLUSTRATIONS

The Stavka Quartermaster-General's Branch		*Frontispiece*
The Old Banner and the New	Facing page	8
The Grand Duke Nicholas Distributes Crosses of St. George	,, ,,	14
Funeral of the First Victims of the March Revolution in Petrograd	,, ,,	44
General Alexeiev	,, ,,	72
General Kornilov	,, ,,	72
General Markov	,, ,,	78
Foreign Military Representatives at the Stavka	,, ,,	144
The Conference of Commanders-in-Chief	,, ,,	166
A Group of "Prisoners" at Berdichev	,, ,,	166
The Old Army: A Review. General Ivanov	,, ,,	192
The Revolutionary Army: A Review. Kerensky	,, ,,	192
Before the Battle in the Revolutionary Army: A Meeting	,, ,,	200
Types of Men in the Revolutionary Army	,, ,,	200
Before the Battle in the Old Army: Prayers	,, ,,	208
Types of Soldiers of the Old Army	,, ,,	210
General Alexeiev's Farewell	,, ,,	254
Kerensky Addressing Soldiers' Meeting	,, ,,	262
General Kornilov's Arrival at Petrograd	,, ,,	280
General Kornilov in the Trenches	,, ,,	280
General Kornilov's Welcome in Moscow	,, ,,	316

LIST OF DIAGRAMS AND MAPS

		PAGE
1.	Diagram of the Comparative Forces of the Germans in Different Theatres of War	32
2.	Diagram Indicating the Political Party Divisions in Russia after the Revolution	90
3.	Map of the Russian European Front in 1917	130
4.	Map of the Russian Caucasian Front in 1917	131
5.	Map of the Russian Front in June and July, 1917	298
6.	Map of the Russian Front till August 19th and after	299

FOREWORD

In the midst of the turmoil and bloodshed in Russia people perish and the real outlines of historical events are obliterated. It is for this reason that I have decided to publish these memoirs, in spite of the difficulties of work in my present condition of a refugee, unable to refer to any archives or documents and deprived of the possibility of discussing events with those who have taken part in them.

The first part of my book deals chiefly with the Russian Army, with which my life has been closely linked up. Political, social and economic questions are discussed only in so far as I have found it necessary to describe their influence upon the course of events.

In 1917 the Army played a decisive part in the fate of Russia. Its participation in the progress of the Revolution, its life, degradation and collapse should serve as a great warning and a lesson to the new builders of Russian life. This applies not only to the struggle against the present tyrants. When Bolshevism is defeated, the Russian people will have to undertake the tremendous task of reviving its moral and material forces, as well as that of preserving its sovereign existence. Never in history has this task been as arduous as it is now, because there are many outside Russia's borders waiting eagerly for her end. They are waiting in vain. The Russian people will rise in strength and wisdom from the deathbed of blood, horror and poverty, moral and physical.

The Russian Turmoil

CHAPTER I.

THE FOUNDATIONS OF THE OLD POWER: FAITH, THE CZAR AND THE MOTHER COUNTRY.

THE inevitable historical process which culminated in the Revolution of March, 1917, has resulted in the collapse of the Russian State. Philosophers, historians and sociologists, in studying the course of Russian life, may have foreseen the impending catastrophe. But nobody could foresee that the people, rising like a tidal wave, would so rapidly and so easily sweep away all the foundations of their existence: the Supreme Power and the Governing classes which disappeared without a struggle; the intelligencia, gifted but weak, isolated and lacking will-power, which at first, in the midst of a deadly struggle, had only words as a weapon, later submissively bent their necks under the knife of the victors; and last, but not least, an army of ten million, powerful and imbued with historic traditions. That army was destroyed in three or four months.

This last event—the collapse of the army—was not, however, quite unexpected, as the epilogue of the Manchurian war and the subsequent events in Moscow, Kronstadt and Sevastopol were a terrible warning. At the end of November, 1905, I lived for a fortnight in Harbin, and travelled on the Siberian Railway for thirty-one days in December, 1907, through a series of " republics " from Harbin to Petrograd. I thus gained a clear indication of what might be expected from a licentious mob of soldiers utterly devoid of restraining principles. All the meetings, resolutions, soviets—in a word, all the manifestations of a mutiny of the military—were repeated in 1917 with photographic accuracy, but with greater impetus and on a much larger scale.

It should be noted that the possibility of such a rapid psychological transformation was not characteristic of the Russian Army alone. There can be no doubt that war-weariness after three years of bloodshed played an important part in these events, as the armies of the whole world were affected by it and were rendered more accessible to the disintegrating influences of extreme Socialist doctrines. In the autumn of 1918 the German Army Corps that occupied the region of the Don and Little Russia were demoralised in one week, and they repeated to a certain extent the process which we had already lived through of meetings, soviets, committees, of doing away with Commanding Officers, and in some units of the sale of military stores, horses and arms. It was not till then that the Germans understood the tragedy of the Russian officers. More than once our volunteers saw the German officers, formerly so haughty and so frigid, weeping bitterly over their degradation.

" You have done the same to us; you have done it with your own hands," we said

" Not we; it was our Government," was their reply.

In the winter of 1918, as Commander-in-Chief of the Volunteer Army, I received an offer from a group of German officers to join our army as volunteers in the ranks.

The collapse of the army cannot be explained away as the psychological result of defeats and disasters. Even the victors experienced disturbances in the army. There was a certain amount of disaffection among the French troops occupying, in the beginning of 1918, the region of Odessa and Roumania, in the French fleet cruising in the Black Sea, among the British troops in the region of Constantinople and Transcaucasia. The troops did not always obey the orders of their Commanding Officers. Rapid demobilisation and the arrival of fresh, partly volunteer elements, altered the situation.

What was the condition of the Russian Army at the outbreak of the Revolution? From time immemorial the entire ideology of our soldiers was contained in the well-known formula: " For God, for the Czar and for the Mother Country." Generation after generation was born and bred on that formula. These ideas, however, did not penetrate deeply enough into the masses of the people and of the army. For many centuries the Russian people had been deeply religious, but their faith was somewhat shaken in the beginning of the Twentieth Century. The Russian people, as the Russian saying goes, was " the bearer of Christ "—a people inwardly disposed towards Universal Brotherhood, great in its simplicity, truthfulness, humility and forgiveness. That people, Christian in the fullest sense of the word, was gradually changing as it came under the influence of material interests, and learnt or was taught to see in the gratifying of those interests the sole

The Grand Duke Nicholas distributes Crosses of St. George.

purpose of life. The link between the people and its spiritual leaders was gradually weakening as these leaders were detached from the people, entered into the service of the Governing powers, and shared the latter's deficiencies. The development of this moral transformation of the Russian people is too deep and too complex to fall within the scope of these memoirs. It is undeniable that the youngsters who joined the ranks treated questions of the Faith and of the Church with indifference. In barracks they lost the habits of their homes, and were forcibly removed from a more wholesome and settled atmosphere, with all its creeds and superstitions. They received no spiritual or moral education, which in barracks was considered a matter of minor importance, completely overshadowed by practical and material cares and requirements. A proper spirit could not be created in barracks, where Christian morals, religious discourses, and even the rites of the Church bore an official and sometimes even compulsory character. Commanding Officers know how difficult it was to find a solution of the vexed question of attendance at Church services.

War introduced two new elements into the spiritual life of the army. On the one hand, there was a certain moral coarseness and cruelty; on the other, it seemed as if faith had been deepened by constant danger. I do not wish to accuse the orthodox military clergy as a body. Many of its representatives proved their high valour, courage and self-sacrifice. It must, however, be admitted that the clergy failed to produce a religious revival among the troops. It is not their fault, because the world-war into which Russia was drawn was due to intricate political and economic causes, and there was no room for religious fervour. The clergy, however, likewise failed to establish closer connection with the troops. After the outbreak of the Revolution the officers continued for a long time to struggle to keep their waning power and authority, but the voice of the priests was silenced almost at once, and they ceased to play any part whatsoever in the life of the troops. I recall an episode typical of the mental attitude of military circles in those days. One of the regiments of the Fourth Rifle Division had built a camp Church quite close to its lines, and had built it with great care and very artistically. The Revolution came. A demagogue captain decided that his company had inadequate quarters and that a Church was a superstition. On his own authority he converted the Church into quarters for his company, and dug a hole where the altar stood for purposes which it is better not to mention. I am not surprised that such a scoundrel was found in the regiment or that the Higher Command was terrorised and silent. But why did two or three thousand orthodox Russians, bred in the mystic rites of their faith, remain indifferent to such a sacrilege? Be that as it may, there can hardly be any doubt that religion ceased to be one of the moral impulses which upheld the spirit of the Russian Army and prompted it to deeds of valour or protected it later from the development of bestial instincts. The orthodox clergy, generally speaking, was thrown overboard during the storm. Some of the high dignitaries of the Church—the Metropolitans—Pitirim and Makarius—the Archbishop Varnava and others, unfortunately were closely connected with the Governing bureaucracy of the Rasputin period of Petrograd history. The lower grades of the clergy, on the other hand, were in close touch with the Russian intellectuals.

I cannot take it upon myself to judge of the extent to which the Russian Church remained an active force after it came under the yoke of the Bolsheviks. An impenetrable veil hangs over the life of the Russian Church in Soviet Russia, but there can be no doubt that spiritual renaissance is progressing and spreading, that the martyrdom of hundreds, nay, thousands, of priests is waking the dormant conscience of the people and is becoming a legend in their minds.

* *

THE CZAR.

It is hardly necessary to prove that the enormous majority of the Commanding Officers were thoroughly loyal to the Monarchist idea and to the Czar himself. The subsequent behaviour of the higher Commanding Officers who had been Monarchists was due partly to motives of self-seeking, partly to pusillanimity and to the desire to conceal their real feelings in order to remain in power and to carry out their own plans. Cases in which a change of front was the result of the collapse of ideals, of a new outlook, or was prompted by motives of practical statesmanship, were rare. For example, it would have been childish to have believed General Brussilov when he asserted that from the days of his youth he had been " a Socialist and a Republican." He was bred in the traditions of the Old Guards, was closely connected with circles of the Court, and permeated with their outlook. His habits, tastes, sympathies and surroundings were those of a *barin*.[*] No man can be a lifelong liar to himself and to others.

---

[*] *Barin* is the Russian word for master. It also means gentleman, and was used by the peasants and by servants in addressing their superiors.

The majority of the officers of the Regular Russian Army had Monarchist principles and were undoubtedly loyal. After the Japanese war, as a result of the first Revolution, the Officers' Corps was, nevertheless, placed, for reasons which are not sufficiently clear, under the special supervision of the Police Department, and regimental Commanding Officers received from time to time " black lists." The tragedy of it was that it was almost useless to argue against the verdict of " unreliability," while, at the same time, it was forbidden to conduct one's own investigation, even in secret. This system of spying introduced an unwholesome spirit into the army. Not content with this system, the War Minister, General Sukhomlinov, introduced his own branch of counter-spies, which was headed unofficially by Colonel Miassoyedov, who was afterwards shot as a German spy. At every military District Headquarters an organ was instituted, headed by an officer of the Gendarmerie dressed up in G.H.Q. uniform. Officially, he was supposed to deal with foreign espionage, but General Dukhonin (who was killed by the Bolsheviks), when Chief of the Intelligence Bureau of the Kiev G.H.Q. before the War, bitterly complained to me of the painful atmosphere created by this new organ, which was officially subordinate to the Quartermaster-General, but in reality looked on him with suspicion, and was spying not only upon the Staff, but upon its own chiefs.

Life itself seemed to induce the officers to utter some kind of protest against the existing order. Of all the classes that served the State, there had been for a long time no element so downtrodden and forlorn or so ill-provided for as the officers of the Regular Russian Army. They lived in abject poverty. Their rights and their self-esteem were constantly ignored by the Senior Officers. The utmost the rank and file could hope for as the crowning of their career was the rank of Colonel and an old age spent in sickness and semi-starvation. From the middle of the nineteenth century the Officers' Corps had completely lost its character as a class and a caste. Since universal compulsory service was introduced and the nobility ceased to be prosperous the gates of military schools were opened wide to people of low extraction and to young men belonging to the lower strata of the people, but with a diploma from the civil schools. They formed a majority in the Army. Mobilisations, on the other hand, reinforced the Officers' Corps by the infusion of a great many men of the liberal professions, who introduced new ideas and a new outlook. Finally, the tremendous losses suffered by the Regular Officers' Corps compelled the High Command to relax to a certain extent the regulations concerning military training and education, and to introduce on a broad scale promotions from the ranks for deeds of valour, and to give rankers a short training in elementary schools to fit them to be temporary officers.

These circumstances, characteristic of all armies formed from the masses, undoubtedly reduced the fighting capacity of the Officers' Corps, and brought about a certain change in its political outlook, bringing it nearer to that of the average Russian intellectual and to democracy. This the leaders of the Revolutionary democracy did not, or, to be more accurate, would not, understand in the first days of the Revolution. In the course of my narrative I will differentiate between the " Revolutionary Democracy "—an agglomeration of socialist parties—and the true Russian Democracy, to which the middle-class intelligencia and the Civil Service elements undoubtedly belong.

The spirit of the Regular Officers was, however, gradually changing. The Japanese War, which disclosed the grave shortcomings of the country and of the Army, the Duma and the Press, which had gained a certain liberty after 1905, played an important part in the political education of the officers. The mystic adoration of the Monarch began gradually to vanish. Among the junior generals and other officers there appeared men in increasing numbers capable of differentiating between the idea of the Monarchy and personalities, between the welfare of the country and the form of government. In officer circles opportunities occurred for criticism, analysis, and sometimes for severe condemnation.

It is to be wondered that in these circumstances our officers remained steadfast and stoutly resisted the extremist, destructive currents of political thought. The percentage of men who reached the depths and were unmasked by the authorities was insignificant. With regard to the throne, generally speaking, there was a tendency among the officers to separate the person of the Emperor from the miasma with which he was surrounded, from the political errors and misdeeds of the Government, which was leading the country steadily to ruin and the Army to defeat. They wanted to forgive the Emperor, and tried to make excuses for him.

In spite of the accepted view, the monarchical idea had no deep, mystic roots among the rank and file, and, of course, the semi-cultured masses entirely failed to realise the meaning of other forms of Government preached by Socialists of all shades of opinion. Owing to a certain innate Conservatism, to habits dating from time immemorial, and to the teaching of the Church, the existing régime was considered as something quite natural and inevitable. In the mind and in the heart of the soldier the idea of a monarch was, if I may so express it, " in a potential state," rising sometimes to a point of high exaltation when the monarch was personally approached (at reviews, parades and casual meetings), and sometimes falling to indifference. At any rate, the Army was in a disposition sufficiently favourable to the idea of a monarchy and to the dynasty, and that disposition could have easily been maintained. But a sticky cobweb of licentiousness and crime was being woven at Petrograd and Czarskoe Selo. The truth, intermingled with falsehood, penetrated into the remotest corners of the country and into the Army, and evoked painful regrets and sometimes malicious rejoicings. The members of the House of Romanov did not preserve the "idea" which the orthodox monarchists wished to surround with a halo of greatness, nobility and reverence. I recall the impression of a sitting of the Duma which I happened to attend. For the first time, Gutchkov uttered a word of warning from the Tribune of the Duma about Rasputin.

" All is not well with our land."

The House, which had been rather noisy, was silent, and every word, spoken in a low voice, was distinctly audible in remote corners. A mysterious cloud, pregnant with catastrophe, seemed to hang over the normal course of Russian history. I will not dwell on the corrupt influences prevailing in Ministerial dwellings and Imperial palaces to which the filthy and cynical impostor found access, who swayed ministers and rulers.

The Grand Duke Nicholas is supposed to have threatened to hang Rasputin should he venture to appear at G.H.Q. General Alexeiev also disapproved strongly of the man. That the influence of Rasputin did not spread to the old Army is due entirely to the attitude of the above-named generals. All sorts of stories about Rasputin's influence was circulated at the front, and the Censor collected an enormous amount of material on the subject, even from soldiers' letters from the front; but the gravest impression was produced by the word " TREASON " with reference to the Empress. In the Army, openly and everywhere, conversations were heard about the Empress' persistent demands for a separate peace and of her treachery towards Lord Kitchener, of whose journey she was supposed to have informed the Germans. As I recall the past, and the impression produced in the Army by the *rumour* of the Empress' treason, I consider that this circumstance had a very great influence upon the attitude of the Army towards the dynasty and the revolution. In the spring of 1917 I questioned

General Alexeiev on this painful subject. His answer, reluctantly given, was vague. He said: " When the Empress' papers were examined she was found to be in possession of a map indicating in detail the disposition of the troops along the entire front. Only two copies were prepared of this map, one for the Emperor and one for myself. I was very painfully impressed. God knows who may have made use of this map."

History will undoubtedly throw light on the fateful influence exercised by the Empress Alexandra upon the Russian Government in the period preceding the Revolution. As regards the question of treason, this disastrous rumour has not been confirmed by a single fact, and was afterwards contradicted by the investigations of a Commission specially appointed by the Provisional Government, on which representatives of the Soviet of workmen and soldiers served.

We now come to the third foundation—the *Mother Country*. Deafened as we were, alas! by the thunder and rattle of conventional patriotic phrases, endlessly repeated along the whole length and breadth of Russia, we failed to detect the fundamental, innate defect of the Russian people—its lack of patriotism. It is no longer necessary to force an open door by proving this statement. The Brest-Litovsk Treaty provoked no outburst of popular wrath. Russian society was indifferent to the separation of the Border States, even those that were Russian in spirit and in blood. What is more, Russian society approved of this dismemberment. We know of the agreement between Poland and Petlura, between Poland and the Soviet. We know that Russian territorial and material riches were sold for a song to international, political usurers. Need we adduce further proofs?

There can be no doubt that the collapse of Russian Statehood as manifested in " self-determination " was in several instances caused by the desire to find a temporary safeguard against the Bedlam of the Soviet Republic. Life, however, unfortunately does not stop at the practical application of this peculiar " sanitary cordon," but strikes at the very idea of Statehood. This occurred even in such stable districts as the Cossack provinces, not, however, among the masses, but among the leaders themselves. Thus at Ekaterinodar in 1920, at the " High Krug " (Assembly) of the three Cossack armies, the mention of Russia was omitted after a heated discussion from the proposed formula of the oath

Is Crucified Russia unworthy of our love?

What, then, was the effect of the Mother Country idea upon the conscience of the old Army? The upper strata of the Russian intellectuals were well aware of the reasons for the world con-

Patriotism

flagration, of the conflict of the Powers for political and economic supremacy, for free routes, for markets and colonies—a conflict in which Russia's part was merely one of self-defence. On the other hand, the average number of the Russian *intelligencia*, as well as officers, were often satisfied merely with the immediate and more obvious and easily comprehensible causes. Nobody wanted the war, except, perhaps, the impressionable young officers yearning for exploits. It was believed that the powers-that-be would take every precaution in order to avoid a rupture. Gradually, however, the fatal inevitability of war was understood. There was no question on our part of aggressiveness or self-interest. To sympathise sincerely with the weak and the oppressed was in keeping with the traditional attitude of Russia. Also, we did not draw the sword—the sword was drawn against us. That is why, when the war began, the voices were silenced of those who feared that, owing to the low level of her culture and economic development, Russia would be unable to win in the contest with a strong and cultured enemy. War was accepted in a patriotic spirit, which was at times akin to enthusiasm. Like the majority of the intellectuals, the officers did not take much interest in the question of war aims. The war began; defeat would have led to immeasurable disaster to our country in every sphere of its life, to territorial losses, political decadence and economic slavery. Victory was, therefore, a necessity. All other questions were relegated to the background. There was plenty of time for their discussion, for new decisions and for changes. This simplified attitude towards the war, coupled with a profound understanding and with a national self-consciousness, was not understood by the left wing of the Russian politicians, who were driven to Zimmerwald and Kienthal. No wonder, therefore, that when the anonymous and the Russian leaders of the Revolutionary democracy were confronted in February, 1917, before the Army was deliberately destroyed, with the dilemma: "Are we to save the country or the Revolution?" they chose the latter.

Still less did the illiterate masses of the people understand the idea of national self-preservation. The people went to war submissively, but without enthusiasm and without any clear perception of the necessity for a great sacrifice. Their psychology did not rise to the understanding of abstract national principles. "The people-in-arms," for that was what the Army really was, were elated by victory and downhearted when defeated. They did not fully understand the necessity for crossing the Carpathians, and had, perhaps, a clearer idea of the meaning of the struggle on the Styr and the Pripet. And yet it found solace in the thought: "We are from Tambov; the Germans will not reach us." It is necessary to repeat this stale saying, because it expresses the deep-rooted psychology of the average Russian. As a result of this predominance of material interests in the outlook of "the people-in-arms," they grasped more easily the simple arguments based on realities in favour of a stubborn fight and of victory, as well as the impossibility of admitting defeat. These arguments were: A foreign German domination, the ruin of the country and of the home, the weight of the taxes which would inevitably be levied after defeat, the fall in the price of grain, which would have to go through foreign channels, etc. In addition, there was some feeling of confidence that the Government was doing the right thing, the more so as the nearest representatives of that power, the officers, were going forward with the troops and were dying in the same spirit of readiness and submission as the men, either because they had been ordered to do so, or else because they thought it their duty. The rank and file, therefore, bravely faced death. Afterwards when confidence was shaken, the masses of the Army were completely perplexed. The formulas, "without annexations and indemnities," "the self-determination of peoples," etc., proved more abstract and less intelligible than the old repudiated and rusty idea of the Mother Country, which still persisted underneath them. In order to keep the men at the front, the well-known arguments of a materialistic nature, such as the threat of German domination, the ruin of the home, the weight of taxes, were expounded from platforms decorated with red flags. They were taught by Socialists, who favoured a war of defence.

Thus the three principles which formed the foundations of the Army were undermined. In describing the anomalies and spiritual shortcomings of the Russian Army, far be it from me to place it below the level of armies of other countries. These shortcomings are inherent in all armies formed from the masses, which are almost akin to a militia, but this did not prevent these armies or our own from gaining victories and continuing the war. It is necessary, however, to draw a complete picture of the spirit of the Army in order to understand its subsequent destiny.

CHAPTER II.

THE ARMY.

THE Russo-Japanese war had a very great influence upon the development of the Russian army. The bitterness of defeat and the clear consciousness that the policy governing military affairs was disastrously out of date gave a great impulse to the junior military elements and forced the slack and inert elements gradually to alter their ways or else to retire. In spite of the passive resistance of several men at the head of the War Ministry and the General Staff, who were either incompetent or else treated the interests of the army with levity and indifference, work was done at full speed. In ten years the Russian army, without of course attaining the ideal, made tremendous progress. It may be confidently asserted that, had it not been for the hard lessons of the Manchurian campaign, Russia would have been crushed in the first months of the Great War.

Yet the cleansing of the commanding personnel went too slowly. Our softness (" Poor devil! we must give him a job "), wire-pulling, intrigues, and too slavish an observance of the rules of seniority resulted in the ranks of senior commanding officers being crowded with worthless men. The High Commission for granting testimonials, which sat twice a year in Petrograd, hardly knew any of those to whom these testimonials were given. Therein lies the reason for the mistakes made at the outbreak of war in many appointments to High Commands. Four Commanders-in-Chief (one of them suffered from mental paralysis—it is true that his appointment was only temporary), several Army Commanders, many Army Corps and Divisional Commanders had to be dismissed. In the very first days of the concentration of the Eighth Army, in July, 1914, General Brussilov dismissed three Divisional and one Army Corps Commanders. Yet nonentities retained their commands, and they ruined the troops and the operations. Under the same General Brussilov, General D., relieved several times of his command, went from a cavalry division to three infantry divisions in turn, and found final repose in German captivity. Most unfortunately, the whole army was aware of the incompetence of these Commanding Officers, and wondered at their appointments. Owing to these deficiencies, the strategy of the entire campaign lacked inspiration and boldness. Such, for example, were the operations of the North-Western front in East Prussia, prompted solely by the desire of G.H.Q. to save the French Army from a desperate position. Such, in particular, was Rennenkampf's shameful manœuvre, as well as the stubborn forcing of the Carpathians, which dismembered the troops of the South-Western front in 1915, and finally our advance in the spring of 1916.

The last episode was so typical of the methods of our High Command and its consequences were so grave that it is worth our while to recall it.

When the armies of the South-Western front took the offensive in May, the attack was eminently successful and several Austrian divisions were heavily defeated. When my division, after the capture of Lutsk, was moving by forced marches to Vladimir Volynsk, I considered—and we all considered—that our manœuvre represented the entire scheme of the advance, that our front was dealing the main blow. We learnt afterwards that the task of dealing the main blow had been entrusted to the Western front, and that Brussilov's armies were only making a demonstration. There, towards Vilna, large forces had been gathered, equipped with artillery and technical means such as we had never had before. For several months the troops had been preparing *places d'armes* for the advance. At last all was ready, and the success of the Southern armies that diverted the enemy's attention and his reserves also promised success to the Western front.

Almost on the eve of the contemplated offensive the historical conversation took place on the telephone between General Evert, C.-in-C. of the Western front, and General Alexeiev, Chief of Staff of the Supreme Commander-in-Chief. The gist of the conversation was the following:

A. Circumstances require an immediate decision. Are you ready for the advance and are you certain to be successful?

E. I have no certainty of success. The enemy's positions are very strong. Our troops will have to attack the positions against which their previous attacks have failed.

A. If that is the case, you must give immediate orders for the transfer of troops to the South-Western front. I will report to the Emperor.

So the operation, so long awaited and so methodically prepared, collapsed. The Western Army Corps, sent to reinforce us, came too late. Our advance was checked. The senseless slaughter on

The Army

the swampy banks of the Stokhod then began. Incidentally, the Guards lost the flower of their men in those battles. Meanwhile, the German Eastern front was going through a period of intense anxiety. " It was a critical time," says Ludendorff in his *Mes Souvenirs de Guerre* " We had spent ourselves, and we knew full well that no one would come to our assistance if the Russians chose to attack us."

An episode may be mentioned in this connection, which occurred to General Brussilov. The story is not widely known, and may serve as an interesting sidelight on the character of the General—one of the leaders of the campaign. After the brilliant operations of the Eighth Army, which ended in the crossing of the Carpathians and the invasion of Hungary, the C.-in-C., General Brussilov, suffered a curious psychological breakdown. Under the impression that a partial reverse had been sustained by one of the Army Corps, he issued an order for a general retreat, and the Army began rapidly to roll back. He was haunted by imaginary dangers of the enemy breaking through, surrounding our troops, of attacks of enemy cavalry which were supposed to threaten the G.H.Q. Twice General Brussilov moved his H.Q. with a swiftness akin to a panicky flight. The C.-in-C. was thus detached from his armies and out of touch with them.

We were retreating day after day in long, weary marches, and utterly bewildered. The Austrians did not outnumber us, and their moral was no higher than ours. They did not press us. Every day, my riflemen and Kornilov's troops in our vicinity delivered short counter-attacks, took many prisoners, and captured machine-guns.

The Quartermaster-General's branch of the Army was even more puzzled. Every day it reported that the news of the retreat was unfounded; but Brussilov at first disregarded these reports, and later became greatly incensed. The General Staff then had recourse to another stratagem: they approached Brussilov's old friend, the veteran General Panchulidzev, Chief of the Army Sanitation Branch, and persuaded him that, if this retreat continued, the Army might suspect treason and things might take an ugly turn. Panchulidzev visited Brussilov. An intensely painful scene took place. As a result, Brussilov was found weeping bitterly and Panchulidzev fainted. On the same day, an order was issued for an advance, and the troops went forward rapidly and easily, driving the Austrians before them. The strategical position was restored as well as the reputation of the Army Commander.

It must be admitted that not only the troops but the Commanders were but scantily informed of the happenings of the front, and had hazy ideas on the general strategical scheme. The troops criticised them only when it was obvious that they had to pay the price of blood for these schemes. So it was in the Carpathians, at Stokhod, during the second attack on Przemyshl in the spring of 1917, etc. The moral of the troops was affected chiefly by the great Galician retreat, the unhappy progress of the war on the Northern and Western fronts—where no victories were won—and by the tedious lingering for over a year in positions of which everyone was sick to death.

I have already mentioned the cadres of commissioned officers. The great and small shortcomings of these cadres increased as the cadres became separated. No one expected the campaign to be protracted, and the Army organisation was not careful to preserve the cadres of officers and non-commissioned officers. They were drafted wholesale into the ranks at the outbreak of war. I remember so well a conversation that took place during the period of mobilisation, which was then contemplated against Austria alone. It occurred in the flat of General V. M. Dragomirov, one of the prominent leaders of the Army. A telegram was brought in announcing that Germany had declared war. There was a dead silence. Everyone was deep in thought. Somebody asked Dragomirov:
" How long do you think the war will last? "
" Four months."
Companies went to the front sometimes with five to six officers. Regular officers, and later the majority of other officers, invariably and in all circumstances gave the example of prowess, pluck and self-sacrifice. It is only natural that most of them were killed. Another reliable element—the N.C.O.'s of the Reserve—was also recklessly squandered. In the beginning of the war they formed sometimes 50 per cent. of the rank and file. Relations between officers and men in the old army were not always based upon healthy principles. It cannot be denied that there was a certain aloofness caused by the insufficient attention paid by the officers to the spiritual requirements of the soldier's life. These relations, however, gradually improved as the barriers of caste and class were broken down. The war drew officers and men ever closer together, and in some regiments, mostly of the line, there was a true brotherhood in arms. One reservation must here be made. The outward intercourse bore the stamp of the general lack of cul-

ture from which not only the masses but also the Russian intellectuals suffered. Heartfelt solicitude, touching care of the men's needs, simplicity and friendliness—all these qualities of the Russian officer, who lay for months on end in the wet, dirty trenches beside their men, ate out of the same pot, died quietly and without a murmur, was buried in the same " fraternal grave "—were marred by an occasional roughness, swearing, and sometimes by arbitrariness and blows.

There can be no doubt that the same conditions existed within the ranks, and the only difference was that the sergeant and the corporal were rougher and more cruel than the officers. These deplorable circumstances coupled with the boredom and stupidity of barrack life, and the petty restrictions imposed upon the men by the military regulations, gave ample scope for underground seditious propaganda in which the soldier was described as the " victim of the arbitrariness of the men with golden epaulettes." The sound feeling and naturally healthy outlook of the men was not mentioned while the discomforts of military life were insisted on in order to foster a spirit of discontent.

This state of affairs was all the more serious because during the war the process of consolidating the different units became more and more difficult. These units, and especially the infantry regiments, suffering terrible losses and changing their personnel ten or twelve times, became to some extent recruiting stations through which men flowed in an uninterrupted stream. They remained there but a short time, and failed to become imbued with the military traditions of their unit. The artillery and some other special branches remained comparatively solid, and this was due in some measure to the fact that their losses were, as compared with the losses suffered by the infantry, only in the proportion of one to ten or one to twenty.

On the whole the atmosphere in the Army and in the Navy was not, therefore, particularly wholesome. In varying degrees, the two elements of the Army—the rank and file and the commanding cadres—were divided. For this the Russian officers, as well as the intellectuals, were undoubtedly responsible. Their misdeeds resulted in the idea gaining ground that the *barin* (master) and the officer were opposed to the *moujik* and the soldier. A favourable atmosphere was thus created for the work of destructive forces.

Anarchist elements were by no means predominant in the Army. The foundations, though somewhat unstable, had to be completely shattered; the new power had to commit a long series of mistakes and crimes to convert the state of smouldering discontent into active rebellion, the bloody spectre of which will for some time to come hang over our hapless Russian land.

Destructive outside influences were not counteracted in the Army by a reasonable process of education. This was due partly to the political unpreparedness of the officers, partly to the instinctive fear felt by the old régime of introducing " politics " into barracks, even with a view to criticising subversive doctrines. This fear was felt not only in respect of social and internal problems but even in respect of foreign policy. Thus, for example, an Imperial order was issued shortly before the war, strictly prohibiting any discussion amongst the soldiers on the subject of the political issues of the moment (the Balkan question, the Austro-Serbian conflict, etc.). On the eve of the inevitable national war, the authorities persistently refrained from awakening wholesome patriotism by explaining the causes and aims of the war, and instructing the rank and file on the Slav question and our long-drawn struggle against Germanism. I must confess that, like many others, I did not carry out that order, and that I endeavoured properly to influence the moral of the Archangel regiment which I then commanded. I published an impassioned article against the order in the Military Press, under the title *Do not quench the spirit.* I feel certain that the statue of Strassbourg in the Place de la Concorde in Paris, draped in a black veil, played an important part in fostering the heroic spirit of the French Army.

Propaganda penetrated into the old Russian Armies from all sides. There can be no doubt that the fitful attempts of the ever-changing governments of Goremykin, Sturmer, Trepov, etc., to arrest the normal course of life in Russia, provided ample material for propaganda and roused the anger of the people, which was reflected in the Army. Socialist and defeatist writers took advantage of this state of affairs. Lenin first contrived to introduce his doctrines into Russia through the Social Democratic party of the Duma. The Germans worked with even greater intensity.

It should, however, be noted that all this propaganda from outside and from within affected chiefly the units of the rear, the garrisons and reserve battalions of the main centres, and especially of Petrograd, and that, before the Revolution, its influence at the front was comparatively insignificant. Reinforcements reached the front in a state of perplexity, but under the influence of a saner atmosphere, and of healthier, albeit more arduous, conditions of warfare, they rapidly improved. The effect of destructive propaganda was, however, noticeable in certain units where the ground was favourable, and two or three cases of insubordination of entire units occurred before the Revolution,

The Army

and were severely repressed. Finally, the bulk of the Army—the peasantry—was confronted with one practical question which *prompted them instinctively to delay the social revolution:* " THE LAND WOULD BE DIVIDED IN OUR ABSENCE. WHEN WE RETURN WE SHALL DIVIDE IT."

*　　*　　*

The inadequate organisation of the rear, the orgy of theft, high prices, profiteering and luxury, for which the front paid in blood, naturally afforded material for propaganda. The Army, however, suffered most heavily from the lack of technical means, especially of ammunition.

It was only in 1917 that General Sukhomlinov's trial disclosed to the Russian Army and to public opinion the main causes of the military catastrophe of 1915. Plans for replenishing the Russian Army stores had been completed, and credits for that purpose assigned as early as in 1907. Curiously enough, these credits were increased on the initiative of the Commission for National Defence, not of the Ministry of War. As a rule, neither the Duma nor the Ministry of Finance ever refused war credits or reduced them. During Sukhomlinov's tenure of office the War Ministry obtained a special credit of 450 million roubles, of which less than 300 millions were spent. Before the war, the question of providing the Army with munitions after the peace-time stores were exhausted was never even raised. It is true that the intensity of firing reached, from the very outbreak of war, unexpected and unheard-of proportions, which upset all the theoretical calculations of military specialists in Russia and abroad. Naturally, heroic measures were necessary in order to deal with this tragic situation.

Meanwhile, the supplies of ammunition for the reinforcements that came to the front—at first only 1/10th equipped, and later without any rifles at all—were exhausted as early as in October, 1914. The Commander-in-Chief of the South-Western front telegraphed to G.H.Q.: " The machinery for providing ammunition has completely broken down. In the absence of fresh supplies, we shall have to cease fighting, or else send troops to the front in an extremely precarious condition." At the same time (the end of September) Marshal Joffre inquired " whether the Imperial Russian Army was adequately supplied with shells for the uninterrupted conduct of war." The War Minister, General Sukhomlinov, replied: " The present condition of the Russian Army in respect of ammunition gives no ground for serious apprehension." Orders were not placed abroad, and Japanese and American rifles were refused " in order to avoid the inconvenience due to different calibres."

When the man who was responsible for the military catastrophe faced his judges in August, 1917, his personality produced a pitiful impression. The trial raised a more serious, painful question: " How could this irresponsible man, with no real knowledge of military matters, and perhaps even consciously a criminal, have remained in power for six years?" How " shamelessly indifferent to good and evil," according to Pushkin's saying, the military bureaucracy must have been, that surrounded him and tolerated the sins of omission and commission, which invariably and systematically injured the interests of the State.

The final catastrophe came in 1915.

I shall never forget the spring of 1915, the great tragedy of the Russian Army—the Galician retreat. We had neither cartridges nor shells. From day to day, we fought heavy battles and did lengthy marches. We were desperately tired—physically and morally. From hazy hopes we plunged into the depths of gloom. I recall an action near Przemyshl in the middle of May. The Fourth Rifle Division fought fiercely for eleven days. For eleven days the German heavy guns were roaring, and they literally blew up rows of trenches, with all their defenders. We scarcely replied at all—we had nothing to reply with. Utterly exhausted regiments were beating off one attack after another with bayonets, or firing at a close range. Blood was flowing, the ranks were being thinned, and graveyards growing. Two regiments were almost entirely annihilated by firing.

I would that our French and British friends, whose technical achievement is so wondrous, could note the following grotesque fact, which belongs to Russian history:

Our only six-inch battery had been silent for three days. When it received FIFTY SHELLS the fact was immediately telephoned to all regiments and companies, and all the riflemen heaved a sigh of relief and joy.

What painful, insulting irony there was in Brussilov's circular, in which the C.-in-C., incapable of providing us with ammunition, and with a view to raising our spirits and our moral, advised us not to lay too much stress upon the German superiority in heavy guns, because there had been many cases of the Germans inflicting but small losses in our ranks by spending an enormous amount of shells. . .

On May 21st, General Yanushkevitch (Chief of the Staff of the Supreme C.-in-C., the Grand Duke Nicholas Nicholaievitch) telegraphed to the War Minister: " The evacuation of Przemyshl is

The Army

an accomplished fact. Brussilov alleges a shortage of ammunition, that *bête noire*, yours and mine . . . a loud cry comes from all the armies : ' Give us cartridges.' "

* * * *

I am not inclined to idealise our Army. I have to speak many sad truths about it. But when the Pharisees—the leaders of the Russian Revolutionary Democracy—endeavour to explain away the collapse of the Army for which they are mainly responsible, by saying that the Army was already on the verge of collapse, they are lying.

I do not deny the grave shortcomings of our system of appointments to the High Command, the errors of our strategy, tactics and organisation, the technical backwardness of our Army, the defects of the Officers' Corps, the ignorance of the rank and file, and the vices of barrack life. I know the extent of desertions and shirking, of which our intellectuals were hardly less guilty than the ignorant masses. The Revolutionary Democracy did not, however, devote special attention to *these* serious defects of the Army. It could not remedy these evils, did not know how to cure them, and, in fact, did not combat them at all. Speaking for myself, I do not know that the Revolutionary Democracy has cured or even dealt seriously and effectively with any one of these evils. What of the famous " Freedom from Bondage " of the soldier ? Discarding all the exaggerations which this term implies, it may be said that the mere fact of the Revolution brought about a certain change in the relations between the officers and the men. In normal circumstances, and without coarse and malicious out side interference, this change might have become a source of great moral strength, instead of a disaster. It was into this sore that the Revolutionary Democracy poured poison. The very essence of the military organisation : its eternal, unchangeable characteristics, discipline, individual authority, and the non-political spirit of the Army, were ruthlessly assailed by the Revolutionary Democracy. These characteristics were lost. And yet it seemed as if the downfall of the old régime opened new and immense possibilities for cleansing and uplifting the Russian people's Army and its Command morally and technically. Like people, like Army.! After all, the old Russian Army, albeit suffering from the deficiencies of the Russian people, had also the people's virtues, and particularly an exceptional power of endurance in facing the horrors of war. The Army fought without a murmur for nearly three years. With extraordinary prowess and self-sacrifice the men went into action with empty hands against the deadly technique of the enemy. The rivers of blood shed by the rank and file atoned for the sins of the Supreme power, the Government, the people, and of the Army itself.*

Our late Allies should never forget that in the middle of January, 1917, the Russian Army was holding on its front 187 enemy divisions, or 49 per cent. of the enemy's forces operating on the European and Asiatic fronts.

The old Russian Army was still strong enough to continue the war and to win victories.

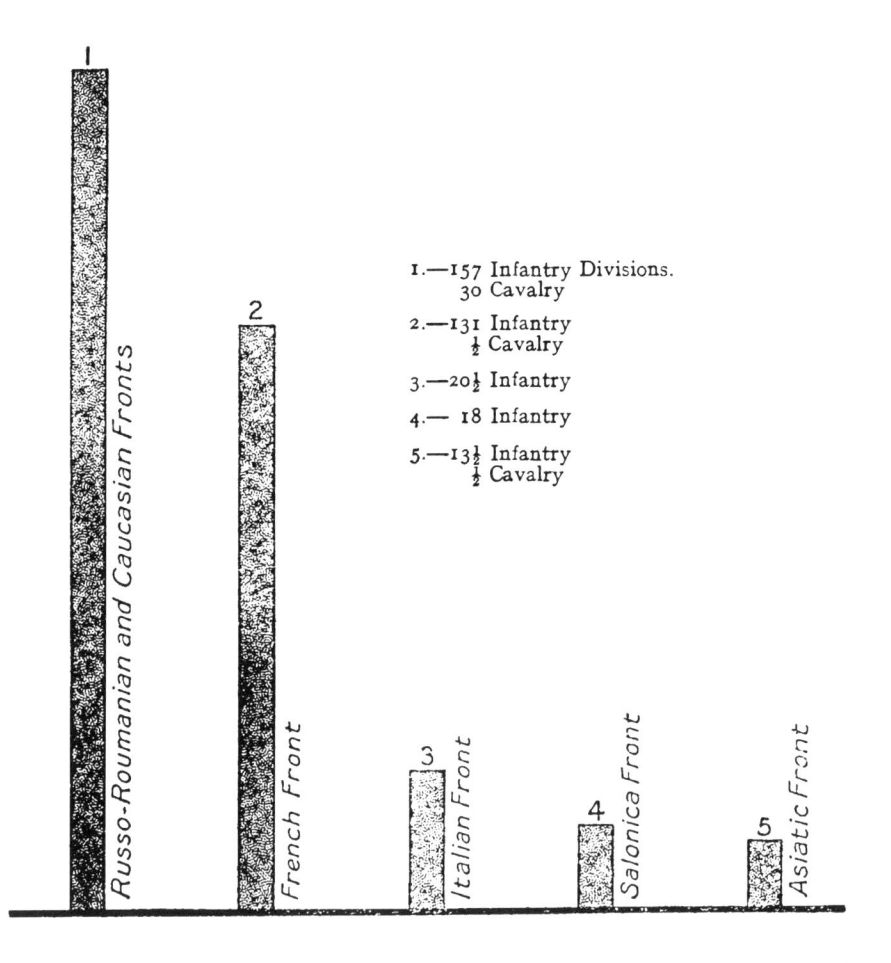

1.—157 Infantry Divisions.
    30 Cavalry
2.—131 Infantry
    ½ Cavalry
3.—20½ Infantry
4.— 18 Infantry
5.—13½ Infantry
    ½ Cavalry

1. Russo-Roumanian and Caucasian Fronts
2. French Front
3. Italian Front
4. Salonica Front
5. Asiatic Front

---

* The French Deputy, Louis Martin, estimates the losses of the Armies in killed alone as follows:—(In millions) Russia 2½, Germany 2, Austria 1½, France 1.4, Great Britain 0.8, Italy 0.6, etc. Russia's share of the martyrdom of all the Allied forces is 40 per cent.

CHAPTER III.

The Old Army and the Emperor.

IN August, 1915, the Emperor, influenced by the entourage of the Empress and of Rasputin, decided to take the Supreme Command of the Army. Eight Cabinet Ministers and some politicians warned the Emperor against this dangerous step, but their pleadings were of no avail. The official motives they adduced were, on the one hand, the difficulty of combining the tasks of governing the country and commanding the Army, and, on the other, the risk of assuming responsibility for the Army at a time when it was suffering reverses and retreating. The real motive, however, was the fear lest the difficult position of the Army be further imperilled by the lack of knowledge and experience of the new Supreme C.-in-C., and that the German-Rasputin clique that surrounded him, having already brought about the paralysis of the Government and its conflict with the Duma, would bring about the collapse of the Army.

There was a rumour, which was afterwards confirmed, that the Emperor came to this decision partly because he feared the entourage of the Empress, and partly because of the popularity of the Grand Duke Nicholas, which was growing in spite of the reverses suffered by the Army.

On August 23rd, an order was issued to the Army and Navy. To the official text, the Emperor added a note in his own hand, a facsimile of which is reproduced overleaf:

This decision, in spite of its intrinsic importance, produced no strong impression upon the Army. The High Commanding Officers and the lower grades of Commissioned Officers were well aware that the Emperor's personal part in the Supreme Command would be purely nominal, and the question in everyone's mind was:

" Who will be the Chief of Staff ? "

The appointment of General Alexeiev appeased the anxiety of the officers. The rank and file cared but little for the technical side of the Command. To them, the Czar had always been the

Supreme Leader of the Army. One thing, however, somewhat perturbed them: the belief had gained ground among the people years before that the Emperor was unlucky.

> Съ твердою вѣрою въ милость Божію и съ непоколебимою увѣренностью въ конечной побѣдѣ будемъ исполнять нашъ святой долгъ защиты Родины до конца и не посрамимъ земли Русской.
>
> — Николай

Translation:—" With firm faith in the grace of God, and with unshaken assurance of final victory, let us fulfil our sacred duty of defending Russia till the end, and let us not bring shame to the Russian land.—NICHOLAS."

In reality, it was General M. V. Alexeiev who took command of the armed forces of Russia. In the history of the Russian war and the Russian turmoil, General Alexeiev holds so prominent a place that his importance cannot be gauged in a few lines. A special historical study would be necessary in order to describe the career of a man whose military and political activities, which some have severely criticised and others extolled, never caused anyone to doubt that (in the words of an Army Order to the Volunteer Army) " his path of martyrdom was lighted by crystalline honesty and by a fervent love for his Mother Country—whether great or downtrodden."

Alexeiev sometimes did not display sufficient firmness in enforcing his demands, but, in respect of the independence of the "Stavka" (G.H.Q.) from outside influences, he showed civic courage which the High Officials of the old régime, who clung to their offices, completely lacked.

One day, after an official dinner at Mohilev, the Empress took Alexeiev's arm, and went for a walk in the garden with him. She mentioned Rasputin. In terms of deep emotion she tried to persuade the General that he was wrong in his attitude towards Rasputin, that "the old man is a wonderful saint," that he was much calumniated, that he was deeply devoted to the Imperial family, and, last but not least, that his visit would bring luck to the "Stavka."

Alexeiev answered dryly that, so far as he was concerned, the question had long since been settled. Should Rasputin appear at G.H.Q., he would immediately resign his post.

"Is this your last word?"

"Yes, certainly."

The Empress cut the conversation short, and left without saying good-bye to the General, who afterwards admitted that the incident had an ill-effect upon the Emperor's attitude towards him. Contrary to the established opinion, the relations between the Emperor and Alexeiev, outwardly perfect, were by no means intimate or friendly, or even particularly confidential. The Emperor loved no one except his son. Therein lies the tragedy of his life as a man and as a ruler.

Several times General Alexeiev, depressed by the growth of popular discontent with the régime and the Crown, endeavoured to exceed the limits of a military report and to represent to the Emperor the state of affairs in its true light. He referred to Rasputin and to the question of a responsible Ministry. He invariably met with the impenetrable glance, so well-known to many, and the dry retort:

"I know."

Not another word.

In matters of Army administration, the Emperor fully trusted Alexeiev, and listened attentively to the General's long, and perhaps even too elaborate, reports. Attentively and patiently he listened, but these matters did not seem to appeal to him. There were differences of opinion in regard to minor matters, appointments to G.H.Q., new posts, etc.

No doubt was left in my mind as to the Emperor's complete indifference in matters of high strategy after I read an important record—that of the deliberations of a Military Council held at G.H.Q. at the end of 1916, under the chairmanship of the

Emperor. All the Commanders-in-Chief and the high officials of G.H.Q. were present, and the plans of the 1917 campaign and of a general advance were discussed.

Every word uttered at the conference was placed on record. One could not fail to be impressed by the dominating and guiding part played by General Gourko—Chief of the General Staff *pro tem.*—by the somewhat selfish designs of various Commanders-in-Chief, who were trying to adapt strategical axioms to the special interests of their fronts, and finally by the total indifference of the Supreme C.-in-C.

Relations similar to those just described continued between the Emperor and the Chief of Staff when General Gourko took charge of that office while Alexeiev, who had fallen seriously ill in the autumn of 1916, was undergoing a cure at Sevastopol, without, however, losing touch with G.H.Q., with which he communicated by direct wire.

Meanwhile, the struggle between the progressive block of the Duma and the Government (General Alexeiev and the majority of the Commanding Officers undoubtedly sympathised with the former) was gradually becoming more and more acute. The record of the sitting of the Duma of November 1st, 1916 (of which the publication was prohibited and an abridged version did not appear in the Press till the beginning of January, 1917), when Shulguin and Miliukov delivered their historical speeches, was circulated everywhere in the Army in the shape of typewritten leaflets. Feeling was already running so high that these leaflets were not concealed, but were read and provoked animated discussions in officers' messes. A prominent Socialist, an active worker of the Union of Towns, who paid his first visit to the Army in 1916, said to me: " I am amazed at the freedom with which the worthlessness of the Government and the Court scandals are being discussed in regiments and messes in the presence of Commanding officers, at Army Headquarters, etc., and that in our country of arbitrary repression . . . at first it seemed to me that I was dealing with ' agents provocateurs.' "

The Duma had been in close connection with the Officers' Corps for a long time. Young officers unofficially partook in the work of the Commission of National Defence during the period of the reorganisation of the Army and revival of the Fleet after the Japanese War. Gutchkov had formed a circle, in which Savitch, Krupensky, Count Bobrinski and representatives of the officers, headed by General Gourko, were included. Apparently, General

The Old Army and the Emperor

Polivanov (who afterwards played such an important part in contributing to the disintegration of the Army, as Chairman of the " Polivanov Commission ") also belonged to the circle. There was no wish to " undermine the foundations," but merely to push along the heavy, bureaucratic van, to give impetus to the work, and initiative to the offices of the inert Military Administration. According to Gutchkov, the circle worked quite openly, and the War Ministry at first even provided the members with materials. Subsequently, however, General Sukhomlinov's attitude changed abruptly, the circle came under suspicion, and people began to call it " The Young Turks."

The Commission of National Defence was, nevertheless, very well informed. General Lukomski, who was Chief of the Mobilisation Section, and later Assistant War Minister, told me that reports to the Commission had to be prepared extremely carefully, and that General Sukhomlinov, trivial and ignorant, produced a pitiful impression on the rare occasions on which he appeared before the Commission, and was subjected to a regular cross-examination.

In the course of his trial, Sukhomlinov himself recounted an episode which illustrates this state of affairs. One day, he arrived at a meeting of the Commission when two important military questions were to be discussed. He was stopped by Rodzianko,* who said to him:

" Get away, get away. You are to us as a red rag to a bull. As soon as you come, your requests are turned down."

After the Galician retreat, the Duma succeeded at last in enforcing the participation of its members in the task of placing on a proper basis all orders for the Army, and the Unions of Zemstvos and Towns were permitted to create the " General Committee for provisioning the Army."

The hard experience of the war resulted at last in the simple scheme of mobilising the Russian industries. No sooner did this undertaking escape from the deadening atmosphere of military offices than it advanced with giant strides. According to official data, in July, 1915, each Army received 33 parks of artillery instead of the requisite 50, whereas, in September, the figure rose to 78, owing to the fact that private factories had been brought into the scheme. I am in a position to state, not only on the strength of figures, but from personal experience, that, at the end of 1916, our Army, albeit falling short of the high standards of the Allied armies in respect of equipment, had sufficient stores of ammunition

---

* President of the Duma.

and supplies wherewith to begin an extensive and carefully-planned operation along the entire front. These circumstances were duly appreciated in the Army, and confidence in the Duma and in social organisations was thereby increased. The conditions of internal policy, however, were not improving. In the beginning of 1917, out of the extremely tense atmosphere of political strife, there arose the idea of a new remedy:

" REVOLUTION."

*   *

Representatives of certain Duma and social circles visited Alexeiev, who was ill at Sevastopol. They told the General quite frankly that a revolution was brewing. They knew what the effect would be in the country, but they could not tell how the front would be impressed, and wanted advice.

Alexeiev strongly insisted that violent changes during the war were inadmissible, that they would constitute a deadly menace to the front, which, according to his pessimistic view, " was already by no means steady," and pleaded against any irretrievable steps for the sake of preserving the Army. The delegates departed, promising to take the necessary measures in order to avert the contemplated revolution. I do not know upon what information General Alexeiev based his subsequent statement to the effect that the same delegates afterwards visited Generals Brussilov and Ruzsky, and after these generals had expressed an opposite view to his, altered their previous decision; but the preparations for the revolution continued.

It is as yet difficult to elucidate all the details of these negotiations. Those who conducted them are silent; there are no records; the whole matter was shrouded in secrecy, and did not reach the bulk of the army. Certain facts, however, have been ascertained.

Several people approached the Emperor, and warned him of the impending danger to the country and the dynasty—Alexeiev, Gourko, the Archbishop Shavelski, Purishkevitch (a reactionary member of the Duma), the Grand Dukes Nicholas Mikhailovitch and Alexander Mikhailovitch, and the Dowager Empress. After Rodzianko's visit to the Army in the autumn of 1916, copies of his letter to the Emperor gained circulation in the Army. In that letter the President of the Duma warned the Emperor of the grave peril to the throne and the dynasty caused by the disastrous activities of the Empress Alexandra in the sphere of internal policy. On November 1st, the Grand Duke Nicholas Mikhailovitch read a letter to the Emperor, in which he pointed out the impossible manner, known to all classes of society, in which Ministers were appointed, through the medium of the appalling people who surrounded the Empress. The Grand Duke proceeded:

" . . . If you could succeed in removing this perpetual interference, the renascence of Russia would begin at once, and you would recover the confidence of the vast majority of your subjects which is now lost. When the time is ripe—and it is at hand—you can yourself grant from the throne the desired responsibility (of the Government) to yourself and the legislature. This will come about naturally, easily, without any pressure from without, and not in the same way as with the memorable act of October 17th, 1905.* I hesitated for a long time to tell you the truth, but made up my mind when your mother and your sisters persuaded me to do so. You are on the eve of new disturbances, and, if I may say so, new attempts. Believe me, if I so strongly emphasise the necessity for your liberation from the existing fetters, I am doing so not for personal motives, but only in the hope of saving you, your throne, and our beloved country from irretrievable consequences of the gravest nature."

All these representations were of no avail.

Several members of the right and of the liberal wing of the Duma and of the progressive bloc, members of the Imperial family, and officers, joined the circle. One of the Grand Dukes was to make a last appeal to the Emperor before active measures were undertaken. In the event of failure, the Imperial train was to be stopped by an armed force on its way from G.H.Q. to Petrograd. The Emperor was to be advised to abdicate, and, in the event of his refusal, he was to be removed by force. The rightful heir, the Czarevitch Alexis, was to be proclaimed Emperor, and the Grand Duke Michael, Regent.

At the same time, a large group of the progressive bloc of the Duma, of representatives of Zemstvos and towns—well versed in the activities of the circle—held several meetings, at which the question was discussed of " the part the Duma was to play after the *coup d'état*."† The new Ministry was then outlined, and of the two suggested candidates for the Premiership, Rodzianko and Prince Lvov, the latter was chosen.

Fate, however, decreed otherwise.

Before the contemplated *coup d'état* took place, there began, in the words of Albert Thomas, " the brightest, the most festive, the most bloodless Russian Revolution."

---

* The Grand Duke here refers to the manifesto drafted by Witte, granting various liberties and decreeing the convocation of the Duma.
† Miliukov ; *History of the Second Russian Revolution*.

CHAPTER IV.

The Revolution in Petrograd.

I DID not learn of the course of events in Petrograd and at G.H.Q. until some time had elapsed, and I will refer to these events briefly in order to preserve the continuity of my narrative. In a telegram addressed to the Emperor by the members of the Council of the Empire on the night of the 28th February, the state of affairs was described as follows:—

" Owing to the complete disorganisation of transport and to the lack of necessary materials, factories have stopped working. Forced unemployment, and the acute food crisis due to the disorganisation of transport, have driven the popular masses to desperation. This feeling is further intensified by hatred towards the Government and grave suspicions against the authorities, which have penetrated deeply into the soul of the nation. All this has found expression in a popular rising of elemental dimensions, and the troops are now joining the movement. The Government, which has never been trusted in Russia, is now utterly discredited and incapable of coping with the dangerous situation."

Preparations for the Revolution found favourable ground in the general condition of the country, and had been made long since. The most heterogeneous elements had taken part in these activities; the German Government, which spared no means for Socialist and defeatist propaganda in Russia, and especially among the workmen; the Socialist parties, who had formed " cells " among the workmen and in the regiments; undoubtedly, too, the Protopopov Ministry, which was said to have been provoking a rising in the streets in order to quell it by armed force, and thus clear the intolerably tense atmosphere. It would seem that all these forces were aiming at the same goal, which they were trying to reach by diverse means, actuated by diametrically opposed motives.

At the same time, the progressive block and social organisations began to prepare for great events which they considered inevitable, and other circles, in close touch with these organisations or sharing their views, were completing the arrangements for a " *Palace coup d'état* " as the last means of averting the impending Revolution.

Nevertheless, the rebellion started as an elemental force and caught everybody unawares. Several days later, when General Kornilov visited the Executive Committee of the Petrograd Soviet of Workmen and Soldiers' Deputies, prominent members of that body incidentally explained that " the soldiers mutinied independently of the workmen, with whom the soldiers had not been in touch on the eve of the rebellion," and that the " mutiny had not been prepared—hence the absence of a corresponding administrative organ."

As regards the circles of the Duma and the social organisations, they were prepared for a *coup d'état*, but not for the Revolution. In the blazing fire of the outbreak they failed to preserve their moral balance and judgment.

The first outbreak began on February 23rd, when crowds filled the streets, meetings were held, and the speakers called for a struggle against the hated power. This lasted till the 26th, when the popular movement assumed gigantic proportions and there were collisions with the police, in which machine-guns were brought into action. On the 26th an ukaze was received proroguing the Duma, and on the morning of the 27th the members of the Duma decided not to leave Petrograd. On the same morning the situation underwent a drastic change, because the rebels were joined by the Reserve battalions of the Litovski, Volynski, Preobrajenski, and Sapper Guards' Regiments. They were Reserve battalions, as the real Guards' Regiments were then on the South-Western Front. These battalions did not differ, either in discipline or spirit, from any other unit of the line. In several battalions the Commanding Officers were disconcerted, and could not make up their minds as to their own attitude. This wavering resulted, to a certain extent, in a loss of prestige and authority. The troops came out into the streets without their officers, mingled with the crowds, and were imbued with the crowds' psychology. Armed throngs, intoxicated with freedom, excited to the utmost, and incensed by street orators, filled the streets, smashed the barricades, and new crowds of waverers joined them. Police detachments were mercilessly slaughtered. Officers who chanced to be in the way of the crowds were disarmed and some of them killed. The armed mob seized the arsenal, the Fortress of Peter and Paul, and the Kresti Prison.

On that decisive day there were no leaders—there was only the tidal wave. Its terrible progress appeared to be devoid of any definite object, plan, or watchword. The only cry that seemed to express the general spirit was " *Long live Liberty.*"

Somebody was bound to take the movement in hand. After violent discussions, much indecision and wavering, that part was assumed by the Duma. A Committee of the Duma was formed, which proclaimed its objects on February 27th in the following guarded words:—

" In the strenuous circumstances of internal strife caused by the activities of the old Government, the temporary Committee of the members of the Duma has felt compelled to undertake the task of restoring order in the State and in society. . . . The Committee expresses its conviction that the population and the army will render assistance in the difficult task of creating a new Government, which will correspond to the wishes of the population, and which will be in a position to enjoy its confidence."

There can be no doubt that the Duma, having led the patriotic and national struggle against the Government detested by the people, and having accomplished great and fruitful work in the interests of the army, had obtained recognition in the country and in the army. The Duma now became the centre of the political life of the country. No one else could have taken the lead in the movement. No one else could have gained the confidence of the country, or such rapid and full recognition as the Supreme Power, as the power that emanated from the Duma. The Petrograd Soviet of Workmen and Soldiers' Deputies was fully aware of this fact, and it did not then claim *officially* to represent the Russian Government. Such an attitude towards the Duma at that moment created the illusion of the *national* character of the Provisional Government created by the Duma. Alongside, therefore, with the troops that mingled with the armed mob and destroyed in their trail everything reminiscent of the old power, alongside with the units that had remained faithful to that power and resisted the mob, regiments began to flock to the Taurida Palace with their commanding officers, bands and banners. They greeted the new power in the person of Rodzianko, President of the Duma, according to the rules of the old ritual. The Taurida Palace presented an unusual sight—legislators, bureaucrats, soldiers, workmen, women; a chamber, a camp, a prison, a headquarters, Ministries. Everyone foregathered there seeking protection and salvation, demanding guidance and answers to puzzling questions which had suddenly arisen. On the same day,

The Revolution in Petrograd

February 27th, an announcement was made from the Taurida Palace:—

" Citizens. Representatives of the workmen, soldiers and people of Petrograd, sitting in the Duma, declare that the first meeting of their representatives will take place at seven o'clock to-night on the premises of the Duma. Let the troops that have joined the people immediately elect their representatives—one to each company. Let the factories elect their deputies—one to each thousand. Factories with less than a thousand workmen to elect one deputy each."

This proclamation had a grave and fateful effect upon the entire course of events. In the first place, it created an organ of unofficial, but undoubtedly stronger, power alongside with the provisional Government—the Soviet of Workmen and Soldiers' deputies, against which the Government proved impotent. In the second place, it converted the political and bourgeois revolution, both outwardly and inwardly, into a social revolution, which was unthinkable, considering the condition of the country at that time. Such a revolution in war time could not fail to bring about terrible upheavals. Lastly, it established a close connection between the Soviet, which was inclined towards Bolshevism and defeatism, and the army, which was thus infected with a ferment which resulted in its ultimate collapse. When the troops, fully officered, smartly paraded before the Taurida Palace, it was only for show. The link between the officers and the men had already been irretrievably broken; discipline had been shattered. Henceforward, the troops of the Petrograd district represented a kind of Pretorian guard, whose evil force weighed heavily over the Provisional Government. All subsequent efforts made by Gutchkov, General Kornilov and G.H.Q. to influence them and to send them to the front were of no avail, owing to the determined resistance of the Soviet.

The position of the officers was undoubtedly tragic, as they had to choose between loyalty to their oath, the distrust and enmity of the men, and the dictates of practical necessity. A small portion of the officers offered armed resistance to the mutiny, and most of them perished. Some avoided taking any part in the events, but the majority in the regiments, where comparative order prevailed, tried to find in the Duma a solution of the questions which perturbed their conscience. At a big meeting of officers held in Petrograd on March 1st, a resolution was carried: " To stand by the people and unanimously to recognise the power of the Executive Committee of the Duma, pending the convocation of the Constituent Assembly; because a speedy organisation of order and of united work in the rear were necessary for the victorious end of the war."

Owing to the unrestrained orgy of power in which the successive rulers appointed at Rasputin's suggestion had indulged during their short terms of office, there was in 1917 no political party, no class upon which the Czarist Government could reply. Everybody considered that Government as the enemy of the people. Extreme Monarchists and Socialists, the united nobility, labour groups, Grand Dukes and half-educated soldiers—all were of the same opinion. I do not intend to examine the activities of the Government which led to the Revolution, its struggle against the people and against representative institutions. I will only draw a summary of the accusations which were justly levelled by the Duma against the Government on the eve of its downfall:

All the Institutions of the State and of society—the Council of the Empire, the Duma, the nobility, the Zemstvos, the municipalities—were under suspicion of disloyalty, and the Government was in open opposition to them, and paralysed all their activities in matters of statesmanship and social welfare.

Lawlessness and espionage had reached unheard-of proportions. The independent Russian Courts of Justice became subservient to " the requirements of the political moment."

Whilst in the Allied countries all classes of society worked whole-heartedly for the defence of their countries, in Russia that work was repudiated with contempt, and the work was done by unskilled and occasionally criminal hands, which resulted in such disastrous phenomena as the activities of Sukhomlinov and Protopopov. The Committee " of Military Industries," which had rendered great services in provisioning the Army, was being systematically destroyed. Shortly before the Revolution its labour section was arrested without any reason being assigned, and this very nearly caused sanguinary disturbances in the capital. Measures adopted by the Government without the participation of social organisations shattered the industrial life of the country. Transport was disorganised, and fuel was wasted. The Government proved incapable and impotent in combating this disorder, which was undoubtedly caused to a certain extent by the selfish and sometimes rapacious designs of industrial magnates. The villages were derelict. A series of wholesale mobilisations, without any exemptions granted to classes which worked for defence, deprived the villages of labour. Prices were unsettled, and the big landowners were given certain privileges. Later, the grain

Funeral of the first victims of the March Revolution in Petrograd.

contribution was gravely mismanaged. There was no exchange of goods between towns and villages. All this resulted in the stopping of food supplies, famine in the towns, and repression in the villages. Government servants of all kinds were impoverishd by the tremendous rise in prices of commodities, and were grumbling loudly.

Ministerial appointments were staggering in their fitfulness, and appeared to the people as a kind of absurdity. The demands of the country for a responsible Cabinet were voiced by the Duma and by the best men. As late as the morning of February 27th, the Duma considered that the granting of the minimum of the political desiderata of Russian society was sufficient to postpone " the last hour in which the fate of the Mother Country and of the dynasty was to be settled." Public opinion and the Press were smothered; the Military Censorship of all internal regions (including Moscow and Petrograd) had made the widest use of its telephones. It was impregnable, protected by all the powers of martial law. Ordinary censorship was no less severe. The following striking fact was discussed in the Duma:

In February, 1917, a strike movement, prompted to a certain extent by the Germans, began to spread in the factories. The Labour members of the Military Industries Committee then drafted a proclamation, as follows:—" Comrades, workmen of Petrograd, we deem it our duty to address to you an urgent request to resume work. The labouring class, fully aware of its present-day responsibilities, must not weaken itself by a protracted strike. The interests of the labouring class are calling upon you to resume work." In spite of Gutchkov's appeal to the Minister of the Interior and to the Chief Censor, this appeal was twice removed from the printing press, and was prohibited.

The question is still open for discussion and investigation as to what proportion of the activities of the old régime in the domain of economics can be attributed to individuals, what to the system, and what to the insuperable obstacles created in the country by a devastating war. But no excuse will ever be found for stifling the conscience, the mind, and the spirit of the people and all social initiative. No wonder, therefore, that Moscow and the provinces joined the Revolution without any appreciable resistance. Outside Petrograd, where the terror of street fighting and the rowdiness of a bloodthirsty mob were absent (there were, however, many exceptions), the Revolution was greeted with satisfaction, and even with enthusiasm, not only by the Revolutionary Democracy, but by the real Democracy, the Bourgeoisie and the Civil Service. There was tremendous animation; thousands of people thronged

the streets. Fiery speeches were made. There was great rejoicing at the deliverance from the terrible nightmare; there were bright hopes for the future of Russia. There was the word:
" LIBERTY."

It was in the air. It was reproduced in speeches, drawings, in music, in song. It was stimulating. It was not yet stained by stupidity, by filth and blood.

Prince Eugene Troubetskoi wrote: " This Revolution is unique. There have been bourgeois revolutions and proletarian revolutions, but such a national Revolution, in the broadest sense of the word, as the present Russian Revolution, there has never been. Everyone took part in this Revolution, everyone made it: the proletariat, the troops, the bourgoisie, even the nobility . . all the live forces of the country. . . . May this unity endure! " In these words the hopes and fears of the Russian intelligencia, not the sad Russian realities, are reflected. The cruel mutinies at Helsingfors, Kronstadt, Reval, and the assassination of Admiral Nepenin and of many officers were the first warnings to the optimists.

• - - - -

In the first days of the Revolution the victims in the Capital were few. According to the registration of the All-Russian Union of Towns, the total number of killed and wounded in Petrograd was 1,443, including 869 soldiers (of whom 60 were officers). Of course, many wounded were not registered. The condition of Petrograd, however, out of gear and full of inflammable material and armed men, remained for a long time strained and unstable. I heard later from members of the Duma and of the Government that the scales were swaying violently, and that they felt like sitting on a powder-barrel which might explode at any moment and blow to bits both themselves and the structure of the new Government which they were creating. The Deputy-Chairman of the Soviet of Workmen and Soldiers' Deputies, Skobelev, said to a journalist:—

" I must confess that, when in the beginning of the Revolution, I went to the entrance of the Taurida Palace to meet the first band of soldiers that had come to the Duma, and when I addressed them, I was almost certain that I was delivering one of my last speeches, and that in the course of the next few days I should be shot or hanged."

Several officers who had taken part in the events assured me that disorder and the universal incapacity for understanding the position in the Capital were so great that *one solid battalion*, commanded by an officer who knew what he wanted, might have upset the entire position. Be that as it may, the temporary Committee of the Duma proclaimed on March 2nd the formation of a Provisional Government. After lengthy discussions with the parallel organs of " Democratic Power," the Soviet of Workmen and Soldiers' Deputies, the Provisional Government issued a declaration : —

" (1) Full and immediate amnesty for all political, religious and terrorist crimes, military mutinies and aggrarian offences, etc.

" (2) Freedom of speech, the Press, meetings, unions and strikes. Political liberties to be granted to all men serving in the Army within the limits of military requirements.

" (3) Cancellation of all restrictions of class, religion and nationality.

" (4) Immediate preparation for the convocation of a Constituent Assembly elected by universal, equal, direct and secret suffrage for the establishment of a form of government and of the Constitution of the country.

" (5) The police to be replaced by a people's Militia, with elected chiefs, subordinate to the organ of Local Self-Government.

" (6) Members of Local Self-Governing Institutions to be elected by universal, equal, direct and secret suffrage.

" (7) The units of the Army that have taken part in the Revolutionary movement are not to be disarmed or removed from Petrograd.

" (8) Military discipline to be preserved on parade and on duty. The soldiers, however, are to be free to enjoy all social rights enjoyed by other citizens.

" The Provisional Government deems it its duty to add that it has no intention of taking advantage of wartime to delay carrying out the aforesaid reforms and measures."

This Declaration was quite obviously drafted under pressure from the " parallel power."

In his book, *Mes Souvenirs de Guerre*, General Ludendorff says : " I often dreamt of that Revolution which was to alleviate the burdens of our war. Eternal chimera ! To-day, however, the dream suddenly and unexpectedly came true. I felt as if a heavy load had fallen off my shoulders. I could not, however, foresee that it would be the grave of our might."

One of the most prominent leaders of Germany—the country that had worked so hard for the poisoning of the soul of the Russian people—has come to the belated conclusion that " Our moral collapse began with the beginning of the Russian Revolution."

CHAPTER V.

The Revolution and the Imperial Family.

ALONE in the Governor's old Palace at Mohilev the Czar suffered in silence; his wife and children were far away, and there was no one with him in whom he was able or willing to confide.

Protopopov and the Government had at first represented the state of affairs as serious, but not alarming—popular disturbances to be suppressed with " a firm hand." Several hundred machine-guns had been placed at the disposal of General Habalov, Commander of the troops of the Petrograd district. Both he and Prince Golitzin, President of the Cabinet, had been given full authority to make use of exceptional means of quelling the riots. On the morning of the 27th General Ivanov had been despatched with a small detachment of troops and a secret warrant, to be made public after the occupation of Czarskoe Selo. The warrant invested him with full military and civic powers. No one could have been less fitted than General Ivanov to occupy so highly important a position, which amounted actually to a Military Dictatorship. Ivanov was a very old man—an honest soldier, unfitted to cope with political complications and no longer in possession of strength, energy, will-power, or determination. . . . His success in dealing with the Kronstadt disturbances of 1906 most probably suggested his present nomination.

Afterwards, when looking over Habalov's and Bieliaiev's* reports, I was aghast at the pusillanimity and the shirking of responsibility which they revealed.

The clouds continue to darken.

On February 26th the Empress wired to the Czar: " Am very anxious about the state of affairs in town. . . ." On the same day Rodzianko sent his historic telegram : " Position serious. Anarchy in the capital. Government paralysed. Transport,

---

* Minister of War

supplies of fuel and other necessaries completely disorganised. General discontent grows. Disorderly firing in the streets. Military units fire at each other. Imperative necessity that some person popular in the country should be authorised to form new Cabinet. No delay possible. Any delay fatal. I pray God that the Monarch be not now held responsible." Rodzianko forwarded copies of his telegram to all the Commanders-in-Chief, asking their support.

Early on the 27th the President of the Duma wired again to the Czar: " Position constantly aggravated. Measures must be taken immediately, as to-morrow may be too late. This hour decides the fate of our country and the dynasty."

It is incredible that, after this, the Czar should not have realised the impending catastrophe, but, in the weakness and irresolution that characterised him, it is probable that he seized the slightest available excuse to postpone his decision, and in a fatalistic manner, left to fate to carry out her secret decrees. . . .

Be that as it may, another impressive warning from General Alexeiev, confirmed by telegrams from the Commanders-in-Chief, yielded no better results, and the Czar, anxious about the fate of his family, left for Czarskoe Selo on the morning of the 29th, without coming to any final decision on the concessions to be granted to his people.

General Alexeiev, although straightforward, wise, and patriotic, was lacking in firmness, and his power and influence with the Emperor were too slight to permit of his insisting on a step the obvious necessity for which was evident even to the Empress. She wired to her husband on the 27th : " Concessions inevitable."

The futile journey was two days in accomplishment. Two days without any correspondence or news as to the course of events, which were developing and changing every hour.

The Imperial train, taking a roundabout course, was stopped at Vishera by orders from Petrograd. On hearing that the Petrograd garrison had acclaimed the Provisional Committee of the Duma, and that the troops of Czarskoe Selo had sided with the Revolution, the Czar returned to Pskov.

At Pskov, on the evening of March 1st, the Czar saw General Rusky, who explained the position to him, but no decision was arrived at, except that on the 2nd of March, at 2 a.m., the Czar again sent for Ruzsky, and handed him an ukase, which made the Cabinet responsible to the Duma. " I knew that this compromise had come too late," said Ruzsky to a correspondent, " but I had no right to express my opinion, not having received any instructions from the Executive Committee of the Duma, so I suggested that the Emperor should see Rodzianko."*

All night long discussions full of deep interest and importance to the fate of the country were held over the wire—between Ruzsky, Rodzianko, and Alexeiev; between Headquarters and the Commanders-in-Chief, and between Lukomsky† and Danilov.‡

They unanimously agreed that the Abdication of the Emperor was unavoidable.

Before midday on March 2nd Ruzsky communicated the opinion of Rodzianko and the Military Commanders to the Czar. The Emperor heard him calmly, with no sign of emotion on his fixed, immovable countenance, but at 3 p.m. he sent Ruzsky a signed Act of Abdication in favour of his son—a document drawn up at Headquarters and forwarded to him at Pskov.

If the sequence of historical events follows immutable laws of its own, there also seems to be a fate influencing casual happenings of a simple, everyday nature, which otherwise seem quite avoidable. The thirty minutes that elapsed after Ruzsky had received the Act of Abdication materially affected the whole course of subsequent events: before copies of the document could be despatched, a communication, announcing the delegates of the Duma, Gutchkov and Shulgin, was received. . . . The Czar again postponed his decision and stopped the publication of the Act.

The delegates arrived in the evening.

Amidst the complete silence of the audience,§ Gutchkov pictured the abyss that the country was nearing, and pointed out the only course to be taken—the abdication of the Czar.

" I have been thinking about it all yesterday and to-day, and have decided to abdicate," answered the Czar. " Until three o'clock to-day I was willing to abdicate in favour of my son, but I then came to realise that I could not bear to part with him. I hope you will understand this ? As a consequence, I have decided to abdicate in favour of my brother."

The delegates, taken aback by such an unexpected turn of events, made no objection. Emotion kept Gutchkov silent. " He felt he could not intrude on paternal relations, and considered that any pressure brought to bear upon the Emperor would be out of place." Shulgin was influenced by political motives.

---

* Chessin : *La Révolution Russe*.
† Quartermaster-General of the Commander-in-Chief of All Fronts.
‡ Chief of Staff of the Northern Front (Com.-in-Ch., General Ruzsky).
§ Count Fredericks, Narishkine, Ruzsky, Gutchkov, Shulgin.

"He feared the little Czar might grow up harbouring feelings of resentment against those who had parted him from his father and mother; also the question whether a regent could take the oath to the Constitution on behalf of an Emperor, who was not of age was a matter of debate."*

"The resentment" of the little Czar concerned a distant future. As to legality, the very essence of a Revolution precludes the legality of its consequences. Also the *enforced* abdication of Nicholas II., his rejection of the rights of inheritance of *his son*, a minor, and, lastly, the transfer of supreme power by Michael Alexandrovitch, a person who *had never* held it, to the Provisional Government by means of an act, in which the Grand Duke "appeals" to Russian citizens to obey the Government, are all of doubtful legality.

It is not surprising that, "in the minds of those living in those first days of the Revolution"—as Miliukov says—"the new Government, established by the Revolution, was looked upon, not as a consequence of the acts of March 2nd and 3rd, but as a result of the events of February 27th. . . ."

I may add that later, in the minds of many Commanding Officers—amongst them, Kornilov, Alexeiev, Romanovsky and Markov, who played a leading part in the attempt to save Russia—legal, party or dynastic considerations had no place. This circumstance is of primary importance for a proper understanding of subsequent events.

About midnight on March 2nd the Czar handed Rodzianko and Ruzsky two slightly amended copies of the Manifesto of his Abdication.

*　　　　　　＊　　　　　　＊

"In the midst of our great conflict with a foreign enemy, who has been striving for close on three years to enslave our country, it has been the will of God to subject Russia to new and heavy trials. Incipient popular disturbances now imperil the further course of the stubborn war. The fate of Russia, the honour of our heroic Army, the entire future of our beloved Land, demand that the war should be carried to a victorious conclusion.

"The cruel foe is nearly at his last gasp, and the hour approaches when our gallant Army, together with our glorious Allies, will finally crush our enemy's resistance. In these decisive days of Russia's existence we feel it our duty to further the firm cohesion and unification of all the forces of the people, and, with

---

* Shulgin's narrative.

the approval of the State Duma, consider it best to abdicate the Throne of Russia and lay down our supreme power. Not wishing to part from our beloved Son, we transmit our inheritance to our Brother, the Grand Duke Michael Alexandrovitch, and give him our blessing in ascending the Throne of the Russian Empire.

" We command our Brother to rule the State in complete and undisturbed union with the representatives of the people in such Legislative Institutions as the People will see fit to establish, binding himself by oath thereto in the name of our beloved country.

" I call all true sons of the Fatherland to fulfil their sacred duty—to obey the Czar in this time of sore distress and help him, together with the representatives of the people, to lead the Russian State along the road to victory, happiness and glory

" May the Lord our God help Russia!
" NICHOLAS."

* * * *

Late at night the Imperial train left for Mohilev. Dead silence, lowered blinds and heavy, heavy thoughts. No one will ever know what feelings wrestled in the breast of Nicholas II., of the Monarch, the Father and the Man, when, on meeting Alexeiev at Mohilev, and looking straight at the latter with kindly, tired eyes, he said irresolutely:—

"*I have changed my mind. Please send this telegram to Petrograd.*"

On a small sheet of paper, in a clear hand, the Czar had himself traced his consent to the immediate accession to the throne of his son, Alexis.

Alexeiev took the telegram, and—did not send it. It was too late; both Manifestoes had already been made public to the Army and to the country.

For fear of " unsettling public opinion," Alexeiev made no mention of the telegram, and kept it in his portfolio until he passed it on to me towards the end of May, when he resigned his post of Supreme Commander-in-Chief. The document, of vast importance to future biographers of the Czar, was afterwards kept under seal at the Operations Department of General Headquarters.

*

Meantime, the members of the Cabinet and of the Provisional Committee* had assembled at the Palace of the Grand Duke

---

* Prince Lvov, Miliukov, Kerensky, Nekrasso, Teresvtchenko, Godnev, Lvov, Gutchkov, and Rodzianko.

Michael Alexandrovitch about midday on May 3rd. Since the 27th of February, the latter had been cut off from all communication with Headquarters or with the Emperor. But the issue of this Conference was practically predetermined by the spirit prevailing in the Soviet of Workmen's Delegates, after the gist of the Manifesto became known to them, by the Resolution of Protest passed by their Executive Committee and forwarded to the Government, by Kerensky's uncompromising attitude, and by the general correlation of forces. Except Miliukov and Gutchkov, all the others, " without the faintest desire of influencing the Grand Duke in any way," eagerly advised him to abdicate. Miliukov warned them that " the support of a symbol familiar to the masses is necessary, if decided authority is to be maintained, and that the Provisional Government, if left alone, might founder in the sea of popular disturbances, and that it might not survive until the Convocation of the Constituent Assembly. . . . "

After another conference with Rodzianko, President of the Duma, the Grand Duke came to his final decision to abdicate.

The " Declaration " of the Grand Duke was published on the same day:

" A heavy burden has been laid on me by the wish of my Brother, who has transferred the Imperial Throne of All Russia to me at a time of unexampled warfare and popular disturbances.

" Animated, together with the nation, by one thought, that the welfare of our country must prevail over every other consideration, I have decided to accept supreme power only if such be the will of our great people, whose part it is to establish the form of government and new fundamental laws of the Russian State through their representatives in the Constituent Assembly.

" With a prayer to God for His blessing, I appeal to all citizens of the Russian State to obey the Provisional Government, which is constituted and invested with full powers by the will of the State Duma, until a Constituent Assembly, convoked at the earliest possible moment by universal, direct, equal and secret suffrage, can establish a form of government which will embody the will of the people."

" MICHAEL."

After his abdication, the Grand Duke resided in the neighbourhood of Gatchino, and stood completely aloof from political life. About the middle of March, 1918, he was arrested by order of the local Bolshevik Committee, taken to Petrograd, and, some time later, exiled to the Government of Perm.

It was rumoured that the Grand Duke, accompanied by his

faithful English valet, had escaped about the middle of July; since then nothing definite has been heard about him. The search organised by the Siberian Government and by that of Southern Russia, as also by the desire of the Dowager Empress, yielded no certain results. The Bolsheviks, for their part, volunteered no official information whatever. But subsequent investigations brought some data to light which indicated that the " release " was a deception, and that the Grand Duke was secretly carried off by Bolsheviks, murdered in the vicinity of Perm, and his body drowned under the ice.

The mystery of the Grand Duke's fate gave rise to fanciful rumours and even to the appearance of impostors in Siberia. During the summer of 1918, at the time of the first successful advance of the Siberian troops, it was widely reported both in Soviet Russia and in the South that the Siberian Anti-Bolshevist forces were led by the Grand Duke Michael Alexandrovitch. Periodically, until late in 1919, his spurious manifestoes appeared in the Provincial Press, chiefly in papers of the extreme Right.

It must be noted, however, that when, in the summer of 1918, the Kiev monarchists carried on an active campaign to impart a monarchical character to the Anti-Bolshevist military movement, they rejected the principle of legitimacy, partly because of the personality of some of the candidates, and, in regard to Michael Alexandrovitch, because he had " tied himself " by a solemn promise to the Constituent Assembly.

In consideration of the complexity and confusion of the conditions that obtained in March, 1917, I have come to the conclusion that a struggle to retain Nicholas II. at the head of the State would have led to anarchy, disruption of the Front, and terrible consequences, both for the Czar and for the country. A Regency, with Michael Alexandrovitch as Regent, might have involved conflict, but no disturbance, and was certain of success. It would have been more difficult to place Michael Alexandrovitch on the throne, but even that would have been possible if a Constitution on broad, democratic lines had been accepted by him.

The members of the Provisional Government and of the Provisional Committee—Miliukov and Gutchkov excepted—terrorised by the Soviets of Workmen's Delegates, and attributing too much importance to them and to the excited workmen and soldier masses in Petrograd, took on themselves a heavy responsibility for the future when they persuaded the Grand Duke to decline the immediate assumption of Supreme Power.

Miliukov : *History of the Second Russian Revolution.*

The Revolution and the Imperial Family   55

I am not referring to Monarchism or to a particular dynasty. These are secondary questions. I am speaking of Russia only.

It is certainly hard to say whether this power would have been lasting and stable, whether it would not have undergone changes later on; but, if it had even succeeded in maintaining the Army during the war, the subsequent course of Russian history might have been one of progress, and the upheavals that now endanger her very existence might have been avoided.

*   *   *   *

On March 7th the Provisional Government issued an order according to which " The ex-Emperor and his Consort are deprived of liberty, and the ex-Emperor is to be taken to Czarskoe Selo." The duty of arresting the Empress was laid on Kornilov, and orthodox Monarchists never forgave him for it. But, strangely enough, Alexandra Fedorovna, after hearing of the warrant, expressed her satisfaction that the renowned General Kornilov, and not a member of the new Government, had been sent to her.

The Emperor was arrested by four members of the Duma.

On March 8th, after leave-takings at Headquarters, the Czar quitted Mohilev amidst the stony silence of the crowd, and under the tearful eyes of his mother, who never saw her son again.

To understand the seemingly incomprehensible behaviour of the Government to the Imperial family during the period of their residence both at Czarskoe Selo and at Tobolsk, the following circumstances must be kept in mind. Notwithstanding that, in the seven and a half months of the existence of the Provisional Government, not one single serious attempt was made to liberate the captives, yet they attracted the exclusive attention of the Soviet of Workmen and Soldiers' Delegates. On March 10th Vice-President Sokolov made the following announcement to a unanimously approving audience: " I was informed yesterday that the Provisional Government had consented to allow Nicholas II. to go to England and that it is discussing arrangements with the British authorities without the knowledge or the consent of the Executive Committee of Workmen's and Soldiers' Delegates. We have mobilised all the military units that we can influence, and have taken measures to prevent Nicholas II. from leaving Czarskoe without our permission. Telegrams have been sent down the railway lines to detain the train of Nicholas II. should it appear. . . . We have despatched our Commissars with the necessary number of troops and armoured cars and have closely surrounded the Alexander Palace. After that we conferred with the Provisional Government, who confirmed all our orders. At present the late Czar is under our protection, as well as under that of the Provisional Government "

On the 1st August, 1917, the Imperial family was exiled to Tobolsk, and, after the establishment of Bolshevist rule in Siberia, they were transferred to Ekaterinburg, and were the victims of incredible insults and cruelty by the mob, until they were put to death.* Thus did Nicholas II. atone for his grievous sins, voluntary and involuntary, against the Russian people.†

In the course of the second Kuban campaign I received the news of the death of the Emperor Nicholas II., and ordered memorial services for the soul of the former leader of the Russian Army to be held in the Volunteer Army. Democratic circles and the Press criticised me severely for this.

The words of wisdom, *Vengeance is mine: I will repay*, were obviously forgotten.

---

* The murder took place on the night of July 16th, 1918.
† Much time, pains and labour were devoted to the task of collecting information about the murdered Imperial family by General Dietrichs.

CHAPTER VI

THE REVOLUTION AND THE ARMY.

ORDER No. 1.

THESE events found me far away from the Capital, in Roumania, where I was commanding the Eighth Army Corps. In our remoteness from the Mother Country we felt a certain tension in the political atmosphere, but we certainly were not prepared for the sudden *dénouement* or for the shape it assumed.

On the morning of March 3rd I received a telegram from Army Headquarters—" For personal information "—to the effect that a mutiny had broken out in Petrograd, that the Duma had assumed power, and that the publication of important State documents was expected. A few hours later the wire transmitted the manifestoes of the Emperor Nicholas the Second and of the Grand Duke Michael. At first an order was given for their distribution, then, much to my amazement (as the telephones had already been spreading the news) the order was countermanded and finally confirmed. These waverings were apparently due to the negotiations between the temporary Committee of the Duma and the Headquarters of the Norman Front about postponing the publication of these Acts owing to a sudden change in the Emperor's fundamental idea, namely, the substitution of the Grand Duke Michael for the Grand Duke Alexis as Heir to the Throne. It proved, however, impossible to delay the distribution. The troops were thunderstruck. No other word can describe the first impression produced by the *manifestoes*. There was neither sorrow nor rejoicing. There was deep, thoughtful silence. Thus did the regiments of the Fourteenth and Fifteenth Divisions take the news of the abdication of their Emperor. Only occasionally on parade did the rifle waver and tears course down the cheeks of old soldiers.

In order accurately to describe the spirit of the moment,

undimmed by the passing of time, I will quote extracts from a letter I wrote to a near relation on March 8th:

" A page of history has been turned. The first impression is stunning because it is so unexpected and so grandiose. On the whole, however, the troops have taken the events quietly. They express themselves with caution; but three definite currents in the mentality of the men can easily be traced: (1) A return to the past is impossible; (2) the country will receive a Constitution worthy of a great people, probably a Constitutional Limited Monarchy; (3) German domination will come to an end and the war will be victoriously prosecuted."

The Emperor's abdication was considered as the inevitable result of the internal policy of the last few years. There was, however, no irritation against the Emperor personally or against the Imperial Family. Everything was forgiven and forgotten. On the contrary, everyone was interested in their fate, and feared the worst. The appointment of the Grand Duke Nicholas as Supreme Commander-in-Chief, and of General Alexeiev as his Chief-of-Staff, was favourably received, alike by officers and men, and interest was manifested in the question as to whether the Army would be represented in the Constituent Assembly. The composition of the Provisional Government was treated more or less as a matter of indifference. The appointment of a civilian to the War Ministry was criticised, and it was only the part he had taken in the Council of National Defence, and his close connection with the officers' circles, that mitigated the unfavourable impression. A great many people have found it surprising and incomprehensible that the collapse of a Monarchist régime several centuries old should not have provoked in the Army, bred in its traditions, either a struggle or even isolated outbreaks, or that the Army should not have created its own Vendée.

I know of three cases only of stout resistance: The march of General Ivanov's detachment on Czarskoe Selo, organised by Headquarters in the first days of the risings in Petrograd, very badly executed and soon countermanded, and two telegrams addressed to the Emperor by the Commanding Officers of the Third Cavalry and the Guards Cavalry Corps, Count Keller (killed in Kiev in 1918 by Petlura's men) and Khan Nachitchevansky. They both offered themselves and their troops for the suppression of the mutiny. It would be a mistake to assume that the Army was quite prepared to accept the provisional " Democratic Republic," that there were no " loyal " units or " loyal " chiefs ready to engage in the struggle. They undoubtedly existed. There were, however, two circumstances which

The Revolution and the Army

exercised a restraining influence. In the first place, both Acts of Abdication were apparently legal, and the second of these Acts, in summoning the people to submit to the Provisional Government " invested with full power," took the wind out of the sails of the monarchists. In the second place, it was apprehended that civil war might open the front to the enemy. The Army was *then* obedient to its leaders, and they—General Alexeiev and all the Commanders-in-Chief—recognised the new power. The newly-appointed Supreme Commander-in-Chief, the Grand Duke Nicholas, said in his first Order of the Day: " The power is established in the person of the new Government. I, the Supreme Commander-in-Chief, have recognised that power for the good of our Mother Country, serving as an example to us of our duty as soldiers. I order all ranks of our gallant Army and Navy implicitly to obey the established Government through their direct Chiefs. Only then will God grant us victory."

* * *

The days went by. I began to receive many—both slight and important—expressions of bewilderment and questions from the units of my corps: Who represents the Supreme Power in Russia? Is it the temporary Committee which created the Provisional Government, or is it the latter? I sent an inquiry, but received no answer. The Provisional Government itself, apparently, had no clear notion of the essence of its power.

For whom should we pray at Divine Service? Should we sing the National Anthem and " O God, Save Thy People! " (a prayer in which the Emperor was mentioned)?

These apparent trifles produced, however, a certain confusion in the minds of the men and interfered with established military routine. The Commanding Officers requested that the oath should be taken as soon as possible. There was also the question whether the Emperor Nicolas had the right to abdicate not only for himself, but for his son, who had not yet attained his majority.

Other questions soon began to interest the troops. We received the first Order of the Day of the War Minister, Gutchkov, with alterations of the Army Regulations in favour of the " Democratisation of the Army " (March 5th). By this Order, inoffensive at first sight, the officers were not to be addressed by the men according to their rank, and were not to speak to the men in the second person singular. A series of petty restrictions established by Army Regulations for the men, such as no smoking in the streets and other public places, no card-playing, and exclusion from Clubs and Meetings, were removed. The consequences came as a surprise to those who were ignorant of the psychology of the rank and file. The Commanding Officers understood that if it were necessary to do away with certain out-of-date forms the process should be gradual and cautious, and should by no means be interpreted as one of " the fruits of the Revolutionary victory." The bulk of the men did not trouble to grasp the meaning of these insignificant changes in the Army Regulations, but merely accepted them as a deliverance from the restrictions imposed on them by routine and by respect to the Senior Officers.

" There is liberty, and that's all there is to it."

All these minor alterations of the Army Regulations, broadly interpreted by the men, affected, to a certain degree, the discipline of the army. But that soldiers should be permitted, during the war and during the Revolution, to join in the membership of various Unions and Societies formed for political purposes, was a menace to the very existence of the army. G.H.Q., perturbed by this situation, had recourse to a measure hitherto unknown in the army—to a kind of plébiscite. All Commanding Officers, including Regimental Commanders, were advised to address direct telegrams to the Minister of War, expressing their views on the new orders. I do not know whether the telegraph was able to cope with this task and whether the enormous mass of telegrams reached their destination, but I know that those that came to my notice were full of criticism and of fears for the future of the army. At the same time, the Army Council in Petrograd, consisting of Senior Generals—the would-be guardians of the experience and traditions of the army—decided at a meeting held on March 10th to make the following report to the Provisional Government: " The Army Council deems it its duty to declare its full solidarity with the energetic measures contemplated by the Provisional Government in re-modelling our armed forces in accordance with the new forms of life in the country and in the army. We are convinced that these reforms will be the best means of achieving rapid victory and the deliverance of Europe from the yoke of Prussian militarism." I cannot help sympathising with a civilian War Minister after such an occurrence. It was difficult for us to understand the motives by which the War Ministry was guided in issuing its Orders of the Day. We were unaware of the unrestrained opportunities of the men who surrounded the War Minister, as well as of the fact that the Provisional Government was already dominated by the Soviet and had entered upon the path of compromise, being invariably on the losing side. At the Congress of the Soviets on March 30th, one

The Revolution and the Army

of the speakers stated that in the Conciliation Commission there never was a case in which the Provisional Commission did not give way on important matters.

* * * * *

ON THE FIRST OF MARCH THE SOVIET OF WORKMEN AND SOLDIERS' DELEGATES ISSUED AN ORDER OF THE DAY No. I., WHICH PRACTICALLY LED TO THE TRANSFER OF ACTUAL MILITARY POWER TO THE SOLDIERS' COMMITTEES, TO A SYSTEM OF ELECTIONS AND TO THE DISMISSAL OF COMMANDING OFFICERS BY THE MEN. THAT ORDER OF THE DAY GAINED WIDE AND PAINFUL NOTORIETY AND GAVE THE FIRST IMPETUS TO THE COLLAPSE OF THE ARMY.

ORDER No. I.

March 1st, 1917.

To the Garrison of the Petrograd District, to all Guardsmen, soldiers of the line, of the Artillery, and of the Fleet, for immediate and strict observance, and to the workmen of Petrograd for information.

The Soviet of Workmen and Soldiers' Delegates has decreed:

(1) That Committees be elected of representatives of the men in all companies, battalions, regiments, parks, batteries, squadrons and separate services of various military institutions, and on the ships of the fleet.

(2) All military units not yet represented on the Soviet of Workmen's Delegates to elect one representative from each company. These representatives to provide themselves with written certificates and to report to the Duma at 10 A.M. on March 2nd.

(3) In all its political activities the military unit is subordinate to the Soviet,* and to its Committees.

(4) The Orders of the Military Commission of the Duma are to be obeyed only when they are not in contradiction with the orders and decrees of the Soviet.

(5) All arms—rifles, machine-guns, armoured cars, etc.—are to be at the disposal and under the control of Company and Battalion Committees, and should never be handed over to the officers even should they claim them.

---

* The term *Soviet* for brevity will be used in the course of the narrative instead of *Soviet of Workmen's and Soldiers' Delegates*.

(6) On parade and on duty the soldiers must comply with strict military discipline; but off parade and off duty, in their political, social and private life, soldiers must suffer no restriction of the rights common to all citizens. In particular, saluting when off duty is abolished.

(7) Officers are no longer to be addressed as " Your Excellency," " Your Honour," etc. Instead, they should be addressed as " Mr. General," " Mr. Colonel," etc.

Rudeness to soldiers on the part of all ranks, and in particular addressing them in the second person singular, is prohibited, and any infringement of this regulation and misunderstandings between officers and men are to be reported by the latter to the Company Commanders.

(Signed) THE PETROGRAD SOVIET.

The leaders of the Revolutionary Democracy understood full well the results of Order No. I. Kerensky is reported to have declared afterwards pathetically that he would have given ten years of his life to prevent the Order from being signed. The investigation made by military authorities failed to detect the authors of this Order. Tchkeidze and other members of the Soviet afterwards denied their personal participation and that of the members of the Committee in the drafting of the Order.

Pilates! They washed their hands of the writing of their own Credo. For their words are placed on record, in the report of the secret sitting of the Government, the Commanders-in-Chief and the Executive Committee of the Workmen and Soldiers' Deputies of May 4th, 1917:

Tzeretelli: You might, perhaps, understand Order No. I if you knew the circumstances in which it was issued. We were confronted with an unorganised mob, and we had to organise.

Skobelev: I consider it necessary to explain the circumstances in which Order No. I. was issued. Among the troops that overthrew the old régime, the Commanding Officers did not join the rebels. In order to deprive the former of their importance, we were forced to issue Order No. I. We had inward apprehensions as to the attitude of the front towards the Revolution. Certain instructions were given, which provoked our distrust. To-day we have ascertained that this distrust was well founded.

A member of the Soviet, Joseph Goldenberg, Editor of *New Life,* was still more outspoken. He said to the French journalist, Claude Anet: (Claude Anet: *La Révolution Russe*) " Order No. I. was not an error, but a necessity. It was not drafted by

Sokolov. It is the expression of the unanimous will of the Soviet. On the day we ' made the Revolution,' we understood that if we did not dismember the old army, it would crush the Revolution. We had to choose between the army and the Revolution. We did not hesitate—we chose the latter, and I dare say that we were right."

Order No. I. was disseminated rapidly and everywhere along the whole front and in the rear, because the ideas which it embodied had developed for many years, in the slums of Petrograd as well as in the remote corners of the Empire, such as Vladivostock. They had been preached by all local army demagogues and were being repeated by all the delegates who visited the front in vast numbers and were provided with certificates of immunity by the Soviet.

The masses of the soldiery were perturbed. The movement began in the rear, always more easily demoralised than the front, among the half-educated clerks, doctors' assistants, and technical units. In the latter part of March in our units, breaches of discipline only became more frequent. The officer in command of the Fourth Army was expecting every hour that he would be arrested at his Headquarters by the licentious bands of men attached to service battalions for special duty, such as tailoring, cooking, bootmaking, etc.

The text of the oath of allegiance to the Russian State was received at last. The idea of Supreme Power was expressed in these words: " I swear to obey the Provisional Government now at the head of the Russian State, pending the expression of the popular will through the medium of the Constituent Assembly." The oath was taken by the troops everywhere without any disturbance, but the idyllic hopes of the Commanding Officers were not fulfilled. There was no uplifting of the spirit and the perturbed minds were not quieted. I may quote two characteristic episodes. The Commander of one of the Corps on the Roumanian front died of heart-failure during the ceremony. Count Keller declared that he would not compel his corps to take the oath because he did not understand the substance and the legal foundations of the Supreme Power of the Provisional Government. (Replying to a question addressed from the crowd as to who had elected the Provisional Government, Miliukov had answered: " We have been elected by the Russian Revolution "). Count Keller said he did not understand how one could swear allegiance to Lvov, Kerensky and other individuals, because they could be removed or relinquish their posts. Was the oath a sham? I think that not only for the monarchists, but for many men who did not look upon the oath as a mere formality, it was in any case a great, moral drama difficult to live through. It was a heavy sacrifice made for the sake of the country's salvation and for the preservation of the army.

In the middle of May I was ordered to attend a Council at the Headquarters of the General-in-Command of the Fourth Army. A long telegram was read from General Alexeiev full of the darkest possible pessimism, recounting the beginning of the administrative machine and of the army. He described the demagogic activities of the Soviet, which dominated the will-power and the conscience of the Provisional Government, the complete impotence of the latter and the interference of both in army administration.

In order to counteract the dismemberment of the army, the despatch was contemplated of members of the Duma and of the Soviet, possessing a certain amount of statesmanlike experience, to the front for purposes of propaganda. .

This telegram impressed us all in the same way: *General Headquarters had ceased to be the chief administrative authority in the army.* And yet a stern warning and remonstrance from the High Command, supported by the army, which in the first fortnight had still retained discipline and obedience might, perhaps, have relegated the Soviet, which over-estimated its importance, to its proper place; might have prevented the " democratisation " of the army and might have exercised a corresponding pressure upon the entire course of political events, albeit devoid of any character of counter-revolution or of military dictatorship. The loyalty of the Commanding Officers and the complete absence of active resistance on their part to the destructive policy of Petrograd exceeded all the expectations of the Revolutionary Democracy.

Kornilov's movement came too late.

We drafted a reply suggesting stringent measures against intrusion into the sphere of military administration. On March 18th I received orders to proceed forthwith to Petrograd and to report to the War Minister. I left on the same night and by means of a complex system of carts, motor cars and railway carriages arrived in the Capital after five days' journey. On my way I passed through the Headquarters of Generals Letchitski, Kaledin, and Brussilov. I met many officers and many men connected with the army. Everywhere I heard the same bitter complaint and the same request:

"Tell *them* that *they* are ruining the army."

The summons I had received gave no indication as to the object of my errand. I was completely in the dark and made all kinds of surmises. In Kiev I was struck by the cry of a newsboy who ran past. He shouted: "Latest news. General Denikin is appointed Chief of the Staff of the Supreme Commander-in-Chief"

CHAPTER VII.

Impressions of Petrograd at the End of March, 1917.

BEFORE his abdication the Emperor signed two ukazes—appointing Prince Lvov President of the Council of Ministers and the Grand-Duke Nicholas Supreme Commander-in-Chief. " In view of the general attitude towards the Romanov Dynasty," as the official Petrograd papers said, and in reality for fear of the Soviet's attempting a military *coup d'état*, the Grand-Duke Nicholas was informed on March 9th by the Provisional Government that it was undesirable that he should remain in supreme command. Prince Lvov wrote: " The situation makes your resignation imperative. Public opinion is definitely and resolutely opposed to any members of the House of Romanov holding any office in the State. The Provisional Government is not entitled to disregard the voice of the people, because such disregard might bring about serious complications. The Provisional Government is convinced that, for the good of the country, you will bow to the necessity and will resign before returning to G.H.Q." This letter reached the Grand-Duke when he had already arrived at G.H.Q. Deeply offended, he immediately handed over to General Alexeiev and replied to the Government: "I am glad once more to prove my love for my country, which Russia *heretofore* has never doubted. . . .'"

The very serious question then arose of who was to succeed him. There was great excitement at G.H.Q., and all sorts of rumours were circulated, but on the day I passed Mohilev nothing was known. On the 23rd I reported to the War Minister Gutehkov, whom I had never met before. He informed me that the Government had decided to appoint General Alexeiev to the Supreme Command. At first there had been differences of opinion. Rodzianko and others were against Alexeiev. Rodzianko suggested Brussilov; but now the choice had definitely fallen on Alexeiev. The Government considered him as a man of lenient disposition, and deemed it necessary to reinforce the Supreme Command by a fighting general as Chief-of-Staff. I had been selected on condition that General Klembovski, who was then Alexeiev's assistant, should remain in charge *pro tem.* until I became familiar with the work. I had been, in part, prepared for this offer by the news columns of the Kiev paper. Nevertheless, I felt a certain emotion, and apprehended the vast amount of work which was being thrust upon me so unexpectedly and the tremendous moral responsibility inherent in such an appointment. At great length and quite sincerely I adduced arguments against the appointment. I said that my career had been spent among my men and at Fighting Headquarters, that during the war I had commanded a division and an army corps, and that I was very anxious to continue this work at the front. I said that I had never dealt with matters of policy, of national defence, or of administration on such a colossal scale. The appointment, moreover, had an unpleasant feature. It appears that Gutchkov had quite frankly explained to Alexeiev the reasons for my appointment on behalf of the Provisional Government, and had given the matter the character of an ultimatum. A grave complication had thus arisen. A Chief-of-Staff was being imposed upon the Supreme C.-in-C., and for motives not altogether complimentary to the latter. My arguments, however, were unavailing. I succeeded in obtaining a delay and the privilege of discussing the matter with General Alexeiev before taking a definite decision. In the War Minister's office I met my colleague, General Krymov, and we were both present while the Minister's assistants reported on uninteresting matters of routine. We then retired into the next room and began to talk frankly.

" For God's sake," said Krymov, " don't refuse the appointment. It is absolutely necessary."

He imparted to me his impressions in abrupt sentences in his own peculiar and somewhat rough language, but with all his usual sincerity. He had arrived on March 14th, summoned by Gutchkov, with whom he had been on friendly terms, and they had worked together. He was offered several prominent posts, had asked leave to look round, and then had refused them all. " I saw that there was nothing for me to do in Petrograd, and I disliked it all." He particularly disliked the men who surrounded Gutchkov.

" I am leaving Colonel Samarine, of the General Staff, as a Liaison Officer. There will be at least one live man."

By the irony of fate that officer whom Krymov trusted so well afterwards played a fatal part, as he was the indirect cause of the

General's suicide. . . . Krymov was very pessimistic in his account of the political situation:

" Nothing will come of it in any case. How can business be done when the Soviet and the licentious soldiery hold the Government pinioned? I offered to cleanse Petrograd in two days with one division; but, of course, not without bloodshed. ' Not for anything in the world,' they said. Gutchkov refused. Prince Lvov, with a gesture of despair, exclaimed: ' Oh! but there would be such a commotion! ' Things will get worse. One of these days I shall go back to my army corps. I cannot afford to lose touch with the troops, as it is upon them that I base all my hopes. My corps maintains complete order and, perhaps, I shall succeed in preserving that spirit."

* * *

I had not seen Petrograd for four years. The impression produced by the Capital was painful and strange. . . . To begin with, the Hotel Astoria, where I stayed, had been ransacked. In the hall there was a guard of rough and undisciplined sailors of the Guards. The streets were crowded, but dirty and filled with the new masters of the situation in khaki overcoats. Remote from the sufferings of the front, they were "deepening and saving" the Revolution. From whom? I had read a great deal about the enthusiasm in Petrograd, but I found none. It was nowhere to be seen. The ministers and rulers were pale, haggard, exhausted by sleepless nights and endless speeches at meetings and councils, by addresses to various delegations and to the mob. Their excitement was artificial, their oratory was full of sonorous phrases and commonplaces, of which the orators themselves were presumably thoroughly sick. Inwardly in their heart of hearts they were deeply anxious. No practical work was being done; in fact, the ministers had no time to concentrate their thoughts upon the current affairs of State in their departments. The old bureaucratic machine, creaking and groaning, continued to work in a haphazard manner. The old wheels were still revolving while a new handle was being applied.

The officers of the regular army felt themselves to be stepsons of the Revolution and were unable to hit upon a proper tone in dealing with the men. Among the higher ranks, and especially the officers of the General Staff, there appeared already a new type of opportunist and demagogue. These men played upon the weaknesses of the Soviet and of the new governing class of workmen and soldiers, to flatter the instincts of the crowd, thereby gaining their confidence and making new openings for themselves

Impressions of Petrograd at the End of March, 1917

and for their careers against the background of revolutionary turmoil. I must, however, admit that in those days the military circles proved sufficiently stolid in spite of all the efforts to dismember them, and that the seeds of demoralisation were not allowed to grow. Men of the type described above, such as the young assistant of the War Minister, Kerensky, as well as Generals Brussilov, Cheremissov, Bonch-Bruevitch, Verkhovsky, Admiral Maximov and others were unable to strengthen their influence and their position with the officers.

The citizen of Petrograd, in the broadest sense of the word, was by no means enthusiastic. The first enthusiasm was exhausted and was followed by anxiety and indecision.

Another feature of the life in Petrograd deserves to be noticed. Men have ceased to be themselves. Most of them seem to be acting a part instead of living a life inspired by the new breath of revolution. Such was the case even in the Councils of the Provisional Government, in which the deliberations were not altogether sincere, so I was told, owing to the presence of Kerensky, the " hostage of democracy " Tactical considerations, caution, partisanship, anxiety for one's career, feelings of self-preservation, nervousness and various other good and bad feelings prompted men to wear blinkers and to walk about in these blinkers as apologists for, or at least passive witnesses of, " the conquests of the Revolution." Such conquests as obviously savoured of death and corruption. Hence the false pathos of endless speeches and meetings; hence these seemingly strange contradictions. Prince Lvov saying in a public speech: " The process of the great Russian Revolution is not yet complete, but every day strengthens our faith in the inexhaustible creative forces of the Russian people, in its statesmanlike wisdom and in the greatness of its soul." . . . The same Prince Lvov bitterly complaining to Alexeiev of the impossible conditions under which the Provisional Government was working, owing to the rapid growth of demagogy in the Soviet and in the country. Kerensky, the exponent of the idea of Soldiers' Committees, and Kerensky sitting in his railway carriage and nervously whispering to his adjutant: " Send these d . . . committees to h . " Tchkheidze and Skobelev warmly advocating full democratisation of the army at a joint sitting of the Soviet, of the Government and of the Commanders-in-Chief, and during an interval in private conversation admitting the necessity of rigid military discipline and of their own incapacity to convince the Soviet of this necessity. . . .

I repeat that even then, at the end of March, one could clearly feel in Petrograd that the ringing of the Easter bells had lasted too long, and that they would have done better to ring the alarm bell. There were only two men of all those to whom I had the occasion to speak who had no illusions whatever: Krymov and Kornilov.

I met Kornilov for the first time on the Galician plains, near Galtich, at the end of August, 1914, when he was appointed to the Command of the 48th Infantry Division and myself to the 4th (Iron) Rifle Brigade. Since that day, for four months, our troops went forward side by side as part of the 14th Corps, fighting incessant, glorious and heavy battles, defeating the enemy, crossing the Carpathians and invading Hungary. Owing to the wide extent of the front we did not often meet; nevertheless, we knew each other very well. I had already then a clear perception of Kornilov's main characteristics as a leader. He had an extraordinary capacity for training troops: out of a second-rate unit from the district of Kazan he made, in several weeks, an excellent fighting division. He was resolute and extremely pertinacious in conducting the most difficult and even apparently doomed operations. His personal prowess, which provoked boundless admiration and gave him great popularity among the troops, was admirable. Finally, he scrupulously observed military ethics with regard to units fighting by his side and to his comrades-in-arms. Many commanding officers and units lacked that quality. After Kornilov's astounding escape from Austrian captivity, into which he fell when heavily wounded, and covering Brussilov's retreat from the Carpathians, towards the beginning of the Revolution, he commanded the 25th Corps. All those who knew Kornilov even slightly felt that he was destined to play an important part in the Russian Revolution. On March 2nd Rodzianko telegraphed direct to Kornilov: " The Temporary Committee of the Duma requests you, for your country's sake, to accept the chief command in Petrograd and to arrive at the Capital at once. We have no doubt that you will not refuse the appointment, and will thereby render an inestimable service to the country." Such a revolutionary method of appointing an officer to a high command, without reference to G.H.Q., obviously produced a bad impression at the " Stavka." The telegram received at the " Stavka " is marked " Undelivered," but on the same day General Alexeiev, having requested the permission of the Emperor, who was then at Pskov, issued an order of the day (No. 334): " . . . I agree to General

Impressions of Petrograd at the End of March, 1917

Kornilov being in temporary high command of the troops of the Petrograd Military District."

I have mentioned this insignificant episode in order to explain the somewhat abnormal relations between two prominent leaders, which were occasioned by repeated, petty, personal friction.

I talked to Kornilov at dinner in the War Minister's house. It was the only moment of rest he could snatch during the day. Kornilov, tired, morose and somewhat pessimistic, discussed at length the conditions of the Petrograd Garrison, and his inter course with the Soviet. The hero-worship with which he had been surrounded in the army had faded in the unhealthy atmosphere of the Capital among the demoralised troops. They were holding meetings, deserting, indulging in petty commerce in shops and in the street, serving as hall-porters and as personal guards to private individuals, partaking in plundering and arbitrary searches, but were not serving. It was difficult for a fighting general to understand their psychology. He often succeeded by personal pluck, disregard of danger, and by a witty, picturesque word in holding the mob, for that was what military units were. There were, however, cases when the troops did not come out of barracks to meet their Commander-in-Chief, when he was hissed and the flag of St. George was torn from his motor-car (by the Finland Regiment of the Guards).

Kornilov's description of the political situation was the same as that given by Krymov: Powerlessness of the Government and the inevitability of a fierce cleansing of Petrograd. On one point they differed: Kornilov stubbornly clung to the hope that he would yet succeed in gaining authority over the majority of the Petrograd Garrison. As we know, that hope was never fulfilled.

CHAPTER VIII.

The Stavka: Its Rôle and Position.

ON March 25th I arrived at the Stavka, and was immediately received by General Alexeiev. Of course he was offended. " Well," he said, " if such are the orders, what's to be done? " Again, as at the War Ministry, I pointed out several reasons against my appointment, among others, my disinclination for Staff work. I asked the General to express his views quite frankly, and in disregard of all conventionalities as my old Professor, because I would not think of accepting the appointment against his will. Alexeiev spoke politely, dryly, evasively, and showed again that he was offended. " The scope," he said, " was wide, work difficult, and much training necessary. Let us, however, work harmoniously." In the course of my long career I have never been placed in such a position, and could not, of course, be reconciled to such an attitude. " In these circumstances," I said, " I absolutely refuse to accept the appointment. In order to avoid friction between yourself and the Government, I will declare that it is entirely my own personal decision."

Alexeiev's tone changed immediately. " Oh! no," he said, " I am not asking you to refuse. Let us work together, and I will help you. Also, there is no reason, if you feel that the work is not to your liking, why you should not take command of the First Army, in which there will be a vacancy two or three months hence. I will have to talk the matter over with General Klembovski. He could not, of course, remain here as my assistant."

Our parting was not quite so frigid; but a couple of days went by and there were no results. I lived in a railway carriage, and did not go to the office or to the mess. As I did not intend to tolerate this silly and utterly undeserved position, I was preparing to leave Petrograd. On March 28th the War Minister came to the Stavka and cut the Gordian knot. Klembovski was

General Kornilov

General Alexeiev.

The Stavka : Its Rôle and Position

offered the command of an army or membership of the War Council. He chose the latter, and on April 5th I took charge as Chief of the Staff. Nevertheless, such a method of appointing the closest assistant to the Supreme Commander-in-Chief, practically by force, could not but leave a certain trace. A kind of shadow seemed to lie between myself and General Alexeiev, and it did not disappear until the last stage of his tenure of office. Alexeiev saw in my appointment a kind of tutelage on the part of the Government. From the very first moment I was compelled to oppose Petrograd. I served our cause and tried to shield the Supreme C.-in-C.—and of this he was often unaware—from many conflicts and much friction, taking them upon myself. As time went by friendly relations of complete mutual trust were established, and these did not cease until the day of Alexeiev's death.

On April 2nd the General received the following telegram: " The Provisional Government has appointed you Supreme Commander-in-Chief. It trusts that, under your firm guidance, the Army and the Navy will fulfil their duty to the country to the end." My appointment was gazetted on April 10th.

*   *   *   *   *

The Stavka, on the whole was not favoured. In the circles of the Revolutionary Democracy it was considered a nest of counter-Revolution, although such a description was utterly undeserved. Under Alexeiev there was a loyal struggle against the disruption of the Army. Under Brussilov—opportunism slightly tainted with subservience to the Revolutionary Democracy. As regards the Kornilov movement, although it was not essentially counter-Revolutionary, it aimed, as we shall see later, at combatting the Soviets that were half-Bolshevik. But, even then, the loyalty of the officers of the Stavka was quite obvious. Only a few of them took an active part in the Kornilov movement. After the office of Supreme Commander-in-Chief was abolished, and the new office created of Supreme Commanding Committees, nearly all the members of the Stavka under Kerensky, and the majority of them under Krylenko, continued to carry on the routine work. The Army also disliked the Stavka —sometimes wrongly, sometimes rightly—because the Army did not quite understand the distribution of functions among the various branches of the Service, and ascribed to the Stavka many shortcomings in equipment, organisation, promotion, awards, etc., whereas these questions belonged entirely to the War Ministry and its subordinates. The Stavka had always been somewhat out of touch with the Army. Under the comparatively normal and smoothly working conditions of the pre-Revolutionary period this circumstance did not greatly prejudice the working of the ruling mechanism; but now, when the Army was not in a normal condition, and had been affected by the whirlwind of the Revolution, the Stavka naturally was behind the times.

Finally, a certain amount of friction could not fail to arise between the Government and the Stavka, because the latter constantly protested against many Government measures, which exercised a disturbing influence on the Army. There were no other serious reasons for difference of opinion, because neither Alexeiev nor myself, nor the various sections of the Stavka, ever touched upon matters of internal policy. The Stavka was non-political in the fullest sense of the word, and during the first months of the Revolution was a perfectly reliable technical apparatus in the hands of the Provisional Government. The Stavka did but safeguard the highest interests of the Army, and, within the limits of the War and of the Army, demanded that full powers be given to the Supreme Commander-in-Chief. I may even say that the personnel of the Stavka seemed to me to be bureaucratic and too deeply immersed in the sphere of purely technical interests; they were not sufficiently interested in the political and social questions which events had brought to the fore.

* * *

In discussing the Russian strategy in the Great War, after August, 1915, one should always bear in mind that it was the personal strategy of General Alexeiev. He alone bears the responsibility before history for its course, its successes and failures. A man of exceptional conscientiousness and self-sacrifice, and devoted to his work, he had one serious failing: all his life he did the work of others as well as his own. So it was when he held the post of Quartermaster-General of the General Staff, of Chief-of-Staff of the Kiev District, and later of the South-Western front and finally of Chief-of-Staff to the Supreme C.-in-C. Nobody influenced strategical decisions, and, as often as not, final instructions, written in Alexeiev's tiny and neat handwriting, appeared unexpectedly on the desk of the Quartermaster-General, whose duty under the law and whose responsibility in these matters were very grave. If such a procedure was to a certain extent justifiable, when the post of Quartermaster-General was occupied by a nonentity, there was no excuse for it when he was superseded by other Quartermasters-General, such as Lukomski or Josephovitch. These men could not accept such a position. The former, as a rule, protested by sending in memoranda embodying his opinion, which was adverse to the plan of operations. Such protests, of course, were purely academic, but presented a guarantee against the judgment of history. General Klembovski, my predecessor, was compelled to demand non-interference with the rightful sphere of his competence as a condition of his tenure of office. Till then, Alexeiev had directed all the branches of administration. When these branches acquired a still broader scope, this proved practically impossible, and I was given full liberty in my work except . . . in respect of strategy. Again, Alexeiev began to send telegrams in his own hand of a strategical nature, orders and directions, the motives of which the Quartermaster-General and myself could not understand. Several times, three of us, the Quartermaster-General, Josephovitch, his assistant, General Markov, and myself, discussed this question. The quick-tempered Josephovitch was greatly excited, and asked to be appointed to a Divisional Command. " I cannot be a clerk," he said. " There is no need for a Quartermaster-General at the Stavka if every clerk can type instructions." The General and myself began to contemplate resignation. Markov said that he would not stay for a single day if we went. I finally decided to have a frank talk with Alexeiev. We were both under the strain of emotion. We parted as friends, but we did not settle the question. Alexeiev said: " Do I not give you a full share of the work? I do not understand you." Alexeiev was quite sincerely surprised because during the war he had grown accustomed to a régime which appeared to him perfectly normal. So we three held another conference. After a lengthy discussion, we decided that the plan of campaign for 1917 had long since been worked out, that preparations for that campaign had reached a stage in which substantial alterations had become impossible, that the details of the concentration and distribution of troops were in the present condition of the Army a difficult matter, allowing for differences of opinion; that we could perhaps manage to effect certain alterations of the plan, and that finally our retirement *in corpore* might be detrimental to the work, and might undermine the position of the Supreme C.-in-C., which was already by no means stable. We therefore decided to wait and see. We did not have to wait very long, because, at the end of May, Alexeiev left the Stavka, and we followed him very soon afterwards.

*

What place did the Stavka occupy as a military and political factor of the Revolutionary period?

The importance of the Stavka diminished. In the days of the Imperial régime, the Stavka, from the military point of view, occupied a predominant position. No individual or institution in the State was entitled to issue instructions or to call to account the Supreme Commander-in-Chief, and it was Alexeiev and not the Czar who in reality held that office. Not a single measure of the War Ministry, even if indirectly affecting the interests of the Army, could be adopted without the sanction of the Stavka. The Stavka gave direct orders to the War Minister and to his Department on questions appertaining to the care of the Army. The voice of the Stavka had a certain weight and importance in the practical domain of administration at the theatre of war, albeit without any connection with the general trend of internal policy. That power was not exercised to a sufficient degree; but on principle it afforded the opportunity of carrying on the defence of the country in co-operation with other branches of the administration, which were to a certain extent subordinate to it. With the beginning of the Revolution, these conditions underwent a radical change. Contrary to the examples of history and to the dictates of military science, the Stavka became practically subordinate to the War Minister. This was not due to any act of the Government, but merely to the fact that the Provisional Government combined supreme power with executive power, as well as to the combination of the strong character of Gutchkov and the yielding nature of Alexeiev. The Stavka could no longer address rightful demands to the branches of the War Ministry which were attending to Army equipments. It conducted a lengthy correspondence and appealed to the Ministry of War. The War Minister, who now signed orders instead of the Emperor, exercised a strong influence upon appointments and dismissals of officers in High Command. These appointments were sometimes made by him after consultation with the fronts, but the Stavka was not informed. Army regulations of the highest importance altering the conditions of the troops in respect of reinforcements, routine and duty, were issued by the Ministry without the participation of the Supreme Command, which learnt of their issue only from the Press. In fact, such a participation would have actually been useless. Two products of the Polivanov Commission—the new Courts and the Committees—which Gutchkov *accidentally* asked me to look through, were returned with a series of substantial objections of my own, and Gutchkov expounded them in vain before the representatives of the Soviet. The only result was that certain changes in the drafting of the regulations were made.

All these circumstances undoubtedly undermined the authority

The Stavka : Its Rôle and Position

of the Stavka in the eyes of the Army, and prompted the Generals in High Command to approach the more powerful Central Government Departments without reference to the Stavka, as well as to display excessive individual initiative in matters of paramount importance to the State and to the Army. Thus, in May, 1917, on the Northern Front, all the pre-War soldiers were discharged instead of the prescribed percentage, and this created grave difficulties on other fronts. On the South-Western Front Ukranian units were being formed. The Admiral in command of the Baltic Fleet ordered the officers to remove their shoulder-straps, etc.

The Stavka had lost influence and power, and could no longer occupy the commanding position of an administrative and moral centre. This occurred at the most terrible stage of the World War, when the Army was beginning to disintegrate, and when not only the entire strength of the people was being put to the test, but the necessity had arisen for a power exceptionally strong and wide in its bearing. Meanwhile, the matter was quite obvious : if Alexeiev and Denikin did not enjoy the confidence of the Government, and were considered inadequate to the requirements of the Supreme Command, they should have been superseded by new men who did enjoy that confidence and who should have been invested with full powers. As a matter of fact, changes were made twice. But only the men were changed, not the principles of the High Command. In the circumstances, when no one actually wielded power, military power was not centred in anybody's hands. Neither the Chiefs who enjoyed the reputation of serving their country loyally and with exceptional devotion, like Alexeiev, and later the " Iron Chiefs," such as Kornilov undoubtedly was and as Brussilov was supposed to be, nor all the Chameleons that fed from the hand of the Socialist reformers of the Army had any real power.

The entire military hierarchy was shaken to its very foundations, though it retained all the attributes of power and the customary routine—instructions which could not move the Armies, orders that were never carried out, verdicts of the Courts which were derided. The full weight of oppression, following the line of the least resistance, fell solely upon the loyal commanding officers, who submitted without a murmur to persecution from above as well as from below. The Government and the War Ministry, having abolished repressions, had recourse to a new method of influencing the masses—to *appeals*. Appeals to the people, to the Army, to the Cossacks, to everybody, flooded the country, inviting all to do their duty. Unfortunately, only those appeals were successful that flattered the meanest instincts of the mob, inviting it to neglect its duty. As a result, it was not counter - Revolution, Buonapartism, or adventure, but the elemental desire of the circles where the ideas of statesmanship still prevailed, to restore the broken laws of warfare, that soon gave rise to a new watchword:

"*Military power must be seized.*"

Such a task was not congenial to Alexeiev or Brussilov. Kornilov subsequently endeavoured to undertake it, and began independently to carry out a series of important military measures and to address ultimatums on military questions to the Government. At first, the only question raised was that of granting "full powers" to the Supreme Command within the scope of its competence.

It is interesting to compare this state of affairs with that of the command of the armies of our powerful foe. Ludendorff, the first Quartermaster-General of the German Army says (*Mes Souvenirs de Guerre*): " In peace-time the Imperial Government exercised full power over its Departments When the War began the Ministers found it difficult to get used to seeing in G.H.Q. a power which was compelled, by the immensity of its task, to act with greater resolution as that resolution weakened in Berlin. Would that the Government could clearly have perceived this simple truth. . . . The Government went its own way, and never abandoned any of its designs in compliance with the wishes of G.H.Q. On the contrary, it disregarded much that we considered necessary for the prosecution of the War."

If we recall that in March, 1918, the deputy of the Reichstag, Haase, was more than justified in saying that the Chancellor was nothing but a figure-head covering the military party, and that Ludendorff was actually governing the country, we will understand the extent of the power which the German Command deemed it necessary to exercise in order to win the World War.

I have drawn a general picture of the Stavka, such as it was when I took charge as Chief-of-Staff. Taking the entire position into consideration, I had two main objects in view: first, to counteract with all my strength the influences which were disrupting the Army, so as to preserve that Army and to hold the Eastern Front in the world struggle; and secondly, to reinforce the rights, the power, and the authority of the Supreme Commander-in-Chief. A loyal struggle was at hand. In that struggle, which only lasted two months, all sections of the Stavka had their share.

General Markov.

CHAPTER IX.

General Markov.

THE duties of the Quartermaster-General in the Stavka were many-sided and complex. As in the European Army, it proved therefore necessary to create the office of a second Quartermaster-General. The first dealt merely with matters concerning the conduct of operations. I invited General Markov to accept this new office. His fate was linked up with mine until his glorious death at the head of a Volunteer Division. That Division afterwards bore with honour his name, which has become legendary in the Volunteer Army. At the outbreak of war he was a lecturer at the Academy of the General Staff. He went to the war as Staff-Officer to General Alexeiev. Then he joined the 19th Division, and in December, 1914' he served under my command as Chief-of-Staff of the 4th Rifle Brigade, which I then commanded. When he came to our Brigade he was unknown and unexpected, as I had asked the Army G.H.Q. for another man to be appointed. Immediately upon his arrival he told me that he had recently undergone a slight operation, was not feeling well, was unable to ride, and would not go up to the front line. I frowned, and the Staff exchanged significant glances. The " Professor," as we afterwards often called him as a friendly jest, was obviously out of place in our midst.

I started one day with my staff, all mounted, towards the line where my riflemen were fiercely fighting, near the town of Friestach. The enemy was upon us, and the fire was intense. Suddenly, repeated showers of shrapnel came down upon us. We wondered what it meant, and there was Markov gaily smiling, openly driving to the firing line in a huge carriage. " I was bored staying in, so I have come to see what is going on here."

From that day the ice was broken, and Markov assumed a proper place in the family of the " Iron Division." I have never met a man who loved military work to such an extent as Markov.

He was young (when he was killed in the summer of 1918 in action he was only 39 years of age), impetuous, communicative, eloquent. He knew how to approach, and closely, too, any *milieu*—officers, soldiers, crowds—sometimes far from sympathetic, and how to instil into them his straightforward, clear, and indisputable articles of faith. He was very quick to grasp the situation in battle, and made work much easier for me. Markov had one peculiarity. He was quite exceptionally straightforward, frank, and abrupt when attacking those who, in his opinion, did not display adequate knowledge, energy, or pluck. While he was at Headquarters the troops therefore viewed him (as in the Brigade) with a certain reserve, and sometimes even with intolerance (as in the Rostov period of the Volunteer Army). No sooner, however, did Markov join the Division than the attitude towards him became one of love on the part of the riflemen, or even enthusiasm on the part of the Volunteers. The Army had its own psychology. It would have no abruptness and blame from Markov as a Staff Officer. But when *their* Markov, in his usual short fur coat with his cap at the back of his head, waving his inevitable whip, was in the rifleman's firing line, under the hot fire of the enemy, he could be as violent as possible, he could shout and swear—his words provoked sometimes sorrow, sometimes mirth, but there was always a sincere desire to be worthy of his praise. I recall the heavy days which the Brigade endured in February, 1915. The Brigade was pushed forward, was surrounded by a semi-circle of hills occupied by the enemy, who was in a position to snipe us. The position was intolerable, the losses were heavy, and nothing could be gained by keeping us on that line. But the 14th Infantry Division next to us reported to the Army H.Q.: " Our blood runs cold at the thought of abandoning the position and having afterwards once more 'to attack the heights which have already cost us rivers of blood." I remained. Matters, however, were so serious that one had to be in close touch with the men. I moved the field H.Q. up to the position. Count Keller, in command of our section, having travelled for eleven hours in deep mud and over mountain paths, arrived at that moment, and rested for a while.

" Let us now drive up to the line."

We laughed.

" How shall we drive? Would you come to the door, enemy machine-guns permitting ? "

Count Keller left fully determined to extricate the Brigade from the trap. The Brigade was melting away. In the rear there was only one ramshackle bridge across the San. We were in the hands of fate. Will the torrent swell? If it does, the bridge will be swept away, and our retreat will be cut off. At this difficult moment the Colonel in command of the 13th Rifle Regiment was severely wounded by a sniper as he was coming out of the house where the H.Q. were stationed. All officers of his rank having been killed, there was nobody to replace him. I was pacing up and down the small hut, in a gloomy mood. Markov rose.

" Give me the 13th Regiment, sir," said Markov.

" Of course, with pleasure."

I had already thought of doing so. But I hesitated to offer it to Markov lest he should think it was my intention to remove him from the Staff. Markov afterwards went with his regiment from one victory to another. He had already earned the Cross of St. George and the sword of St. George, but for nine months the Stavka would not confirm his appointment, because he had not reached the dead line of seniority.

I recall the days of the heavy Galician retreat, when a tidal wave of maddened peasants, with women, children, cattle and carts, was following the Army, burning their villages and houses. Markov was in the rear, and was ordered promptly to blow up the bridge at which this human tide had stopped. He was, however, moved by the sufferings of the people, and for six hours he fought for the bridge at the risk of being cut off, until the last cart of the refugees had crossed the bridge.

His life was a perpetual fiery impulse. On one occasion I had lost all hope of ever seeing him again. In the beginning of September, 1915, in the course of the Lutsk operation, in which our Division so distinguished itself, between Olyka and Klevan, the left column commanded by Markov broke the Austrian line and disappeared. The Austrians closed the line. During the day we heard no news, and the night came. I was anxious for the fate of the 13th Regiment, and rode to a high slope, observing the enemy's firing line in the silent distance. Suddenly, from afar, from the dense forest, in the far rear of the Austrians, I heard the joyous strains of the Regimental March of the 13th. What a relief it was!

" I got into such a fix," said Markov afterwards, " the devil himself could not have known which were my riflemen and which were Austrians. I decided to cheer up my men and to collect them by making the band play."

Markov's column had smashed the enemy, had taken two thousand prisoners and a gun, and had put the Austrians to disorderly flight towards Lutsk.

In his impulsiveness he sometimes went from one extreme to another, but, as soon as matters grew really desperate, he immediately regained self-possession. In October, 1915, the 4th Rifle Division was conducting the famous Chartoriisk operation, had broken the enemy on a front about twelve miles wide and over fifteen miles deep. Brussilov, having no reserves, hesitated to bring up troops from another front in order to take advantage of this break. Time was short. The Germans centred their reserves, and they were attacking me on all sides. The situation was difficult. Markov, from the front line, telephoned: "The position is peculiar. I am fighting the four quarters of the earth. It is so hard as to be thoroughly amusing." Only once did I see him in a state of utter depression, when, in the spring of 1915, near Przemyshl, he was removing from the firing line the remnants of his companies. He was drenched with the blood of the C.O. of the 14th Regiment, who had been standing by, and whose head had been torn off by a shell.

Markov never took any personal precautions. In September, 1915, the Division was fighting in the direction of Kovel. On the right our cavalry was operating, was moving forward irresolutely, and was perturbing us by incredible news of the appearance of important enemy forces on its front, on our bank of the River Styr. Markov became annoyed with this indecision, and reported to me: "I went to the Styr with my orderly to give the horses a drink. Between our line and the Styr there is no one, neither our cavalry nor the enemy."

I reported him for promotion to General's rank, as a reward for several battles, but my request was not granted on the plea that he was "a youngster." Verily youth was a great defect. In the spring of 1916 the Division was feverishly preparing for the break-through at Lutsk. Markov made no secret of his innermost wish: "It is to be either one or the other—a wooden cross or the Cross of St. George of the Third Degree." But the Stavka, after several refusals, compelled him to accept "promotion"—once again the office of Divisional Chief-of-Staff. (This measure was due to a great dearth of officers of the General Staff, because the normal activities of the Academy had come to an end. Colonels and Generals were made to hold for a second time and on special conditions the office of Chief of Divisional Staff before they were appointed to Divisional Commands.) After several months on the Caucasian Front, where Markov suffered from inaction, he lectured for some time at the Academy, which had then reopened, and later returned to the Army. At the outbreak of the Revolution he was attached to the Commanding Officer of the Tenth Army as General for special missions.

* * * *

In the beginning of March a mutiny broke out at Briansk in the big garrison. It was attended by pogroms and by the arrest of officers. The townfolk were terribly excited. Markov spoke several times in the crowded Council of Military Deputies. After tempestuous and passionate debates, he succeeded in obtaining a resolution for restoring discipline and for freeing twenty of those arrested. Nevertheless, after midnight several companies in arms moved to the railway station in order to do away with Markov and with the arrested officers. The mob was infuriated and Markov seemed to be doomed, but his resourcefulness saved the situation. Trying to make his voice heard above the tumult, he addressed an impassioned appeal to the mob. The following sentence occurred in his speech: " Had any of my ' Iron ' Riflemen been here, he would have told you who General Markov is."
" I served in the 13th Regiment," came a voice from the crowd.

Markov pushed aside several men who were surrounding him, advanced rapidly towards the soldier, and seized him by the scruff of the neck.

" You? You? Then why don't you thrust the bayonet into me? The enemy's bullet has spared me, so let me perish by the hand of my own rifleman "

The mob was still more intoxicated, but with admiration. Accompanied by tempestuous cheering, Markov and the arrested officers left for Minsk.

Markov was lifted by the wave of events, and gave himself entirely to the struggle, without a thought for himself or for his family. Faith and despair succeeded each other in his mind; he loved his country and felt sorry for the Army, which never ceased to occupy a prominent place in his heart and in his mind.

Reference will be made more than once in the course of this narrative to the personality of Markov, but I could not refrain from satisfying my heart's desire in adding a few laurels to his wreath—the wreath that was placed upon his tomb by two faithful friends, with the inscription:—

" He lived and died for the good of his country."

CHAPTER X.

The Power—The Duma—The Provisional Government—The High Command—The Soviet of Workmen's and Soldiers' Delegates.

RUSSIA'S exceptional position, confronted on the one hand with a world war and on the other with a revolution, made the establishment of a strong power an imperative necessity.

The Duma, which, as I have already said, unquestionably enjoyed the confidence of the country, refused, after lengthy and heated discussions, to head the Revolutionary power. Temporarily dissolved by the Imperial ukaze of February 27th, it remained loyal, and " did not attempt to hold an official sitting," as it " considered itself a legislative institution of the old régime, co-ordinated by fundamental law with the obviously doomed remnants of autocracy." (Miliukov, *History of the Second Russian Revolution*.) The subsequent decrees emanated from the " private conference of the members of the Duma." This body elected the " temporary Committee of the Duma," which exercised supreme power in the first days of the Revolution.

When power was transferred to the Provisional Government, the Duma and the Committee retired to the background, but did not cease to exist, and endeavoured to give moral support and a *raison d'être* to the first three Cabinets of the Government. On May 2nd, during the first Government crisis, the Committee still struggled for the right to *appoint* members of the Government; subsequently it reduced its demands to that of the right to *participate* in the formation of the Government. Thus, on July 7th, the Committee of the Duma protested against its exclusion from the formation of a new Provisional Government by Kerensky, as it considered such a course as " legally inadmissible and politically disastrous." The Duma, of course, was fully entitled to participate in the direction of the life of the country, as, even in the camp of its enemies, the signal service was recognised which the Duma had rendered to the Revolution " In converting to it the entire front and all the officers " (Stankevitch: *Reminiscences*). There can be no doubt that, had the Soviet taken the lead in the Revolution, there would have been a fierce struggle against it, and the Revolution would have been squashed. It might, perhaps, have then given the victory to the Liberal Democracy, and would have led the country to a normal evolutionary development. Who knows?

The members of the Duma themselves felt the strain of inactivity which was at first voluntary and later compulsory. There were many absentees, and the President of the Duma had to combat this attitude. Nevertheless, the Duma and the Committee were quite alive to the importance of the trend events were taking. They issued resolutions condemning, warning, and appealing to the common sense, the heart, and the patriotism of the people, of the Army, and of the Government. The Duma, however, had already been swept aside by the Revolutionary elements. Its statesmanlike appeals, full of the clear consciousness of impending perils, had ceased to impress the country, and were ignored by the Government. Even a Duma so peaceable that it did not even fight for power aroused the apprehensions of the Revolutionary Democracy, and the Soviets led a violent campaign for the abolition of the Council of the State and of the Duma. In August the Duma relaxed its efforts in issuing proclamations, and when Kerensky dissolved the Duma at the bidding of the Soviets, nineteen days before the expiration of its five years' term, on October 6th, this news did not produce any appreciable effect in the country. Rodzianko kept alive for a long time the idea of the Fourth Duma or of the Assembly of all Dumas as the foundation of the power of the State. He stuck to this idea throughout the Kuban campaigns and the Ekaterinodar Volunteer period of the anti-Bolshevik struggle. But the Duma was dead. . . .

None can tell whether the Duma's abdication of power was inevitable in the days of March, and whether it was rendered imperative by the relative strength of the forces that struggled for power, whether the " class " Duma could have retained the Socialist elements in its midst and have continued to wield a certain influence in the country, acquired as a result of its fight against autocracy. It is at least certain that, in the years of trouble in Russia, when no normal, popular representation was possible, all Governments invariably felt the necessity for some substitute for this popular representation, were it only as a kind of tribune from which expression could be given to different currents of thought, a rock upon which to stand and to divine moral responsibilities. Such was the " Temporary Council of the Russian Republic " at Petrograd in October, 1917, which, however, had been started by the Revolutionary Democracy, as a counter-blast to the contemplated Bolshevik Second Congress of Soviets. Such was the partial constituent Assembly of 1917, which was held on the Volga in the summer of 1918, and such the proposed convocation of the High Council and Assembly (*Sobor*) of the Zemstvos in the South of Russia and in Siberia in 1919. Even the highest manifestation of collective dictatorship —" the Soviet of People's Commissars "—which reached a level of despotism and had suppressed social life and all the live forces of the country to an extent unknown in history, and reduced the country to a graveyard, still considered it necessary to create a kind of theatrical travesty of such a representative institution by periodically convoking the " All-Russian Congress of Soviets."

The authority of the Provisional Government contained the seed of its own impotence. As Miliukov has said, that power was devoid of the " symbol " to which the masses were accustomed. The Government yielded to the pressure of the Soviet, which was systematically distorting all State functions and making them subservient to the interests of class and party.

Kerensky, the " hostage of Democracy," was in the Government. In a speech delivered in the Soviet he thus defined his rôle: " I am the representative of Democracy, and the Provisional Government should look upon me as expressing the demands of Democracy, and should particularly heed the opinions which I may utter." Last, but not least, there were in the Government representatives of the Russian Liberal Intelligencia, with all its good and bad qualities, and with the lack of will-power characteristic of that class, the will-power which, by its boundless daring, its cruelty in removing obstacles, and its tenacity in seizing power, gives victory in the struggle for self-preservation to class, caste and nationality. During the four years of the Russian turmoil the Russian Intelligentsia and Bourgeoisie lived in a state of impotence and of non-resistance, and surrendered every stronghold; they even submitted to physical extermination and extinction. Strong will-power appeared to exist only on the two extreme flanks of the social front. Unfortunately it was a will to destroy and not to create. One flank has already produced Lenin, Bronstein, Apfelbaum, Uritzki, Dzerjinski, and Peters. . . . The other flank, defeated in March, 1917, may not yet have said its last word. The Russian Revolution was undoubtedly national in its origin, being a mode of expressing the universal protest against the old régime. But, when the time came for reconstruction, two forces came into conflict which embodied and led two different currents of political thought, two different outlooks. According to the accepted phrase, it was a struggle between the Bourgeoisie and the Democracy. But it would be more correct to describe it as a struggle between the Bourgeois and the Socialist Democracies. Both sides derived their leading spirits from the same source—the Russian Intelligentsia—by no means numerous and heterogeneous, not so much in respect of class and wealth as of political ideas and methods of political contest. Both sides inadequately reflected the thoughts of the popular masses in whose name they spoke. At first these masses were merely an audience applauding the actors who most appealed to its impassioned, but not altogether idealistic, instincts. It was only after this psychological training that the inert masses, and in particular the Army, became, in the words of Kerensky, " an elemental mass melted in the fire of the Revolution and . . . exercising tremendous pressure which was felt by the entire organism of the State." To deny this would be tantamount to the denial, in accordance with Tolstoi's doctrine, of the influence of leaders upon the life of the people. This theory has been completely shattered by Bolshevism, which has conquered for a long time the masses of the people with whom it has nothing in common and who are inimical to the Communist creed.

In the first weeks of the new Government the phenomenon became apparent, which was described in the middle of July by the Committee of the Duma in its appeal to the Government in the following words: " The seizure of the power of the State by irresponsible organisations, the creation by these organisations of a dual power in the centre, and of the absence of power in the country."

The power of the Soviet was also conditional in spite of a series of Government crises and of opportunities thereby provided for seizing that power and wielding it without opposition and unreservedly (the Provisional Government offered no resistance). The Revolutionary Democracy, as represented by the Soviet, categorically declined to assume that rôle because it realised quite clearly that it lacked the strength, the knowledge, and the skill to govern the country in which it had as yet no real support. Tzeretelli, one of the leaders of Revolutionary Democracy, said: " The time is not yet ripe for the fulfilment of the ultimate aims of the proletariat and for the solution of class questions. We understand that a Bourgeois Revolution is in progress . . . as we are unable fully to attain to our bright ideal . . . and we *do not wish to assume that responsibility for the collapse of the movement*, which we could not avoid if we made the desperate attempt to impose our will upon events at the present moment." Another representative, Nahamkes, said that they preferred " to compel the Government to comply with their demands by means of perpetual organised pressure." A member of the Executive Committee of the Soviet, Stankevitch, thus describes the Soviet in his *Reminiscences*, which reflect the incorrigible idealism of a Socialist who is off the rails and who has now reached the stage of excusing Bolshevism, but who nevertheless impresses one as being sincere: " The Soviet, a gathering of illiterate soldiers, took the lead because it asked nothing and because it was only a screen covering what was actually complete anarchy." Two thousand soldiers from the rear and eight hundred workmen from Petrograd formed an institution which pretended to guide the political, military, economic and social life of an enormous country. The records of the meetings of the Soviet, as reported in the Press, testify to the extraordinary ignorance and confusion which reigned at these meetings. One could not help being painfully impressed by such a " representation " of Russia. An impotent and subdued anger against the Soviet was growing in the circles of the Intelligencia, the Democratic Bourgeoisie and the Officers. All their hatred was concentrated upon the Soviet, which they abused in terms of excessive bitterness. That hatred, often openly expressed, was wrongly interpreted by the Revolutionary Democracy as abhorrence of the very *idea of Democratic Representation*. In time the supremacy of the Petrograd Soviet, which ascribed to itself the exceptional merit of having destroyed the old régime, began to wane. A vast network of Committees and Soviets, which had flooded the country and the Army, claimed the right to participate in the work of the State. In April, therefore, a Congress was held of the delegates of Workmen and Soldiers' Soviets. The Petrograd Soviet was reorganised on the basis of a more regular representation, and in June the All-Russian Congress of Representatives of the Soviets was opened. The composition of this fuller representation of Democracy is interesting:—

Revolutionary Socialists	285
Social Democrats (Mensheviks)	248
Social Democrats (Bolsheviks)	105

The Duma

Internationalists	32
Other Socialists	73
United Social Democrats	10
Members of the " Bund "	10
Members of the " Edimstvo " (Unity) group	3
Popular Socialists	3
Trudovik (Labour)	5
Communist Anarchists	1

Thus, the overwhelming masses of Non-Socialist Russia were not represented at all; even the elements that were either non-political or belonged to the groups of the right and were elected by the Soviets and Army Committees as non-party members, hastened for motives altogether in the interests of the State to profess the Socialistic creed. In these circumstances the Revolutionary Democracy could hardly be expected to exercise self-restraint, and there could be no hope of keeping the popular movement within the limits of the Bourgeois Revolution. In reality the ramshackle helm was seized by a block of Social Revolutionaries and Mensheviks, in which first the former and then the latter predominated. It is that narrow partisan block which held in bondage the will of the Government and is primarily responsible for the subsequent course of the Revolution.

The composition of the Soviet was heterogeneous: intellectuals, bourgeoisie, workmen, soldiers and many deserters. The Soviet and the Congresses, and especially the former, were a somewhat inert mass, utterly devoid of political education. Action, power and influence afterwards passed therefore into the hands of Executive Committees in which the Socialist intellectual elements were almost exclusively represented. The most devastating criticism of the Executive Committee of the Soviet came from that very institution, and was made by one of its members, Stankevitch: the meetings were chaotic, political disorganisation, indecision, haste, and fitfulness showed themselves in its decisions, and there was a complete absence of administrative experience and true democracy. One of the members advocated anarchy in the " Izvestia," another sent written permits for the expropriation of the landlords, a third explained to a military delegation which had complained of the Commanding Officers that these officers should be dismissed and arrested, etc.

" The most striking feature of the Committee is the preponderance of the alien element," wrote Stankevitch. " Jews, Georgians, Letts, Poles, and Lithuanians were represented out of

Russia during the turmoil.

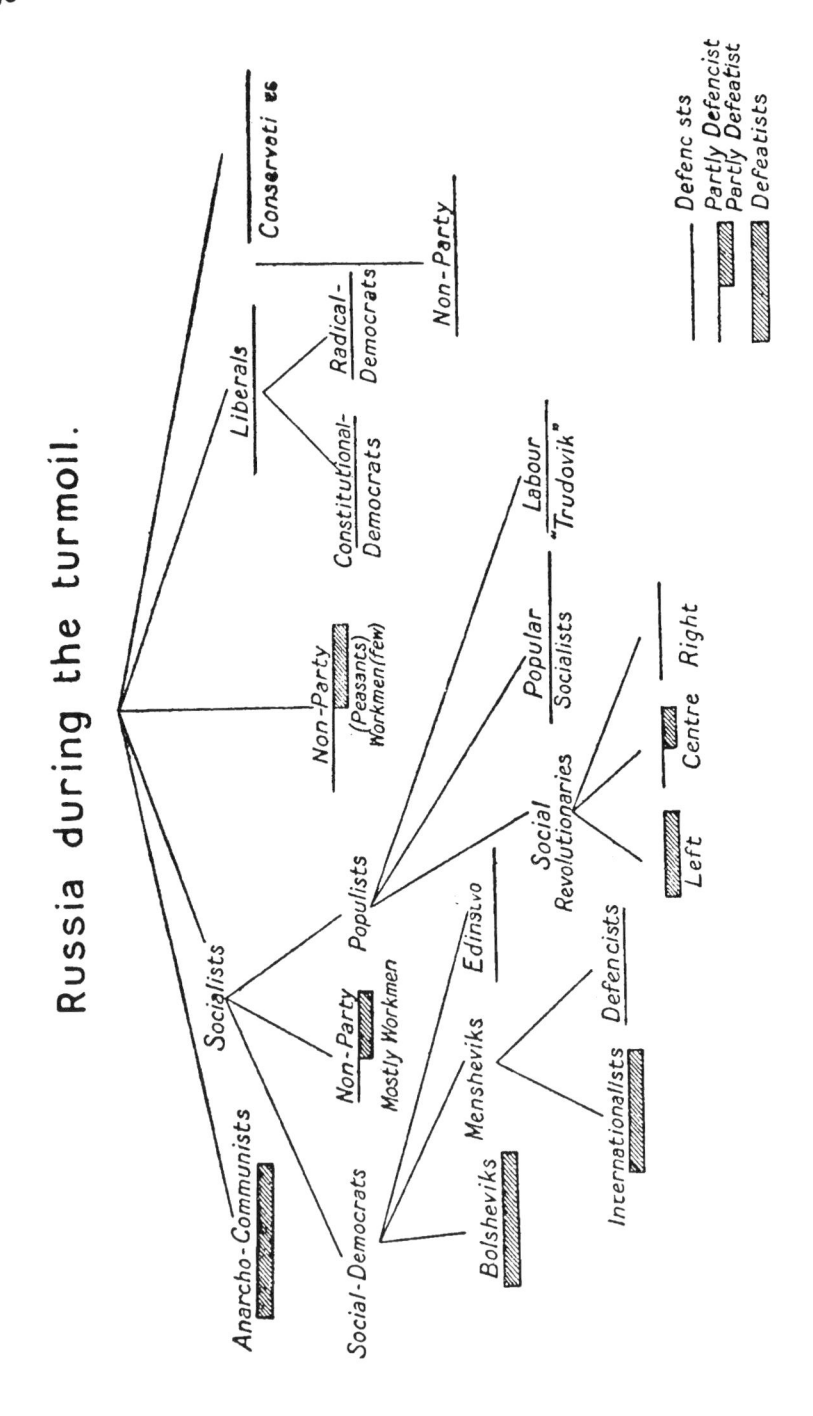

Diagram showing political groupings:

- **Conservatives**
- **Liberals**
  - Constitutional-Democrats
  - Radical-Democrats
  - Non-Party
- **Non-Party** (Peasants, Workmen (few))
- **Socialists**
  - Anarcho-Communists *(Defeatists)*
  - Social-Democrats
    - Non-Party — Mostly Workmen *(Partly Defencist / Partly Defeatist)*
    - Bolsheviks *(Defeatists)*
    - Mensheviks
      - Edinstvo
      - Defencists
      - Internationalists *(Partly Defeatist)*
  - Populists
    - Labour "Trudovik"
    - Popular Socialists
    - Social Revolutionaries
      - Right
      - Centre *(Partly Defencist)*
      - Left *(Partly Defeatist)*

Legend:
- —— Defencists
- Partly Defencist
- Partly Defeatist
- ▨ Defeatists

The Soviet

all proportion to their numbers in Petrograd and in the country."

The following is a list of the first Presidium of the All-Russian Central Committee of the Soviets:—

- 1 Georgian
- 5 Jews
- 1 Armenian
- 1 Pole
- 1 Russian (if his name was not an assumed one).

This exceptional preponderance of the alien element, foreign to the Russian national idea, could not fail to tinge the entire activities of the Soviet with a spirit harmful to the interests of the Russian State. The Provisional Government was the captive of the Soviet from the very first day, as it had under-estimated the importance and the power of that institution, and was unable to display either determination or strength in resisting the Soviet. The Government did not even hope for victory in that struggle, as, in its endeavour to save the country, it could not very well proclaim watchwords which would have suited the licentious mob and which emanated from the Soviet. The Government talked about duty, the Soviet about rights. The former " prohibited," the latter " permitted." The Government was linked with the old power by the inheritance of statesmanship and organisation, as well as the external methods of administration; whereas the Soviet, springing from mutiny and from the slums, was the direct negation of the entire old régime. It is a delusion to think, as a small portion of the moderate democracy still appear to do, that the Soviet played the part of " restraining the tidal wave of the people." *The Soviet did not actually destroy the Russian State, but was shattering it, and did so to the extent of smashing the Army and imposing Bolshevism on it.* Hence the duplicity and insincerity of its activities. Apart from its declarations, all the speeches, conversations, comments, and articles of the Soviet and of the Executive Committee, of its groups and individuals, came to the knowledge of the country and of the Front, and tended towards the destruction of the authority of the Government. Stankevitch wrote that not deliberately, but persistently, the Committee was dealing death-blows to the Government.

Who, then, were the men who were trying to democratise the Army Regulations, smashing all the foundations of the Army, inspiring the Polivanov Commission, and tying the hands of two War Ministers? The following is the personnel elected in the beginning of April from the Soldiers' Section of the Soviet to the Executive Committee:—

War-time Officers	1
Clerks	2
Cadets	2
Soldiers from the rear	9
Scribes and men on special duty	5

I will leave their description to Stankevitch, who said: " At first hysterical, noisy, and unbalanced men were elected, who were utterly useless to the Committee. . . ." New elements were subsequently added. " The latter tried consciously, and in the measure of their ability, to cope with the ocean of military matters. Two of them, however, seemed to have been inoffensive scribes in Reserve Battalions, who had never taken the slightest interest in the War, the Army, or the political Revolution." The duplicity and the insincerity of the Soviet were clearly manifested in regard to the War. The intellectual circles of the Left and of the Revolutionary Democracy mostly espoused the idea of Zimmerwald and of Internationalism. It was natural, therefore, that the first word which the Soviet addressed on March 14, 1917, " To the Peoples of the Whole World," was:

" PEACE."

The world problems, infinitely complex, owing to the national, political, and economic interests of the peoples who differed in their understanding of the Eternal Truth, could not be solved in such an elementary fashion. Bethmann-Holweg was contemptuously silent. On March 17th, 1917, the Reichstag, by a majority against the votes of both Social Democratic parties, declined the offer of peace without annexations. Noske voiced the views of the German Democracy in saying: " We are offered from abroad to organise a Revolution. If we follow that advice the working classes will come to grief." Among the Allies and the Allied Democracies the Soviet manifesto provoked anxiety, bewilderment, and discontent, which were vividly expressed in the speeches made by Albert Thomas, Henderson, Vandervelde, and even the present-day French Bolshevik, Cachin, upon their visits to Russia. The Soviet subsequently added to the word " Peace " the definition, " Without annexations and indemnities on the basis of the self-determination of peoples." The theory of this formula promptly clashed with the actual question of Western and Southern Russia occupied by the Germans; of Poland, of

Roumania, Belgium, and Serbia, devastated by the Germans; of Alsace-Lorraine and Posen, as well as of the servitude, expropriations, and compulsory labour which had been imposed upon all the countries invaded by the Germans. According to the programme of the German Social Democrats, which was at length published in Stockholm, the French in Alsace-Lorraine, the Poles in Posen, and the Danes in Schleswig were only to be granted national autonomy under the sceptre of the German Emperor. At the same time, the idea of the independence of Finland, Russian Poland, and Ireland was strongly advocated. The demand for the restoration of the German colonies was curiously blended with the promises of independence for India, Siam, Korea. . . .

The sun did not rise at the bidding of Chanticleer. The *ballon d'essai* failed. The Soviet was forced to admit that "time is necessary in order that the peoples of all countries should rise, and with an iron hand compel their rulers and capitalists to make peace. . . Meanwhile, the comrade-soldiers who have sworn to defend Russian liberties should not refuse to advance, as this may become a military necessity. . . ." The Revolutionary Democracy was perplexed, and their attitude was clearly expressed in the words of Tchkeidze: "We have been preaching against the War all the time. How can I appeal to the soldiers to continue the War and to stay at the Front?"

Be that as it may, the words "War" and "Advance" had been uttered. They divided the Soviet Socialists into two camps, the "Defeatists" and "Defensists."* Theoretically, only the right groups of the Social Revolutionaries, the popular Socialists, the "Unity" ("Edistvo") group, and the Labour party ("Trudoviki") belonged to the latter. All other Socialists advocated the immediate cessation of the war and the "deepening" of the Revolution by means of internal Class War. In practice, when the question of the continuation of the war was put to the vote, the Defensists were joined by the majority of the Social Revolutionaries and of the Social Democrat Mensheviks. The resolutions, however, bore the stamp of ambiguity—neither war nor peace. Tzeretelli was advocating "a movement against the war in all countries, Allied and enemy." The Congress of the Soviets at the end of May passed an equally ambiguous resolution, which, after demanding that annexations and indemnities should be renounced by all belligerents, pointed out that, "so long as the

---

* The word *Defensists* is used as a translation of the newly-coined Russian word *oboronetz*, which means "He who is in favour of a defensive war."

war lasts, the collapse of the Army, the weakening of its spirit, strength and capacity for *active* operations would constitute a strong menace to the cause of Freedom and to the vital interests of the country." In the beginning of June the Second Congress passed a new resolution. On the one hand, it emphatically declared that " the question of the advance should be decided solely from the point of view of purely military and strategical considerations "; on the other hand, it expressed an obviously Defeatist idea · " Should the war end by the complete defeat of one of the belligerent groups, this would be a source of new wars, would increase the enmity between peoples, and would result in their complete exhaustion, in starvation and doom." The Revolutionary Democracy had obviously confused two ideas: the *strategic victory* signifying the end of the war and *the terms of the Peace Treaty*, which might be humane or inhuman, righteous or unjust, far-seeing or short-sighted. In fact, what they wanted was war and an advance, but *without a victory*. Curiously enough, the Prussian Deputy, Strebel, the editor of *Vorwaerts*, invented the same formula as early as in 1915. He wrote: " I openly profess that a complete victory of the Empire would not benefit the Social Democracy."

There was not a single branch of administration with which the Soviet and the Executive Committee did not interfere with the same ambiguity and insincerity, due on the one hand to the fear of any action contrary to the fundamentals of their doctrine, and on the other to the obvious impossibility of putting these doctrines into practice. The Soviet did not, and could not, partake in the creative work of rebuilding the State. With regard to Economics, Agriculture, and Labour, the activities of the Soviet were reduced to the publication of pompous Socialist Party programmes, which the Socialist Ministers themselves clearly understood to be impracticable in the atmosphere of War, Anarchy, and Economic crisis prevailing in Russia. Nevertheless, these Resolutions and Proclamations were interpreted in the factories and in the villages as a kind of " Absolution." They roused the passions and provoked the desire, immediately and arbitrarily, to put them into practice. This provocation was followed by restraining appeals. In an appeal addressed to the sailors of Kronstadt on May 26th, 1917, the Soviet suggested " that they should demand immediate and implicit compliance with all the orders of the Provisional Government given in the interests of the Revolution and of the security of the country. . "

All these literary achievements are not, however, the only form of activity in which the Soviet indulged. The characteristic feature of the Soviet and of the Executive Committee was the complete absence of discipline in their midst. With reference to the special Delegation of the Committee, whose object it was to be in contact with the Provisional Government, Stankevitch says: " What could that Delegation do? While it was arguing and reaching a complete agreement with the Ministers, dozens of members of the Committee were sending letters and publishing articles; travelling in the provinces, and at the Front in the name of the Committee; receiving callers at the Taurida Palace, everyone of them acting independently and taking no heed of instructions, Resolutions, or decisions of the Committee."

Was the Central Committee of the Soviet invested with actual power? A reply to this question can be found in the appeal of the Organising Committee of the Labour Socialist Democratic Party of July 17th. " The watchword ' All-Power to the Soviets,' to which many workmen adhere, is a dangerous one. *The following of the Soviets represents a minority in the population*, and we must make every effort in order that the Bourgeois elements, who are still willing and capable of joining us in preserving the conquests of the Revolution, shall share with us the burdens of the inheritance left by the old régime, which we have shouldered, and the enormous responsibility for the outcome of the Revolution which we bear in the eyes of the people." The Soviet, and later the All-Russian Central Committee, could not, and would not, by reason of its composition and their political ideas, exercise a powerful restraining influence upon the masses of the people, who had thrown off the shackles and were perturbed and mutinous. The movement had been inspired by the members of the Soviet, and the influence and authority of the Soviet were, therefore, entirely dependent on the extent to which they were able to flatter the instincts of the masses. These masses, as Karl Kautsky, an observer from the Marxist Camp, has said, " were concerned merely with their requirements and their desires as soon as they were drawn into the Revolution, and they did not care a straw whether their demands were practicable or beneficial to society." Had the Soviet endeavoured to resist with any firmness or determination whatsoever the pressure of the masses, it would have run the risk of being swept away. Also, day after day and step by step, the Soviet was coming under the influence of Anarchist and Bolshevik ideas.

CHAPTER XI.

The Bolshevik Struggle for Power—The Power of the Army and the Idea of a Dictatorship.

IN the first period—from the beginning of the Revolution until the *coup d'état* of November—the Bolsheviks were engaged in struggling to seize power by destroying the Bourgeois régime and disorganising the Army, thus paving the way for the *avénement* of Bolshevism, as Trotsky solemnly expressed it. On the day after his arrival in Russia Lenin published his programme, of which I will here mention the salient points

(1) The War waged by the " Capitalist Government " is an Imperialistic, plundering War. No concessions, therefore, should be made to Revolutionary " Defensism." The representatives of that doctrine and the Army in the field should be made clearly to understand that the War cannot end in a truly Democratic peace, without coercion, *unless* Capitalism is destroyed.

The troops must fraternize with the enemy.

(2) The first stage of the Revolution by which the Bourgeoisie came into power must be followed by the second stage in which power must pass into the hands of the Proletariat and of the poorest peasants.

(3) No support should be given to the Provisional Government, and the fallacy of its promises should be exposed.

(4) The fact must be acknowledged that, in the majority of the Soviets, the Bolshevik party is in a minority. The policy must therefore be continued of criticising and exposing mistakes, while at the same time advocating the necessity for the transfer of Supreme Power to the Soviet.

(5) Russia is not a Parliamentary Republic—that would have been a step backwards—but a Republic of the Soviets of Workmen's and Peasants' Deputies.

The police (Militia?), the Army, and the Civil Service must be abolished.

(6) With regard to the agrarian question, the Soviets of farm-labourers' deputies must come to the fore. All landowners' estates must be confiscated, and all land in Russia nationalised and placed at the disposal of Local Soviets of Peasants' Deputies. The latter to be elected among the poorest peasants.

(7) All the banks in the country must be united in one National Bank, controlled by the Soviet.

(8) Socialism must not be introduced now, but a step must be taken towards the ultimate control by the Soviet of all industries and of the distribution of materials.

(9) The State shall become a Commune, and the Socialist Democratic Bolshevik Party shall henceforward be called " The Communist Party."

I shall not dwell upon this programme, which was put into practice, with certain reservations, in November, 1917. During the first period the activities of the Bolsheviks, which are of great importance, were based upon the following three principles:

(1) The overthrow of the Government and the demoralisation of the Army.

(2) The promotion of class war in the country and discontent in the villages.

(3) The seizure of power by the minority, which, according to Lenin, was to be " well-organised, armed and centralised," *i.e.*, the Bolshevik party. (This was, of course, a negation of Democratic forms of Government.)

The ideas and aims of the party were, of course, beyond the understanding not only of the ignorant Russian peasantry, but even of the Bolshevik underlings scattered throughout the land. The masses wanted simple and clear watchwords to be immediately put into practice, which would satisfy their wishes and demands arising from the turmoil of the Revolution. That " simplified " Bolshevism inherent in all popular movements against the established power in Russia was all the easier to institute in that it had freed itself from all restraining moral influences and was aiming primarily at destruction pure and simple, ignoring the consequences of military defeat and of the ruin of the country. The Provisional Government was the first target. In the Bolshevik Press, at public meetings, in all the activities of the Soviets and Congresses, and even in their conversations with the members of the Provisional Government, the Bolshevik leaders stubbornly and arrogantly advocated its removal, describing it as an instrument of counter-Revolution and of International reaction. The

Bolsheviks, however, refrained from decisive action, as they feared the political backwardness of the country as a whole. They began what soldiers call " a reconnaissance," and carried it out with great intensity. They seized several private houses in Petrograd, and organised a demonstration on the 20th and 21st of April. That was the first " review " of the proletariat, at which an estimate was made of the Bolshevik forces. The excuse for this demonstration, in which the workmen and the troops participated, was given by Miliukov's Note on International Policy. I say *excuse* because the real reason lay in the fundamental divergence of opinion mentioned above. Everything else was only a pretext. As a result of the demonstration there were great disturbances and armed conflicts in the capital, and many casualties. The crowds carried placards bearing the inscriptions : " Down with the Miliukov Policy of Conquests," and " Down with the Provisional Government."

The review was a failure. In the course of the debate in the Soviet on this occasion, the Bolsheviks demanded that the Government be deposed, but there was a note of hesitation in their speeches : " The proletariat should first discuss the existing conditions and form an estimate of its strength." The Soviet passed a resolution condemning both the Government's policy of conquest and the Bolshevik demonstration, while at the same time " congratulating the Revolutionary Democracy of Petrograd, which had proved its intense interest in international politics by meetings, resolutions and demonstrations."

Lenin was planning another armed demonstration on a large scale on June 10th during the Congress of the Soviets; but it was countermanded, as the great majority of the Congress was opposed to it. The demonstration was likewise intended as a means of seizing power. This internal struggle between the two wings of the Revolutionary Democracy, which were bitterly antagonistic to one another, is extremely interesting. The Left wing made every endeavour to induce the " Defensist " block, which was preponderant, to break with the Bourgeoisie and to assume power. The block was also resolutely opposed to such a course.

Within the Soviets new combinations were coming into being. On certain questions the Social Revolutionaries of the Left and the Social Democrats—Internationalists—were leaning towards the Bolsheviks. Nevertheless, until September the Bolsheviks were not in a majority in the Petrograd Soviet or in many provincial Soviets. It was only on September 25th that Bronstein Trotsky succeeded Tchkeidze as Chairman of the Petrograd

The Bolshevik Struggle for Power

Soviet. The motto, "All Power to the Soviets," sounded from their lips like self-sacrifice or provocation. Trotsky explained this contradiction by saying that, owing to constant re-elections, the Soviets reflected the true (?) spirit of the masses of workmen and soldiers, who were leaning to the Left, whereas, after the break with the Bourgeoisie, extremist tendencies were bound to prevail in the Soviets. As the true aspect of Bolshevism gradually revealed itself these dissensions deepened, and were not limited to the Social Democratic programme or to party tactics. It was a struggle between Democracy and the Proletariat, between the majority and a minority, which was intellectually backward, but strong in its mutinous daring and headed by strong and unprincipled men. It was a struggle between the democratic principles of Universal Suffrage, political liberties, equality, etc., and the dictatorship of a privileged class, madness, and imminent slavery. On the 2nd July there was a second Ministerial crisis, for which the outward cause was the disapproval of the Liberal Ministers of the Act of Ukrainian Autonomy. On July 3rd-5th the Bolsheviks made another riot in the Capital, in which workmen, soldiers and sailors participated. It was done this time on a large scale, and was accompanied by plunder and murder. There were many victims, and the Government was in great difficulty. Kerensky was at that time visiting us on the Western Front. His conversations with Petrograd over the direct wire indicated that Prince Lvov and the Government were deeply depressed. Prince Lvov summoned Kerensky to return to Petrograd at once, but warned him that he could not be responsible for his safety. The rebels demanded that the Soviet and the Central Executive Committee of the Congress should assume power. These wings of the Revolutionary Democracy returned another categorical refusal. The movement found no support in the provinces, and the mutiny was quelled chiefly by the Vladimir military school and the Cossack regiments. Several companies of the Petrograd garrison likewise remained loyal. Bronstein Trotsky wrote that the movement was premature because there were too many passive and irresolute elements in the garrison; but that it had nevertheless been proved that, " except the cadets, no one wanted to fight against the Bolsheviks *for the Government and for the leading parties in the Soviet.*"

The tragedy of the Government headed by Kerensky, and of the Soviet, lay in the fact that the masses would not follow abstract watchwords. They proved equally indifferent to the country and to the Revolution, as well as to the International, and had no intention of shedding their blood and sacrificing their lives for any of these ideas. The crowd followed those who gave practical promises and flattered its instincts.

When we speak of " power," with reference to the first period of the Russian Revolution, we actually mean only its outward forms; for under the exceptional conditions imposed by a World War on a scale unequalled in history, when 20 per cent. of the entire male population was under arms, the power was really concentrated in the hands of the Army. That Army had been led astray, had been demoralised by false doctrines, had lost all sense of duty, and all fear of authority. Last, but not least, it had no leader. The Government, Kerensky, the Commanding Corps, the Soviet, Regimental Committees—for many reasons none of these could claim that title. The dissensions between all these contending forces were reflected in the minds of the men, and hastened the ruin of the Army. It is useless to make any surmises which cannot be proved by realities, especially in the absence of historical perspective; but there can be no doubt the question, whether or not it would have been possible to erect a dam which would have stemmed the tide and preserved discipline in the Army, will continue to arouse attention. Personally, I believe that it was possible. At first the Supreme Command might have done it, as well as the Government, had it shown sufficient resolve to squash the Soviets or sufficient strength and wisdom to draw them into the orbit of statesmanship and of truly democratic constructive work.

There can be no doubt that, in the beginning of the Revolution, the Government was recognised by all the sane elements of the population. The High Command, the officers, many regiments, the Bourgeoisie, and those Democratic elements which had not been led astray by militant Socialism adhered to the Government. The Press in those days was full of telegrams, addresses and appeals from all parts of Russia, from various Social, Military and class organisations and institutions whose democratic attitude was undoubted.

As the Government weakened and was driven into two successive coalitions, that confidence correspondingly decreased and could not find compensation in fuller recognition by the Revolutionary Democracy; because anarchist tendencies, repudiating all authority, were gaining ground within these circles. In the beginning of May, after the armed rising in the streets of Petrograd, which took place without the knowledge of the Soviet, but with the participation of its members; after the resignation of Miliukov and Gutchkov, the complete impotence of the Provisional Government became so clearly apparent that Prince Lvov appealed to the Soviet, with the consent of the Duma Committee and of the Constitutional Democratic Party. He invited " the active creative forces of the country to participate directly in the government which had hitherto refrained from any such participation."

After some hesitation, the Soviet deemed it necessary to accept the offer, thereby assuming direct responsibility for the fate of the revolution. (Four members of the Soviet accepted Ministerial posts.) The Soviet declined to assume full power " because the transfer of power to the Soviets in that period of the revolution would have weakened it and would have prematurely estranged the elements capable of serving it, which would constitute a menace to the revolution." The impression produced by such declarations upon the Bourgeoisie and upon the " hostages " in the Coalition Government can be imagined. Although the Soviet expressed full confidence in the Government and appealed to the democracy to grant it full support, which would guarantee the authority of the Government, that Government was already irretrievably discredited. The Socialist circles which had sent their representatives to join it neither altered nor strengthened its intellectual level. On the contrary, it was weakened, inasmuch as the gulf was widened which separated the two political groups represented in the Government. While officially expressing confidence in the Government, the Soviet continued to undermine its power and became somewhat lukewarm towards the Socialist Ministers, who had been compelled by circumstances to deviate, to a certain extent, from the programme of the Socialist party. The people and the Army did not pay much attention to these events, as they were beginning to forget that there was any power at all, owing to the fact that the existence of that power had no bearing upon their everyday life.

The blood shed during the Petrograd rising organised by the anarchist-Bolshevik section of the Soviet on July 4th-5th, Prince Lvov's resignation, and the formation of a new coalition in which the Socialists, nominated by the Soviet, definitely predominated were but stepping stones towards the complete collapse of the power of the State. As I have already said, the first Government crisis was occasioned by events which, however important politically, were only " excuses." In the new Coalition the Democratic Bourgeoisie played but a secondary part, and its " temporary " assistance was only required in order that responsibility might be shared; while everything was decided behind the curtain, in the circles closely connected with the Soviet. Such a coalition could have no vitality and could not reconcile even the opportunist elements of the Bourgeoisie with the Revolutionary Democracy. Apart from political and social considerations, the relative strength of the forces which were brought into play was influenced by the growing discontent of the masses with the activities of the Government owing to the general condition of the country. The masses accepted the revolution not as an arduous, transitory period, linked up with the past and present political development of Russia and of the world, but as an independent reality of the day, carrying in its trail real calamities such as the War, banditism, lawlessness, stoppage of industry, cold and hunger. The masses were unable to grasp the situation in its complex entirety and could not differentiate between elemental, inevitable phenomena inherent in all revolutions and the will for good or evil of departments of the Government, institutions or individuals. They felt that the situation was intolerable and tried to find a remedy. As a result of the universal recognition of the impotence of the existing power, a new idea began to occupy the minds of the people:

A DICTATORSHIP.

I emphatically declare that in the social and military circles with which I was in touch the tendency towards a dictatorship was prompted by a patriotic and clear consciousness of the abyss into which the Russian people was rapidly sinking. *It was not in the slightest degree inspired by any reactionary or counter-revolutionary motives.* There can be no doubt that the movement found adherents among the reactionaries and among mere opportunists; but both these elements were accessory and insignificant. Kerensky thus interpreted the rise of the movement which he described as " the tide of conspiracy ": " The Tarnopol defeat created a movement in favour of conspiracies, while the Bolshevik rising of July demonstrated to the uninitiated the *depth of the disruption of Democracy, the impotence of the revolution* against anarchy, as well as the strength of the organised minority which acted spontaneously." It would be difficult to find a better excuse for the movement. In the atmosphere of popular discontent, universal disorder and approaching anarchy, endeavours at creating a dictatorship were the natural outcome of the existing conditions. These endeavours had their origin in a search for a *strong national and democratic power, but not a reactionary one.*

On the whole the Revolutionary Democracy lived in an atmosphere poisoned by the fear of a counter-revolution. All its cares, measures, resolutions and appeals, as well as the disruption of the Army and the abolition of the police in the villages, tended towards a struggle with this imaginary foe, which was supposed to menace the conquests of the revolution. Were the conscious leaders of the Soviet really convinced that such a danger existed, or were they fanning this unfounded fear as a tactical move? I am inclined to accept the second solution, because it was quite obvious, not only to myself, but to the Soviet as well, that the activities of the Democratic Bourgeoisie meant not counter-revolution, but merely opposition. And yet in the Russian partisan press and in wide circles outside Russia it is precisely in the former sense that the pre-November period of the Revolution was interpreted. The Provisional Government proclaimed a broad, Democratic programme upon its formation. In the circles of the Right this programme was criticised and there was discontent; but no active opposition. In the first four or five months after the beginning of the Revolution there was not a single important counter-revolutionary organisation in the country. These organisations became more or less active and other secret circles, especially officers' circles, were formed in July in connection with the plans for a Dictatorship. There can be no doubt that many people with pronounced tendencies towards a restoration joined these circles. But their main object was to combat the unofficial government, which was a class government, as well as the personnel of the Soviet and the Executive Committee. Had these circles not collapsed prematurely owing to their weakness, numerical insignificance and lack of organisation, some of the members of those institutions might very possibly have been destroyed. While constantly resisting counter-revolution from the Right, the Soviet gave every opportunity for the preparations for a real counter-revolution emanating from its own midst, from the Bolsheviks.

I remember that different persons who came to the Stavka began to discuss the question of a dictatorship and to throw out feelers, as it were, approximately in the beginning of June. All these conversations were stereotyped to such an extent that I have no difficulty in summarising them.

" Russia is moving towards inevitable ruin. The Government is utterly powerless. We must have a strong power. Sooner or later we shall have to come to a Dictatorship."

Nobody mentioned restoration or a change of policy in a reactionary direction. The names were mentioned of Kornilov and Brussilov. I warned them against hasty decisions. I must confess that we still entertained the illusory hope that the Government—by internal evolution, under the influence of a new, armed demonstration on the part of the anti-National extremist elements towards which they were so lenient—would realise the futility and hopelessness of continuing in their present position and would come to the idea of power vested in one man, which might be achieved in a constitutional manner. The future seemed pregnant with disaster in the absence of a truly lawful power. I pointed out that there were no military leaders enjoying sufficient authority with the demoralised soldiery, but that if, a military dictatorship should become necessary for the State and practicable, Kornilov was already very much respected by the officers, whereas Brussilov's reputation had been injured by his opportunism.

In his book Kerensky says that " Cossack circles and certain politicians " had suggested repeatedly to him that the impotent Government should be replaced by a personal dictatorship. It was only when society was disappointed in him as the " possible organiser and chief agent for altering the system of Government " that " a search began for another individual."

There can be no doubt that the men and social circles that appealed to Kerensky in the question of a dictatorship were not his apologists and did not belong to the " Revolutionary Democracy," but the mere fact of their appeal is sufficient proof that their motives could not have been reactionary, and that it reflected the sincere desire of the Russian patriotic elements to see a strong man at the helm in days of storm and strife.

Perhaps there may also have been another motive; there had been a short period, approximately in June, when not only the Russian public, but also the officers had succumbed to the charm of the War Minister's impassioned oratory and pathos. The Russian officers, who were being sacrificed wholesale, had forgotten and forgiven and were desperately hoping that he would save the Russian Army. And their promise to die in the front line was by no means an empty one. During Kerensky's visits to the front, it was a painful sight to see these doomed men, their eyes shining with exaltation, and their hearts beating with hope, a hope that was destined to be so bitterly and mercilessly disappointed.

It is to be noted that Kerensky, seeking in his book to justify the temporary " concentration of power " which he assumed on August 27th, says: " In the struggle against the conspiracy conducted by a single will, the State was compelled to set against it a will capable of resolute and quick action. No collective power, much less a Coalition, can possess such a single will."

I think that the internal condition of the Russian State threatened with a monstrous joint conspiracy of the German General Staff and the anti-national and anti-constitutional elements of the Russian exiles was sufficiently grave to warrant the demand for a strong power " capable of resolute and quick action."

CHAPTER XII.

The Activities of the Provisional Government—Internal Politics, Civil Administration—The Town, the Village and the Agrarian Problem.

I WILL deal in this and in the subsequent chapters with the internal condition of Russia in the first period of the Revolution only in so far as it affected the conduct of the World War. I have already mentioned the duality of the Supreme Administration of the country and the incessant pressure of the Soviet upon the Provisional Government. A member of the Duma, Mr. Shulgin, wittily remarked: " The old régime is interned in the fortress of Peter and Paul, and the new one is under domiciliary arrest." The Provisional Government did not represent the people as a whole; it could not and would not forestall the will of the Constituent Assembly by introducing reforms which would shake the political and social structure of the State to its very foundations. It proclaimed that " not violence and compulsion, but the voluntary obedience of free citizens to the power which they had themselves created, constituted the foundation of the new administration of the State. Not a single drop of blood has been shed by the Provisional Government which has erected no barrier against the free expression of public opinion. . . ." This non-resistance to evil at the moment when a fierce struggle, unfettered by moral or patriotic considerations, was being conducted by some groups of the population for motives of self-preservation and by others for the attainment by violence of extreme demands, was undoubtedly a confession of impotence. In the subsequent declarations of the second and third Coalition Governments mention was made "of stringent measures " against the forces of disorganisation in the country. These words, however, were never translated into deeds.

The idea of not forestalling the will of the Constituent Assembly was not carried out by the Government, especially in the domain of national self-determination. The Government proclaimed the independence of Poland, but made "the consent to such alterations of the territory of the Russian State as may be necessary for the creation of independent Poland " dependent upon the All-Russian Constituent Assembly. That proclamation, the legal validity of which is contestable, was, however, in full accord with the juridical standpoint of society. With regard to Finland, the Government did not alter her legal status towards Russia, but confirmed the rights and privileges of the country, cancelled all the limitations of the Finnish Constitution and intended to convoke the Finnish Chamber (" Seim ") that was to confirm the new constitution of the Principality. The Government subsequently adhered to their intention to entertain favourably all the just demands of the Finns for local reconstruction. Nevertheless, both the Provisional Government and Finland were engaged in a protracted struggle for power on account of the universal desire for the immediate satisfaction of the interests of the separate nationalities. On July 6th the Finnish Assembly passed a law (by the majority of Social-Democratic votes) proclaiming the assumption by that body of supreme power after the abdication " of the Finnish Grand-Duke " (the official title of the Russian Emperor). Only foreign affairs, military legislation and administration were left to the Provisional Government. This decision corresponded to a certain degree with the resolution of the Congress of Soviets, which demanded that full independence should be granted to Finland before the convocation of the Constituent Assembly, with the above-mentioned restrictions. The Russian Government answered this declaration of the actual independence of Finland by dissolving the Assembly, which met, however, once again in September of its own free will. In this struggle, the intensity of which varied according to the rise and fall of the political barometer in Petrograd, the Finnish politicians, disregarding the interests of the State and having no support whatsoever in the Army, counted exclusively upon the loyalty or, to be more correct, the weakness of the Provisional Government. Matters never reached the stage of open rebellion. The conscious elements of the population kept the country within the limits of reasonableness, not out of loyalty, but perhaps because they feared the consequences of civil war and especially of the sabotage in which the licentious soldiers and sailors would have presumably indulged.

May and June were spent in a struggle for power between the Government and the self-appointed Central Rada (Assembly). The All-Ukrainian Military Congress, also convened arbitrarily on June 8th, demanded that the Government should immediately comply with all the demands of the Central Rada and the Congresses, and suggested that the Rada should cease to address the

Government, but should begin at once to organise the autonomous administration of the Ukraine. On June 11th the autonomous Constitution of the Ukraine was adopted and a Secretariat (Council of Ministers) formed under the chairmanship of Mr. Vinnichenko. After the Government envoys—the Ministers Kerensky, Tereschenko and Tzeretelli—had negotiated with the Rada, a proclamation was issued on July 2nd, which forestalled the decision of the Constituent Assembly and proclaimed the autonomy of the Ukraine with certain restrictions. The Central Rada and the Secretariat were gradually seizing the administration, creating a dual power on the spot and discrediting the All-Russian Government. They thus provoked civil strife and provided moral excuses for every endeavour to shirk civic and military duties to the common Mother Country. The Central Rada, moreover, contained from the outset sympathisers with Germany and was undoubtedly connected through the "Union for the Liberation of the Ukraine" with the headquarters of the Central Powers. Bearing in mind the ample material collected by the Stavka, Vinnichenko's half-hearted confession to a French correspondent (?) with regard to Germanophil tendencies in the Rada, and finally the report of the Procurator of the Kiev Court of Appeal at the end of August, 1917, I cannot doubt that the Rada played a criminal part. The Procurator complained that the complete destruction of the machinery of intelligence and of criminal investigation deprived the Government prosecutors of the possibility of investigating the situation; he said that not only German espionage and propaganda, but the mutinies of the Ukrainian troops, as well as the destination of obscure funds of undoubted Austro-German origin . . . could be traced to the Rada.

*   *   *

The Ministry of the Interior, which, in the old days, practically controlled the Autocracy and provoked universal hatred, now went to the other extreme. It all but abolished itself, and the functions of that branch of the administration were divided among local, self-appointed organisations. The history of the organs of the Ministry of the Interior is, in many ways, similar to the fate of the Supreme Command. On March 5th the Minister-President issued an order for the suppression of the offices of Governor and of Inspector of Police ("Ispravnik"), which were to be replaced by the presidents of the Provincial and District self-governing Councils ("Oupravas"), and for the police to be replaced by a militia organised by Social Institutions. This measure, adopted owing to the universal dislike for the agents of the old régime, was, in fact, the only actual manifestation of the Government's will; because the status of the Commissars was not established by law until the month of September. The instructions and orders of the Government were, on the whole, of an academic nature, because life followed its own course, and was regulated, or, to be more correct, muddled up, by local revolutionary changes of the law. The office of Government Commissars became a sinecure from the very outset. They had no power or authority, and became entirely dependent upon revolutionary organisations. When the latter passed a vote of censure upon the activities of a Commissar, he could practically do nothing more. The organisations elected a new one, and his confirmation in office by the Provisional Government was a mere formality. In the first six weeks seventeen Provincial Commissars and a great many District Commissars were thus removed. Later, in July, Tzeretelli, during his tenure of the office of Minister of the Interior, which lasted for a fortnight, gave official sanction to this procedure and sent a circular to the Local Soviets and Committees, inviting them to send in to him the names of desirable candidates, which were to replace the unsuitable ones. Thus there remained no representatives of the Central power on the spot. In the beginning of the Revolution the so-called " Social Committees " or " Soviets of Social Organisation " really represented a social Institution comprising the union of towns and *Zemstvos*, of Municipal Dumas, professional Unions, Co-operatives, Magistrates, etc. Things went from bad to worse when these Social Committees were dissolved into class and party organisations. Local power passed into the hands of the Soviets of Workmen and Soldiers and in places before the law had been produced to " democratised " Socialistic Dumas, closely reminiscent of semi-Boshevik Soviets.

The regulations issued by the Government on April 15th, on the organisation of Municipal Self-Government, comprised the following main points:

(1) All citizens of both sexes, having attained the age of twenty, were given the suffrage in the town.
(2) No domiciliary qualification was established.
(3) A proportional system of elections was introduced.
(4) The Military were given the suffrage in the localities in which the respective garrisons were quartered.

I will not examine in detail these regulations, which are probably the most Democratic ever known in Municipal Law, because the experience gained in their application was too short to afford any ground for discussion. I will only note one phenomenon which accompanied the introduction of these regulations in the autumn of 1917. The free vote in many places became a mockery. Throughout the length and breadth of Russia, all the non-Socialist and politically neutral parties were under suspicion and were subjected to persecution. They were not allowed to conduct propaganda, and their meetings were dispersed. Electioneering was characterised by blatant abuses. Occasionally election agents were subjected to violence and lists of candidates destroyed. At the same time the licentious and demoralised soldiery of many garrisons—chance guests in the town in which, as often as not, they had only appeared a day or two before—rushed to the polls and presented lists drawn up by the extreme Anti-National parties. There were cases when military units, arriving after the elections, demanded a re-election and accompanied this demand by threats and sometimes murders. There can be no doubt that, among the circumstances that affected the August elections in Petrograd to the Municipal Duma, to which sixty-seven Bolsheviks out of two hundred were elected, the presence in the Capital of numerous demoralised garrisons was not the least important. The authorities were silent because they were absent. The *Petite Bourgeoisie*, the intellectual workers, in a word, the Town Democracy in the widest sense, was the weakest party and was always defeated in that Revolutionary struggle. The mutinies, rebellions, and separations of various Republics—the precursors of the bloody Soviet Régime—had the most painful effect on the life of that portion of the community. The " self-determination " of the soldiers caused uneasiness and even fear of unrestricted violence. Even travelling was unsafe and difficult, because the railways fell into the hands of deserters. The " self-determination " of the workmen resulted in the impossibility of obtaining supplies of the most necessary commodities, owing to a tremendous rise in prices. The " self-determination " of the villages produced a stoppage of supplies, and the villages were thus left to starve; not to mention the moral ordeal of the class which was subjected to insults and degradation. The Revolution had raised hopes for the betterment of the conditions of life for everyone except the *Bourgeois* Democracy, because even the moral conquests proclaimed by the new Revolutionary power— liberty of speech, of the Press and of meetings, etc.—soon belonged exclusively to the Revolutionary Democracy. The upper *Bourgeoisie* (intellectually superior) was organised to a certain extent by means of the Constitutional Democratic Party, but the *Petite Bourgeoisie* (the *Bourgeois* Democracy) had no organisation whatsoever and no means for an organised struggle. The Democratic Municipalities were losing their true Democratic aspect—not as a result of the new Municipal law, but of Revolutionary practice—and became mere class organs of the Proletariat, or the representatives of purely Socialistic parties, completely out of touch with the people.

Self-government in the districts and in the villages in the first period of the Revolution was of more or less the same nature. Towards the autumn there should have been a Democratic system of *Zemstvo* Administration, on the same basis as that in the municipalities. The District (Volost) *Zemstvo* was to undertake the administration of local agriculture, education, order and safety. As a matter of fact, the villages were administered—if such a word can be applied to Anarchy—by a complex agglomeration of revolutionary organisations, such as peasant Congresses, Supply and Land Committees, Popular Soviets, Village Councils, etc. Very often another peculiar organisation—that of the deserters—dominated them all. At any rate, the All-Russian Union of Peasants agreed with the following declaration made by the left wing: " All our work for the organisation of various Committees will be of no avail if these Social Organisations are to remain under the constant threat of being terrorised by accidental armed bands."

The only question that deeply perturbed the minds of the peasantry and overshadowed all other events, was the old, painful, traditional question:

THE QUESTION OF THE LAND.

It was an exceptionally complex and tangled question. It arose more than once in the shape of fruitless mutinies, which were ruthlessly suppressed. The wave of agrarian troubles which swept over Russia in the years of the First Revolution (1905-6) and left a trail of fire and ruined estates was an indication of the consequences that were bound to follow the Revolution of 1917. It is difficult to form an exhaustive idea of the motives which prompted the land-owners to defend their rights so stubbornly and so energetically: was it atavism, a natural yearning for the land, statesmanlike considerations as to the desirability of increasing the productivity of the land by introducing higher methods of agriculture, a desire to maintain a direct influence over the people, or was it merely selfishness? . . One thing is certain—the agrarian reforms were overdue. Retribution could not fail to overtake the Government and the Ruling Classes for the long years of poverty, oppression, and, what is most important, the incredible moral and intellectual darkness in which the peasant masses were kept, their education being entirely neglected.

The peasants demanded that all land should be surrendered to them, and would not wait for the decision of the Central Land Committee or of the Constituent Assembly. This impatience was undoubtedly due, to a great extent, to the weakness of the Government and to outside influences, which will be described later. There was no divergence of opinion as to the fundamental idea of the reforms. The Liberal Democracy and the *Bourgeoisie*, the Revolutionary Democracy and the Provisional Government, all spoke quite definitely about " handing the land over to the workers." With the same unanimity these elements favoured the idea of leaving the final decision on the reform of the land and legislation on the subject to the Constituent Assembly. This irreconcilable divergence of opinion arose by reason of the very essence of land reform. Liberal circles in Russia stood for the private ownership of the land—an idea which found increasing favour with the peasants—and demanded that the peasants should receive allotments rather than that the land should be entirely redistributed. On the other hand, the Revolutionary Democracy advocated, at all meetings of every party, class and profession, the adoption of the Resolution of the All-Russian Congress of Peasants, which was passed on May 25th, with the approval of the Minister Tchernov on " the transfer of all lands . . . *to the people as a whole, as their patrimony, on the basis of equal possession without any payment.*" The peasants did not or would not understand this Social Revolutionary Resolution, which caused dissensions. The peasants were private owners by nature and could not understand the principle of nationalisation. The principle of equal possession meant that many millions of peasants, whose allotments were larger than the normal, would lose their surplus allotments, and the whole question of the redistribution of the land would lead to endless civil war; because there were innumerable peasants who had no land at all, and only 45,000,000 dessiatines of arable land which did not belong to the peasants to divide among 20,000,000 peasant households.

The Provisional Government did not consider itself entitled to solve the land problem. Under the pressure of the masses, it transferred its rights partly to the Ministry of Agriculture, partly to the Central Land Committee, which was organised on the basis of broad, democratic representation. The latter was entrusted with the task of collecting data and of drawing up a scheme of land reform, as well as of regulating the existing conditions with regard to the land. In practice, the use of the land transfer, rent, employment of labour, etc., were dealt with by the Local Land Committees. These bodies contained illiterate elements—the intellectuals as a rule were excluded—which had selfish motives and had no perception either of the extent or of the limits of their powers. The Central Representative Institutions and the Ministry of Agriculture, under Tchernov, issued appeals against arbitrariness and for the preservation of the land, pending the decision of the Constituent Assembly. At the same time they overtly encouraged " temporary possession of the land," as seizure of the land was then described, on the excuse that the Government were obliged to sell as much land as possible. The propaganda that was conducted on a large scale in the villages by irresponsible representatives of Socialist and Anarchist circles completed Tchernov's work.

The results of this policy were soon apparent. In one of his circulars to Provincial Commissars, the Minister of the Interior, Tzeretelli, admitted that complete anarchy reigned in the villages: " Land is being seized and sold, agricultural labourers are forced to stop working, and landowners are faced with demands which are economically impossible. Breeding stock is being destroyed and implements plundered. Model farms are being ruined. Forests are being cut down irrespective of ownership, timber and logs are being stolen, and their shipment prevented. No sowing is done on privately-owned farms, and harvests of grain and hay are not reaped." The Minister accused the Local Committees and the Peasant Congresses of organising arbitrary seizures of the land, and came to the conclusion that the existing conditions of agriculture and forestry " would inevitably bring about endless calamities for the Army and the country, and threatened the very existence of the State." If we recall the fires, the murders, the lynchings, the destruction of estates, which were often filled with treasures of great historical and artistic value, we shall have a true picture of the life of the villages in those days.

The question of the ownership of the land by the landlords was thus not merely a matter of selfish class interest, all the more as, not only the landlords but the wealthy peasants were subjected to violence by order of the Committees, and in spite of them. One village rose against another. It was not a question of the transfer of riches from one class or individual to another, but of the destruction of treasures, of agriculture, and of the economic stablity of the State. The instincts of proprietorship inherent in the peasantry irresistibly grew as these seizures and partitions took place. The mental attitude of the peasantry upset all the plans of the Revolutionary Democracy. By converting the peasants into a *Petite Bourgeoisie*, it threatened to postpone to an indefinite date the triumph of Socialism. The villagers were obsessed by the idea of land distribution and by their own interests, and were not in the least concerned with the War, with politics, or with social questions which did not directly affect them. The workers of the village were being killed and maimed at the front, and the village, therefore, considered the War as a burden. The authorities disallowed seizures of the land and imposed restrictions in the shape of monopolies and fixed prices for corn. The peasantry, therefore, bore a grudge against the Government. The towns ceased to supply manufactured goods and the villages were estranged from the towns and ceased to supply them with grain. This was the only real " conquest " made by the Revolution, and those who profited by it grew very anxious as to the attitude of future Governments towards the arbitrary solution of the land question. They therefore actively encouraged anarchy in the villages, condoned seizures and undermined the authority of the Provisional Government. By this means they hoped to bring the peasants over to their side as supporters, or, at least, as a neutral element, in the impending decisive struggle for power.

*   *   *   *   *

The abolition of the police by the order issued on April 17th was one of the acts of the Government which seriously complicated the normal course of life. In reality, this act only confirmed the conditions which had arisen almost everywhere in the first days of the Revolution, and were directly due to the wrath of the people against the Executive of the old régime, and especially of those who had been oppressed and persecuted by the police and had suddenly found themselves on the crest of the wave. It would be a hopeless task to defend the Russian police as an institution. It could only be considered good by comparing it with the militia and with the Extraordinary Bolshevik Commission. . .

In any case it would have been useless to resist the abolition of the police, because it was a psychological necessity. There can be no doubt that the attitude and actions of the old police were due less to their political opinions than to the instructions of their employers and to their own personal interests. No wonder, therefore, that the gendarmes and the policemen, insulted and persecuted, introduced a very bad element into the Army, into which they were subsequently forcibly drafted. The Revolutionary Democracy, in self defence, grossly exaggerated their counter-revolutionary activities in the Army; nevertheless, it is absolutely true that a great many ex-officers of the police and of the gendarmerie, partly, perhaps, from motives of self-defence, chose for themselves a most lucrative profession—that of the demagogue and the agitator. The fact is that the abolition of the police in the very midst of the turmoil—when crime was on the increase and the guarantees of public safety and of the safety of individual property were weakened—was a real calamity. The militia, indeed, far from being a substitute for the police, was a caricature of them. In Western countries the police is placed as a united force under the orders of a Department of the Central Government. The Provisional Government placed the militia under the orders of *Zemstvo* and Municipal Administrations. The Government Commissars were only entitled to make use of the militia for certain definite purposes. The cadres of the militia were filled by untrained men, devoid of technical experience, and, as often as not, criminals. By virtue of the new law, there were admitted to the militia persons under arrest or who had served a term of imprisonment for comparatively grave offences. The system of recruiting practised by some forcibly " democratised " *Zemstvo* and Municipal institutions tended quite as much as the new law towards the deterioration of the personnel of the militia.

The Chief of the Central Administration of the Militia himself admitted that escaped convicts were sometimes placed in command of the militia. The villages were sometimes without any militia at all, and they administered themselves as best they could.

In its proclamation of April 25th the Provisional Government gave an accurate description of the condition of the country in stating that " the growth of new social ties was slower than the process of disruption caused by the collapse of the old régime." In every feature of the life of the people this fact was clearly to be observed.

CHAPTER XIII.

THE ACTIVITIES OF THE PROVISIONAL GOVERNMENT: FOOD SUPPLIES, INDUSTRY, TRANSPORT AND FINANCE.

IN the early spring of 1917 the deficiency in supplies for the Army and for the towns was rapidly growing. In one of its appeals to the peasants the Soviet said: " The enemies of freedom, the supporters of the deposed Czar, are taking advantage of the shortage of food in the towns *for which they are themselves responsible* in order to undermine your freedom and ours. They say that the Revolution has left the country without bread. . . ." This simple explanation, adduced by the Revolutionary Democracy in every crisis, was, of course, one-sided. There was the inheritance of the old régime as well as the inevitable consequences of three years of war, during which imports of agricultural implements had come to a standstill, labourers were taken from the land, and, as a result, the area under crops was diminished. But these were not the only reasons for the food shortage in a fertile country—a shortage which in the autumn was considered by the Government as disastrous. The food policy of the Government and the fluctuation of prices, the depreciation of the currency and a rise in the price of commodities entirely out of proportion to the fixed prices for grain also largely contributed to this result. This rise in prices was due to general economic conditions, and especially to a very rapid rise in wages; to the agrarian policy of the Government, the inadequacy of the area under crops, to the turmoil in the villages, and to the breakdown of transport. Private trade was abolished and the entire matter of food supplies was handed over to Food Supply Committees— undoubtedly democratic in character, but, with the exception of the representatives of the Co-operatives, inexperienced and devoid of a creative spirit. There are many more reasons, great and small, which may be included in the formula: The Old Régime, the War and the Revolution.

On March 29th the Provisional Government introduced the grain monopoly. The entire surplus of grain, excluding normal

The Provisional Government

supplies, seed corn and fodder, reverted to the State. At the same time the Government once again raised the fixed price of grain, and promised to introduce fixed prices for all necessary commodities, such as iron, textiles, leather, kerosine oil, etc. This last measure, which was universally recognised as just, and to which the Minister of Supplies attributed a very great importance, proved impossible of application owing to the confused condition of the country. Russia was covered by a huge network of Food Supply Institutions, which cost 500,000,000 roubles a year, but could not cope with their work. The villages, on the other hand, had ceased to pay taxes and rents, were flooded with paper money, for which they could get no equivalent in manufactured goods, and were by no means anxious to supply grain. Propaganda and appeals were of no avail, and, as often as not, force had to be applied.

In its Proclamation of August 29th the Government admitted that the country was in a desperate position; the Government stores were emptying; towns, provinces, and armies at the Front were in dire need of bread, *although, in fact, there was sufficient bread in the country.* Some had not delivered last year's harvest; some were agitating and preventing others from doing their duty. In order to avert grave danger, the Government once more raised the fixed prices and threatened to apply stringent measures against the offenders, and to regulate prices and the distribution of articles required by the villages. But the vicious circle of conflicting political, social and class interests was narrowing, like to a tight noose, round the neck of the Government, paralysing its will-power and energy.

*   *   *

The condition of industry was no less acute, and it was steadily falling into ruin. Here, as in the matter of supplies, the calamity cannot be ascribed to one set of causes, as happened when the employers and the workmen levelled accusations against one another. The former were charged with taking excessive profits and having recourse to sabotage in order to upset the Revolution, while the latter were blamed for slackness and greed and for deriving selfish gains from the Revolution. The causes may be divided into three categories.

Owing to various political and economic reasons and to the fact that the old Government did not devote sufficient attention to the development of the natural resources of the country, our industries were not placed on a solid basis, and were to a great extent dependent upon foreign markets even for such material as might easily have been found in Russia. Thus in 1912 there was a serious shortage of pig-iron, and in 1913 of fuel. From 1908 to 1913 imports of metals from abroad rose from 29 to 34 per cent. Before the War we imported 48 per cent. of cotton. We needed 2,750,000 pouds* of wool from abroad out of a total of the 5,000,000 pouds produced.

The War unquestionably affected industry very deeply. Normal imports came to a standstill. The mines of Dombrovsk were lost. Owing to strategical requirements, transport was weakened, supplies of fuel and of raw materials diminished. Most of the factories had to work for the Army, and their personnel was curtailed by mobilisations. From an economic point of view, the militarisation of industry was a heavy burden for the population, because, according to the estimates made by one of the Ministers, the Army absorbed 40 to 50 per cent. of the total of goods produced by the country. Finally, the War widened the gulf between the employers and the workmen, as the former made immense profits, whereas the latter were impoverished, and their condition was further aggravated by the suspension of certain professional guarantees on account of the War by the fact that certain categories of workmen were drafted by conscription to definite industrial concerns, and by the general burden of inflated prices and inadequate food supplies.

Even in these abnormal circumstances Russian industries to some extent fulfilled the requirements of the moment, but the Revolution dealt them a death blow, which caused their gradual dislocation and ultimate collapse. On the one hand, the Provisional Government was legislating for the establishment of a strict Government control of the industries of the country and for regulating them by heavily taxing profits and excess war profits, as well as by Government distribution of fuel, raw materials and food. The latter measure caused the trading class to be practically eliminated and to be replaced by democratic organisations. Whether excess profits disappeared as a result of this policy, or were merely transferred to another class, it is not easy to decide. On the other hand, the Government were deeply concerned with the protection of labour, and were drafting and passing various laws concerning the freedom of unions, labour exchanges, conciliation boards, social insurance, etc. Unfortunately, the impatience and the desire for " law-making " which had seized the villages were also apparent in the factories. Heads of industrial concerns were dismissed wholesale, as well as the

---

* A " poud " is equal to 40 pounds.

administrative and technical staffs. These dismissals were accompanied by insults and sometimes by violence, out of revenge for past offences, real or imaginary. Some of the members of the staffs resigned of their own accord, because they were unable to endure the humiliating position into which they were forced by the workmen. Given our low level of technical and educational standards, such methods were fraught with grave danger. As in the Army, so in the factories, Committees replaced by elections the dismissed personnel with utterly untrained and ignorant men. Sometimes the workmen completely seized the industrial concerns. Ignorant and unprovided with capital, they led these concerns to ruin, and were themselves driven to unemployment and misery. Labour discipline in the factories completely vanished, and no means was left of exercising moral, material or judicial pressure or compulsion. The "consciousness" alone of the workers proved inadequate. The technical and administrative personnel which remained or was newly elected could no longer direct the industries and enjoyed no authority, as it was thoroughly terrorised by the workmen. Naturally, therefore, the working hours were still further curtailed, work became careless, and production fell to its lowest ebb. The metallurgical industries of Moscow fell 32 per cent. and the productivity of the Petrograd factories 20 to 40 per cent. as early as in the month of April. In June the production of coal and the general production of the Donetz basin fell 30 per cent. The production of oil in Baku and Grozni also suffered. The greatest injury, however, was inflicted upon the industries by the monstrous demands for higher wages, completely out of proportion to the cost of living and to the productivity of labour, as well as to the actual paying capacity of the industries. These demands greatly exceeded all excess profits. The following figures are quoted in a Report to the Provisional Government: In eighteen concerns in the Donetz Basin, with a total profit of 75,000,000 roubles per annum, the workmen demanded a wage increase of 240,000,000 roubles per annum; the total amount of increased wages in all the mining and metallurgical factories of the South was 800,000,000 roubles per annum. In the Urals the total Budget was 200,000,000, while the wages rose to 300,000,000. In the Putilov factory alone, in Petrograd, before the end of 1917, the increase in wages amounted to 90,000,000 roubles. The wages rose from 200 to 300 per cent. The increase in the wages of the textile workers of Moscow rose 500 per cent., as compared to 1914. The burden of these increases naturally fell on the Government, as most of the factories were working for the defence of the country. Owing to the condition of industry described above, and to the psychology of the workmen, industrial concerns collapsed, and the country experienced an acute shortage of necessary commodities, with a corresponding increase in prices. Hence the rise in the price of bread and the reluctance of the villages to supply the towns.

At the same time Bolshevism introduced a permanent ferment into the labouring masses. It flattered the lowest instincts, fanned hatred against the wealthy classes, encouraged excessive demands, and paralysed every endeavour of the Government and of the moderate Democratic organisations to arrest the disruption of industry: "All for the Proletariat and through the Proletariat." Bolshevism held up to the working class vivid and entrancing vistas of political domination and economic prosperity, through the destruction of the Capitalist régime and the transfer to the workmen of political power, of industries, of the means of production, and of the wealth of the country. And all this was to come at once, immediately, and not as a result of a lengthy, social, economic process and organised struggle. The imagination of the masses, unfettered by knowledge or by the authority of leading professional unions, which were morally undermined by the Bolsheviks, and were on the verge of collapse, was fired by visions of avenging the hardships and boredom of heavy toil in the past, and of enjoying amenities of a *Bourgeois* existence, which they despised and yet yearned for with equal ardour. It was "Now or Never: All or Nothing!" As life was destroying allusions, and the implacable law of economics was meting out the punishment of high prices, hunger and unemployment, Bolshevism was the more convincingly insisting upon the necessity of rebellion and explaining the causes of the calamity and the means of averting it. The causes were: the policy of the Provisional Government, which was trying to reintroduce enslavement by the Bourgeoisie, the sabotage of the employers, and the connivance of the Revolutionary Democracy, including the Mensheviks, which had sold itself to the Bourgeoisie. The means was the transfer of power to the Proletariat.

All these circumstances were gradually killing Russian Industry.

In spite of all these disturbances, the dislocation of industry was not immediately felt in the Army to an appreciable degree, because attention was concentrated upon the Army at the expense of the vital necessities of the country itself, and also because for several months there had been a lull at the Front. In June, 1917, therefore, we were provided adequately, if not amply, for an important offensive. Imports of war material through

The Provisional Government

Archangel, Murmansk, and partly through Vladivostok had increased, but had not been sufficiently developed by reason of the natural shortcomings of maritime routes, and of the low carrying capacity of the Siberian and of the Murmansk Railways. Only 16 per cent. of the actual needs of the Army were satisfied. The military administration, however, clearly saw that we were living on the old stores collected by the patriotic impulse and effort of the country in 1916. By August, 1917, the most important factories for the production of war materials had suffered a check. The production of guns and of shells had fallen 60 per cent., and of aircraft 80 per cent. The possibility of continuing the War under worse material conditions was, however, amply proved later by the Soviet Government, which had been using the supplies available in 1917 and the remnants of Russian Industrial production for the conduct of civil war for more than three years. This, of course, was only possible through such an unexampled curtailment of the consuming market that we are practically driven back to primitive conditions of life.

Transport was likewise in a state of dislocation. As early as May, 1917, at the Regular Congress of Railway Representatives at the Stavka, the opinion was expressed, and confirmed by many specialists, that, unless the general conditions of the country changed, our railways would come to a standstill within six months. Practice has disproved theory. For over three years, under the impossible conditions of Civil War and of the Bolshevik Régime, the railways have continued to work. It is true that they did not satisfy the needs of the population even in a small measure, but they served the strategical purposes. That this situation cannot last, and that the entire network of the Russian Railways is approaching its doom, is hardly open to doubt. In the history of the disintegration of the Russian Railway System the same conditions are traceable which I have mentioned in regard to the Army, the villages, and especially the industries: the inheritance of the unwise policy of the past in regard to railways, the excessive demands of the War, the wear and tear of rolling stock, and anarchy on the line, due to the behaviour of a licentious soldiery; the general economic condition of the country, the shortage of rails, of metal and of fuel; the " democratisation " of Railway Administration, in which the power was seized by various Committees; the disorganisation of the administrative and technical personnel, which was subjected to persecution; the low producing power of labour and the steady growth of the economic demands of the railway employees and workmen.

In other branches of the Administration the Government offered a certain resistance to the systematic seizure of power by private organisations, but in the Ministry of Railways that pernicious system was introduced by the Government itself, in the person of the Minister Nekrassov. He was the friend and the inspirer of Kerensky, alternately Minister of Railways and of Finance, Assistant and Vice-President of the Council of Ministers, Governor-General of Finland, Octobrist, Cadet (Constitutional Democrat), and Radical Democrat, holding the scales between the Government and the Soviet. Nekrassov was the darkest and the most fatal figure in the Governing Circles, and left the stamp of destruction upon everything he touched—the All-Russian Executive Committee of the Union of Railways, the autonomy of the Ukraine, or the Kornilov movement.

The Ministry had no economic or technical plan. As a matter of fact, no such plan could ever be carried out, because Nekrassov decided to introduce into the Railway Organisation, hitherto strongly disciplined, " the new principles of Democratic Organisation, instead of the old watchwords of compulsion and fear "(?). Soviets and Committees were implanted upon every branch of the Railway Administration. Enormous sums were spent upon this undertaking, and, by his famous circular of May 27th, the Minister assigned to these organisations a very wide scope of control and management, as well as of the " direction " which they were henceforward entitled to give to the responsible personnel in the Administration. Executive functions were subsequently promised to these organisations. . . . " Meanwhile the Ministry of Railways and its subordinate branches will work in strict accordance with the ideas and wishes of the United Railway Workers." Nekrassov thus handed over to a private organisation the most important interests of the State—the direction of the Railway policy, the control of the Defence, of industries, and of all other branches dependent upon the railway system. As one of our contemporary critics has said, this measure would have been entirely justified had the whole population of Russia consisted of railway employees. This reform, carried out by Nekrassov on a scale unprecedented in history, was something worse than a mere blunder. The general trend of Ministerial policy was well understood. In the beginning of August, at the Moscow Congress, which was turned into a weapon for the Socialist parties of the Left, one of the leaders declared that " the Railway Union must be fully autonomous and no authority except that of the workers

The Provisional Government

themselves should be entitled to interfere with it." In other words, a State within a State.

Disruption ensued. A new phase of the arbitrariness of ever-changing organisations was introduced into the strict and precise mechanism of the railway services in the centre as well as throughout the country. I understand the democratisation that opens to the popular masses wide access to science, technical knowledge, and art, but I do not understand the democratisation of these achievements of human intellect.

There followed anarchy and the collapse of Labour discipline. As early as in July the position of the railways was rendered hopeless through the action of the Government.

After holding the office of Minister of Railways for four months, Nekrassov went to the Ministry of Finance, of which he was utterly ignorant, and his successor, Yurenev, began to struggle against the usurpation of power by the railwaymen, as he considered " the interference of private persons and organisations with the executive functions of the Department as a crime against the State." The struggle was conducted by the customary methods of the Provisional Government, and what was lost could no longer be recovered. At the Moscow Congress the President of the Union of the Railwaymen, fully conscious of its power, said that the struggle against democratic organisations was a manifestation of counter-Revolution, that the Union would use every weapon in order to counteract these endeavours, and " would be strong enough to slay this counter-Revolutionary hydra." As is well known, the All-Russian Executive Committee of the Union of Railways subsequently became a political organisation pure and simple, and betrayed Kornilov to Kerensky and Kerensky to Lenin. With a zeal worthy of the secret police of the old régime, it hunted out Kornilov's followers, and finally met an inglorious end in the clutches of Bolshevik Centralisation.

* * * ⁕

We now come to another element in the life of the State—Finance. Every normal financial system is dependent upon a series of conditions: general political conditions, offering a guarantee of the external and internal stability of the State and of the country; strategical conditions, defining the measure of efficiency of the National Defence; economic conditions, such as the productivity of the country's industries and the relation of production to consumption; the conditions of labour, of transport, etc. The Government, the Front, the villages, the factories, and the transport offered no necessary guarantees, and the Ministry of Finance could but have recourse to palliatives in order to arrest the disruption of the entire system of the currency and the complete collapse of the Budget, pending the restoration of comparative order in the country. According to the accepted view, the main defects of our pre-War Budget were that it was based upon the revenue of the spirit monopoly (800,000,000 roubles), and that there was scarcely any direct taxation. Before the War the Budget of Russia was about $3\frac{1}{2}$ milliards of roubles; the National Debt was about $8\frac{1}{2}$ milliards, and we paid nearly 400,000,000 roubles interest per annum; half of that sum went abroad, and was partially covered by $1\frac{1}{2}$ milliards of our exports. The War and Prohibition completely upset our Budget. Government expenses during the War reached the following figures:

$\frac{1}{2}$ 1914	5 milliards of roubles.	
1915	12	,, ,,
1916	18	,,
Seven months, 1917	18	,, ,,

The enormous deficit was partially covered by loans and by paper currency. The expenses of the War were met, however, out of the so-called "War Fund." At the Stavka, in accordance with the dictates of practical wisdom, expenditure was under the full control of the Chief-of-Staff of the Supreme Commander-in-Chief, who determined the heads of expenditure in his Orders, schedules, and estimates.

The Revolution dealt the death-blow to our finance. As Shingarev, the Minister of Finance, said, the Revolution " induced everyone to claim more rights, and stifled any sense of duty. Everybody demanded higher wages, but no one dreamt of paying taxes, and the finances of the country were thus placed in a hopeless position." There was a real orgy; everyone was desperately trying to grab as much as possible from the Treasury under the guise of democratisation, taking advantage of the impotence of the Government and of powerlessness to resist. Even Nekrassov had the courage to declare at the Moscow Congress that " Never in history had any Czarist Government been as generous and prodigal as the Government of Revolutionary Russia," and that " the new Revolutionary régime is much more expensive that the old one." Suffice it to quote a few " astronomic " figures in order to gauge the insuperable obstacles in the way of a reasonable Budget. The decline of production and the excessive rise in wages resulted in the necessity of enormous expenditure for subsidies to expiring concerns and for over-payments for means of production. These over-payments in the Donetz Basin alone amounted to 1,200,000,000 roubles; the increase in the soldiers' pay, 500,000,000 roubles; railwaymen's pay, 350,000,000 roubles; Post Office employees, 60,000,000 roubles. After a month the latter demanded another 105,000,000 roubles, while the entire revenue of the Posts and Telegraphs was 60,000,000 roubles. The Soviet demanded 11 milliards (in other words, nearly the total of the Budget for 1915) for allowances to soldiers' wives, whereas only 2 milliards had been spent till 1917 under this head. The Food Supply Committees cost 500,000,000 roubles per annum, and the Land Committee 140,000,000 roubles, etc., etc. Meanwhile the revenue was falling steadily. Thus, for example, the Land Tax fell 32 per cent. in the first few months of the Revolution; the revenue from town property, 41 per cent.; the House Tax, 43 per cent., etc. At the same time, our internal troubles caused the depreciation of the rouble and a fall in the price of Russian securities abroad. The Provisional Government based its financial policy upon " reorganisation of the Financial System on democratic lines and the direct taxation of the propertied classes " (Death Duties, Excess Profits Taxes, Income Taxes, etc.). The Government, however, would not adopt the measure recommended by the Revolutionary Democracy—a compulsory loan or a high Capital Levy—a measure distinctly tainted with Bolshevism. All these just taxes, introduced or planned, did not suffice even partially to satisfy the growing needs of the State. In the month of August the Finance Ministry was compelled to increase indirect taxation on certain monopolies, such as tea, sugar, and matches. These measures were, of course, extremely burdensome, and therefore highly unpopular.

Expenditure was growing, revenue was not forthcoming. The Liberty Loan was not progressing favourably, and there could be no hope for foreign loans on account of the condition of the Russian Front. Internal loans and Treasury Bonds yielded $9\frac{1}{2}$ milliards in the first half of 1917. Ordinary revenue was expected to yield 5,800,000,000 roubles. There remained one weapon established by the historical tradition of every revolution —the Printing Press.

Paper currency reached colossal proportions:

$\frac{1}{2}$ 1914	1,425,000,000	roubles.
1915	2,612,000,000	,,
1916	3,488,000,000	,,
$\frac{1}{2}$ 1917 ...	3,990,000,000	,,

According to the estimates of July, 1917, the total of paper currency was 13,916,000,000 roubles (the gold reserve was 1,293,000,000 roubles), as against 2 milliards before the War. Four successive Finance Ministers were unable to drag the country out of the financial morass. This might possibly have been achieved by the awakening of the national spirit and an understanding of the interests of the State, or by the growth of a wise and strong power which could have dealt a final blow to the anti-State, selfish motives of the Bourgeois elements that based their well-being upon the War and upon the blood of the people, as well as of the Democracy, which, in the words of Shingarev, " so severely condemned through its representatives in the Duma the very same poison (paper currency) which it was now drinking greedily at the moment when that Democracy had become its own master."

CHAPTER XIV.

The Strategical Position of the Russian Front.

THE first and fundamental question with which I was confronted at the Stavka was *the objective of our Front.* The condition of the enemy did not appear to us as particularly brilliant. But I must confess that the truth as at present revealed exceeds all our surmises, especially according to the picture drawn by Hindenburg and Ludendorff of the condition of Germany and of her Allies in 1917. I will not dwell upon the respective numerical strength, armaments, and strategical positions on the Western Front. I will only recall that in the middle of June Hindenburg gave rather a gloomy description of the condition of the country in his telegram to the Emperor. He said: " We are very much perturbed by the depression of the spirits of the people. That spirit must be raised, *or we shall lose the War.* Our Allies also require support, lest they desert us. . . . Economic problems must be solved, which are of paramount importance to our future. The question arises—Is the Chancellor capable of solving them? A solution must be found *or else we perish.*"

The Germans were anticipating a big offensive of the British and the French on the Western Front, where they had concentrated their main attention and their main forces, leaving on the Eastern Front after the Russian Revolution only such numbers as were scarcely sufficient for defence. And yet the position on the Eastern Front continued to create a certain nervousness at the German G.H.Q. Will the Russian people remain steadfast, or will the Defeatist tendencies prevail? Hindenburg wrote: " As the condition of the Russian Army prevented us from finding a clear answer to that question, our position in regard to Russia remained insecure."

In spite of all its defects, the Russian Army in March, 1917, was a formidable force, with which the enemy had seriously to reckon. Owing to the mobilisation of industry, to the activities of the War-Industries Committees, and partly to the fact that the

War Ministry was showing increased energy, our armaments had reached a level hitherto unknown. Also, the Allies were supplying us with artillery and war materials through Murmansk and Archangel on a larger scale. In the spring we had the powerful Forty-Eighth Corps—a name under which heavy artillery of the highest calibre for special purposes, " Taon," was concealed. In the beginning of the year the engineering troops were reorganised and amplified. At the same time new infantry divisions were beginning to deploy. This measure, adopted by General Gourko during his temporary tenure of office as Chief-of-Staff of the Supreme C.-in-C., consisted in the reduction of regiments from four battalions to three, as well as the reduction of the number of guns to a division. A third division was thus created in every Army Corps, with artillery. There can be no doubt that, had this scheme been introduced in peace-time, the Army Corps would have been more pliable and considerably stronger. It was a risky thing to do in war-time. Before the spring operations the old divisions were disbanded, whereas the new ones were in a pitiable state in regard to armaments (machine-guns, etc.), as well as technical strength and equipment. Many of them had not been sufficiently blended together—a circumstance of particular importance in view of the Revolution. The position was so acute that in May the Stavka was compelled to sanction the disbanding of those of the Third Division which should prove feeble, and to distribute the men among units of the line. This idea, however, was hardly ever put into practice, as it encountered strong opposition on the part of units already disaffected by the Revolution. Another measure which weakened the ranks of the Army was the dismissal of the senior men in the ranks.

This decision, fraught with incalculable consequences, was taken on the eve of a general offensive. It was due to a statement made at a Council at the Stavka by the Minister of Agriculture (who was also in charge of supplies) that the condition of supplies was critical, and that he could not undertake the responsibility of feeding the Army unless about a million men were removed from the ration list. In the debate attention was drawn to the presence in the Army of an enormous number of non-combatants, quite out of proportion to the numbers of fighting men, and to the inclusion in the Army of a quantity of auxiliary bodies, which were hardly necessary, such as of Labour Organisations, Chinese, and other alien Labour Battalions, etc. Mention was also made of the necessity of having a younger Army. I very much feared this trend of mind, and gave orders to the Staff to draw up accurate lists of all the above-named Capitalists. While this work was still

The Strategical Position of the Russian Front

in preparation the War Minister issued, on April 5th, an Order of the Day giving leave, in the internal districts, to soldiers over forty to work in the fields till May 15th. Leave was afterwards extended till June 15th, but practically hardly anyone returned. On April 10th the Provisional Government discharged all men over forty-three. Under the pressure of the men it became unavoidable to spread the provisions of the first Order to the Army, which would not be reconciled to any privileges granted to the rear. The second Order gave rise to a very dangerous tendency, as it practically amounted to a *beginning of demobilisation*. The elemental desire of those who had been given leave to return to their homes could not be controlled by any regulations, and the masses of these men, who flooded the railway stations, caused a protracted disorganisation of the means of transport. Some regiments formed out of Reserve battalions lost most of their men. In the rear of the Army transport was likewise in a state of confusion. The men did not wait to be relieved, but left the lorries and the horses to their fate; supplies were plundered and the horses perished. The Army was weakened as a result of these circumstances, and the preparations for the defensive were delayed.

The Russian Army occupied an enormous Front, from the Baltic to the Black Sea and from the Black Sea to Hamadan. Sixty-eight infantry and nine cavalry corps occupied the line. Both the importance of and the conditions obtaining on these Fronts varied. Our Northern Front, including Finland, the Baltic and the line of the Western Dvina, was of great importance, as it covered the approaches to Petrograd. But the importance at that Front was limited to defensive purposes, and for that reason it was impossible to keep at that Front large forces or considerable numbers of guns. The conditions of that Theatre—the strong defensive line of the Dvina—a series of natural positions in the rear linked up with the main positions of the Western Russian Front, and the impossibility of any important operations in the direction of Petrograd without taking possession of the Sea, which was in our hands—all this would have justified us in considering that the Front was, to a certain extent, secure, had it not been for two circumstances, which caused the Stavka serious concern: The troops of the Northern Front, owing to the vicinity of Revolutionary Petrograd, were more demoralised than any other, and the Baltic Fleet and its bases—Helsingfors and Kronstadt, of which the latter served as the main base of Anarchism and Bolshevism—were either " autonomous " or in a state of semi-Anarchy. While preserving to a certain degree the

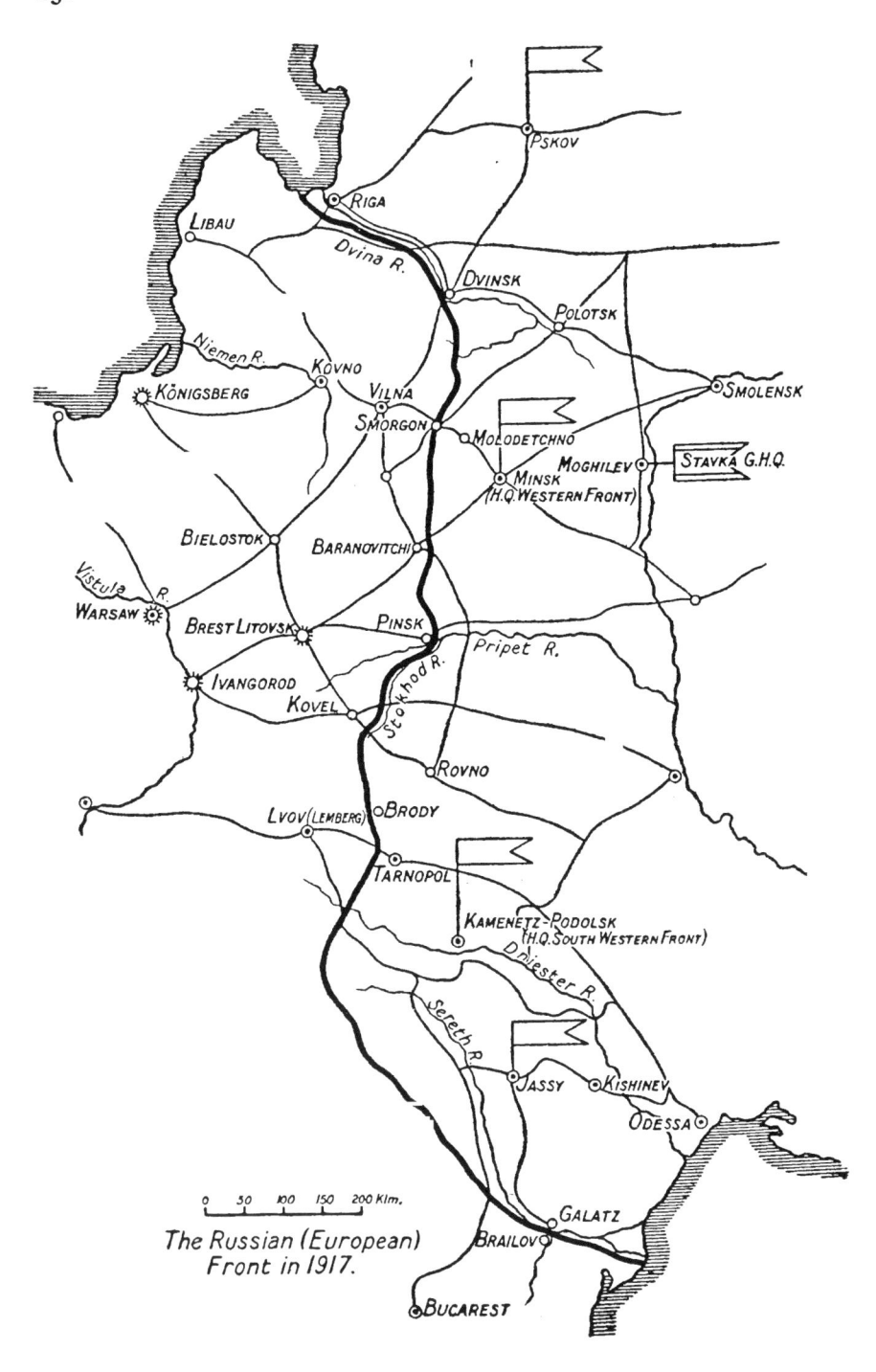

The Russian (European) Front in 1917.

The Strategical Position of the Russian Front

outward form of discipline, the Baltic Fleet was actally in a state of complete insubordination. The Admiral in command, Maximov, was entirely in the hands of the Central Committee of Sailors. Not a single order for Naval operations could be carried out without the sanction of that Committee, not to speak of Naval actions. Even the work of laying and repairing minefields—the

The Russian Caucasian Front in March 1917

main defence of the Baltic—met with opposition from Sailors' Organisations and the crews. Not only the general decline of discipline, but the well-planned work of the German General Staff were quite obvious, and apprehensions were entertained lest Naval secrets and codes be revealed to the enemy. At the same time, the troops of the Forty-Second Corps, quartered along the Finnish Coast and on the Monzund Islands, had been idle for a long time and their positions scattered. With the beginning of the Revolution they were, therefore, rapidly demoralised, and some of them were nothing but physically and morally degenerate crowds. To relieve or to move them was an impossibility. I recall that in May, 1917, I made several unavailing endeavours to send an Infantry Brigade to the Monzund Islands. Suffice it to say that the Army Corps Commander would not make up his mind to inspect his troops and get into touch with them—a circumstance which is typical of the troops as well as of the personality of their Commander. In a word, the position on the Northern Front in the spring of 1917 was the following: We received daily reports of the Channel between the Islands of the Gulf of Riga and the mainland being blocked with ice, and this ice appeared to be the chief real obstacle to an invasion of the German Fleet and Expeditionary Forces.

The Western Front extended from the Disna to the Pripet. On this long line two sectors—Minsk-Vilna and Minsk-Baranovitchi—were of the greatest importance to us, as they represented the two directions in which our troops, as well as the Germans, might undertake offensive operations, for which there had already been precedents. The other sections of the Front, and especially the Southern—the Pollessie, with its forests and marshes—owing to the conditions of the country and of the railways, were passive. Along the River Pripet, its tributaries and canals, a kind of half-peaceful intercourse with the Germans had long since been established, as well as a secret exchange of goods, which was of some advantage to the " Comrades." For example, we received reports that Russian soldiers from the Line, with bags, appeared daily in the market of Pinsk, and that their advent was for many reasons encouraged by the German authorities. There was another vulnerable point—the bridge-head on the Stokhod by the station, Chrevishe-Golenin, occupied by one of the Army Corps of General Lesh. On March 21st, after strong artillery preparation and a gas attack, the Germans fell upon our Corps and smashed it to pieces. Our troops had heavy casualties, and the remnants of the Corps retreated behind the Stokhod. The Stavka did not get an accurate list of the casualties, because it was impossible to ascertain the numbers of killed or wounded under the head of " Missing." The German Official Communiqué gave a list of prisoners—150 officers and about 10,000 men. Owing to the conditions in that theatre of war, this tactical success was of no strategical importance, and could lead to no dangerous developments. Nevertheless, we could not but wonder at the frankness of the cautious

Norddeutsche Allgemeine Zeitung, the official organ of the German Chancellor, which wrote: " The Communiqué of the Stavka of the Russian Supreme Command of March 29th is mistaken in interpreting the operations undertaken by the German troops, and dictated by a tactical necessity which had arisen only within the limits of a given sector, was an operation of general importance." The paper knew the facts of which we were not certain and which have now been explained by Ludendorff. From the beginning of the Russian Revolution, Germany had a new aim: *Unable to conduct operations on both the main Fronts*, she had decided *attentively to follow and to encourage the process of demoralisation in Russia, striking at her not by arms, but by developing propaganda.* The battle of the Stokhod was fought on the personal initiative of General Linsingen, and the German Government was frightened because it considered that " at a moment when fraternisation was proceeding at full speed " German attacks might revive the dying flames of patriotism in Russia and postpone her collapse. The Chancellor asked the German G.H.Q. to make as little as possible of that success, and the G.H.Q. cancelled all further offensives " in order not to dash the hopes for peace which were about to be realised."

Our reverse on the Stokhod produced a strong impression in the country. It was the first fighting experience of the " Freest Revolutionary Army in the world. . . ." The Stavka merely gave the facts in a spirit of impartiality. In the circles of the Revolutionary Democracy the reverse was explained partly by the treachery of the Commanding Officers and partly by a conspiracy to emphasise by this example the impracticability of the new Army Regulations and the danger of the collapse of discipline, partly by the incompetence of the military authorities. The Moscow Soviet wrote to the Stavka accusing one of the assistants of the War Minister who had commanded a division on that Front of being a traitor. Others attributed our defeat solely to the demoralisation of the troops. In reality, the reasons for the defeat were twofold: The *tactical* reason—the doubtful practicability of occupying a narrow bridge-head when the river was swollen, the insecurity of the rear and perhaps inadequate use of the troops and of technical means; and the *psychological* reason, the collapse of the *moral* and of the discipline of the troops. The last circumstance, apparent in the enormous number of prisoners, gave both the Russian Stavka and Hindenburg's headquarters much food for thought.

The South-Western Front, from the Pripet to Moldavia, was the most important, and attracted the greatest attention. From that Front, operating lines of the highest importance led to the

North-West, into the depths of Galicia and Poland, to Cracow, Warsaw and Brest-Litovsk. The advance along these lines was covered from the South by the Carpathians, separated the Southern Austrian group of armies from the Northern German, and threatened the rear and the communications of the latter. These operating lines, upon which no serious obstacles were encountered, led us to the Front of the Austrian troops, whose fighting capacity was lower than the Germans. The rear of our South-Western Front was comparatively well-organised and prosperous. The psychology of the troops, of the Command, and of the Staffs always differed considerably from the psychology of other Fronts. In the glorious, but joyless, campaign only the armies of the South-Western Front had won splendid victories, had taken hundreds of thousands of prisoners, had made victorious progress hundreds of miles deep into the enemy territory, and had descended into Hungary from the Carpathians. These troops had formerly always believed in success. Brussilov, Kornilov, Kaledin had made their reputations on that Front. Owing to all these circumstances the South-Western Front was regarded as the natural base and the centre of the impending operations. Consequently, troops, technical means, the greater part of the heavy artillery (" Taon ") and munitions were concentrated at that Front. The region between the Upper Seret and the Carpathians was, therefore, being prepared for the offensive, *Places d'armes* erected, roads made. Further south there was the Roumanian Front, stretching to the Black Sea. After the unsuccessful campaign of 1916 our troops occupied the line of the Danube, the Seret and the Carpathians, and it was sufficiently fortified. Part of General Averesco's Roumanian troops occupied the Front between our Fourth and Ninth Armies, and part were being organised under the direction of the French General, Berthelot, assisted by Russian Gunner Instructors. The reorganisation and formation proceeded favourably, the more so as the Roumanian soldier is excellent war material. I became acquainted with the Roumanian Army in November, 1916, when I was sent with the Eighth Army Corps to Busco, into the thick of the retreating Roumanian Armies. Curiously enough, I was ordered to advance in the direction of Bucarest until I came into contact with the enemy, and to cover that direction with the assistance of the retreating Roumanian troops. For several months I fought by Buseo, Rymnik and Fokshany, having two Roumanian Corps at times under my command and Avaresco's Army on my flank. I thus gained a thorough knowledge of the Roumanian troops. In the beginning of the campaign the Roumanian Army showed complete

The Strategical Position of the Russian Front

disregard of the experience of the World War. In matters of equipment and ammunition their levity was almost criminal. There were several capable Generals, the officers were effeminate and inefficient, and the men were splendid. The artillery was adequate, but the infantry was untrained. These are the main characteristics of the Roumanian Army, which soon afterwards acquired better organisation and improved in training and equipment. The relations between the actual Russian Commander-in-Chief, who was designated as the Assistant C.-in-C., and the King of Roumania, who was nominally in Chief Command, were fairly cordial. Although the Russian troops began to commit excesses, which had a bad effect upon the attitude of the Roumanians, the condition of the Front did not, however, cause serious apprehension. Owing to the general conditions at the Theatre of War, only an advance in great strength in the direction of Bucarest and an invasion of Transylvania could have had a political and strategical effect. But new forces could not be moved to Roumania, and the condition of the Roumanian Railways excluded all hope of the possibility of transport and supplies on a large scale. The theatre, therefore, was of secondary importance, and the troops of the Roumanian Front were preparing for a local operation, with a view to attracting the Austro-German forces.

The Caucasian Front was in an exceptional position. It was far distant. For many years the Caucasian Administration and Command had enjoyed a certain degree of autonomy. From August, 1916, the Army was commanded by the Grand-Duke Nicholas, a man of commanding personality, who took advantage of his position whenever there was a difference of opinion between himself and the Stavka. Finally, the natural conditions of the theatre of war and the peculiarities of the enemy rendered that Front entirely different from the European. All this led to a kind of remoteness and aloofness of the Caucasian Army and too abnormal relations with the Stavka. General Alexeiev repeatedly stated that, in spite of all his efforts, he was unable clearly to discern the situation in the Caucasus. The Caucasus lived independently, and told the Government only as much as it considered necessary; and the reports were coloured in accordance with local interests.

In the spring of 1917 the Caucasian Army was in a difficult position, not by reason of the strategical or fighting advantages of the enemy—the Turkish Army was by no means a serious menace—but of internal disorganisation. The countryside was roadless and bare. There were no supplies or forage, and the difficulties of transport made the life of the troops very arduous. The Army Corps on the Right Flank was comparatively well supplied, owing to facilities for transport across the Black Sea, but the other Army Corps, and especially those of the Left Flank, fared very badly. Owing to geographical conditions, light transport required an enormous number of horses, while there was no fodder on the spot. Railways of all kinds were being built very slowly, partly owing to a lack of railway material and partly because that material had been wasted by the Caucasian Front upon the Trapezund Railway, which was of secondary importance, owing to the parallel Maritime transport. In the beginning of May General Yudenitch reported that, owing to disease and loss of horses, transport was completely disorganised, batteries in position had no horses, half of the transport was non-existent, and 75,000 horses were needed. Tracks, rolling stock and forage were urgently required. In the first half of April 30,000 men (22 per cent.) of the Infantry of the Line had died of typhus and scurvy. Yudenitch therefore foreshadowed the necessity of a compulsory retreat to points of supply, the centre towards Erzerum and the Right Flank to the frontier. The solution suggested by General Yudenitch could not be accepted, both for moral reasons and because our retreat would have freed Turkish troops for action on other Asiatic Fronts. This circumstance particularly worried the British Military Representative at the Stavka, who repeatedly conveyed to us the desire of the British G.H.Q. that the Left Flank of our troops should advance in the valley of the River Diala for a combined operation with General Maude's Mesopotamian contingent against Halil Pasha's Army. This advance was necessary to the British rather for political considerations than for strategical requirements. The actual condition of our Left Flank Army Corps was, moreover, truly desperate, and in May tropical heat set in in the valley of the Diala. As a result the Caucasian Front was unable to advance, and was ordered actively to defend its position. The advance of the Army Corps of the Left Flank, in contact with the British, was made conditional upon the latter supplying the troops. As a matter of fact, in the middle of April, a partial retreat took place in the direction of Ognot and Mush; at the end of April the Left Flank began its fruitless advance in the valley of the Diala, and subsequently a condition arose on the Caucasian Front which was something between War and Peace.

In conclusion, mention must be made of another portion of the Armed Forces of Russia in that theatre—the Black Sea Fleet. In May and in the beginning of June serious disturbances had

The Strategical Position of the Russian Front 137

already occurred, which led to the resignation of Admiral Koltchak. The Fleet, however, was still considered strong enough to carry out its task—to hold the Black Sea and also to blockade the Turkish and Bulgarian coasts and guard the maritime routes to the Caucasian and Roumanian Fronts.

I have given a short summary of the conditions of the Russian Front without indulging in a detailed examination of strategical possibilities. Whatever our strategy during that period may have been, it was upset by the masses of the soldiery, for from Petrograd to the Danube and the Diala demoralisation was spreading and growing. In the beginning of the Revolution it was impossible to gauge the extent of its effects upon various fronts and upon future operations. But many were those whose minds were poisoned by a suspicion as to the futility of all our plans, calculations and efforts.

CHAPTER XV

THE QUESTION OF THE ADVANCE OF THE RUSSIAN ARMY.

WE were thus confronted with a crucial question: SHOULD THE RUSSIAN ARMY ADVANCE?

On March 27th the Provisional Government issued a proclamation " To the Citizens " on the subject of war aims. The Stavka could not detect any definite instructions for governing the Russian Army in the midst of a series of phrases in which the true meaning of the appeal was obscured in deference to the Revolutionary Democracy. " The Defence at all costs of our national patrimony and the liberation of the country from the enemy who has invaded it is the first and vital aim of our soldiers, who are defending the freedom of the people. .
Free Russia does not aim at domination over other peoples, at depriving them of *their* national patrimony, or at the forcible seizure of foreign territories. She aims at a lasting peace, on the basis of the self-determination of peoples. The Russian people do not wish to increase their external power at the expense of other peoples . . but will not allow their Mother Country to come out of the great struggle downtrodden and weakened. These principles will constitute the basis of the Foreign Policy of the Provisional Government . . . *while all the obligations to our Allies will be respected."*

In the Note of April 18th, addressed to the Allied Powers by the Foreign Minister, Miliukov, we find yet another definition: " The universal desire of the people to carry the World War to a victorious conclusion . . . has grown owing to the consciousness of the common responsibility of everyone. This desire has become more active, because it is concentrated on the aim which is immediate and clear to everyone—*that of repelling the enemy who has invaded the territory of our Mother Country."* These, of course, were mere phrases, which described the War aims in cautious, timorous and nebulous words, allowing of any interpretation, and deprived, moreover, any foundation in fact.

The Question of the Advance of the Russian Army

The will for victory in the people and in the Army had not only not grown, but was steadily decreasing, as a result of weariness and waning patriotism, as well as of the intense work of the abnormal coalition between the representatives of the extreme elements of the Russian Revolutionary Democracy and the German General Staff. That coalition was formed by ties which were unseen and yet quite perceptible. I will deal with that question later, and will only say here that the destructive work, in accordance with the Zimmerwald programme, for ending the War began long before the Revolution and was conducted from within as well as from without. The Provisional Government was trying to pacify the militant element of the Revolutionary Democracy by expounding meaningless and obscure formulas with regard to the War aims, but it did not interfere with the Stavka in regard to the choice of strategical means. We were, therefore, to decide the question of the advance independently from the prevailing currents of political opinion. The only clear and definite object upon which the Commanding Staffs could not fail to agree was to defeat the enemy in close union with the Allies. Otherwise our country was doomed to destruction.

Such a decision implied an advance on a large scale because victory was impossible without it, and a devastating war might otherwise become protracted. The responsible organs of the Democracy, the majority of whom had Defeatist tendencies, tried correspondingly to influence the masses. Even the moderate Socialist circles were not altogether free from these tendencies. The masses of the soldiery utterly failed to understand the ideas behind of the Zimmerwald programme; but the programme itself offered a certain justification for the elementary feelings of self-preservation. In other words, it was a question with them of saving their skin. The idea of an advance could not, therefore, be particularly popular with the Army, as demoralisation was growing. There was no certainty not only that the advance would be successful, but even that the troops would obey the order to go forward. The colossal Russian Front was still steady
by the force of inertia. The enemy feared it, as, like ourselves, he was unable to gauge its potential strength. What if the advance were to disclose our impotence?

Such were the motives adduced against an advance. But there were too many weighty reasons in favour of it, and these reasons were imperative. The Central Powers had exhausted their strength, moral and material, and their man power. If our advance in the autumn of 1916, which had no decisive strategical results, had placed the enemy forces in a critical position, what might not happen now, when we had become stronger and, technically better equipped, when we had the advantage in numbers, and the Allies were planning a decisive blow in the spring of 1917? The Germans were awaiting the blow with feverish anxiety, and in order to avert it they had retreated thirty miles on a front of 100 miles between Arras and Soissons to the so-called Hindenburg line, after causing incredibly ruthless and inexcusable devastation to the relinquished territory. This retreat was significant, as it was an indication of the enemy's weakness, and gave rise to great hopes. *We had to advance.* Our intelligence service was completely destroyed by the suspicions of the Revolutionary Democracy, which had foolishly believed that this service was identical with the old secret police organisation, and had therefore abolished it. Many of the delegates of the Soviet were in touch with the German agents. The fronts were in close contact, and espionage was rendered very easy. In these circumstances our decision not to advance would have been undoubtedly communicated to the enemy, who would have immediately commenced the transference of his troops to the Western Front. This would have been tantamount to treason to our Allies, and would have inevitably led to a separate peace—with all its consequences—if not officially, at least practically. The attitude of the revolutionary elements in Petrograd in this matter was, however, so unstable that the Stavka had at first suspected—without any real foundation—the Provisional Government itself.

This caused the following incident: At the end of April, in the temporary absence of the Supreme C.-in-C., the Chief of the Diplomatic Chancery reported to me that the Allied Military Attaches were greatly perturbed because a telegram had just been received from the Italian Ambassador at Petrograd, in which he categorically stated that the Provisional Government had decided to conclude a separate peace with the Central Powers. When the receipt of a telegram had been ascertained, I sent a telegram to the War Minister, because I was then unaware of the fact that the Italian Embassy, owing to the impulsiveness of its personnel, had more than once been the channel through which false rumours had been spread. My telegram was most emphatic, and ended thus: " Posterity will stigmatise with deep contempt the weak-kneed, impotent, irresolute generation which was good enough to destroy the rotten régime, but not good enough to preserve the honour, the dignity, and the very existence of Russia." The misunderstanding was painful indeed; the news was false, the Government was not thinking of a separate peace. Later, at the

The Question of the Advance of the Russian Army

fateful sitting of the Conference at the Stavka of Commanders-in-Chief and members of the Government, on July 16th, I had an opportunity of expressing my views once more. I said: "
There is another way—the way of treason. It would give a respite to our distressed country. . . . But the curse of treachery will not give us happiness. At the end of that way there is slavery—political, economical, and moral."

I am aware that in certain Russian circles such a straightforward profession of moral principles in politics was afterwards condemned. It was stated that such idealism is misplaced and pernicious, that the interests of Russia must be considered above all " conventional political morality." . . . A people, however, lives not for years, but for centuries, and I am certain that, had we then altered the course of our external policy, the sufferings of the Russian people would not have been materially affected, and the gruesome, blood-stained game with marked cards would have continued . . . at the expense of the people. The psychology of the Russian military leaders did not allow of such a change, of such a compromise with conscience. Alexeiev and Kornilov, abandoned by all and unsupported, continued for a long time to follow that path, trusting and relying upon the common-sense, if not the noble spirit, of the Allies and preferring to be betrayed rather than betray.

Was that playing the part of a Don Quixote? It may be so. But the other policy would have had to be conducted by other hands less clean. As regards myself, three years later, having lost all my illusions and borne the heavy blows of fortune, having knocked against the solid wall of the overt and blind egoism of fhe " friendly " powers, and being therefore free from all obligations towards the Allies, almost on the eve of the final betrayal by these powers of the real Russia, I remained the convinced advocate of *honest policy*. Now the tables are turned. At the end of April, 1920, I had to try and convince British Members of Parliament that a healthy national policy cannot be free from all moral principles, and that an obvious crime was being committed because no other name could be given to the abandonment of the armed forces of the Crimea to the discontinuance of the struggle against Bolshevism, its introduction into the family of civilised nations, and to its indirect recognition; that this would prolong for a short while the days of Bolshevism in Russia, but would open wide the gates of Europe to Bolshevism. I am firmly convinced that the Nemesis of history will not forgive THEM, as it would not have then forgiven us. The beginning of 1917 was a moment of acute peril for the Central Powers and a decisive moment for the

Entente. The question of the Russian advance greatly perturbed the Allied High Command. General Barter, the Representative of Great Britain, and General Janin, the French Representative at Russian Headquarters, often visited the Supreme C.-in-C. and myself, and made inquiries on the subject. But the statements of the German Press, with reference to pressure from the Allies and to ultimatums to the Stavka, are incorrect. These would have simply been useless, because Janin and Barter understood the situation, and knew that it was the condition of the Army that hindered the beginning of the advance. They tried to hurry and to increase technical assistance, while their more impulsive compatriots—Thomas, Henderson, and Vandervelde—were making hopeless endeavours to fan the flame of patriotism by their impassioned appeals to the Representatives of the Russian Revolutionary Democracy and to the troops.

The Stavka also took into consideration the strong probability that the Russian Army would have rapidly and finally collapsed had it been left in a passive condition and deprived of all impulses for active hostilities, whereas a successful advance might lift and heal the *moral,* if not through sheer patriotism, at least through the intoxication of a great victory. Such feelings might have counteracted all international formulas sown by the enemy on the fertile soil of the Defeatist tendencies of the Socialistic Party. Victory would have given external peace, and some chance of peace within. Defeat opened before the country an abyss. The risk was inevitable, and was justified by the aim of saving Russia. The Supreme Commander-in-Chief, the Quartermaster-General, and myself fully agreed as to the necessity of an advance. And this view was shared in principle by the Senior Commanding Officers. Different views were held on various Fronts as to the degree of fighting capacity of the troops and as to their preparedness. I am thoroughly convinced that the decision itself independently of its execution rendered the Allies a great service, because the forces, the means, and the attention of the enemy were kept on the Russian Front, which, although it had lost its former formidable power, still remained a potential danger to the enemy. The same question, curiously enough, was confronting Hindenburg's Headquarters. Ludendorff writes: " The general position in April and in May precluded the possibility of important operations on the Eastern Front." Later, however, " . . . there were great discussions on the subject at G.H.Q. Would not a rapid advance on the Eastern Front with the available troops, reinforced by a few divisions from the West, offer a better chance than mere waiting? It was a most propitious moment, as some

The Question of the Advance of the Russian Army

people said, for smashing the Russian Army, when its fighting capacity had deteriorated. . . . I disagreed, in spite of the fact that our position in the West had improved. I would not do anything that might destroy the real chances of peace." Ludendorff means, of course, separate peace. What such a peace was to be we learnt later, at Brest-Litovsk.

The Armies were given directions for a new offensive. The general idea was to break through the enemy positions on sectors specially prepared on all European fronts, to advance on a broad front in great strength on the South-Western Front, in the direction from Kamemetz-Podolsk to Lvov, and further to the line of the Vistula, while the striking force of our Western Front was to advance from Molodetchno to Vilna and the Niemen, throwing back northwards the German Armies of General Eichorn. The Northern and the Roumanian Fronts were to co-operate by dealing local blows and attracting the forces of the enemy. The time for the advance was not definitely fixed, and a broad margin was allowed. But the days went by, and the troops, who had hitherto obeyed orders and carried out the most difficult tasks without a murmur, the same troops that had hitherto withstood the onset of the Austro-German Armies with naked breasts, without cartridges or shells, now stood with their will-power paralysed and their reason obscured. The offensive was still further delayed.

Meanwhile the Allies, who had been preparing a big operation for the spring, as they had counted upon strong reinforcements being brought up by the enemy in the event of the complete collapse of the Russian Front, began the great battle in France, as had been planned, at the end of March, and *without awaiting the final decision on our advance*. The Allied Headquarters, however, did not consider simultaneous action as a necessary condition of the contemplated operations, even before disaffection had begun in the Russian Army. Owing to the natural conditions of our Front we were not expected to begin the advance before the month of May. Meanwhile, according to the general plan of campaign for 1917, which had been drawn up in November, 1916, at the Conference at Chantilly, General Joffre intended to begin the advance of the Anglo-French Army at the end of January and the beginning of February. General Nivelle, who superseded him, altered the date to the end of March after the Conference at Calais of February 14th, 1917. The absence of co-ordination between the Western and Eastern European Fronts was bearing bitter fruit. It is difficult to tell whether the Allies would have deferred their spring offensive for two months, and whether the advances of a combined operation with the Russian

Front would have been a compensation for the delay, which gave Germany the opportunity of reinforcing and reorganising her armies. One thing is certain—that that lack of co-ordination gave the Germans a great respite. Ludendorff wrote: " I detest useless discussions, but I cannot fail to think of what would have happened had Russia advanced in April and May and had won a few minor victories. We would have been faced, as in the autumn of 1916, with a fierce struggle. Our munitions would have reached a very low ebb. After careful consideration, I fail to see how our High Command could have remained the master of the situation had the Russians obtained in April and May even the same scant successes which crowned their efforts in June. In April and May of 1917, in spite of our victory (?) on the Aisne and in Champagne, it was only the Russian Revolution that saved us."

* * * * *

Apart from the general advance on the Austro-German Front, another question of considerable interest arose in April—that of an *independent operation for the conquest of Constantinople.* Inspired by young and spirited naval officers, the Foreign Minister, Miliukov, repeatedly negotiated with Alexeiev, and tried to persuade him to undertake that operation, which he considered likely to be successful, and which would, in his opinion, confront the Revolutionary Democracy, which was protesting against annexations, with an accomplished fact. The Stavka disapproved of this undertaking, as the condition of our troops would not permit of it. The landing of an Expeditionary Force—in itself a very delicate task—demanded stringent discipline, preparation, and perfect order. What is more, the Expeditionary Force, which would lose touch with the main Army, should be imbued with a very strong sense of duty. To have the sea in the rear is a circumstance which depresses even troops with a very strong *moral.* These elements had already ceased to exist in the Russian Army. The Minister's requests were becoming, however, so urgent that General Alexeiev deemed it necessary to give him an object-lesson, and a small Expedition was planned to the Turkish coast of Asia Minor. As far as I can remember, Zunguldak was the objective. This insignificant operation required a detachment consisting of one Infantry Regiment, one Armoured Car Division, and a small Cavalry contingent, and was to have been carried out by the troops of the Roumanian Front. After a while the Headquarters of that Front had shamefacedly to report that the detachment could not be formed because the troops declined to join the Expeditionary Force. This episode was due to a foolish interpretation

Foreign military representatives at the Stavka. Standing on the pathway, from left to right: Lieut.-Col Marsengo (Italy); 2. General   anin (France ; 3. General Alexeiev   4. General Barter Great Britain) ; 5. General Rome Longhena (Italy

The Question of the Advance of the Russian Army

of the idea of peace without annexations, which distorted the very principles of strategy and was also, perhaps, due to the same instinct of self-preservation. It was another ill omen for the impending general advance. That advance was still being prepared, painfully and desperately.

The rusty, notched Russian sword was still brandished. The question was, when would it stop and upon whose head would it fall?

CHAPTER XVI.

MILITARY REFORMS—THE GENERALS—THE DISMISSAL FROM THE HIGH COMMAND.

PREPARATIONS for the advance continued alongside of the so-called " Democratisation." These phenomena must be here recorded, as they had a decisive effect upon the issue of the summer offensive and upon the final destinies of the Army. Military reforms began by the dismissal of vast numbers of Commanding Generals. In military circles this was described, in tragic jest, as " The slaughter of the innocents." It opened with the conversation between the War Minister, Gutchkov, and the General on duty at the Stavka, Komzerovski. At the Minister's request the General drew up a list of the Senior Commanding Officers, with short notes (records of service). This list, afterwards completed by various people who enjoyed Gutchkov's confidence, served as a basis for the " slaughter." In the course of a few weeks 150 Senior Officers, including seventy Commanders of Infantry and Cavalry Divisions, were placed on the Retired List. In his speech to the Delegates of the Front on April 29th, 1917, Gutchkov gave the following reasons for this measure: " It has been our first task, after the beginning of the Revolution, to make room for talent. Among our Commanding Officers there were many honest men; but some of them were unable to grasp the new principles of intercourse, and in a short time more changes have been made in our commanding personnel than have ever been made before in any army. . . . I realised that there could be no mercy in this case, and I was merciless to those whom I considered incapable. Of course, I may have been wrong. There may have been dozens of mistakes, but I consulted knowledgeable people and took decisions only when I felt that they were in keeping with the general opinion. At any rate, we have promoted all those who have proved their capacity among the Commanding Officers. I disregarded hierarchical considerations. There are men who commanded regiments in the beginning of the War and are now commanding armies.

We have thus attained not only an improvement, but something different and equally important. By proclaiming the watchword 'Room for talent' we have instilled joy into the hearts, and have induced the officers to work with impetus and inspiration."

What did the Army gain by such drastic changes? Did the *cadres* of the Commanding Officers really improve? In my opinion that object was not attained. New men appeared on the scene, owing to the newly-introduced right of selecting assistants, not without the interference of our old friends—family ties, friendship and wire-pulling. Could the Revolution give new birth to men or make them perfect? Was a mechanical change of personnel capable of killing a system which for many years had weakened the impulse for work and for self-improvement? It may be that some talented individuals did come to the fore, but there were also dozens, nay, hundreds, of men whose promotion was due to accident and not to knowledge or energy. This accidental character of appointments was further intensified when later Kerensky abolished for the duration of the War all the existing qualifications, as well as the correlation of rank and office. The qualification of knowledge and experience was also thereby set aside. I have before me a list of the Senior Commanding Officers of the Russian Army in the middle of May, 1917, when Gutchkov's "slaughter" had been accomplished. The list includes the Supreme Commander-in-Chief, the Commanders-in-Chief of Fronts, Armies and Fleets, and their Chiefs of Staff—altogether forty-five men:

OPPORTUNISTS.

The Commanding Personnel.	Approving of Democratisation.	Non-Resisters to Democratisation.	Opponents of Democratisation.	Total.
The Supreme C.-in-C. Army Commanders Fleet Commanders Chiefs of Staff	9 6	5 6	7 7	
	15	11	14	40

I have excluded five names, as I have no data about them.

These men were the brain, the soul and the will-power of the Army. It is difficult to estimate their military capacity according to their last tenures of office, because strategy and military science in 1917 had almost entirely ceased to be applied and became slavishly subservient to the soldiery, but I know the activities of these men in regard to the struggle against democratisation—*i.e.*, the disruption of the Army, and the above table indicates the three groups into which they were divided. Subsequently, after 1918, some of these men took part in the struggle or kept aloof from it.

OPPORTUNISTS.

The Commanding Personnel.	Approving of Democratisation.	Non-Resisters to Democratisation.	Opponents of Democratisation.	Total.
In Anti-Bolshevik Organisations	2		10	19
With the Bolsheviks	6			7
Retired from the struggle	-		3	14

Such are the results of the changes in the High Command, where men were in the public eye and where their activities attracted the critical attention not only of the Government, but of military and social circles. I think that in the lower grades things were no better. The question of the justice of this measure may be open to discussion, but, personally, I have no doubt whatsoever about its extreme impracticability. The dismissal *en masse* of Army Chiefs definitely undermined the faith in the Commanding Staffs, and afforded an excuse for the abitrariness and violence of the Committees and of the men towards individual representatives of the Commanding Staff. Constant changes and transfers removed most officers from their units, where they may have enjoyed respect and authority acquired by military prowess. These men were thrown into new circles strange to them, and time was needed, as well as difficult work, in the new and fundamentally changed atmosphere in order to regain that respect and authority. The formation of Third Infantry Divisions was still proceeding, and was also occasioning constant changes in the Commanding Personnel. That chaos was bound to ensue as a result of all these circumstances is fairly obvious. So delicate a machine as the Army was in the days of War and Revolution

Military Reforms

could only be kept going by the force of inertia, and could not withstand new commotions. Pernicious elements, of course, should have been removed and the system of appointments altered, and the path opened for those who were worthy; beyond that the matter ought to have been allowed to follow its natural course without laying too much stress upon it and without devising a new system. Apart from the Commanding Officers who were thus removed, several Generals resigned of their own accord—such as Letchitzki and Mistchenko—who could not be reconciled to the new régime, and many Commanders who were evicted in a Revolutionary fashion by the direct or indirect pressure of the Committee or of the soldiery. Admiral Koltchak was one of them. Further changes were made, prompted by varying and sometimes self-contradictory views upon the Army Administration. These changes were, therefore, very fitful, and prevented a definite type of Commanding Officer from being introduced.

Alexeiev dismissed the Commander-in-Chief, Ruzsky, and the Army Commander, Radko-Dmitriev, for their weakness and opportunism. He visited the Northern Front, and, having gained an unfavourable impression of the activities of these Generals, he discreetly raised the question of their being " overworked." That is the interpretation given by the Army and Society to these dismissals.

Brussilov dismissed Yudenitch for the same reasons. I dismissed an Army Commander (Kvietsinski) because his will and authority were subservient to the disorganising activities of the Committees who were democratising the Army.

Kerensky dismissed the Supreme Commander-in-Chief and the Commanders-in-Chief, Gourko and Dragomirov, because they were strenuously opposed to the democratisation of the Army. He also dismissed Brussilov for the opposite motives, because Brussilov was an Opportunist, pure and simple.

Brussilov dismissed the Commander of the Eighth Army, General Kaledin—who later became the Ataman of the Don and was universally respected—on the plea that he had " lost heart " and did not approve of democratisation. This dismissal of a General with a magnificent War record was effected in a rude and offensive manner. He was at first offered the command of another Army, and then offered to retire. Kaledin then wrote to me: " My record entitles me to be treated otherwise than as a stop-gap, without taking my own views into consideration."

General Vannovski, who was relieved of the command of an Army Corps by the Army Commander because he refused to acknowledge the priority of the Army Committee, was immediately appointed by the Stavka to a Higher Command and given an Army on the South-Western Front.

General Kornilov, who had refused the Chief Command of the troops of the Petrograd District, " because he considered it impossible to be a witness of and a contributor to the disruption of the Army by the Soviet," was afterwards appointed to the Supreme Command at the Front. Kerensky removed me from the office of Chief-of-Staff of the Supreme C.-in-C. because I did not share the views of the Government and openly disapproved of its activities, but, at the same time, he allowed me to assume the high office of Commander-in-Chief of our Western Front.

Things also happened of an entirely different nature. The Supreme Commander-in-Chief, General Alexeiev, made several unavailing efforts to dismiss Admiral Maximov, who had been elected to the command of the Baltic Fleet and was entirely in the hands of the mutinous Executive Committee of the Baltic Fleet. It was necessary to remove that officer, who had brought about so much evil, influenced, no doubt, by his surroundings, because the Committee refused to release him, and Maximov refused all summonses to come to the Stavka on the plea that the condition of the Fleet was critical. In the beginning of June Brussilov managed to remove him from the Fleet . . . at the price of appointing him Chief of the Naval Staff of the Supreme C.-in-C. Many other examples might be quoted of incredible contrasts in principles of Army Administration occasioned by the collision of two opposing forces and two schools of thought.

I have already said that the entire Commanding Staff of Generals was strictly loyal to the Provisional Government. General Kornilov, the would-be " rebel," addressed the following speech to a Meeting of Officers: " The old régime has collapsed. The people are building a new structure of liberty, and it is the duty of the people's Army wholeheartedly to support the new Government in its difficult, creative work." The Commanding Staff may have taken some interest in questions of general policy and in the Socialistic experiments of the Coalition Governments, but no more than was taken by all cultured Russians, and they did not consider themselves entitled or obliged to induce the troops to participate in the solution of social problems. Their only concern was to preserve the Army and the Foreign policy which contributed to the victory. Such a connection between the Commanding Staff and the Government, at first " a love match " and later one of convenience, prevailed until the General Offensive in June, while there still remained a flicker of hope that the mood of the Army would change. That hope was destroyed by events, and, after the advance, the attitude of the Commanding Staff was somewhat shaken. I may add that the *entire* Senior Commanding Staff considered as inadmissable the democratisation of the Army which the Government was enforcing. From the table which I have quoted it can be seen that 65 per cent. of the Commanding Officers did not raise a sufficiently strong protest against the disruption of the Army. The reasons were manifold and entirely different. Some did it for tactical considerations, as they thought that the Army was poisoned and that it should be healed by such dangerous antidotes. Others were prompted by purely selfish motives. I do not speak from hearsay, but because I know the *milieu* and the individuals, many of whom have discussed the matter with me with perfect frankness. Cultured and experienced Generals could not frankly and scientifically advocate such " military " views as, for example, Klembovski's suggestion that a triumvirate should be placed at the head of the Army, consisting of the Commander-in-Chief, a Commissar, and an elected soldier; Kvietzinski's suggestion that the Army Committee should be invested with special plenary power by the War Minister and the Central Committee of the Soviet, which would entitle them to act in the name of that Committee; or Viranovski's suggestion that the entire Commanding Staff should be converted into " technical advisers " and their power transferred entirely to the Commissars and the Committee.

The loyalty of the High Commanding Staff can be gauged from the following fact: At the end of April General Alexeiev, despairing of the possibility of personally preventing the Government from adopting measures which tended to disrupt the Army, and before issuing the famous Proclamation of the Rights of the Soldier, wired in cipher to all the Commanders-in-Chief a draft of a strong and resolute collective appeal from the Army to the Government. This appeal pointed to the abyss into which the Army was being hurled. In the event of the draft being approved, it was to have been signed by all Senior ranks, including Divisional Commanders. The Fronts, however, for various reasons, disapproved of such means of influencing the Government. General Ragosa, the temporary C.-in-C. of the Roumanian Front, who was afterwards Ukrainian War Minister under the Hetman, replied that the Russian people seemed to be ordained by the Almighty to perish, and it was therefore useless to struggle against Fate. With a sign of the Cross, one should patiently await the dictates of Fate! This was literally the sense of his telegram.

Such was the attitude and the confusion in the higher ranks of the Army. As regards the Commanders, who fought unremittingly against the disruption of the Army, many of them struggled against the tide of democratisation, as they considered it their duty to the people. They did this in disregard of the success or failure of their efforts, of the blows of Fate, or of the dark future, of which some already had a premonition, and which was already approaching with disaster in its train. On they went, with heads erect, misunderstood, slandered and savagely hated, as long as life and courage permitted.

CHAPTER XVII.

"Democratisation of the Army"—Administration, Service and Routine.

IN order to carry out the democratisation of the Army and the reform of the War Ministry in accordance with the new régime, Gutchkov established a Commission under the Chairmanship of the late War Minister, Polivanov, who died at Riga in 1920, where he was the expert of the Soviet Government in the Delegation for making peace with Poland. The Commission was composed of representatives of the Military Commission of the Duma and of representatives of the Soviet. There was a similar Commission in the Ministry of the Navy under the Chairmanship of Savitch, a prominent member of the Duma. I know more about the work of the First Commission, and will therefore dwell upon it. The regulations drafted by the Commission were not confirmed until they had been approved by the Military Section of the Executive Committee of the Soviet, which enjoyed great authority and often indulged in independent military law-making. No future historian of the Russian Army will be able to avoid mention of the Polivanov Commission—this fatal Institution whose stamp is affixed to every one of the measures which destroyed the Army. With incredible cynicism, not far removed from treachery, this Institution, comprising many Generals and officers appointed by the War Minister, systematically and daily introduced pernicious ideas and destroyed the rational foundations of military administration. Very often drafts of regulations, which appeared to the Government as excessively demagogic and were not sanctioned, appeared in the Press and came to the knowledge of the masses of the soldiery. They were instilled into the Army, and subsequently caused pressure to be brought to bear upon the Government by the soldiery. The military members of the Commission seemed to be competing with one another in slavish subservience to the new masters, and endorsed by their authority the destructive ideas. Men who reported to the

Committee have told me that civilians occasionally protested during the debates and warned the Committee against going too far, but no such protests ever came from the military members. I fail to understand the psychology of the men, who came so rapidly and unreservedly under the heel of the mob. The list of military members of the Commission of the month of May indicates that most of them were Staff Officers and representatives of other Departments, mostly of Petrograd (twenty-five); only nine were from the Army, and these do not seem to have been drawn from the line. Petrograd has its own psychology different from that of the Army. The most important and detrimental Democratic regulations were passed concerning the organisation of Committees, disciplinary action, the reform of the Military Courts, and, finally, the famous " Declaration of the Rights of the Soldier."

Military Chiefs were deprived of disciplinary power. It was transferred to Regimental and Company Disciplinary Courts, which also had to settle "misunderstandings" between officers and men. There is no need to comment upon the importance of this curtailment of the disciplinary power of the officers; it introduced complete anarchy in the internal life of regimental units, and the officer was discredited *by the law.* The latter circumstance is of paramount importance, and the Revolutionary Democracy took full advantage of this procedure in all its attempts at law-making. The reform of the Courts aimed at weakening the influence of military judges by appointment upon the course of the trial, the introduction of juries and the general weakening of military justice. Field Courts-Martial were abolished, which meted out quick punishment on the spot for obvious and heavy crimes, such as treason, desertion, etc.

The democratisation of the Military Courts might be excused to a certain extent by the fact that confidence in the officers, having been undermined, it was necessary to create judicial Courts of a mixed composition on an elective basis, which in theory were supposed to enjoy to a greater extent the confidence of the Revolutionary Democracy. But that object was not attained, because the Military Courts—one of the foundations of order in the Army—fell entirely into the hands of the mob. The investigating organs were completely destroyed by the Revolutionary Democracy, and investigation was strongly resisted by the armed men and sometimes by the Regimental Revolutionary Institutions. The armed mob, which included many criminal elements, exercised unrestrained and ignorant pressure upon the conscience of the judges, and passed sentences in advance of the verdicts of the judges. Army Corps Tribunals were destroyed, and members of the jury who had dared to pass a sentence distasteful to the mob were put to flight. These were common occurrences. The case was heard in Kiev of the well-known Bolshevik, Dzevaltovski, a captain of the Grenadier Regiment of the Guards, who was accused, with seventy-eight other men, of having refused to join in the advance and of having dragged his regiment and other units to the rear. The circumstances of the trial were these: In Court there was a mob of armed soldiers, who shouted approval of the accused on his way from the prison to the Court. Dzevaltovski called, together with his escort, at the Local Soviet, where he received an ovation. Finally, while the jury were deliberating, the Armed Reserve Battalions paraded before the Court with the band and sang the "International." Dzevaltovski and all his companions were, of course, found "Not guilty." Military Courts were thus gradually abolished.

It would be a mistake, however, to ascribe this new tendency solely to the influence of the Soviets. It may also be explained by Kerensky's point of view. He said: " I think that no results can be achieved by violence and by mechanical compulsion in the present conditions of warfare, where huge masses are concerned. The Provisional Government in the three months of its existence has come to the conclusion that it is necessary to appeal to the common-sense, the conscience and the sense of duty of the citizens, and that it is the only means of achieving the desired results."

In the first days of the Revolution the Provisional Government abolished Capital Punishment by the Ukase of March 12th. The Liberal Press greeted this measure with great pathos. Articles were written expressing strongly humanitarian views, but scant understanding of realities, of the life of the Army, and also scant foresight. V. Nabokoff, the Russian Abolitionist, who was General Secretary to the Provisional Government, wrote: " This happy event is a sign of true magnanimity and of wise foresight Capital Punishment is abolished unconditionally and for ever. . . . It is certain that in no other country has the moral condemnation of this, the worst kind of murder, reached such enormous proportions as in Russia. . . . Russia has joined the States that no longer know the shame and degradation of judicial murder." It is interesting to note that the Ministry of Justice drafted two laws, in one of which Capital Punishment was maintained for the most serious military offences—espionage and treason. But the Department of Military Justice, headed by

General Anushkin, emphatically declared in favour of complete abolition of Capital Punishment.

July came. Russia had already become used to Anarchist outbreaks, but was nevertheless horror-stricken at the events that took place on the battlefields of Galicia, near Kalush and Tarnopol. The telegrams of the Government Commissars, Savinkov and Filonenko, and of General Kornilov, who demanded the immediate reintroduction of Capital Punishment, were as a stroke of a whip to the " Revolutionary Conscience." On July 11th, Kornilov wrote· " The Army of maddened, ignorant men, who are not protected by the Government from systematic demoralisation and disruption, and who have lost all sense of human dignity, is in full flight. On the fields, which can no longer be called battlefields, shame and horror such as the Russian Army has never known reign supreme. . The mild Government measures have destroyed discipline, and are provoking the fitful cruelty of the unrestrained masses. These elemental feelings find expression in violence, plunder and murders. . . . Capital Punishment would save many innocent lives at the price of a few traitors and cowards being eliminated."

On July 12th the Government restored Capital Punishment and Revolutionary Military Tribunals, which replaced the former Field Courts-Martial. The difference was that the judges were elected (three officers and three men) from the list of the juries or from Regimental Committees. This measure, the restoration of Capital Punishment, due to pressure having been brought to bear upon the Government by the Military Command, the Commissars, and the Committees, was, however, foredoomed to failure. Kerensky subsequently tried to apologise to the Democracy at the " Democratic Conference ": " Wait till I have signed a single death sentence, and I will then allow you to curse me. " On the other hand, the very personnel of the Courts and their surroundings, described above, made the very creation of these Courts impossible: there were hardly any judges capable of passing a death sentence or any Commissars willing to endorse such a sentence. On the Fronts which I commanded there were, at any rate, no such cases. After the new Revolutionary Military Tribunals had been functioning for two months, the Department of Military Justice was flooded with reports from Military Chiefs and Commissars on the " blatant infringements of judicial procedure, upon the ignorance and lack of experience of the judges."

The disbandment of mutinous regiments was one of the punitive measures carried out by the Supreme Administration or Command. This measure had not been carefully thought out, and led to thoroughly unexpected consequences—it provoked mutinies, prompted by a desire to be disbanded. Regimental honour and other moral impulses had long since been characterised as ridiculous prejudices. The actual advantages of disbanding, on the other hand, were obvious to the men: regiments were removed from the firing line for a long time, disbanding continued for months, and the men were sent to new units, which were thus filled with vagabond and criminal elements. Responsibility for this measure can be equally divided between the War Ministry, the Commissars, and the Stavka. The whole burden of it finally fell once more upon the guiltless officers, who lost their regiments —which were their families—and their appointments, and were compelled to wander about in new places or find themselves in the desolate condition of the Reserve.

Apart from this undesirable element, units were filled with the late inmates of convict prisons, owing to the broad amnesty granted by the Government to criminals, who were to expiate their crimes by military service. My efforts to combat this measure were unavailing, and resulted in the formation of a special regiment of convicts—a present from Moscow—and in the formation of solid anarchist cadres in the Reserve Battalions. The *naïf* and insincere argument of the Legislator that crimes were committed because of the Czarist Régime, and that a free country would convert the criminal into a self-sacrificing hero, did not come true. In the garrisons, where amnestied criminals were for some reason or other more numerous, they became a menace to the population before they ever saw the Front. Thus, in June, in the units quartered at Tomsk, there was an intense propaganda of wholesale plunder and of the suppression of all authority. Soldiers formed large robber bands and terrorized the population. The Commissar, the Chief of the garrison, and all the local Revolutionary Organisations started a campaign against the plunderers; after much fighting, no less than 2,300 amnestied criminals were turned out of the garrison.

Reforms were intended to affect the entire administration of the Army and of the Fleet, but the above-mentioned Committees of Polivanov and Savitch failed to carry them out, as they were abolished by Kerensky, who recognised at last all the evil they had wrought. The Committees merely prepared the Democratisation of the War and Naval Councils by introducing elected soldiers into them. This circumstance is the more curious because, according to the Legislator's intention, these Councils were to consist of men of experience and knowledge, capable of solving questions of organisation, service, and routine, of military and naval legislation, and of making financial estimates of the cost of the armed forces of Russia. This yearning of the uncultured portion of Democracy for spheres of activity foreign to it was subsequently developed on an extensive scale. Thus, for example, many military colleges were, to a certain extent, managed by Committees of servants, most of whom were illiterate. Under the Bolshevik Régime, University Councils numbered not only Professors and students, but also hall-porters.

I will not dwell upon the minor activities of the Committees, the reorganisation of the Army, and the new regulations, but will describe the most important measure—the Committees and the " Declaration of the Rights of the Soldier."

CHAPTER XVIII.

The Declaration of the Rights of the Soldier and Committees.

ELECTIVE bodies from the Military Section of the Soviet to Committees and Soviets of various denominations in regimental units and in the Departments of the Army, the Fleet and the rear, were the most prominent factor of " Democratisation." These institutions were partly of a mixed type, and included both officers and men and partly soldiers and workers' institutions pure and simple. Committees and Soviets were formed everywhere as the common feature of Revolutionary Organisations, planned before the Revolution and sanctioned by the Order No. 1. Elections from the troops to the Soviet in Petrograd were fixed for February 27th, and the first Army Committees came into being on March 1st, in consequence of the above-mentioned Order No. 1. Towards the month of April self-appointed Soviets and Committees, varying in denomination, personnel and ability, existed in the Army and in the rear, and introduced incredible confusion into the system of military hierarchy and administration. In the first month of the Revolution the Government and the military authorities did not endeavour to put an end to or to restrict this dangerous phenomenon. They did not at first realise its possible consequences, and counted upon the moderating influence of the Officer element. They occasionally took advantage of the Committees for counteracting acute manifestations of discontent among the soldiers, as a doctor applies small doses of poison to a diseased organism. The attitude of the Government and of the military authorities towards these organisations was irresolute, but was one of semi-recognition. On April 9th, addressing the Army Delegates, Gutchkov said at Yassy: " A Congress will soon be held of the Delegates of all Army Organisations, and general regulations will then be drawn up. Meanwhile, you should *organise as best you can*, taking advantage of the existing organisations and working for general unity."

In April the position became so complicated that the authorities could no longer shirk the solution of the question of Committees. At the end of March there was a Conference at the Stavka, attended by the Supreme Commander-in-Chief, the War Minister, Gutchov, his Assistants, and officers of the General Staff. I was also present in my capacity as future Chief-of-Staff to the Supreme C.-in-C. A draft was presented to the Conference, brought from Sevastopol by the Staff-Colonel Verkhovski (afterwards War Minister). The draft was modelled upon the regulations already in force in the Black Sea Fleet. The discussion amounted to the expression of two extreme views—mine and those of Colonel Verkhovski. The latter had already commenced those slightly demagogic activities by which he had at first gained the sympathies of the soldiers and of the sailors. He had had a short experience in organising these masses. He was persuasive because he used many illustrations—I do not know whether the facts he mentioned were real or imaginary—his views were pliable, and his eloquence was imposing. He idealised the Committees, and argued that they were very useful, even necessary and statesmanlike, inasmuch as they were capable of bringing order into the chaotic movements of the soldiery. He emphatically insisted upon the competence and the rights of these Committees being broadened.

I argued that the introduction of Committees was a measure which the Army organisation would be unable to understand, and that it amounted to disruption of the Army. If the Government was unable to cope with the movement, it should endeavour to paralyse its dangerous consequences. With that end in view, I advocated that the activities of the Committees should be limited to matters of internal organisation (food supplies, distribution of equipment, etc.), that the officer element should be strengthened, and that the Committees should remain within the sphere of the lower grades of the Army, in order to prevent them from spreading and acquiring a preponderating influence upon larger formations such as Divisions, Armies, and Fronts. Unfortunately, I only succeeded in compelling the Conference to accept my views to an insignificant degree, and on March 30th the Supreme C.-in-C. issued an Order of the Day on the " transition to the new forms of life," and appealing to the officers, men, and sailors wholeheartedly to unite in the work of introducing strict order and solid discipline within the units of the Army and Navy.

The main principles of the regulations were the following :

(1) The *fundamental objects* of the organisation were (*a*) to increase the fighting power of the Army and of the Navy in order to win the War; (*b*) to devise new rules for the life of the soldier-

The Declaration of Rights

citizen of Free Russia; and (c) to contribute to the education of the Army and of the Fleet.

(2) The *structure* of the organisation: Permanent sections—Company, Regimental, Divisional, and Army Committees. Temporary sections—Conferences, attached to the Stavka, of Army Corps, of the Fronts, and of the Centre. The latter to form permanent Soviet.

(3) The Conferences to be called by the respective Commanding Officers or on the initiative of the Army Committees. All the resolutions of the Conferences and Committees to be confirmed by the respective military authorities prior to publication.

(4) The *competence* of the Committees was limited to enforcing order and fighting power (discipline, resistance to desertion, etc.), routine (leave, barrack life, etc.), internal organisation (control of food supplies and equipment), and education.

(5) *Questions of training* were unreservedly excluded from discussion.

(6) The *personnel of the Committees* was determined in proportion to elected representatives—one officer to two men.

In order to give an idea of the slackening of discipline in the higher ranks I may mention that, immediately after receiving these regulations, and obviously under the influence of Army organisations, General Brussilov issued the following order: " Officers to be excluded from Company Committees, and in higher Committees the proportion lowered from one-third to one-sixth. "

In less than a fortnight, however, the War Ministry, in disregard of the Stavka, published its own regulations, drafted by the famous Polivanov Committee, with the assistance of Soviet representatives. In these new regulations substantial alterations were made: the percentage of officers in Committees was reduced; Divisional Committees abolished; " the taking of rightful measures against abuses by Commanding Officers in the respective units " were added to the powers of the Committees; the Company Committees were not permitted to discuss the matter of military preparedness and other purely military matters affecting the unit, but no such reservation was made with regard to Regimental Committees; the Regimental Commanding Officer was entitled to appeal against but not to suspend the decisions of the Committee; finally, the Committees were given the task of negotiating with political parties of every description in the matter of sending delegates, speakers, and pamphlets explaining the political programme before the elections to the Constituent Assembly.

These regulations, which were tantamount to converting the Army in war-time into an arena of political strife and depriving the Commanding Officer of all control over his unit, constituted, in fact, one of the main turning points on the path of destruction of the Army.

The following appreciation of these regulations by the Anarchist, Makhno (the Order of the Day of one of his subordinate Commanders of November 10th, 1919), is worthy of note: " As any party propaganda at the present moment strongly handicaps the purely military activities of the rebel armies, I emphatically declare to the population that all party propaganda is strictly prohibited pending the complete victory over the White Armies. . . ."

Several days later, in view of a protest from the Stavka, the War Ministry issued orders for the immediate suspension of the regulations concerning the Committees. Where the Committees had already been formed, they were allowed to carry on in order to avoid misunderstandings. The Ministry decided to alter the section of the regulations concerning the Committees, in accordance with the orders of the Supreme Commander-in-Chief, in which fuller consideration was given to the interests of the troops. Thus, in the middle of April there was an infinite variety in the organisation of the Army. Some institutions were illegal, others were sanctioned by the Stavka, and others still by the War Ministry. All these contradictions, changes, and re-elections might have led to ridiculous confusion had not the Committees simplified matters: they simply cast off all restrictions and acted arbitrarily. Wherever troops or Army departments were quartered among the population local Soldiers' Soviets or Soviets of Soldiers and Workmen were formed, which recognised no regulations, and were particularly intent upon covering deserters and mercilessly exploiting municipalities, Zemstvos, and the population. The authorities never opposed them, and it was only at the end of August that the War Ministry lost patience with the abuses of these " Institutions of the Rear," and informed the Press that it *intended* to undertake the drafting of special regulations concerning these Institutions.

Who were the members of the Committees? The combatant element, living for and understanding the interests of the Army and imbued with its traditions, was scantily represented. Valour, courage and a sense of duty were rated very low on the market of Soldiers' Meetings. The masses of the soldiery, who were, alas! ignorant, illiterate, and already demoralised and distrusted their Chiefs, elected mostly men who imposed on them by smooth

The Declaration of Rights

talking, purely external political knowledge derived from the revelation of Party propaganda; chiefly, however, by shamelessly bowing to the instincts of the men. How could a real soldier, appealing to the sense of duty, to obedience and to a struggle for the Mother Country, compete with such demagogues? The officers did not enjoy the confidence, they did not wish to work in the Committees, and their political education was probably inadequate. In the Higher Committees one met honest and sensible soldiers more often than officers, because a man wearing a soldier's tunic was in a position to address the mob in a manner in which the officer could never dare to indulge. The Russian Army was henceforward administered by Committees formed of elements foreign to the Army and representing rather Socialist Party organs. It was strange and insulting to the Army that Congresses of the Front, representing several million combatants and many magnificent units with a long and glorious record, and comprising officers and men of whom any Army might be proud, were held under the Chairmanship of such men as civilian Jews and Georgians, who were Bolsheviks, Mensheviks, or Social Revolutionaries—Posner on the Western Front, Gegetchkory on the Caucasian, and Doctor Lordkipanitze on the Roumanian

What, then, were these Army Organisations doing that were supposed to reconstruct " the freest Army in the world "? I will quote a list of questions discussed at Conferences of the Front and which influenced the Front and Army Committees·

(1) The attitude towards the Government, the Soviet and the Constituent Assembly.
(2) The attitude towards War and Peace.
(3) The question of a Democratic Republic as a desirable form of Government.
(4) The question of the land.
(5) The Labour question.

These intricate and burning political and social questions, to which a radical solution was being given and which created partisanship and class strife, were thus introduced into the Army that was facing a strong and cruel enemy. The effect was self-evident. But even in strictly military matters certain utterances were made at the Conference at Minsk, which attracted the particular attention of the military and civil authorities, and caused us gravely to ponder. It was suggested that the rank of officer, individual disciplinary power, etc., should be abolished, and that the Committees should be entitled to remove Commanding Officers of whom they disapproved. From the very first days of their existence the Committees fought stubbornly to obtain full power not only with regard to the administration of the Army, but even for the formula: " All Power to the Soviets." At first, however, the attitude of the Army Committees towards the Provisional Government was perfectly loyal, and the lower the Committee the more loyal it was. The Petrograd papers of March 17th were full of resolutions proclaiming unrestricted obedience to the Provisional Government, of telegrams greeting and of records of delegations sent by the troops, who were perturbed by rumours of the opposition of the Soviet. This attitude later underwent several changes, due to the propaganda of the Soviet. A powerful influence was exercised by the resolution of the Congress of Soviets, which I have already quoted, and which appealed to the Russian Revolutionary Democracy to organise under the guidance of the Soviets and to be prepared to resist all the attempts of the Government to avoid the control of the Democracy or the fulfilment of their pledges.

The Higher Committees indulged chiefly in political activities and in the strengthening of Revolutionary tendencies in the Army, while the Lower Committees gradually became absorbed in matters of service and routine, and were weakening and discrediting the authority of the Commanding Officers. The right to remove these officers was practically established, because the position of those who had received a vote of censure became intolerable. Thus, for instance, on the Western Front, which I commanded, about sixty Senior Officers resigned—from Army Corps to Regimental Commanders. What was, however, infinitely more tragic was the endeavour of the Committees, on their own initiative and under pressure from the troops, to interfere with purely military and technical Orders, thus rendering military operations difficult or even impossible. The Commanding Officer who was discredited, fettered and deprived of power, and, therefore, of responsibility, could no longer confidently lead the troops into the field of victory and death   As there was no authority the Commanding Officers were compelled to have recourse to the Committees, which sometimes did exercise a restraining influence over the licentious soldiery, resisted desertion, smoothed friction between officers and men, appealed to the latter's sense of duty—in a word, tried to arrest the collapse of the crumbling structure. These activities of some of

The Declaration of Rights

the Committees still misled their apologists, including Kerensky. It is no use to argue with men who think that a structure may be erected by one laying bricks one day and pulling them to pieces on the next.

The work, overt and unseen, of Army Committees, alternating between patriotic appeals and internationalist watchwords, between giving assistance to Commanding Officers and dismissing them, between expressions of confidence in, or of distrust of, the Provisional Government, and ultimatums for new boots or travelling allowances for members of Committees. . The historian of the Russian Army, in studying these phenomena, will be amazed at the ignorance of the elementary rules governing the very existence of an armed force, which was displayed by the Committees in their decisions and in their writings.

The Committees of the Rear and of the Fleet were imbued with a particularly demagogic spirit. The Baltic Fleet was in a state approaching anarchy all the time; the Black Sea Fleet was in a better condition, and held out until June. It is difficult to estimate the mischief made by these Committees and Soviets in the Rear, scattered all over the country. Their overbearing manner was only comparable with their ignorance. I will mention a few examples illustrating these activities.

The Regional Committee of the Army, the Fleet and the Workmen of Finland issued a declaration in May, in which, not content with the autonomy granted to Finland by the Provisional Government, they demanded her complete independence, and declared that "they would give every support to all the Revolutionary Organisations working for a speedy solution of that question."

The Central Committee of the Baltic Fleet, in conjunction with the above-mentioned Committee, made a declaration, which coincided with the Bolshevik outbreak in Petrograd in the beginning of June They demanded "all power to the Soviets. We shall unite in the Revolutionary struggle of our working Democracy for power, and will not allow the ships to be called out by the Provisional Government for the suppression of the mutiny to leave Petrograd."

The Committee of the Minsk Military District, shortly before the advance, gave leave to all the Reservists to proceed to their farms. I gave orders for the trial of the Committee, but the order was of no avail, because, in spite of all my representations, the War Ministry had not established any legal responsibility for the Committees, whose decisions were recorded by vote and occasionally by secret ballot. I will mention yet another curious episode. The Committee of one of the Cavalry Depôts on my Front decided that horses should be watered only once a day, so most of the horses were lost.

It would be unjust to deny that the organisations of the Rear occasionally did adopt reasonable measures, but these instances are few indeed, and they were drowned in the general wave of anarchy which these organisations had raised. The attitude of the Committees towards the War, and in particular towards the proposed advance, was, of course, a momentous matter. In Chapter X. I have already described the self-contradictions of the Soviets and Congresses, as well as the ambiguous and insincere directions which they gave to the Army Organisations, and which amounted to the acceptance of War and of the advance, but without victory. The same ambiguity prevailed in the High Committees, with the exception, however, of the Committee of our Western Front, which passed in June a truly Bolshevik Resolution to the effect that War has been engendered by the plundering policy of the Government; that the only means of ending the War was for the united Democracies of all countries to resist their Governments; and that a decisive victory of one or the other of the contending groups of Powers would only tend to increase militarism at the expense of Democracy.

As long as the Front was quiet the troops accepted all these discourses and Resolutions in a spirit of comparative indifference. But when the time came for the advance, many people thought of saving their skins, and the ready formulas of Defeatism proved opportune. Besides the Committees, who were continuing to pass patriotic Resolutions, certain organisations reflecting the views of the units of the Army, or their own, violently opposed the idea of an advance. Entire regiments, divisions, and even Army Corps, especially on the Northern and Western Russian Fronts, refused to conduct preparatory work or to advance to the firing line. On the eve of the advance we had to send large forces for the suppression of units that had treacherously forgotten their duty.

I have already mentioned the attitude of many Senior Commanders towards the Committees. The best summary of these views can be found in the appeal of General Fedotov, in temporary command of an Army, to the Army Committee: " Our Army is at present organised as no other Army in the world. . . , Elected bodies play an important part. We—*the former leaders* —can only give the Army our military knowledge of strategy and tactics. You—the Committees—are called upon to organise the Army and to create its internal strength. Great indeed is the part which you—the Committees—are called upon to play in the

The Conference of Commanders-in-Chief. Standing on the pathway, from left to right: Generals Denikin, Danilov, Hanjin. Seated (left): Doukhonin, Gourko, Brussilov. Centre: Alexeiev. Right: Dragomirov, Scherbatchev.

A group of "prisoners" at Berdichev. From left to right: Captain Kletzando, General Elsner, General Vannovsky, General Denikin, General Erdeli, General Markov, General Orlov.

creation of a new and strong Army. History will recognise this. . . ."

Before the Army Organisations were sanctioned the Commander of the Caucasian Front issued an Order for the decisions of the self-appointed Tiflis Soldiers' Soviet to be published in the Orders of the Day, and for all regulations appertaining to the Organisation and routine of the Army to be sanctioned by that Soviet. Is one to wonder that such an attitude of a certain portion of the Commanding Staffs gave an excuse and a foundation for the growing demands of the Committees?

As regards the Western and South-Western Fronts, which I commanded, I definitely refused to have anything to do with the Committees, and suppressed, whenever possible, such of their activities as were contrary to the interests of the Army One of the prominent Commissars, a late member of the Executive Committee of the Soviet, Stankevitch, wrote: " Theoretically, it became increasingly apparent that either the Army must be abolished or else the Committees. In practice, one could do neither one nor the other. The Committees were a vivid expression of the incurable sociological disease of the Army, and a sign of its certain collapse and paralysis. Was it not for the War Ministry to hasten the death by a resolute and hopeless surgical operation?"

The once great Russian Army of the first period of the Revolution dwindled inevitably to nothing under such conditions as these:

There was no Mother Country. The leader had been crucified. In his stead a group appeared at the Front of five Defensists and three Bolsheviks, and made an appeal to the Army:

" Forward, to battle for liberty and for the Revolution, but . without inflicting a decisive defeat upon the enemy," cried the former.

" Down with the War and all power to the Proletariat! " shouted the others.

The Army listened and listened, but would not move. And then . . . it dispersed!

CHAPTER XIX.

The Democratisation of the Army: The Commissars.

THE next measure for the democratisation of the Army was the introduction of the Institution of Commissars. The idea was derived from the history of the French Revolutionary Wars, and was fostered in various circles at different times; it was prompted chiefly by *distrust of the Commanding Staffs*. Pressure was brought to bear from below. The Conference of the Delegates of the Front addressed an emphatic demand to the Soviet in the middle of April that Commissars should be introduced in the Army. The excuse was that it was no longer possible to preserve order in respect of the attitude of the men towards individual Commanding Officers, and that, if cases of arbitrary dismissal had as yet been avoided, it was only due to the fact that the Army expected the Soviet and the Government to take the necessary steps and did not wish to handicap their work. At the same time, the Conference suggested the absurd idea of the simultaneous appointment to the Army of three kinds of Commissars: (1) from the Provisional Government, (2) from the Soviets, and (3) from the Army Committees. The Conference went very far in their demands, and demanded that the Commissariats, as controlling organs, should: discuss *all* matters appertaining to the competence of the Commanders of Armies and Fronts; counter-sign *all* Army Orders; investigate the activities of the Commanding Staffs, with the right to recommend their dismissal.

Protracted negotiations on this matter ensued between the Soviet and the Government, and at the end of April it was agreed that Commissars would be appointed to the Army—one from the Provisional Government and one from the Soviet. This decision, however, was subsequently altered, probably as the result of the formation of a Coalition Ministry (May 5th). One Commissar was appointed by agreement between the Government and the Soviet. He represented both these bodies, and was responsible

The Democratisation of the Army

to them. At the end of June the Provisional Government introduced the office of Commissar of the Fronts, and thus defined their function: according to the instructions of the War Ministry, they were to see that all political questions arising within the Armies of the Front should be given a uniform solution, and that the work of the Army Commissars should be co-ordinated. At the end of July a final touch was given by the appointment of a High Commissar attached to the Stavka, and the entire official correspondence was concentrated in the political section of the War Ministry. No law, however, was passed defining the rights and the duties of the Commissars. The Commanding Staffs, at any rate, were unaware of such laws, and this alone gave rise to all the misunderstandings and conflicts that followed. The Commissars had secret instructions to watch the Commanding Staffs and Headquarters in respect of their political reliability. From that point of view the democratic régime went further, perhaps, than the autocratic. Of this I became convinced during my command of the Western and South-Western Fronts, in reading the telegrams exchanged between the Commissariats and Petrograd. These telegrams—may the Commissars forgive me!—were handed to me, de-coded, by my Staff, immediately after their despatch. This part of the Commissars' duty required a certain training in political intelligence, but their overt duties were infinitely more complex: they demanded statesmanship, a clear knowledge of the aims to be pursued, an understanding of the psychology, not merely of the officers and men, but of the Senior Commanding Staff, acquaintance with the fundamental principles of service and routine in the Army, great tact, and, finally, the personal qualities of courage, strong will, and energy. Only such qualifications were capable of mitigating to a certain degree the disastrous consequences of a measure which deprived (to be more accurate, sanctioned the deprivation of) the Commanding Officers of the possibility of influencing the troops—that influence being the only means of strengthening the hope and faith in victory.

Such elements were not to be found, unfortunately, in the circles connected with the Government and the Soviet and enjoying their confidence. The personnel of the Commissars whom I met may be described thus: War-time officers, doctors, solicitors, newspaper men, exiles and *emigrés* completely out of touch with Russian life, members of militant Revolutionary organisations, etc. These men had, obviously, inadequate knowledge of the Army. All these men belonged to Socialist parties, from Social-Democrat Mensheviks to the group " Edinstvo " (unity), War party blinkers, and very often did not follow the political lines of the Government because they considered themselves tied by Soviet and party discipline. Owing to political differences of opinion, the attitude of the Commissars towards the War also varied. Stankevitch, one of the Commissars, who carried out his duties in his own way most conscientiously, when proceeding to visit an advancing Division was beset with doubts: " The soldiers believe that we do not wish to deceive them; they force themselves, therefore, to forget their doubts, and they go forward to death and murder. But we, are we entitled not only to encourage them, but to take upon ourselves the decision?" According to Savinkov (who was Commissar of the Seventh Army of the South-Western Front, and later War Minister), not all the Commissars agreed upon the question of Bolshevism, and not all of them considered a resolute struggle against the Bolsheviks possible or desirable. Savinkov was an exception. Although not a soldier by profession, he was steeled in struggle and wanderings, in constant danger, and his hands were stained with the blood of political victims. This man, however, understood the laws of the struggle, threw off the yoke of the party, and fought more resolutely than others against the disorganisation of the Army. But the personal touch in his attitude towards the events was somewhat too marked. None of the Commissars, with the exception of very few men of the Savinkov type, displayed personal strength or energy. They were men of words, not of deeds. Their lack of training would not have had such negative results had it not been for the fact that, their functions not being clearly defined, they gradually began to interfere with every feature of the life and service of the troops, partly on their own initiative, partly at the instigation of the men and of the Army Committees, and partly even of Commanding Officers, who were trying to escape responsibility. Questions of appointments, dismissals, and even operative plans attracted the attention of the Commissars, not only from the point of view of " covert counter-Revolution," but from the point of view of practicability. The confusion in their minds was so great that the weaker elements among the Commanding Staffs were sometimes completely disheartened. I remember one case during the July retreat on the South-Western Front. One of the Army Corps Commanders rashly destroyed a well-equipped military railway, thereby placing the Army in an exceedingly difficult position. He was dismissed by the Army Commander, and afterwards expressed to me his sincere astonishment: " Why had he been dismissed? He had acted—upon the instructions of the Commissar."

The Democratisation of the Army

The Commissars carried out the ideas of the Soviet and wholeheartedly defended the sacred newly-acquired rights of the soldier, but failed to fulfil their primary duty—direct the political life of the Army. Very often the most destructive propaganda was permitted. Soldiers' meetings and Committees were allowed to pass all kinds of anti-National and anti-Government resolutions, and the Commissars only interfered when the tension of the atmosphere resulted in an armed mutiny. Such a policy puzzled the troops, the Committees, and the Commanding Officers.

The institution of Commissars did not attain its purpose. Among the soldiers the Commissars could not be popular because they were to a certain extent an instrument of compulsion, and occasionally of suppression. At the same time, the extent of their power was not well defined, and they could not gain proper authority over the most undisciplined units. This was confirmed later after the seizure of power by the Bolsheviks, when the Commissars were the first to flee from their posts in a great hurry and in secret.

There thus appeared in the Russian Army, instead of one authority, three different authorities, which excluded one another —the Commanding Officer, the Committee, and the Commissar. They were shadowy authorities. Another authority was overhanging, and was oppressing them morally with all its insensate weight—the power of the mob.

*   *   *

In examining the question of the new Institutions—Commissars and Committees—and of their bearing upon the destinies of the Russian Army, I have done so solely from the point of view of the preservation of our Armed Forces as an important factor in the future of our country. It would, however, be a mistake to overlook the connection between these measures and the entirety of laws which govern the life of the people and the course of the Revolution. These measures, moreover, bear the stamp of logic and of inevitability owing to the part which the Revolutionary Democracy had chosen to play. Therein lies the tragedy of the situation. The Socialist Democracy did not possess any elements sufficiently trained to become the instruments of Army Administration. At the same time, it did not have the courage or the possibility to quell the resistance of the Bourgeois Democracy and of the Commanding Staffs, and to compel them to work for the glorification of Socialism, as the Bolsheviks afterwards did, who forced the remnants of the Russian *intelligencia* and of the officers to serve Communism by applying methods of sanguinary and ruthless extermination. When the Revolutionary Democracy actually assumed power and set up to fulfil certain aims it was well aware of the fact that those elements in the administration and the Command who were called upon to carry out these aims did not share the views of the Revolutionary Democracy. Hence the inevitable distrust of these elements and the desire to weaken their influence and their authority. What methods did the Democracy have recourse to? As the Central Revolutionary organ was utterly devoid of statesmanship and of patriotism, it applied in its struggle against political opponents destructive methods, completely disregarding the fact that by these methods they were destroying the country and the Army. Another circumstance must be borne in mind—the Revolution that had shaken the State to its very foundations and upset the established class relations occurred at the moment when the flower of the Nation—over 10,000,000 men—were under arms. Elections to the Constituent Assembly were impending. In these circumstances it was impossible to avoid politics being introduced into the Army, as it is impossible to arrest the course of a river. But it would have been possible to divert it to proper channels. In this matter, however, the two contending forces (that which wished to preserve the State and the Demagogic Force) also collided, as both endeavoured to influence the attitude of the Army, which was a decisive factor in the Revolution.

These were the propositions which pre-ordained and explained the subsequent course of the Democratisation of the Army. The Socialist Democracy, which governed at first behind the scenes and then overtly, was endeavouring to strengthen its position and to bow to the instincts of the crowd, destroyed the military power and connived at the Institution of Elective Military Organisations, which were less dangerous and more open to its influence than the Commanding Staffs, although they did not answer the requirements of the Soviet. The necessity of military authority of some sort was clearly realised. The Commanding Staffs were distrusted, and there was a desire to create a buffer between the two artificially separated elements of the Army. These considerations inspired the creation of the office of Commissars, who bore the dual responsibility before the Soviet and the Government. Neither the men nor the officers were satisfied with these institutions, which fell together with the Provisional Government, were revived with certain modifications in the Red Army, and once again swept away by the tide of events.

" Peoples cannot choose their Institutions, as man cannot choose his age. Peoples obey the Institutions to which they are tied by their past, their creed, by the economic laws and surroundings in which they live. There are many examples in history when the people have destroyed by violent Revolution the Institutions which it has taken a dislike for. But there is not a case in history of these new institutions forcibly imposed upon the people becoming permanent and solid. After a while the past comes again into force, because we are created entirely by that past and it is our supreme ruler."*

It is obvious that the Russian National Army will be revived not only on democratic, but on historical foundations.

---

* Gustave Le-Bon, *The Psychology of Socialism*.

CHAPTER XX.

The Democratisation of the Army—The Story of "The Declaration of the Rights of the Soldier."

THE ill-famed law, emanating from the Polivanov Committee and known as the " Declaration of the Rights of the Soldier," was confirmed by Kerensky on May 9th. I will give the main points of that law:

(1) " All soldiers of the Army enjoy full rights of citizenship."

(2) Every soldier is entitled to the membership of any political, national, religious, economic, or professional organisation, society or union.

(3) Every soldier off duty has the right freely and openly to express in word, writing, or in the Press his political, religious, social and other views.

(4) All printed matter (periodicals and other) should be delivered to the addressees.

(5) Soldiers are not to be appointed as orderlies. Officers are entitled to have one servant, appointed by mutual consent (of the soldier and of the officer); wages also to be settled by mutual consent, but there should be no more than one servant to each officer, Army doctor, Army clerk, or Priest.

(6) Saluting is abolished for men as well as for units.

(7) No soldier is to be punished or fined without trial. At the Front the Commanding Officer is entitled, on his own responsibility, to take the necessary steps, including armed force, against disobedient subordinates. Such steps are not to be considered as disciplinary punishments. Internal administration, punishments, and control in cases defined by Army regulations, belong to elective Army Organisations.

This " Declaration of Rights," of which the above is but a brief summary, gave official sanction to the malady with which the Army was stricken, and which spread in varying degrees owing to mutinies, violence, and " by Revolutionary methods," as the current expression goes. It dealt a death-blow to the old Army.

The Democratisation of the Army

It introduced boundless political discussions and social strife into the unbalanced ARMED MASSES which had already become aware of their rough physical power. " The Declaration " admitted and sanctioned wide propaganda by speech and pamphlet of anti-national, immoral and anti-Social doctrines, and even the doctrines that repudiated the State and the very existence of the Army. Finally, it deprived Commanding Officers of disciplinary power, which was handed over to elective bodies, and once again insulted and degraded the Commanding Staff. In his remarks attached to the text of the " Declaration," Kerensky says: " Let the freest Army and Navy of the World prove that there is strength and not weakness in Liberty, let them forge a new iron discipline of duty and raise the Armed Power of the country."

And the " Great Silent One," as the French picturesquely describe the Army, began to talk and to shout louder and louder still, enforcing its demands by threats, by arms, and by shedding the blood of those who dared to resist its folly.

At the end of April the final draft of the " Declaration " was sent by Gutchkov to the Stavka for approval. The Supreme Commander-in-Chief and myself returned an emphatic disapproval, in which we gave vent to all our moral sufferings and our grief for the dark future of the Army. Our conclusion was that the " Declaration " " was the last nail driven into the coffin which has been prepared for the Russian Army." On May 1st Gutchkov resigned from the War Ministry, as he did not wish " to share the responsibility for the heavy sin which was committed against the Mother Country," and in particular to sign the " Declaration."

*   *   *   *

The Stavka sent copies of the draft " Declaration " to the Commander-in-Chief of the Fronts for reference, and they were called by General Alexeiev to Moghilev, in order to discuss the fateful position. This historical Conference took place on May 2nd. The speeches, in which the collapse of the Russian Army was described, were restrained and yet moving, as they reflected deep sorrow and apprehension. Brussilov, in a low voice expressing sincere and unfeigned pain, ended thus: " All this can yet be borne, and there still remains some hope of saving the Army and leading it forward, provided the ' Declaration ' is not issued. If it is, there is no salvation, and I would not remain in office for a single day." This last sentence provoked a warm protest from General Stcherbatchov, who argued that no one should resign, that, however arduous and hopeless the position may be, the leaders cannot abandon the Army. . . . Somebody suggested that all the Commanders-in-Chief should immediately proceed to Petrograd, and address to the Provisional Government a stern warning and definite demands. The General who suggested this thought that such a demonstration would produce a very strong impression and might arrest the progress of destructive legislation. Others thought that it was a dangerous expedient and our last trump card, and that, should the step prove ineffective, the High Command would be definitely discredited. The suggestion, however, was accepted, and, on the 4th May, a Conference took place of all the Commanders-in-Chief (with the exception of the Caucasian Front), the Provisional Government, and the Executive Committee of the Soviet. I am in possession of the record of that Conference, of which I give extensive extracts below. The condition of the Army, such as it appeared to its leaders, in the course of events, and without, therefore, any historical perspective, is therein described, as well as the characteristics of the men who were then in power. The trend of the speeches made by the Commander-in-Chief was the same as in the Stavka, but they were less emphatic and less sincere. Brussilov smoothed over his accusations, lost his pathos, " warmly greeted the Coalition Ministry," and did not repeat his threat of resignation.

THE RECORD.

General Alexeiev.—I consider it necessary to speak quite frankly. We are all united in wishing for the good of our country. Our paths may differ, but we have a common goal of ending the War in such a manner as to allow Russia to come out of it unbroken, albeit tired and suffering. Only victory can give us the desired consummation. Only then will creative work be possible. But victory must be achieved, and that is only possible if the orders of the Commanding Officers are obeyed. If not, it is not an Army, but a mob. To sit in the trenches does not mean to reach the end of the War. The enemy is transferring, in great haste, division after division from our Front to the Franco-British Front, and we continue to sit still. Meanwhile, the conditions are most favourable for our victory, but we must advance in order to win it. Our Allies are losing faith in us. We must reckon with this in the diplomatic sphere, and I particularly in the military one. It seemed as if the Revolution would raise our spirits, would give us impetus, and therefore victory. In that, unfortunately, we have so far been mistaken. Not only is there no enthusiasm or impetus, but the lowest instincts have come to the fore, such

The Democratisation of the Army

as self-preservation. The interests of the Mother Country and its future are not being considered. . . . You will ask what has happened to the authority, to principles, or even to physical compulsion? I am bound to state that the reforms to which the Army has as yet failed to adapt itself have shaken it, have undermined order and discipline. Discipline is the mainstay of the Army. If we follow that path any further there will be a complete collapse.
. The Commanders-in-Chief will give you a series of facts describing the condition of the Armies. I will offer a conclusion and will give expression to our desires and demands, which must be complied with.

General Brussilov.—I must first of all describe to you the present condition of the officers and men. Cavalry, artillery and engineering troops have retained about 50 per cent. of their cadres. But in the infantry, which is the mainstay of the Army, the position is entirely different. Owing to enormous casualties in killed, wounded and prisoners, as well as many deserters, some regiments have changed their cadres nine or ten times, so that only from three to ten men remain of the original formation. Reinforcements are badly trained and their discipline is still worse. Of the regular officers from two to four remain and in many cases they are wounded. Other officers are youngsters commissioned after a short training and enjoying no authority owing to their lack of experience. It is upon these new cadres that the task has fallen to remodel the Army on a new basis, and that task has so far proved beyond their capacity. Although we felt that a change was necessary and that it had already come too late, the ground was nevertheless unprepared. The uneducated soldier understood it as a deliverance from the officers' yoke. The officers greeted the change with enthusiasm. Had this not been so, the Revolution may not have probably passed so smoothly. The result, however, was that freedom was only given to the men, whereas the officers had to be content to play the part of pariahs of liberty. The unconscious masses were intoxicated with liberty. Everyone knows that extensive rights have been granted, but they do not know what these rights are, and nobody bothers about duties. The position of the officers is very difficult. From 15 to 20 per cent. have rapidly adapted themselves to the new conditions, because they believed that these conditions were all to the good. Those of the officers who were trusted by the men did not lose that trust. Some, however, became too familiar with the men, were too lenient and even encouraged internal dissensions amongst the men. But the majority of the officers, about 75 per cent., were unable to adapt themselves. They were offended, retired to the background and do not know what to do now. We are trying to bring them into contact with the soldiers once more, because we need the officers for continued fighting, and we have no other cadres. Many of the officers have no political training, do not know how to make speeches—and this, of course, handicaps the work of mutual understanding. It is necessary to explain and to instil into the masses the idea that freedom has been granted to *everyone*. I have known our soldiers for forty-five years, I love them and I will do my best to bring them into close touch with the officers, but the Provisional Government, the Duma and particularly the Soviet should also make every effort in order to assist in that work which must be done as soon as possible in the interests of the country. It is also necessary, owing to the peculiar fashion in which the illiterate masses have understood the watchword " without annexations and indemnities." One of the regiments has declared that not only would it refuse to advance, but desired to leave the front and to go home. The Committees opposed this tendency, but were told that they would be dismissed. I had a lengthy argument with the regiment, and when I asked the men whether they agreed with me, they begged leave to give me a written answer. A few minutes later they presented to me a poster: " Peace at any price and down with the War." In the course of a subsequent talk I had with one of the men, he said to me: " If there are to be no annexations, why do we want that hill top?" My reply was: " I also do not want the hill top, but we must beat the enemy who is occupying it." Finally, the men promised to hold on, but refused to advance, arguing that " the enemy is good to us and has informed us that he will not advance provided we do not move. It is important that we should go home to enjoy freedom and the land. Why should we allow ourselves to be maimed?" Is it to be an offensive or a defensive campaign? Success can be only obtained by an offensive. If we conduct a passive defence the front is bound to be broken. If discipline is strong a break-through may yet be remedied. But we must not forget that we have no well-disciplined troops, that they are badly trained and that the officers have no authority. In these circumstances an enemy success may easily become a catastrophe. The masses must, therefore, be persuaded that we must advance instead of remaining on the defensive.

We thus have many shortcomings, but numerical superiority is still on our side. If the enemy succeeds in breaking the French and the British, he will throw his entire weight upon us and we will then be lost. We need a strong government upon which we could rely, and we whole-heartedly greet the coalition government. The power of the State can only be strong when it leans upon the Army, which represents the armed forces of the nation.

General Dragomirov.—The prevailing spirit in the Army is the desire of peace. Anyone might be popular in the Army who would preach peace without annexations and would advocate self-determination. The illiterate masses have understood the idea of " no annexations " in a peculiar fashion. They do not understand the conditions of different peoples, and they repeatedly ask the question: " Why do not the Allied democracies join in our declarations? " The desire for peace is so strong that reinforcements refuse to accept equipment and arms and say: " They are no good to us as we do not intend to fight." Work has come to a standstill and it is even necessary to see to it that trenches are not dismantled and that roads are mended. In one of the best regiments we found, on the sector which it had occupied, a red banner inscribed: " Peace at all costs." The officer who tore that banner had to flee for his life. During the night men from that regiment were searching for the officer at Dvinsk, as he had been concealed by the Headquarters Staff. The dreadful expression " Adherents of the old régime " caused the best officers to be cast out of the Army. We all wanted a change, and yet many excellent officers, the pride of the Army, had to join the Reserve simply because they tried to prevent the disruption of the Army, but failed to adapt themselves to the new conditions. What is much more fatal is the growth of slackness and of a lingering spirit. Egoism is reaching terrible proportions, and each unit thinks only of its own welfare; endless deputations come to us daily, demanding to be relieved, to remove Commanding Officers, to be re-equipped, etc. All these deputations have to be addressed, and this hinders our work. Orders that used to be implicitly obeyed now demand lengthy arguments; if a battery is moved to a different sector, there is immediate discontent, and the men say: " You are weakening us—you are traitors." Owing to the weakness of the Baltic Fleet, we found it necessary to send an Army Corps to the rear to meet the eventual landing of an enemy force, but we were unable to do so, because the men said: " Our line is long enough as it is and if we lengthen it still more we will be unable to hold the enemy." Formerly we had no difficulty whatsoever in regrouping the troops. In September, 1915, eleven Army Corps were removed from the Western front, and this saved us from a defeat which might have decided the fate of the War. At present such a thing would be impossible, as every unit raises objections to the slightest move. It is very difficult to compel the men to do anything in the interests of the Mother Country. Regiments refuse to relieve their comrades in the firing line under various excuses—such as bad weather, or the fact that not all their men had had their baths. On one occasion a unit refused to go to the front on the plea that it had already been in the firing line at Easter time. We are compelled to ask the Committees of various regiments to argue the matter out. Only a small minority of officers is behaving in an undignified manner, trying to make themselves popular by bowing to the instincts of the men. The system of elections has not been introduced in its entirety, but many unpopular officers have been summarily dismissed as they were accused of being adherents to the old régime; other Commanding Officers, who had been considered incompetent and liable to dismissal, have been made to stay. It was quite impossible not to grant the demands for their retention. With regard to excesses there have been individual cases of shootings of officers.

Things cannot continue on these lines. We want strong power. We have fought for the country. You have taken the ground from under our feet. Will you kindly restore it? Our obligations are colossal, and we must have the power in order to be able to lead to victory the millions of soldiers who are entrusted to our care.

General Stcherbatchov.—The illiteracy of the soldiery is the main reason of all these phenomena. It is not, of course, the fault of our people that it is illiterate. For this the old régime is entirely responsible, as it looked upon education from the point of view of the Ministry of the Interior. Nevertheless, we have to reckon with the fact that the masses do not understand the gravity of our position, and that they misinterpret even such ideas as may be considered reasonable. . . . If we do not wish Russia to collapse, we must continue the struggle and we must advance. Otherwise we shall witness a grotesque sight. The representatives of oppressed Russia fought heroically; but having overthrown the government that was striving for peace with dishonour, the citizens of free Russia are refusing to fight and to safeguard their liberties. This is grotesque, strange, incomprehensible. But it is so. The reason is that discipline has gone and there is no faith in the Commanding Officers. Mother Country, to most men, is an empty sound. These conditions are most painful, but they are particularly painful on the Roumanian front, where one has to reckon not only with military surroundings of specific difficulty, but also with a very complex political atmosphere. Our people are used to plains, and the mountainous nature of the theatre of war has a depressing effect upon the troops. We often hear the complaint: "Do not keep us in these cursed mountains." We have

The Democratisation of the Army

only one railway line to rely upon for supplies, and have great difficulty in feeding the troops. This, of course, enhances discontent. The fact that we are fighting on Roumanian territory is interpreted as a fight " for Roumania," which is also an unpopular idea. The attitude of the local population is not always friendly, and the men come to the conclusion that they are being refused assistance by those on whose behalf they are fighting. Friction thus arises and deepens, because some of the Roumanians blame us for the defeats which they have themselves suffered and owing to which they have lost most of their territory and of their belongings. The Roumanian Government and the Allied representatives are well aware of the ferment in our Army, and their attitude towards us is changing. I personally noticed that a shadow has fallen between us, and that the former respect and faith in the prowess of the Russian Army have vanished. I still enjoy great authority, but if the disruption of the Army continues not only shall we lose our Allies but make enemies of them, and there would then be a danger of peace being made at our expense. In 1914 we advanced across the whole of Galicia. In 1915, in our retreat, we took at the South-Western front 100,000 prisoners. You may judge what that retreat was like and what was the spirit of the troops. In the summer of 1916 we saved Italy from disaster. Is it possible that we may now abandon the Allied cause and be false to our obligations? The Army is in a state of disruption, but that can be remedied. Should we succeed, within a month and a half our brave officers and men would advance again. History will wonder at the inadequate means with which we achieved brilliant results in 1916. If you wish to raise the Russian Army and to convert it into a strong organised body which will dictate the terms of peace, you must help us. All is not lost yet, but only on condition that the Commanding Officers will regain prestige and confidence. We hope that full powers in the Army will once again be vested in the Supreme Commander-in-Chief, who alone can manage the troops. We will obey the will of the Provisional Government, but you must give us strong support.

General Gourko.—If you wish to continue the War till the desired end, you must restore the power of the Army. We have received the draft of the " Declaration " (of the rights of the soldier). Gutchkov would not sign it and has resigned. I am bound to say that if a civilian has resigned and refused to sign that declaration—to us, the Army Chiefs, it is inacceptable. It simply completely destroys everything that is left. I will recount to you an episode which occurred while I was temporarily holding the office of Chief-of-Staff of the Supreme C.-in-C.

On February 13th I had a long talk with the late Czar, trying to persuade him to grant a responsible ministry. As a last trump card, I alluded to our international position, to the attitude of our Allies and to the probable consequences of this measure. But my card was already beaten. I will now endeavour to describe our international position. We have no direct indication of the attitude of our Allies towards our intentions to give up the struggle. We cannot, of course, force them to express their innermost thoughts. As in time of war, one is often compelled to come to a decision " for the enemy," I will now try to argue " for the Allies."

It was easy to begin the Revolution, but we have been submerged by its tidal wave. I trust that common sense will help us to survive this. If not, if the Allies realise our impotence, the principles of practical policy will force upon them the only issue —a separate peace. That would not be on their part a breach of obligations, because we had promised to fight together and have now come to a standstill. If one of the parties is fighting and the other is sitting in the trenches, like a Chinese dragon, waiting for the result of the fight—you must agree that the fighting side may begin to think of making separate peace. Such a peace would, of course, be concluded at our expense. The Austrians and the Germans can get nothing from our Allies: their finance is in a state of collapse and they have no natural riches. Our finances are also in a state of collapse, but we have immense untouched natural resources. Our Allies would, of course, come to such a decision only as a last resort, because it would be not peace, but a lengthy armistice. Bred as they are upon the ideals of the nineteenth century, the Germans, having enriched themselves at our expense, would once again fall upon us and upon our late Allies. You may say that if this is possible why should we not conclude a separate peace first. Here I will mention first of all the moral aspect of the question. The obligation was undertaken by Russia, not merely by the late autocrat. I was aware—long before you had heard of it—of the duplicity of the Czar, who had concluded soon after the Russo-Japanese War of 1904-5 an alliance with the Emperor William, while the Franco-Russian Alliance was still in existence. The free Russian people, responsible for its acts, cannot renounce its obligations. But setting aside the moral aspect, there remains the material problem. If we open negotiations they cannot remain secret, and our Allies would hear of it within two or three days. They would also enter into a parley, and a kind of auction sale would begin. The Allies are, of course, richer than ourselves, but on their side the struggle has not yet ended; besides, our enemies could get much more at our expense.

The Democratisation of the Army 183

It is precisely from the internationl point of view that we must prove our capacity for a continued struggle. I will not continue to revolutionise the Army, because if I should we might find ourselves powerless not only to advance but even to remain on the defensive. The latter is infinitely more difficult. In 1915 we retreated and orders were obeyed. You were entitled to expect this, because we had trained the Army. The position has now been altered; you have created something new and have deprived us of power. You can no longer hold us responsible, and the responsibility must fall heavily upon your heads. You say that the Revolution is still proceeding. Listen to us. We are better acquainted with the psychology of the troops, we have gone with them through thick and thin. Stop the Revolution and give us, the military Chiefs, a chance to do our duty and to bring Russia to such a condition in which you may continue your work. Otherwise, we will hand over to you not Russia, but a field in which our enemies will sow and reap, and Democracy itself will curse you. It will be Democracy that will suffer if the Germans win. Democracy will be starving—while the peasants will always manage to feed themselves on their own land. It was said of the old régime that it " played into the hands of William." Will it be possible to level the same accusation against you? William is fortunate indeed, as both Monarchs and Democracies are playing into his hands. The Army is on the eve of disruption. Our Mother Country is in danger and is nearing a collapse. You must help. It is easy to destroy, and if you know how to destroy—you should also know how to rebuild.

General Alexeiev.—The main points have been stated, and they are true. The Army is on the brink of the abyss. Another step and it will fall into the abyss and will drag along Russia and all her liberties, and there will be no return. Everyone is guilty, and the guilt lies heavily upon all that has been done in that direction for the last two and a half months. We have made every effort and are now devoting all our strength to the task of restoring the Army. We trust that Mr. Kerensky will apply all his qualities of mind and character and all his influence to that consummation, and will help us. But that is not enough. Those who have been disrupting the Army must also help. Those who have issued the Order No. 1 must issue a series of orders and comments. If the " Declaration " is published, as Gutchkov said, the last flimsy foundations will fall into dust and the last hope will be dashed. Be patient, there is time still. That which has been granted in the last two and a half months has not as yet taken root. We have regulations defining rights and duties. All the regulations that are issued nowadays only mention rights. You must do away with the idea that peace will come by itself. Those who say " down with the War " are traitors, and those who say " there should be no advance " are cowards. We still have men with sincere convictions. Let them come to us not as passing stars, but let them live with us and dispel the misunderstandings that have arisen. You have the Press. May it encourage patriotism and demand that everyone do his duty.

Prince Lvov.—We have heard the Commanders-in-Chief, we understand all they have said and will do our duty to our country till the end.

Tzeretelli.—There is no one here who has contributed to the disruption of the Army and played into the hands of William. I have heard the accusation that the Soviet has contributed to the disruption of the Army. And yet everyone agrees that the Soviet is the only institution that enjoys authority at present. What would happen were there no Soviet? Fortunately, Democracy has come to the rescue and we still have hope in salvation. What can you do? There are only two paths for you to follow. One is to reject the policy of the Soviets. But you would then have no source of power wherewith to hold the Army and to lead it for the salvation of Russia. Your other path is the true path, which we have tried; the path of unity with the desires and expectations of the people. If the Commanding Officers have failed to make it quite clear that the whole strength of the Army for the defence of the country lay in the advance, there is no magic wand capable of doing it. It is alleged that the watchword " Without annexations or indemnities " has demoralised the Army and the masses. It is quite likely that it has been misunderstood, but it should have been explained that this was the ultimate aim; we cannot renounce that watchword. We are aware that Russia is in danger, but her defence is a matter for the people as a whole. The Power must be united and must enjoy the confidence of the people, but this can only be achieved if the old policy is completely discarded. Unity can only be based on confidence, which cannot be bought. The ideals of the Soviet are not those of separate and small groups—they are the ideals of the country. To renounce them is to renounce the country. You might, perhaps, understand Order No. 1 if you knew the conditions in which it was issued. We were confronted with an unorganised mob and we had to organise it. The masses of the soldiery do not wish to go on with the War. They are wrong, and I cannot believe that they are prompted by cowardice. It is the result of distrust. Discipline should remain. But if the soldiers realise that you are not fighting against Democracy, they will trust you. By this means the Army may yet be saved. By this means the authority of the Soviet will be strengthened. There is only one way of salvation, the way of confidence and of the Democratisation of the country and of the Army. It is by accepting those principles that the Soviet has gained the confidence of the people and is now in a position to carry out its ideas. As long as that is so, not all is lost. You must try to enhance the confidence in the Soviet.

Skobelev.—We have not come here to listen to reproaches. We know what is going on in the Army. The conditions which you have described are undoubtedly ominous. It will depend upon the spirit of the Russian people whether the ultimate goal will be reached and whether we shall come out of the present difficulty with honour. I consider it necessary to explain the circumstances in which Order No. 1 was issued. In the troops which had overthrown the old régime, the Commanding Officers had not joined the mutineers; we were compelled to issue that Order so as to deprive these officers of authority. We were anxious about the attitude of the front towards the Revolution and about the instructions that were being given. We have proved to-day that our misgivings were not unfounded. Let us speak the truth: the activities of the Commanding Staff have prevented the Army, in these two and a half months, from understanding the Revolution. We quite realise the difficulties of your position. But when you say that the Revolution must be stayed, we are bound to reply that the Revolution cannot begin or end to order. Revolution may take its normal course when the mental process of the Revolution spreads all over the country, when it is understood by the 70 per cent. of illiterate people.

Far be it from us to demand that all Commanding Officers be elected. We agree with you that we have power and have succeeded in attaining it. When you will understand the aims of the Revolution and will help the people to understand our watchword, you will also acquire the necessary power. The people must know what they are fighting for. You are leading the Army for the defeat of the enemy, and you must explain that a strategical advance is necessary in order that the watchwords that have been proclaimed may be vindicated. We trust the new War Minister and hope that a revolutionary Minister will continue our work and will hasten the mental process of the Revolution in the heads of those who think too slowly.

The War Minister—Kerensky.—As Minister and Member of the Government, I must say that we are trying to save the country and to restore the fighting capacity and activities of the Russia-

Army. *We assume responsibility, but we also assume the right to lead the Army* and to show it the path of future development. Nobody has been uttering reproaches here. Everyone has described what he has lived through and has tried to define the causes of events, but our aims and desires are the same. The Provisional Government recognises that the Soviet has played a prominent part and admits its work of organisation—otherwise I would not be War Minister. No one can level accusations at the Soviet. But no one can accuse the Commanding Staffs either, because the officers have borne the brunt of the Revolution quite as much as the rest of the Russian people. Everyone understands the position. Now that my comrades are joining the Government, it will be easier to attain our common aims. There is but one thing for us to do—to save our freedom. I will ask you to proceed to your commands and to remember that the whole of Russia stands behind you and behind the Army. It is our aim to give our country complete freedom. But this cannot be done unless we show the world at large that we are strong in spirit.

General Gourko (replying to Skobelev and Tzeretelli).—We are discussing the matter from different angles. Discipline is the fundamental condition of the existence of the Army. The percentage of losses which a unit may suffer without losing its fighting capacity is the measure of its endurance. I have spent eight months in the South African Republics and have seen regiments of two different kinds: (1) Small, disciplined and (2) Volunteer, undisciplined. The former continued to fight and did not lose their fighting power when their losses amounted to 50 per cent. The latter, although they were volunteers who knew what they were fighting for, left the ranks and fled from the battlefield after losing 10 per cent. No force on earth could induce them to fight. That is the difference between disciplined and undisciplined troops. We demand discipline. We do all we can to persuade. But your authoritative voice must be heard. We must remember that if the enemy advances, we shall fall to pieces like a pack of cards. If you will not cease to revolutionise the Army—you must assume power yourselves.

Prince Lvov.—Our ends are the same and everyone will do his duty. I thank you for your visit and for giving us your views.

* * * * *

The Conference came to a close. The Commanders-in-Chief rejoined their fronts, fully conscious that the last card had been beaten. At the same time, the Soviet orators and the Press started

The Democratisation of the Army

a campaign of abuse against Generals Alexeiev, Gourko and Dragomirov, which rendered their resignations imperative. On the 9th of May, as I already mentioned, Kerensky confirmed the " Declaration " while issuing an Order of the Day on the inadmissibility of senior Commanding Officers relinquishing their posts " in order to shirk responsibility." What was the impression produced by that fateful Order?

Kerensky *afterwards* tried to adduce the excuse that the regulation was drafted before he had assumed office and was approved of by the Executive Committee as well as by " military authorities," and that he had no reason to refuse to confirm it; in a word, that he was compelled to do so. But I recall more than one of Kerensky's speeches in which, believing his course to be the right one, he prided himself on his courage in issuing a Declaration " which Gutchkov had not dared to sign, and which had evoked the protests of all the Commanding Officers." On May 13th the Executive Committee of the Soviets responded to the Declaration by an enthusiastic proclamation which dwelt mainly upon the question of saluting. Poor, indeed, was the mind that inspired this verbiage: " Two months we have waited for this day. Now the soldier is by law a citizen. . . . Henceforward the citizen soldier is free from the servile saluting, and will greet anyone he chooses as an equal and free man. In the Revolutionary Army discipline will live through popular enthusiasm and not by means of compulsory saluting. . " Such were the men who undertook to reorganise the Army.

As a matter of fact, the majority of the Revolutionary Democracy of the Soviets were not satisfied with the Declaration. They described it as " a new enslavement of the soldier," and a campaign was opened for further widening of these rights. Members of the Defencist coalition demanded that the Regimetal Committees should be empowered to challenge the appointments of the Commanding Officers and to give them attestations, as well as that freedom of speech should be granted on service. Their chief demand, however, was for the exclusion of Paragraph 14 of the Declaration entitling the Commanding Officer to use arms in the firing line against insubordination. I need hardly mention the disapproval of the Left, " Defeatist " Section of the Soviet.

The Liberal Press utterly failed to appraise the importance of the Declaration and never treated it seriously. The official organ of the Constitutional Democratic Party (*Retch*, May 11th) had an article which expressed great satisfaction that the Declaration " afforded every soldier the chance of taking part in the political life of the country, definitely freed him from the shackles of the old régime and led him from the stale atmosphere of the old barracks into the fresh air of liberty." It also said that " throughout the world all other armies are remote from politics, whilst the Russian Army will be the first to enjoy the fullness of political rights." Even the Conservative paper (*Novoc Vremia*) said in a leading article: " It is a memorable day; to-day the great Army of mighty Russia becomes truly the Army of the Revolution. . . . Intercourse between warriors of all ranks will henceforward be placed upon the common foundation of a sense of duty binding on every citizen, irrespective of rank. And the Revolutionary Army of regenerated Russia will go forward to the great ordeal of blood with faith in victory and in peace." Difficult, indeed, was the task of the Commanding Officers who were endeavouring to preserve the Army when they found that the fundamental principles upon which the very existence of the Army depended were misunderstood so grossly, even in circles which had heretofore been considered as the mainstay of Russian statesmanship.

The Commanding Officers were still more disheartened, and the Army fell into the abyss with ever-increasing rapidity.

CHAPTER XXI.

The Press and Propaganda.

IN the late World War, along with aeroplanes, tanks, poison gases and other marvels of military *technique*, a new and powerful weapon came to the fore, viz: *p r o p a g a n d a*. Strictly speaking, it was not altogether new, for as far back as 1826 Canning said, in the House of Commons: " Should we ever have to take part in a war we shall gather under our flag all the rebels, all those who, with or without cause, are discontented in the country that goes against us." But now this means of conflict attained an extraordinary development, intensity and organisation, attacking the most morbid and sensitive points of national psychology. Organised on a large scale, supplied with vast means, the propaganda organs of Great Britain, France and America, especially those of Great Britain, carried on a terrible warfare by word of mouth, in the Press, in the films and   . with gold, extending this warfare over the territories of the enemy, the Allies and the neutrals, introducing it into all spheres—military, political, moral and economic. The more so, that Germany especially gave grounds enough for propaganda to have a plentiful supply of irrefragable, evidential material at its disposal. It is difficult to enumerate, even in their general features alone, that enormous arsenal of ideas which, step by step, drop by drop, deepened class differences, undermined the power of the State, sapped the moral powers of the enemy and their confidence in victory, disintegrated their alliance, roused the neutral powers against them and finally raised the falling spirits of their allied peoples. Nevertheless, we should not attach exceptional importance to this external moral pressure, as the leaders of the German people are now doing, to justify themselves: Germany has suffered a political, economic, military and moral defeat. It was only the interaction of all these factors that determined the fatal issue of the struggle, which, towards its end, became a lingering death-agony. One could only marvel at the vitality of the German people, which, by its intellectual power and the stability of its political thought, held out so long, until at last, in November, 1918, "a double death-blow, both at the front and in the rear," laid it in the dust. In connection with this, history will undoubtedly note a great analogy between the parts played by the "Revolutionary Democracies" of Russia and of Germany in the destinies of these peoples. After the *débâcle* the leader of the German Independent Social Democrats acquainted the country with the great and systematic work which they had carried on, from the beginning of 1918, for the breaking down of the German Army and Navy, to the glory of the social revolution. In this work one is struck by the similarity of method and *modus operandi* with those practised in Russia.

While unable to resist British and French propaganda, the Germans were very successful in applying this means to their Eastern antagonist, the more so that: "Russia created her own misfortunes," said Ludendorff, "and the work which we carried on there was not too hard."

The results of the interaction of the skilful hand of Germany with the movements which arose, less from the fact itself of the Revolution than from the individual character of the Russian rebellion, exceeded the highest hopes of the Germans.

The work was carried on in three directions—political, military and social. In the first we note the idea, quite clearly and definitely formulated and systematically carried out by the German Government, *of the dismemberment of Russia*. Its realisation took shape in the proclamation, on November 15, 1916, of the Kingdom of Poland* *with a territory which was to extend eastward " as far as possible ";* in the creation of the States of Courland and Lithuania—"independent," but in union with Germany; in the sharing of the White Russian provinces between Poland and Lithuania, and, finally, in the prolonged and very persistent preparation of the secession of Little Russia, which took place later, in 1918. While the former facts had a meaning only in principle, concerning, as they did, territories actually occupied by the Germans and defined the character of the future "annexations," the attitude assumed by the Central Powers with respect to Little Russia exercised a direct influence on the stability of our South-Western front, creating political complications in the country and separatist tendencies in the Army. I shall return to this question later.

---

* The restoration of Poland in her *ethnographic* frontiers was intended by Russia also.

The Press and Propaganda

The German Headquarters included an excellently organised " press-bureau," which, besides influencing and directing the home Press, also guided German propaganda, which penetrated mainly into Russia and France. Miliukov quotes a circular issued by the German Foreign Office to all its representatives in neutral countries: " You are informed that on the territory of the country to which you are accredited, special offices have been instituted for the organisation of propaganda in the States, now fighting with the German coalition. The propaganda will be engaged in exciting the social movement and, in connection with the latter, strikes, revolutionary outbreaks, separatism, among the constituent parts of these States, and civil war, as well as agitation in favour of disarmament and the cessation of the present sanguinary slaughter. You are instructed to afford all possible protection and support to the directors of the said propaganda offices."

It is curious that, in the summer of 1917, the British Press took up arms against Sir George Buchanan and the British Propaganda Ministry for their inertness in the matter of influencing the Democracy of Russia and of fighting German propaganda in that country. One of the papers pointed out that the British bureau of Russian propaganda had at its head a novelist and literary beginners who had " as much idea of Russia as of Chinese metaphysics."

As for us, neither in our Government departments nor at the Stavka did we have any organ whatever which was even in some degree reminiscent of the mighty Western propaganda institutions. One of the sections of the Quartermaster-General's department had charge of technical questions, concerning relations with the Press, and was left without importance, influence, or any active task. The Russian Army, well or badly, fought in primitive ways, without ever having recourse to that " poisoning of the enemy's spirit," which was so widely practised in the West. And it paid for this with superfluous torrents of blood. But if opinions may differ regarding the morality of destructive propaganda, we cannot but note our complete inertness and inactivity in another and perfectly pure sphere. We did absolutely nothing to acquaint foreign public opinion with the exceptionally important part played by Russia and the Russian Army in the World War, with the enormous losses suffered and the sacrifices made by the Russian people, with those constant majestic deeds of self-sacrifice, incomprehensible, perhaps, to the cold understanding of our Western friends, which the Russian Army made whenever the Allied front was within a hair's-breadth of defeat. . . . Such a want of comprehension of the part played by Russia I have met with almost everywhere, in wide social circles, long after the conclusion of peace, in my wanderings over Europe.

The following small episode is a burlesque, but very characteristic instance of this. On a banner presented to Marshal Foch " from American friends " are depicted the flags of all countries, lands and colonies, which in one way or another came within the orbit of the Entente; the Russian flag occupies the forty-sixth place, after Hayti and Uruguay and immediately after San-Marino.

Is this ignorance or triviality?

We did nothing to lay a firm moral foundation for national unity during our occupation of Galicia, did not draw public opinion to our side during the occupation of Roumania by the Russian troops, did nothing to restrain the Bulgarian people from betraying the interests of the Slavonic races. Finally, we took no advantage of the presence on Russian soil of an enormous number of prisoners, to give them at least a correct idea of Russia.

The Stavka, firmly barricaded within the sphere of purely military questions connected with the carrying out of the campaign, made no attempt to gain any influence over the general course of political events, which agrees completely with the service idea of a national army. But, at the same time, the Stavka distinctly avoided influencing the public spirit of the country so as to lead this powerful factor to moral co-operation in the struggle. There was no connection with the leading organs of the Press, which was represented at the Stavka by men possessing neither weight nor influence.

When the thunderstorm of the Revolution broke and the political whirlwind swept up and convulsed the Army, the Stavka could remain inert no longer. It had to respond. The more so, that suddenly no source of moral power was to be found in Russia which might have protected the Army. The Government, especially the War Office, rushed irresistibly down the path of opportunism; the Soviets and the Socialist Press undermined the Army; the Bourgeois Press now cried " videant consules ne quid Imperio detrimenti caparet," now naïvely rejoiced at the " democratisation and liberation " which were taking place. Even in what might have been considered the competent spheres of the higher military bureaucracy of Petrograd there reigned such a variety of views, as plunged the public opinion of the country into perplexity and bewilderment.

It turned out, however, that for the conflict the Stavka possessed neither organisation nor men, neither technique nor knowledge and experience. And, worst of all, the Stavka was in some way or other shoved and thrown aside by the madly-

The Old Army: a review. General Ivanov.

The Revolutionary Army: a review. Kerensky.

careering chariot of life. Its voice grew weaker and sank into silence.

The second Quartermaster-General—General Markov—had a serious task before him—he had to create the necessary apparatus, to establish communications with the important papers, to supply the Stavka with a " megaphone " and raise the condition of the Army Press, which was leading a wretched existence and which the army organisations were trying to destroy. Markov took up the task warmly, but failed to do anything serious, as he only remained in office two months. Every step of the Stavka in this direction called forth from the Revolutionary Democracy a disingenuous accusation of counter-revolutionary action. And Liberal Bourgeois Moscow, to which he turned for aid, in the form of intellectual and technical assistance in his task, replied with eloquent promises, but did absolutely nothing.

Thus the Stavka had no means at all, not only for actively combating the disintegration of the Army, but for resisting German propaganda, which was spreading rapidly.

Ludendorff says frankly and with a national egotism rising to a high degree of cynicism: " I did not doubt that the *débâcle* of the Russian Army and the Russian people was fraught with great danger for Germany and Austria-Hungary. . . . *In sending Lenin to Russia* our Government assumed an enormous responsibility! This journey was justified from a military point of view; *it was necessary that Russia should fall.* But our Government should have taken measures that this should not happen to Germany." *

Even now the boundless sufferings of the Russian people, now " out of the ranks," did not call forth a single word of pity or regret from its moral corrupters. . . .

With the beginning of the campaign, the Germans altered the direction of their work with respect to Russia. Without breaking their connections with the well-known reactionary circles at Court, in the Government and in the Duma, using all means for influencing these circles and all their motives—greed, ambition, German atavism, and sometimes a peculiar understanding of patriotism—the Germans entered at the same time into close fellowship with the Russian Revolutionaries in the country, and especially abroad, amongst the multitudinous emigrant colony.

---

* *Mes Souvenirs de Guerre.*

Directly or indirectly, all were drawn into the service of the German Government—great agents in the sphere of spying and recruiting, like Parvus (Helfand); provocateurs, connected with the Russian Secret Police, like Blum; propaganda agents— Oulianoff (Lenin), Bronstein (Trotsky), Apfelbaum (Zinovieff), Lunacharsky, Ozolin, Katz (Kamkoff), and many others. And in their wake went a whole group of shallow or unscrupulous people, cast over the frontier and fanatically hating the *régime* which had rejected them—hating it to the degree of forgetfulness of their native land, or squaring accounts with this *régime*, acting sometimes as blind tools in the hands of the German General Staff. What their motives were, what their pay, how far they went—these are details; what is important is that they sold Russia, serving those aims which were set before them by our foe. They were all closely interlaced with one another and with the agents of the German Secret Service, forming with them one unbroken conspiracy.

The work began with a widespread Revolutionary and Separatist (Ukrainian) propaganda among the prisoners of war. According to Liebknecht, " the German Government not only helped this propaganda, but carried it on itself." These aims were served by the Committee of Revolutionary Propaganda, founded in 1915 at The Hague by the Union for the Liberation of the Ukraine in Austria by the Copenhagen Institute (Parvus's organisation), and a whole series of papers of a Revolutionary and Defeatist character, partly published at the expense of the German Staff, partly subsidised by it—the *Social Democrat* (Geneva—Lenin's paper), *Nashe Slovo* (Paris—Trotsky's paper), *Na Tchoozhbeenie* (Geneva—contributions from Tchernoff, Katz and others), *Russkii Viestnik, Rodnaya Retch, Nedielia*, and so forth. Similar to this was the activity—the spread of Defeatist and Revolutionary literature, side by side with purely charitable work—of the Committee of Intellectual Aid to Russian Prisoners of War in Germany and Austria (Geneva), which was in connection with official Moscow and received subsidies from it.

To define the character of these publications it is enough to quote two or three phrases expressing the views of their inspirers. Lenin said in the *Social Democrat:* " The least evil will be the defeat of the Czarist monarchy, the most barbarous and reactionary of all Governments." Tchernoff, the future Minister of Agriculture, declared in the *Mysl* that he had one Fatherland only—the International!

Along with literature the Germans invited Lenin's and Tchernoff's collaborators, especially from the editorial staff of *Na*

The Press and Propaganda

Tchoozhbeenie, to lecture in the camps, while a German spy, Consul Von Pelehe, carried on a large campaign for the recruiting of agitators for propaganda in the ranks of the Army—among the Russian emigrants of conscript age and of Left Wing politics.

All this was but preparatory work. The Russian Revolution opened boundless vistas for German propaganda. Along with honest people, once persecuted, who had struggled for the good of the people, there rushed into Russia all that revolutionary riff-raff which absorbed the members of the Russian secret police, the international informers and the rebels.

The Petrograd authorities feared most of all the accusation of want of Democratic spirit. Miliukov, as Minister, stated repeatedly that " the Government considers unconditionally possible the return to Russia of all emigrants, regardless of their views on the War and independently of their registration in the International Control List.* This Minister carried on a dispute with the British, demanding the release of the Bolsheviks, Bronstein (Trotsky), Zourabov and others, who had been arrested by the British.

Matters were more complicated in the case of Lenin and his supporters. Despite the demands of the Russian Government, the Allies would undoubtedly have refused to let them through. Therefore, as Ludendorff acknowledges, the German Government despatched Lenin and his companions (the first group consisted of seventeen persons) to Russia, allowing them free transit through Germany. This undertaking, which promised extraordinarily important results, was richly financed with gold and credit through the Stockholm (Ganetsky-Fuerstenberg) and Copenhagen (Parvus) centres and through the Russian Siberian Bank. That gold which, as Lenin expressed it, "does not smell."

In October, 1917, Bourtsev published a list of 159 persons brought through Germany to Russia by order of the German General Staff. Nearly all of them, according to Bourtsev, " were revolutionaries who, during the War, had carried on a defeatist campaign in Switzerland and were now William's voluntary or involuntary agents." Many of them at once assumed a prominent position in the Social Democratic party, in the Soviet, the Committee† and the Bolshevik Press. The names of Lenin, Tseder-

---

* These lists contained the names of those suspected of relations with the enemy Governments.

† Among the members of the Committee were, for instance, Zourabov and Perzitch, who had served under Parvus.

baum (Martov), Lunacharsky, Natanson, Riazanov, Apfelbaum (Zinoviev) and others soon became the most fateful in Russian history.

On the day of Lenin's arrival in Petrograd the German paper *Die Woche* devoted an article to this event, in which he was called " a true friend of the Russian people and an honourable antagonist." And the Cadet semi-official organ, the *Retch*, which afterwards boldly and unwaveringly waged war against the Lenin party, greeted his arrival with the words: " Such a generally acknowledged leader of the Socialist party ought now to be in the arena, and his arrival in Russia, whatever opinion may be held of his views, should be welcomed."

On April 3rd Lenin arrived in Petrograd, where he was received with much state, and in a few days declared his theses, part of which formed the fundamental themes of German propaganda: " Down with war and all power to the Soviet! "

Lenin's first actions seemed so absurd and so clearly anarchistic that they called forth protests not only in the whole of the Liberal Press, but also in the greater part of the Socialist Press.

But, little by little, the Left Wing of the Revolutionary Democracy, reinforced by German agents, joined overtly and openly in the propaganda of its chief, without meeting any decisive rebuff either from the double-minded Soviet or the feeble Government. The great wave of German and mutinous propaganda engulfed more and more the Soviet, the Committee, the Revolutionary Press, and the ignorant masses, and was reflected, consciously or unconsciously, even among those who stood at the helm of the State.

From the very first Lenin's organisation, as was said afterwards, in July, in the report of the Procurator of the Petrograd High Court of Justice, " aiming at assisting the States warring against Russia in their hostile actions against her, entered into an agreement with the agents of the said States to forward the disorganisation of the Russian Army and the Russian rear, for which purpose it used the financial means received from these States to organise a propaganda among the population and the troops. . . . and also, for the same purpose, organised in Petrograd, from July 3rd to 5th, an armed insurrection against the Supreme Power existing in the State."

The Stavka had long and vainly raised its voice of warning. General Alexeiev had, both personally and in writing, called on the Government to take measures against the Bolsheviks and the spies. Several times I myself applied to the War Office, sending in, among other things, evidential material concerning Rakovsky's

The Press and Propaganda

spying and documents certifying the treason of Lenin, Skoropis-Yoltoukhovsky and others. The part played by the Union for the Liberation of the Ukraine (of which, besides others, Melenevsky and V. Doroshenko were members)* as an organisation of the Central Powers for propaganda, spying and recruiting for "Setch Ukraine units," was beyond all doubt. In one of my letters (May 16th), based on the examination of a Russian officer, Yermolenko, who had been a prisoner of war and had accepted the part of a German agent for the purpose of disclosing the organisation, the following picture was revealed: "Yermolenko was transferred to our rear, on the front of the Sixth Army, to agitate for a speedy conclusion of a separate peace with Germany. Yermolenko accepted this commission at the insistence of his comrades. Two officers of the German General Staff, Schiditzky and Lubar, informed him that a similar agitation was being carried on in Russia by the sectional president of the Union for the Liberation of the Ukraine, A. Skoropis-Yoltoukhovsky, and by Lenin, as agents of the German General Staff. Lenin had been instructed to seek to undermine by all means the confidence of the Russian people in the Provisional Government. The money for this work was received through one Svendson, an employee of the German Embassy in Stockholm. These methods were practised before the Revolution also. Our command turned its attention to the somewhat too frequent appearance of "escaped prisoners." Many of them having surrendered to the enemy, passed through a definite course of intelligence work, and having received substantial pay and "papers," were permitted to pass over to us through the line of trenches.

Being altogether unable to decide what was a case of courage and what of treachery, we nearly always sent all escaped prisoners from the European to the Caucasian Front.

All the representations of the High Command as to the insufferable situation of the Army, in the face of such vast treachery, remained without result. Kerensky carried on free debates in the Soviet with Lenin on the subject whether the country and the Army should be broken down or not, basing his action on the view that he was the "War Minister of the Revolution," and that "freedom of opinion was sacred to him, whencesoever it might proceed." Tzeretelli warmly defended Lenin:

---

* It is curious that Bronstein (Trotsky)—a person sufficiently competent in the matter of secret communications with the Staffs of our antagonists—said in the *Izvestia* for July 8th, 1917: "In the paper *Nashe Slovo* I have exposed and pilloried Skoropis-Yoltoukhovsky, Potok and Melenevsky as agents of the Austrian General Staff."

" I do not agree with Lenin and his agitation. But what has been said by Deputy Shulgin is a slander against Lenin, *Never has Lenin called for actions which would infringe upon the course of the Revolution. Lenin is carrying on an idealist propaganda.*"

This much-talked-of freedom of opinion extremely simplified the work of German propaganda, giving rise to such an unheard-of phenomenon as the open preaching in German, at public meetings and in Kronstadt, of a separate peace and of distrust of the Government, by an agent of Germany, the President of the Zimmerwald and Kienthal Conference, Robert Grimm!

What a state of moral prostration and loss of all national dignity, consciousness, and patriotism is presented by the picture of Tzeretelli and Skobelev " vouching " for the *agent provocateur;* of Kerensky importuning the Government to grant Grimm the right of entry into Russia; of Tereshtchenko permitting it, and of Russians listening to Grimm's speeches—without indignation, without resentment.

During the Bolshevik insurrection of July the officials of the Ministry of Justice, exasperated by the laxity of the leaders of the Government, decided, with the knowledge of their Minister, Pereverzev, to publish my letter to the Minister of War and other documents, exposing Lenin's treason to his country. The documents being a statement signed by two Socialists, Alexinsky and Pankratov, were given to the printers. The premature disclosure of this fact called forth a passionate protest from Tchkheidze and Tzeretelli, and terrible anger on the part of the Ministers Nekrassov and Tereshtchenko. The Government forbade the publication of information which sullied the good name of comrade Lenin, and had recourse to reprisals against the officials of the Ministry of Justice. However, the statement appeared in the Press. In its turn the Executive Committee of the Soviet of Workmen's and Soldiers' Delegates exhibited a touching care, not only for the inviolability of the Bolsheviks, but even for their honour, by issuing on July 5th a special appeal calling on people " to refrain from the spreading of accusations reflecting dishonour " on Lenin and " other political workers " pending the investigation of the matter by a special commission. This consideration was openly expressed in a resolution passed by the Central Executive Committees (on July 8th), which, while condemning the attempt of the Anarchist-Bolshevist elements to overthrow the Government, expressed the fear that the " inevitable " measures to which the Government and the military authorities

The Press and Propaganda

must have recourse . . . would create a basis for the demagogic agitation of the counter-Revolutionaries who, for the time being, gathered round the flag of the Revolutionary régime, but who might pave the way for a military Dictatorship."

However, the exposure of the direct criminal participation of the leaders of Bolshevism in acts of mutiny and treason may have obliged the Government to begin repressions. Lenin and Apfelbaum (Zinoviev) escaped to Finland, while Bronstein (Trotsky), Kozlovsky, Raskolnikov, Remniov, and many others were arrested. Several Anarchist-Bolshevist newspapers were suspended.

These repressions, however, were not of a serious character. Many persons known to have been leaders in the mutiny were not charged at all, and their work of destruction was continued with consistency and energy.

While carrying the war into our country the Germans persistently and methodically put into practice another watchword—peace at the Front. Fraternisation had taken place earlier as well, before the Revolution; but it was then due to the hopelessly wearisome life in the trenches, to curiosity, to a simple feeling of humanity even towards the enemy—a feeling exhibited by the Russian soldier more than once on the battlefield of Borodino, in the bastions of Sevastopol, and in the Balkan mountains. Fraternisation took place rarely, was punished by the commanders, and had no dangerous tendencies in it. But now the German General Staff organised it on a large scale, systematically and along the whole Front, with the participation of the higher Staff organs and the commanders, with a detailed code of instructions, which included the observation of our forces and positions, the demonstration of the impressive armament and strength of their own positions, persuasion as to the aimlessness of the War, the incitement of the Russian soldiers against the Government and their commanders, in whose interest exclusively this " sanguinary slaughter " was being continued. Masses of the Defeatist literature manufactured in Germany were passed over into our trenches, and at the same time agents of the Soviet and the Committee travelled quite freely along the Front with similar propaganda, with the organisation of " exhibition fraternisation," and with whole piles of *Pravda, Trench Pravda, Social Democrat,* and other products of our native Socialist intellect and conscience —organs which, in their forceful argumentation, left the Jesuitical eloquence of their German brethren far behind. At the same time a general meeting of simple " delegates from the Front " in Petrograd was passing a resolution in favour of allowing fraternisation for the purpose of revolutionary propaganda among the enemy's ranks!

One cannot read without deep emotion of the feelings of Kornilov, who, for the first time after the Revolution, in the beginning of May, when in command of the Eighth Army, came into contact with this fatal phenomenon in the life of our Front. They were written down by Nezhintsev, at that time captain of the General Staff and later the gallant commander of the Kornilov Regiment, who in 1918 fell in action against the Bolsheviks at the storm of Ekaterinodar.

" When we had got well into the firing zone of the position," writes Nezhintsev, " the General (Kornilov) looked very gloomy. His words, ' disgrace, treason,' showed his estimate of the dead silence of the position. Then he remarked:

" ' Do you feel all the nightmare horror of this silence? You understand that we are watched by the enemy artillery observers and that we are not fired at. Yes, the enemy are mocking us as weaklings. Can it be that the Russian soldier is capable of informing the enemy of my arrival at the position?'

" I was silent, but the sacred tears in the eyes of this hero touched me deeply, and at this moment I vowed in my mind that I would die for him and for our common Motherland. General Kornilov seemed to feel this. He turned to me suddenly, pressed my hand, and turned away, as if ashamed of his momentary weakness.

" The acquaintance of the new Commander with the infantry began with the units in the Reserve, when formed in rank, holding a meeting and replying to all appeals for the necessity of an advance by pointing out how useless it was to continue a Bourgeois war, carried on by ' militarists.' When, after two hours of fruitless discussion, General Kornilov, worn out morally and physically, proceeded to the trenches, he found a scene there which could scarcely have been foreseen by any soldier of this age.

" We entered into a system of fortifications where the trench-lines of both sides were separated or, more correctly, joined by lines of barbed wire . The appearance of General Kornilov was greeted . . by a group of German officers, who gazed insolently on the Commander of the Russian Army; behind them stood some Prussian soldiers. The General took my field-glasses and, ascending the parapet, began to examine the arena of the

Before the battle in the Revolutionary Army: a meeting.

Types of men in the Revolutionary Army.

fights to come. When someone expressed a fear that the Prussians might shoot the Russian Commander, the latter replied:

" ' I would be immensely glad if they did; perhaps it might sober our befogged soldiers and put an end to this shameful fraternisation.'

" At the positions of a neighbouring regiment the Commander of the Army was greeted by the *bravura* march of a German Jaeger regiment, to whose band our ' fraternising ' soldiers were making their way. With the remark, ' This is treason! ' the General turned to an officer standing next him, ordering the fraternisers from both sides to be told that if this disgraceful scene did not cease at once he would turn the guns loose on them. The disciplined Germans ceased playing and returned to their own trenches, seemingly ashamed of the abominable spectacle. But our soldiers—oh! they held meetings for a long time, complaining of the way their ' counter-Revolutionary commanders oppressed their liberty.' "

In general I do not cherish feelings of revenge. Yet I regret exceedingly that General Ludendorff left the German Army prematurely, before its break-up, and did not experience directly in its ranks those inexpressibly painful moral torments which we Russian officers have suffered.

Besides fraternisation, the enemy High Command practised, on an extensive scale and with provocatory purpose, the dispatch of flags of truce directly to the troops, or rather to the soldiers. Thus, about the end of April on the Dvinsk Front there came with a flag of truce a German officer, who was not received. He managed, however, to address to the crowd of soldiers the words: " I have come to you with offers of peace, and am empowered to speak even with the Provisional Government, but your commanders do not wish for peace." These words were spread rapidly, and caused agitation among the soldiers and even threats to desert the Front. Therefore when, a few days later, in the same section, *parliamentaires* (a brigade commander, two officers, and a bugler) made their appearance again, they were taken to the Staff quarters of the Fifth Army. It turned out, of course, that they had no authorisations, and could not even state more or less definitely the object of their coming, since " the sole object of the pseudo-*parliamentaires* appearing on our Front," says an order of the Commander-in-Chief, " has been to observe our dispositions and our spirit, and, by a lying exhibition of their pacific feelings, to incline our troops to an inaction profitable to the Germans and ruinous to Russia and her freedom." Similar cases occurred on the Fronts of the Eighth, Ninth, and other Armies.

It is characteristic that the Commander-in-Chief of the Eastern German Front, Prince Leopold of Bavaria, found it possible to take a personal part in this course of provocation. In two radiograms, bearing the systematic character of the customary proclamations and intended for the soldiers and the Soviet, he stated that the High Command was ready to meet half-way " the repeatedly expressed desire of the Russian Soldiers' Delegates to put an end to bloodshed "; that " military operations between us (the Central Powers) and Russia could be put an end to *without Russia breaking with her Allies* "; that " if Russia wants to know the particulars of our conditions, let her give up her demand for their publication. . ." And he finishes with a threat: " Does the new Russian Government, instigated by its Allies, wish to satisfy itself whether divisions of heavy guns are still to be found on our Eastern Front? "

Earlier, when leaders did discreditable things to save their armies and their countries, at least they were ashamed of it and kept silence. Nowadays military traditions have undergone a radical change.

To the credit of the Soviet it must be said that it took a proper view of this provocationary invitation, saying in reply: " The Commander-in-Chief of the German troops on the Eastern Front offers us ' a separate truce and secrecy of negotiations.' But Russia knows that the *débâcle* of the Allies will be the beginning of the *débâcle* of her own Army, and the *débâcle* of the Revolutionary troops of Free Russia would mean not only new common graves, but the failure of the Revolution, the fall of Free Russia."

From the very first days of the Revolution a marked change naturally took place in the attitude of the Russian Press. It expressed itself on the one hand in a certain differentiation of all the Bourgeois organs, which assumed a Liberal-Conservative character, the *tactics* of which were adopted by an inconsiderable part of the Socialist Press, of the type of Plekhanov's *Yedinstvo;* and on the other in the appearance of an immense number of Socialist organs.

The organs of the Right Wing underwent a considerable evolution, a characteristic indication of which was the unexpected declaration of a well-known member of the *Novoye Vremya* staff,

Mr. Menshikov: "We must be grateful to destiny that the Monarchy, which for a thousand years has betrayed the people, has at last betrayed itself and put a cross on its own grave. To dig it up from under that cross and start a great dispute about the candidates for the fallen throne would be, in my opinion, a fatal mistake." In the course of the first few months the Right Press partly closed down—not without pressure and violence on the part of the Soviets—partly it assumed a pacific-Liberal attitude. It was only in September, 1917, that its tone grew extremely violent in connection with the final exposure of the weakness of the Government, the loss of all hope of a legal way out of the "no thoroughfare" which had arisen, and the echoes of Kornilov's venture. The attacks of the extremist organs on the Government passed into solid abuse of it.

Though differing in a greater or lesser degree in its understanding of the social problems which the Revolution had to solve, though guilty, perhaps, along with Russian society, of many mistakes, yet the Russian Liberal Press showed an exceptional unanimity in the more important questions of a constitutional and national character: full power to the Provisional Government, Democratic reforms in the spirit of the programme of March 2nd,* war until victory along with the Allies, an All-Russia Constituent Assembly as the source of the supreme power and of the constitution of the country. In yet another respect has the Liberal Press left a good reputation behind it in history: in the days of lofty popular enthusiasm, as in the days of doubt, vacillation and general demoralisation, which distinguished the Revolutionary period of 1917, no place was found in it, nor in the Right Press either, for the distribution of German gold. . . .

The appearance, on a large scale, of the new Socialist Press was accompanied by a series of unfavourable circumstances. It had no normal past, no traditions. Its prolonged life below the surface, the exclusively destructive method of action adopted by it, its suspicious and hostile attitude towards all authority, put a certain stamp on the whole tendency of this Press, leaving too little place and attention for creative work. The complete discord in thought, the contradictions and vacillation which reigned both within the Soviet and also among the party groups and within the parties, were reflected in the Press, just as much as the elemental pressure from below of irresistible, narrowly egotistic class demands; for neglect of these demands gave rise to the

---

* V. chap. IV.—Of course articles 7 and 8 did not meet with the approval of public opinion.

threat, which was once expressed by the " beauty and pride of the Revolution," the Kronstadt sailors to Tchernov, the Minister: " If you will not give us anything, Michael Alexandrovitch will." Finally, the Press was not uninfluenced by the appearance in it of a number of such persons as brought into it an atmosphere of uncleanness and perfidy. The papers were full of names, which had emerged from the sphere of crime, of the Secret Police and of international espionage. All these gentlemen—Tchernomazov (a provocator in the Secret Police and director of the pre-Revolutionary *Pravdo*), Berthold (the same and also editor of the *Communist*), Dekonsky, Malinovsky, Matislavsky, those colleagues of Lenin and Gorky—Nahamkes, Stoutchka, Ouritsky, Gimmer (Soukhanov), and a vast number of equally notorious names—brought the Russian Press to a hitherto unknown degree of moral degradation.

The difference was only a matter of scope. Some papers, akin to the Soviet semi-official organ, the *Izvestia of the Workmen's and Soldiers' Delegates*, undermined the country and the Army, while others of the *Pravda* type (the organ of the Bolshevik Social Domocrats) broke them down.

At the same time as the *Izvestia* would call on its readers to support the Provisional Government, while secretly ready to strike a blow at it, the *Pravda* would declare that " the Government is counter-Revolutionary, and therefore there can be no relations with it. The task of the Revolutionary Democracy is to attain to the dictatorship of the proletariat." And Tchernov's Socialist Revolutionary organ, the *Delo Naroda*, would discover a neutral formula: all possible support to the Coalition Government, but " there is not, and cannot be, any unanimity in this question; more than that, there must not be, in the interests of the double defence."

At the same time as the *Izvestia* began to preach an advance, but without a final victory, not abandoning, however, the intention of " deciding over the heads of the Government and the ruling classes the conditions on which the War might be stopped," the *Pravda* called for universal fraternisation, and the Socialist Revolutionary, *Zemlia i Volia*, alternately grieved that Germany still wished for conquest, or demanded a separate peace. Tchernov's paper, which in March had considered that, " should the enemy be victorious, there would be an end to Russian freedom," now, in May, saw in the preaching of an advance " the limit of unblushing gambling on the fate of the Fatherland, the limit of irresponsibility and demagogy." Gorky's paper, *Novaya Zhizn*, speaking through Gimmer (Soukhanov), rises to cynicism when it says:

The Press and Propaganda

" When Kerensky gives orders for *Russian soil to be cleared of enemy troops*, his demands far exceed the limits of military *technique*. He calls for a political act, one which has never been provided for by the Coalition Government. For clearing the country by an advance signifies ' complete victory ' . . ." Altogether the *Novaya Zhizn* supported German interests with especial warmth, raising its voice in all cases when German interests were threatened with danger, either on the part of the Allies or on ours. And when the advance of the disorganised Army ended in failure—in Tarnopol and Kalush—when Riga had fallen, the Left Press started a bitter campaign against the Stavka and the commanding personnel, and Tchernov's paper, in connection with the proposed reforms in the Army, cried hysterically : " Let the proletarians know that it is proposed again to give them up to the iron embrace of beggary, slavery and hunger. .
Let the soldiers know that it is proposed again to enslave them with the ' discipline ' of their commanders and to force them to shed their blood without end, so long as the belief of the Allies in Russia's ' gallantry ' is restored." The most straightforward of all, however, was afterwards the *Iskra*, the organ of the Menshevist Internationalists (Martov-Zederbaum), which, on the day of the occupation of the island of Oesel by a German landing-party, published an article entitled " Welcome to the German Fleet ! "

The Army had its own military Press. The organs of the Army staffs and of those at the Front, which used to appear before the Revolution, were of the nature of purely military bulletins. Beginning with the Revolution, these organs, with their weak literary forces, began to fight for the existence of the Army, conscientiously, honestly, but not cleverly. Meeting with indifference or exasperation on the part of the soldiers, who had already turned their backs on the officers, and especially on the part of the Committee organs of the " Revolutionary " movement, which existed side by side with them, they began to weaken and die out, until at last, in the days of August, an order from Kerensky closed them altogether; the exclusive right of publishing Army newspapers was transferred to the Army Committee and the Committees of the troops at the Front. The same fate befell the *News of the Active Army*, the Stavka organ, started by General Markov and left without support from the weighty powers of the Press of the capital.

The Committee Press, widely spread among the troops at the expense of the Government, reflected those moods of which I have spoken earlier in the chapter on the Committees, ranging from Constitutionalism to Anarchism, from complete victory to an immediate conclusion of peace, without orders. It reflected—but in a worse, more sorry form, as regards literary style and content—that disharmony of thought and those tendencies towards extreme theories which characterised the Socialist Press of the Capital. In this respect, in accordance with the personnel of the Committees, and to some extent with their proximity to Petrograd, the respective Fronts differed somewhat from one another. The most moderate was the South-Western Front, somewhat worse, the Western, while the Northern Front was pronouncedly Bolshevist. Besides local talent, the columns of the Committee Press were in many cases opened wide to the resolutions not only of the extreme national parties, but even of the German parties.

It would be incorrect, however, to speak of the immediate action of the Press on the masses of the soldiers. It did not exist any more than there were any popular newspapers which these masses could understand. The Press exercised an influence principally on the semi-educated elements in the ranks of the Army. This sphere turned out to be nearer to the soldiers, and to it passed a certain share of that authority which was enjoyed earlier by the officers. Ideas gathered from the papers and refracted through the mental prism of this class passed in a simplified form to the soldiery, the vast majority of which unfortunately consisted of ignorant and illiterate men. And among these masses all these conceptions, stripped of cunningly-woven arguments, premises and grounds, were transformed into wondrously simple and terrifically logical conclusions.

In them dominated the straightforward negation: " Down! "

Down with the Bourgeois Government, down with the counter-Revolutionary Commanders, down with the "sanguinary slaughter," down with everything of which they were sick, of which they were wearied, all that in one way or another interfered with their animal instincts and hampered " free will "—down with them all!

In such an elementary fashion did the Army at innumerable soldiers' meetings settle all the political and social questions that were agitating mankind.

* * *

The curtain has fallen. The Treaty of Versailles has for a time given pause to the armed conflict in Central Europe. Evident to the end that, having regained their strength, the nations may again take up their arms, so as to burst the chains in which defeat has fettered them.

The Press and Propaganda

The idea of the "world-peace," which the Christian churches have been preaching for twenty centuries, is buried for years to come.

To us, how childishly naïve now seem the efforts of the humanists of the nineteenth century, who by prolonged, ardent propaganda sought to soften the horrors of war and to introduce the limiting norms of International Law! Yes, now, when we know that one may not only infringe the neutrality of a peaceful, cultured country, but give it to be ravaged and plundered; when we can sink peaceable ships, with women and children on board, by means of submarines; poison people with suffocating gases and tear their bodies with the fragments of explosive bullets; when a whole country, a whole nation, is quoted by cold, political calculation merely as a "Barrier" against the invasion of armed force and pernicious ideas, and is periodically either helped or betrayed in turn.

But the most terrible of all weapons ever invented by the mind of man, the most shameful of all the methods permitted in the late World War was *the poisoning of the soul of a people!*

Germany assigns the priority of this invention to Great Britain. Let them settle this matter between themselves. But I see my native land crushed, dying in the dark night of horror and insanity And I know her tormentors.

Two theses have arisen before mankind in all their grim power and all their shameless nakedness:

All is permissible for the advantage of one's country!

All is permissible for the triumph of one's party, one's class!

All, even the moral and physical ruin of an enemy country, even the betrayal of one's native land and the making on its living body of *social experiments,* the failure of which threatens it with paralysis and death.

Germany and Lenin unhesitatingly decided these questions in the affirmative. The world has condemned them; but are all those who speak of the matter so unanimous and sincere in their condemnation? Have not these ideas left somewhat too deep traces in the minds, not so much perhaps of the popular masses as of their leaders? I, at least, am led to such a conclusion by all the present soulless world policy of the Governments, especially towards Russia, by all the present utterly selfish tactics of the class organisations.

This is terrible.

I believe that every people has the right to defend its existence, sword in hand; I know that for many years to come war will be the customary method of settling international disputes, and that methods of warfare will be both honourable and, alas! dishonourable. But there is a certain limit, beyond which even baseness ceases to be simply baseness and becomes insanity. This limit we have already reached. And if religion, science, literature, philosophers, humanitarians, teachers of mankind do not arouse a broad, idealistic movement against the Hottentot morality with which we have been inoculated, the world will witness the decline of its civilisation.

Before the battle in the Old Army Prayers.

CHAPTER XXII.

The Condition of the Army at the July Advance.

HAVING outlined a whole series of conditions which exercised an influence on the life, spirit, and military efficiency of the once famous Russian Army, I shall now pass to the sorrowful tale of its fall.

I was born in the family of an officer of the line, and for twenty-two years (including the two years of the Russo-Japanese War) before the European War served in the ranks of modest line units and in small Army Staffs. I shared the life, the joys and the sorrows of the officer and the soldier, and devoted many pages in the Military Press to their life which was my own. From 1914 to 1920, almost without interval, I stood at the head of the troops and led them into battle on the fields of White Russia, Volynia, Galicia, in the mountains of Hungary, in Roumania, and then—then in the bitter internecine war which, with bloody share, ploughed up our native land.

I have more grounds and more right to speak of the Army and in the name of the Army than all those strangers of the Socialist Camp, who, in their haughty self-conceit, as soon as they touched the Army, began breaking down its foundations, judging its leaders and fighters and diagnosing its serious disease, who even now, after grievous experiments and experiences, have not given up the hope of transforming this mighty and terrible weapon of national self-preservation into a means for satisfying party and social appetites. For me, the Army is not only an historical, social, national phenomenon, but nearly the whole of my life, in which lie many memories, precious and not to be forgotten, in which all is bound up and interlaced into one general mass of swiftly passing days of sadness and of joy, in which there are hundreds of cherished graves, of buried dreams and unextinguishable faith.

The Army should be approached cautiously, never forgetting

that not only its historical foundations, but even such details of its life as may, perhaps, seem strange and absurd, have their meaning and significance.

When the Revolution began that old veteran, beloved by both officers and soldiers, General P. I. Mishtchenko, being unable to put up with the new régime, retired from the Army. He lived at Temir-Han Shoura, never went outside his garden fence, and always wore his General's uniform and his crosses of St. George, even in the days of Bolshevik power. One day the Bolsheviks came to search his house, and, among other things, wanted to deprive him of his shoulder straps and decorations. The old General retired to a neighbouring room and shot himself.

Let whoever will laugh at " old-fashioned prejudices." We shall reverence his noble memory.

And so the storm-cloud of the Revolution broke.

There was no doubt whatever that such a cataclysm in the life of the nation could not but have a grave effect. The Revolution *was bound* to convulse the Army, greatly weakening and breaking all its historic ties. Such a result was normal, natural and unavoidable, independently of the condition of the Army at the moment, independently of the mutual relations of Commanders and subordinates. We can speak only of the circumstances which arrested or hastened the disintegration of the Army.

A Government appeared.

Its source might have been one of three elements: The High Command (a military dictatorship), the Bourgeois State Duma (the Provisional Government), or the Revolutionary Democracy (the Soviet). It was the Provisional Government that was acknowledged. The attitude of the other two elements towards it was different; the Soviet practically robbed the Government of its power, while the High Command submitted to it implicitly, and was therefore obliged to carry out its plans.

The Government had two courses open to it; it could combat the disintegrating influences which began to appear in the Army by stern and ruthless measures, or it could encourage them. Owing to pressure from the Soviet and partly through want of firmness and through misunderstanding of the laws of existence of armed forces, the Government chose the second course.

This circumstance decided the fate of the Army. All other circumstances could but influence the duration of the process of disruption and its depth.

The festive days of touching and joyous union between the officers and the soldiers vanished rapidly, being replaced by tiresome, weary week-days. But they had been in the past, those days

Types of soldiers of the Old Army. This company was sent to the West European Front.

of joy, and, therefore, no impassable abyss existed between the two Ranks, over which the inexorable logic of life had long been casting a bridge. The unnecessary, obsolete methods, which had introduced an element of irritation into the soldiery, fell away at once, as of themselves; the officers became more thoughtful and industrious.

Then came a torrent of newspapers, appeals, resolutions, orders, from some unknown authority, and with them a whole series of new ideas, which the soldier masses were unable to digest and assimilate. New people appeared, with a new speech, so fascinating and promising, liberating the soldiers from obedience and inspiring hope that they would be saved from deadly danger immediately. When one Regimental Commander naïvely inquired whether these people might not be tried by Field Court-Martial and shot, his telegram, after passing through all official stages, called forth the reply from Petrograd that these people were inviolable, and had been sent by the Soviet to the troops for the very purpose of explaining to them the true meaning of current events.

When such leaders of the Revolutionary Democracy, as have not yet lost their feeling of responsibility for crucified Russia, now say that the movement, caused by the deep class differences between the officers and the soldiers and by "the enslavement" of the latter, was of an elemental nature, which they could not resist, this is deeply untrue.

All the fundamental slogans, all the programmes, tactics, instructions and text-books, forming the foundation of the "democratisation" of the Army, had been drawn up by the military sections of the secret Socialist parties long before the War, outside of "elemental" pressure, on the grounds of clear, cold calculation, as a product of "Socialist reasoning and conscience."

True, the officers strove to persuade the men not to believe the "new words" and to do their duty. But from the very beginning the Soviets had declared the officers to be foes of the Revolution; in many towns they had been subjected to cruel torture and death, and this with impunity. Evidently not without some reason, when even the "Bourgeois" Duma issued such a strange and unexpected "announcement" as the following: "This first day of March, rumours were spread among the soldiers of the garrison of Petrograd to the effect that the officers in the regiments were disarming the soldiers. These rumours were investigated and found to be false. As President of the Military Commission of the Provisional Committee of the State

Duma, I declare that the most decided measures *will be* taken to prevent such action on the part of the officers, up to the shooting of those guilty of it. Signed, COLONEL ENGELHARDT."

Next came Order No. I., the Declaration and so forth.

Perhaps, however, it might have been possible to combat all this verbal ocean of lies and hypocrisy which flowed from Petrograd and from the local Soviets and was echoed by the local demagogues had it not been for a circumstance which paralysed all the efforts of the Commanders, viz., the animal feeling of self-preservation which had flooded the whole mass of the soldiers. This feeling had always existed. But it had been kept under and restrained by examples of duty fulfilled, by flashes of national self-consciousness, by shame, fear and pressure. When all these elements had disappeared, when for the soothing of a drowsy conscience there was a whole arsenal of new conceptions, which justified the care for one's own hide and furnished it with an ideal basis, then the Army could exist no longer. This feeling upset all the efforts of the Commanders, all moral principles and the whole regiment of the Army.

In a large, open field, as far as the eye can see, run endless lines of trenches, sometimes coming close up to each other, interlacing their barbed wire fences, sometimes running far off and vanishing behind a verdant crest. The sun has risen long ago, but it is still as death in the field. The first to rise are the Germans. In one place and another their figures look out from the trenches; a few come out on to the parapet to hang their clothes, damp after the night, in the sun. A sentry in our front trench opens his sleepy eyes, lazily stretches himself, after looking indifferently at the enemy trenches. A soldier in a dirty shirt, bare-footed, with coat slung over his shoulders, cringing under the morning cold, comes out of his trench and plods towards the German positions, where, between the lines, stands a " post-box "; it contains a new number of the German paper, *The Russian Messenger*, and proposals for barter.

All is still. Not a single gun is to be heard. Last week the Regimental Committee issued a resolution against firing, even against distance firing; let the necessary distances be estimated by the map. A Lieutenant-Colonel of the gunners—a member of the Committee—gave his full approval to this resolution. When yesterday the Commander of a field battery began firing at a new enemy trench, our infantry opened rifle fire on our observation post and wounded the telephone operator. During the night the infantry lit a fire on the position being constructed for a newly arrived heavy battery.*

Nine a.m. The first Company gradually begins to awaken. The trenches are incredibly defiled; in the narrow communication trenches and those of the second line the air is thick and close. The parapet is crumbling away. No one troubles to repair it; no one feels inclined to do so, and there are not enough men in the Company. There is a large number of deserters; more than fifty have been allowed to go. Old soldiers have been demobilised, others have gone on leave with the arbitrary permission of the Committee. Others, again, have been elected members of numerous Committees, or gone away as delegates; a while ago, for instance, the Division sent a numerous delegation to "Comrade" Kerensky to verify whether he had really given orders for an advance. Finally, by threats and violence, the soldiers have so terrorised the regimental surgeons that the latter have been issuing medical certicates even to the "thoroughly fit."

In the trenches the hours pass slowly and wearily, in dullness and idleness. In one corner men are playing cards, in another a soldier returned from leave is lazily and listlessly telling a story; the air is full of obscene swearing. Someone reads aloud from the *Russian Messenger* the following:

"The English want the Russians to shed the last drop of their blood for the greater glory of England, who seeks her profit in everything. . . . Dear soldiers, you must know that Russia would have concluded peace long ago had not England prevented her. . . . We must turn away from her—the Russian people demand it; such is their sacred will."

Someone or other swears.

"Don't you wish for peace. *They* make peace, the ——; we shall die here, without getting our freedom!"

Along the trenches came Lieutenant Albov, the Company Commander. He said to the groups of soldiers, somewhat irresolutely and entreatingly:

"Comrades, get to work quickly. In three days we have not made a single communication trench to the firing line."

The card players did not even look round; someone said in a low voice, "All right." The man reading the newspaper rose and reported, in a free and easy manner:

---

* Generally speaking, the special services, and especially the artillery, retained their likeness to human beings, as well as a certain amount of discipline, much longer than the infantry.

"The Company does not want to dig, because that would be preparation for an advance, and the Committee has resolved. . . ."

"Look here, you understand nothing at all about it, and, moreover, why do you speak for the whole Company? Even if we remain on the defensive we are lost in case of an alarm; the whole Company cannot get out to the firing line along a single trench."

He said this, and with a gesture of despair went on his way. Matters were hopeless. Every time he tried to speak with them for a time, and in a friendly way, they would listen to him attentively; they liked to talk to him, and, on the whole, his Company looked on him favourably in their own way. But he felt that between him and them a wall had sprung up, against which all his good impulses were shattered. He had lost the path to their soul—lost it in the impassable jungle of darkness, roughness, and that wave of distrust and suspicion which had overwhelmed the soldiers. Was it, perhaps, that he used the wrong words, or was not able to say what he meant? Scarcely that. But a little while before the War, when he was a student and was carried away by the popular movement, he had visited villages and factories and had found "real words" which were clear and comprehensible to all. But, most of all, with what words can one move men to face death when all their feelings are veiled by one feeling—that of self-preservation?

The train of his thoughts was broken by the sudden appearance of the Regimental Commander.

"What the devil does this mean? The man on duty does not come forward. The men are not dressed. Filth and stench. What are you about, Lieutenant?"

The grey-headed Colonel cast a stern glance on the soldiers which involuntarily impressed them. They all rose to their feet. He glanced through a loop-hole and, starting back, asked nervously:

"What is that?"

In the green field, among the barbed wire, a regular bazaar was going on. A group of Germans and of our men were bartering vodka, tobacco, lard, bread. Some way off a German officer reclined on the grass—red-faced, sturdy, with an arrogant look on his face—and carried on a conversation with a soldier named Soloveytchick; and, strange to say, the familiar and insolent Soloveytchick stood before the Lieutenant respectfully.

The Colonel pushed the observer aside and, taking his rifle from him, put it through the loop-hole. A murmur was heard

among the soldiers. They began to ask him not to shoot. One of them, in a low voice, as if speaking to himself, remarked:
" This is provocation."
The Colonel, crimson with fury, turned to him for a moment and shouted:
" Silence ! "
All grew silent and pressed to the loop-hole. A shot was heard, and the German officer convulsively stretched himself out and was still; blood was running from his head. The haggling soldiers scattered.

The Colonel threw the rifle down and, muttering through his teeth " Scoundrels! " strode further along the trenches. The " truce " was infringed.

The Lieutenant went off to his hut. His heart was sad and empty. He was oppressed by the realisation of his unwantedness and uselessness in these absurd surroundings, which perverted the whole meaning of that service to his country, which alone justified all his grave troubles and the death which might perhaps be near. He threw himself on his bed, where he lay for an hour, for two hours, striving to think of nothing, to forget himself.

But from beyond the mud wall, where the shelter lay, there crept someone's muffled voice, which seemed to wrap his brain in a filthy fog

" It is all very well for them, the ——. They receive their hundred and forty roubles a month clear, while we—so generous of them—get seven and a half. Wait a bit, our turn will come."

Silence.

" I hear they are sharing the land in our place in the province of Kharkov. If I could only get home."

There was a knock at the door. The Sergeant-Major had come.

" Your honour (so he always addressed his Company Commander in the absence of witnesses), the Company is angry, and threatens to leave the position if it is not relieved at once. The Second Battalion should have relieved us at five o'clock, and it is not here yet. Couldn't they be rung up ? "

" They will not go away. All right, I shall inquire; but, all the same, it is too late now. After this morning's incident the Germans will not allow us to be relieved by day."

" They will allow us. The Committee members know about it already. I think "—he lowered his voice—" that Soloveytchick has managed to slip across and explain matters. It is rumoured that the Germans have promised to overlook it, on condition that next time the Colonel comes to visit the trenches we should let them know, and they will throw a bomb. You had better repoi it or else, who knows?"

" All right."

The Sergeant-Major was preparing to leave. The Lieutenant stopped him.

" Matters are bad, Petrovitch. They do not trust us."

" God alone knows whom they trust; only last week the Sixth Company elected their Sergeant-Major themselves, and now they are making a mock of him; they won't let him say a word."

" What will things be afterwards?"

The Sergeant-Major blushed, and said softly·

" Then the Soloveytchicks will rule over us, and we shall be, so to speak, dumb animals before them—that is how matters will be, your honour."

The relief came at last. Captain Bouravin, the Commander of the Fifth Company, came into the hut. Albov offered to show him the section and explain the disposition of the enemy.

" Very well, though that does not matter, because I am not really in command of the Company—I am boycotted."

" How? "

" Just so. They have elected the 2nd Lieutenant, my subaltern, as Company Commander, and degraded me as a supporter of the old régime, because, you see, I had drill twice a day—you know that the marching contingents come up here absolutely untrained. Indeed, the 2nd Lieutenant was the first to vote for my removal. ' We have been slave-driven long enough,' said he. ' Now we are free. We must clean out everyone, beginning with the head. A young man can manage the regiment just as well, so long as he is a true Democrat and supports the freedom of the soldier.' I would have left, but the Colonel flatly refused to allow it, and forbids me to hand over the company. So now, you see, we have two commanders. I have stood the situation for five days. Look here, Albov, you are not in a hurry, are you? Very good, then; let us have a chat. I am feeling depressed. Albov, have you not yet thought of suicide?"

" Not as yet."

Bouravin rose to his feet.

" Understand me, they have desecrated my soul, outraged my human dignity, and so every day, every hour, in every word, glance or gesture one sees a constant outrage. What have I done to them? I have been in the service for eight years; I have no family, no house or home. All this I have found in the regiment, my own regiment. Twice I have been badly wounded, and before my wounds were healed have rushed back to the regiment—so there you are! And I loved the soldier—I am ashamed to speak of it myself, but they must remember how, more than once, I have crept out under the barbed wire to drag in the wounded. And now! Well, yes, I reverence the regimental flag and hate their crimson rags. I accept the Revolution. But to me Russia is infinitely dearer than the Revolution. All these Committees and meetings, all this adventitious rubbish which has been sown in the Army I am organically unable to swallow and digest. But, after all, I interfere with no one; I say nothing of this to anyone, I strive to convince no one. If only the War could be ended honourably, and then I am ready to break stones on the highway, only not to remain in an Army democratised in such a manner. Take my subaltern; he discusses everything with them—nationalisation, socialisation, labour control. Now I cannot do so—I never had time to study it, and I confess I never took any interest in the matter. You remember how the Army Commander came here and, amidst a crowd of soldiers, said: ' Don't say "General"; call me simply Comrade George.' Now I cannot do such things; besides, all the same, they would not believe me. So I am silent. But they understand and pay me off. And, you know, with all their ignorance, what subtle psychologists they are! They are able to find the place where the sting hurts most. Now, yesterday for instance . . ."

He stooped down to Albov's ear, and continued in a whisper:

" I returned from our mess. In my tent, at the head of my bed, I have a photograph—well, just a treasured memory. There they had drawn an obscenity! "

Bouravin rose and wiped his brow with his handkerchief.

" Well, let us take a look at the positions. God willing, we shall not have to stand it long. No one in the Company wants to go scouting. I go myself every night; sometimes there is a volunteer who accompanies me—he has a hunter's strain in him. Should anything happen, please, Albov, see to it that a little packet—it is in my bag—is sent to its destination."

The company, without waiting for the completion of the relief, wandered away in disorder. Albov plodded after them.

The communication trench ended in a broad hollow. Like a great ant-hill the regimental bivouac stretched in rows of huts, tents, smoking camp-kitchens and horse-lines. They had once been carefully masked by artificial plantations, which had now withered, lost their leaves, and were merely leafless poles. On an open green soldiers were drilling here and there—listlessly, lazily, as if to create an impression that they were doing something; after all, it would be awkward to be doing absolutely nothing at all. There were few officers about; the good ones were sick of the trivial farce into which real work was now transformed, while the inferior ones had a moral justification for their laziness and idleness. In the distance something between a mob and a column marched along the road towards the regimental staff quarters, carrying crimson flags. Before them went a huge banner bearing the inscription, in white letters, visible in the distance: " Down with War ! "

These were reinforcements coming up. At once, all the soldiers drilling on the green, as if at a signal, broke their ranks and ran towards the column.

" Hey, countrymen! What province are you from ? "

An animated conversation began on the usual anxious themes: how did matters stand with the land; would peace be concluded soon? Much interest, also, was shown in the question as to whether they had brought any home-brewed spirits, as " their own regimental " home brew, manufactured in fairly large quantities at " the distillery " of the Third Battalion, was very disgusting, and gave rise to painful symptoms.

Albov made his way to the mess-room. The officers were gathering for dinner. What had become of the former animation, friendly talk, healthy laughter and torrents of reminiscences of a stormy, hard, but glorious life of war? The reminiscences had faded, the dreams had flown away, and stern reality crushed them all down with its weight.

They spoke in low voices, sometimes breaking off or expressing themselves figuratively: the mess servants might denounce them, and also new faces had appeared among themselves. Not so long ago the Regimental Committee, on the report of a servant, had tried an officer of the regiment, who wore the Cross of St. George and to whom the regiment owed one of its most famous victories. This Lieutenant-Colonel had said something about " mutinous slaves." And though it was proved that those were not his own words and that he had only quoted a speech made by Comrade Kerensky, the Committee " expressed its indignation at him "; he had to leave the regiment.

The personnel of the officers, too, was much changed. Of the original staff, some two or three remained. Some had perished, others had been crippled, others again, having earned " distrust," were wandering about the Front, importuning Staffs, joining shock battalions, entering institutions in the rear, while some of the weaker brethren had simply gone home. The Army had ceased to need the bearers of the traditions of its units, of its

The Condition of the Army at the July Advance

former glory—of those old Bourgeois prejudices, which had been swept into the dust by the Revolutionary creative power.

Everyone in the regiment knows already of that morning's event in Albov's Company. He is questioned about details. A Lieutenant-Colonel sitting next him wagged his head.

"Well done, our old man. There was something in the Fifth Company, too. But I am afraid it will end badly. Have you heard what was done to the Commander of the Doubov Regiment, because he refused to confirm an elected Company Commander and put three agitators under arrest? *He was crucified.* Yes, my boy! They nailed him to a tree and began, in turn, to stick their bayonets into him, to cut off his ears, his nose, his fingers."

He seized his head in his hands.

"My God! Where do these men get so much brutality, so much baseness?"

At the other end of the table the ensigns are carrying on a conversation on that ever harassing theme—where to get away to.

"Have you applied for admission to the Revolutionary Battalion?"

"No, it is not worth while. It seems that it is being formed under the superintendence of the Executive Committee, with Committees, elections and " Revolutionary " discipline. It does not suit me."

"They say that shock units are being formed in Kornilov's Army and at Minsk also. That would be good. . ."

"I have applied for transfer to our rifle brigade in France. Only I do not know what I am to do about the language."

"Alas! my boy, you are too late," remarked the Lieutenant-Colonel from the other end of the table. "The Government has long ago sent 'emigrant comrades' there to enlighten minds. And now our brigades, somewhere in the South of France, are in the situation of something like either prisoners of war or disciplinary battalions."

This talk, however, was realised by all to be of a purely platonic character, in view of the hopelessness of a situation from which there was no escape. It was only a case of dreaming a little, as Tchekhov's *Three Sisters* once dreamed of Moscow. Dreaming of such a wondrous place, where human dignity is not trampled into the mud daily, where one can live quietly and die honourably, without violence and without outrage to one's service. Such a very little thing.

"Mitka, bread!" boomed out the mighty bass of 2nd Lieutenant Yassny.

He is quite a character, this Yassny. Tall and sturdy, with a thick crop of hair and a copper-coloured beard, he is altogether an embodiment of the strength and courage of the soil. He wears four crosses of St. George, and has been promoted from the rank of Sergeant for distinction in action. He does not adapt himself to his new surroundings in the least, said " levorution " for " revolution " and " mettink " for " meeting," and cannot reconcile himself to the new order. Yassny's undoubted " democratic " views, his candour and sincerity, have given him an exceptionally privileged position in the regiment. Without enjoying any special influence, he can, however, condemn, rudely, harshly, sometimes with an oath, both people and ideas, which are jealously guarded and worshipped by the regimental " Revolutionary Democracy." The men are angry, but suffer him.

" There is no bread, I say."

The officers, absorbed in their thoughts and in their conversation, had not even noticed that they had eaten their soup without bread.

" There will be no bread to-day," answered the waiter.

" What is the meaning of this? Call the mess-sergeant."

The mess-sergeant came, and began to justify himself in a bewildered manner; he had sent in a request that morning for two poods of bread. The head of the Commissariat had endorsed it " to be issued," but the clerk, Fedotov, a member of the Commissariat Committee, had endorsed it in his turn " not to be issued." So the storehouse would not issue any bread.

No one made any objection, so painfully ashamed was everyone both of the mess-sergeant and of those depths of inanity which had suddenly broken into their life and swamped it with a grey, filthy slime. Only Yassny's bass voice rang out distinctly under the arches of the mess-room:

" What swine! "

Albov was just preparing for a nap after dinner when the flap of his tent was lifted, and through the aperture appeared the bald head of the Chief of the Commissariat—a quiet, elderly Colonel, who had joined the Army again from the retired list.

" May I come in? "

" I beg your pardon, Colonel."

" Never mind, my dear fellow, don't get up. I have just come in for a second. You see, to-day at six o'clock there is to be a regimental meeting. It will hear the Report of the Committee for verifying the Commissariat, and apparently they will go for me.

The Condition of the Army at the July Advance

I am no speech-maker, but you are a master of it. Take my part, should it be necessary."

" Certainly. I did not intend going, but once it is necessary, I shall be there."

" Thank you, then, my dear fellow."

By six o'clock the square next to the regimental Staff quarters was completely covered with men. At least two thousand had turned up. The crowd moved, chattered, laughed—just such a Russian crowd as on the Khodynka in Moscow or the *Champs de Mars* in Petrograd at a holiday entertainment. The Revolution could not transform it all at once, either mentally or spiritually. But, having stunned it with a torrent of new words and opened up before it unbounded possibilities, the Revolution had destroyed its equilibrium and made it nervously susceptible and stormily reactive to all methods of external influence. An ocean of words —both morally lofty and basely criminal—flowed through their minds as through a sieve, which passed through the trend of the new ideas and retained only those grains which had a real applied meaning in their daily life, in the surroundings of the soldier, the peasant, the workman. Hence the absolute absence of results from the torrents of eloquence which flooded the Army at the instance of the Minister of War; hence, too, the illogical warm sympathy with both speakers of clearly opposed politics.

Under such conditions, what practical meaning could the crowd find in such ideas as duty, honour, interests of the State, on the one hand; annexations, indemnities, the self-determination of peoples, conscious discipline, and other dim conceptions on the other.

The whole regiment had turned out; the soldiers were attracted by the meeting, as by any other spectacle. Delegates had been sent by the Second Battalion, which was in the trenches— about one-third of the battalion. In the middle of the square stood a platform for the speakers; it was decorated with red flags, faded with time and rain; they have been there since the platform was erected for a review by the Commander of the Army. Reviews are now held not among the ranks, but from a tribune. To-day the agenda of the meeting contain two questions: " (1) The Report of the Commissariat Committee on the anomalies in the supply of Officers' rations; and (2) the report of Comrade Sklianka, an orator specially invited from the Moscow Soviet to speak about the formation of a Coalition Ministry."

During the preceding week a stormy meeting, which nearly ended in a riot, had been held in connection with the complaint of one of the companies that the soldiers had to eat lentils, which they hated, and thin soup, simply because all the groats and butter were taken for the officers' mess. This was clearly nonsense. Nevertheless, it was resolved to appoint a Committee for investigation, which would report to a general meeting of the regiment. The Report was drawn up by a member of the Committee, Lieutenant-Colonel Petrov, who had been removed the year before from the post of Chief of the Commissariat and was now settling accounts with his successor. In a petty, cavilling way, with a sort of mean irony, he enumerated slight, irrelevant, inaccuracies in the Commissariat Department of the regiment—there were no serious ones—and dragged out his Report endlessly in his creaking, monotonous voice. The crowd, which at first had kept quiet, now hummed again, having ceased to listen. From different sides voices were heard:

" Enough ! "

" That will do ! "

The Chairman of the Commission ceased reading and suggested that " those comrades who wished " should express their opinions. A tall, stout soldier ascended the platform, and began speaking in a loud, hysterical voice:

" Comrades, you have heard? That is where the soldiers' property goes. We suffer, our clothes are worn out, we are covered with lice, we go hungry, while they pull the last piece of food out of our mouths."

As he spoke a spirit of nervous excitement kept growing in the crowd, muffled murmurs ran through it, and shouts of approval burst from it here and there.

" When will there be an end to all this? We are worn out, weary to death."

Suddenly 2nd Lieut. Yassny's deep voice was heard from the rear ranks, drowning the voices both of the speaker and of the crowd.

" What is your Company? "

Some confusion took place. The orator was dumb. Shouts of indignation were flung at Yassny.

" What is your Company, I ask you? "

" The Seventh ! "

Voices were heard in the ranks·

" We have no such man in the Seventh Company."

" Wait a bit, my friend," boomed Yassny, " was it not you that came in to-day with the new lot you were carrying a large placard? When have you had time to get worn out, poor fellow? "

The spirit of the crowd changed in an instant. It began to hiss, laugh, shout, and crack jokes. The unsuccessful orator disappeared in the crowd. Someone shouted:

" Pass a resolution ! "

Lieutenant-Colonel Petrov mounted the platform again, and began to read out a ready resolution for transferring the officers' mess to privates' rations. But no one listened to him now. Two or three voices shouted " That's right ! " Petrov hesitated a little, then put the paper in his pocket and left the platform. The second question, concerning the removal of the Chief of the Commissariat and the immediate election of his successor (the author of the report was the candidate proposed) remained unread. The Chairman of the Committee then announced:

" Comrade Sklianka, member of the Executive Committee of the Moscow Council of Workmen's and Soldiers' Delegates, will now address the meeting."

They were tired of their own speakers—it was always one and the same thing—and the arrival of a new man, somewhat advertised by the Committee, aroused general interest. The crowd closed up round the platform and was still. A small, black-haired man, nervous and short-sighted, who constantly adjusted the eye-glasses which kept slipping off his nose, mounted the platform, or rather quickly ran up on to it. He began speaking rapidly, with much spirit and much gesticulation.

" Soldier comrades ! Three months have passed already since the Petrograd workers and Revolutionary soldiers threw off the yoke of the Czar and of all his Generals. The Bourgeoisie, in the person of Tereshtchenko, the well-known sugar refiner; Konovalov, the factory owner; the landowners, Gutchkov, Rodzianko, Miliukov, and other traitors to the interests of the people, having seized the supreme power, have tried to deceive the popular masses.

" The demand of the people that negotiations be commenced at once for that peace which we are offered by our German worker and soldier brethren—who are just as much bereft of all that makes life worth living as we are—has ended in a fraud—a telegram from Miliukov to England and France to say that the Russian people are ready to fight until victory is attained.

" The unfortunate people understood that the supreme power had fallen into even worse hands, $i.e.$, into those of the sworn foes of the workman and the peasant. Therefore the people shouted mightily : ' Down with you, hands off ! '

" And the accursed Bourgeoisie shook at the mighty cry of the workers and hypocritically invited to a share in their power the so-called Democracy—the Socialist-Revolutionaries and the Mensheviks, who always associated with the Bourgeoisie for the betrayal of the interests of the working people."

Having thus outlined the process of the formation of the Coalition Ministry, Comrade Sklianka passed in greater detail to the fascinating prospects of rural and factory anarchy, where " the wrath of the people sweeps away the yoke of capital " and where " Bourgeois property gradually passes into the hands of its real masters—the workmen and the poorer peasants."

" The soldiers and the workmen still have enemies," he continued. " These are the friends of the overthrown Czarist Government, the hardened admirers of shooting, the knout, and blows. The most bitter foes of freedom, they have now donned crimson rosettes, call you ' comrades ' and pretend to be friends, but cherish the blackest intentions in their hearts, preparing to restore the rule of the Romanovs.

" Soldiers, do not trust these wolves in sheep's clothing! They call you to fresh slaughter. Well, follow them if you like! Let them pave the path for the return of the bloody Czar with your corpses. Let your orphans, your widows and children, deserted by all, pass again into slavery, hunger, beggary, and disease ! "

The speech undoubtedly had a great success. The atmosphere grew red-hot, the excitement increased—that excitement of the " molten mass," in the presence of which it is impossible to foresee either the limits or the tension, or the tracks along which the torrent will pour. The crowd was noisy and agitated, accompanying with shouts of approval or curses against " the enemies of the people " those parts of the speech which especially touched its instincts, its naked, cruel egotism.

Albov, pale, with burning eyes, made his appearance on the platform. He spoke excitedly of something or other to the chairman, who then addressed the crowd. The chairman's words were inaudible amidst the noise; for a long time he waved his hands and the flag which he had pulled down, until at last the noise had subsided somewhat.

" Comrades, Lieutenant Albov wishes to address you ! "

Shouts and hisses were heard.

" Down with him ! We do not want him ! "

But Albov was already on the platform, gripping hard, bending downwards towards the sea of heads. And he said:

" No, I will speak, and you dare not refuse to listen to one of those officers whom this man has been abusing and dishonouring here before you. Who he may be, whence he has come, who pays him for his speeches, so profitable to the Germans, not one of you knows. He has come here, befogged you, and will go on his way to sow evil and treason. And you have believed him. And we, who along with you have now carried our heavy cross into the fourth year of the War—we are now to be regarded as your enemies? Why? Is it because we never sent you into action, but led you, bestrewing with officers' corpses the whole of the path covered by the regiment? Is it because that, of the officers who led you in the beginning, there is not one left in the regiment who is not maimed?"

He spoke with deep sincerity and pain in his voice. There were moments when it seemed as if his words were breaking through the withered crust of those hardened hearts, as if a break would again take place in the attitude of the crowd.

"He, your 'new friend,' is calling you to mutiny, to violence, to robbery. Do you understand who will benefit when, in Russia, brother rises against brother, so as to turn to ashes, in sack and fire, the last property left not only to the 'capitalists,' but to the poverty-stricken workers and peasants? No, it is not by violence, but by law and right, that you will acquire land and liberty and a tolerable existence. Your enemies are not here, among the officers, but there—beyond the barbed wire. And we shall not attain either to freedom or to peace by a dishonourable, cowardly standing in one and the same place, but in the general mighty rush of an *advance*."

Was it that the impression of Sklianka's speech was still too vivid or that the regiment took offence at the word "cowardly"—for the most arrant coward will never forgive such a reminder—or, finally, was it the fault of the magic word "advance," which for some time past had ceased to be tolerated in the Army? But anyhow Albov was not allowed to continue his speech.

The crowd bellowed, belched forth curses, pressed forward more and more, advancing toward the platform, and broke down the railing. An ominous roar, faces distorted with fury, and hands stretched forth towards the platform. The situation was becoming critical. 2nd Lieut. Yassny pushed his way through to Albov, took him by the arm, and forcibly led him to the exit. The soldiers of the First Company had already rushed up to it from all sides, and with their aid Albov, with great difficulty, made his way out of the crowd, amidst a shower of choice abuse. Someone shouted out after him:

"Wait a bit, you——; we will settle accounts with you!"

Night. The bivouac had grown quiet. Clouds had covered the sky. It was dark. Albov, sitting on his bed in his narrow tent, illuminated by the stump of a candle, was writing a report to the Commander of the Regiment:

" The officers—powerless, insulted, meeting with distrust and disobedience from their subordinates—can be of no further use. I beg of you to apply for my reduction to the ranks, so that there I might fulfil my duty honestly and to the end."

He lay down on his bed. He gripped his head in his hands. A kind of uncanny, incomprehensible emptiness seized him, just as if some unseen hand had drawn out of his head all thought, out of his heart all pain. What was that? A noise was heard, the tent-pole fell down, the light went out. A number of men on the tent. Hard, cruel blows were showered on the whole of his body. A sharp, intolerable pain shot through his head and his chest. Then his whole face seemed covered with a warm, sticky veil, and soon everything became still and calm again, as if all that was terrible and hard to bear had torn itself away, had remained here, on earth, while his soul was flying away somewhere and was feeling light and joyous.

Albov awoke to feel something cold touching him: a private of his company, Goulkin, an elderly man, was sitting at the foot of his bed and wiping away the blood from his head with a wet towel. He noticed that Albov had regained consciousness.

" Look how they have mangled the man, the scum! It can have been no other than the Fifth Company—I recognised one of them. Does it hurt you much? Perhaps you would like me to go for the doctor? "

" No, my friend, it does not matter. Thank you! " and Albov pressed his hand.

" And their Commander, too, Captain Bouravin, has met with a misfortune. During the night they carried him past us on a stretcher, wounded in the abdomen; the *sanitar* said that he would not live. He was returning from reconnoitring, and the bullet took just at our very barbed wire. Whether it was a German one or whether our own people did not recognise him—who knows? "

He was silent for a while.

" What has come to the people one simply can't understand. And all this is just put on. It is not true—that which they say against the officers—we understand that ourselves. Of course, there are all sorts among you. But we know them very well. Don't we see for ourselves that you, now, are for us with all your heart. Or let us say 2nd Lieut. Yassny. Could such a one sell himself? And yet, try to say a word, to take your part—there would be no living for us. There is a great deal of hooliganism now. It is only hooligans that men listen to. My idea is that all this is taking place because men have forgotten God. Men have nothing to be afraid of."

Albov closed his eyes from weakness. Goulkin hastily arranged the blanket, which had slipped to the floor, made the sign of the cross over him, and quietly slipped out of the tent.

But sleep would not come. His heart was full of an inexhaustible sadness and an oppressive feeling of loneliness. He yearned so much to have some living being at hand, so that he might silently, wordlessly feel its proximity, and not remain alone with his dreadful thoughts. He regretted that he had not detained Goulkin.

All was quiet. The whole camp was sleeping. Albov leaped from his bed and lit the candle again. He was seized with a dull, hopeless despair. He had no more faith in anything. Impenetrable darkness lay before him. To make his exit from life? No, that would be surrender. He must go on, with clenched teeth and hardened heart, until some stray bullet—Russian or German —broke the thread of his wearisome days.

Dawn was coming on. A new day was beginning, new Army week-days, horribly like their predecessors.

* * * *

Afterwards?

Afterwards the " molten element " overflowed its banks completely. Officers were killed, burnt, drowned, torn asunder and had their heads broken through with hammers, slowly, with inexpressible cruelty.

Afterwards—millions of deserters. Like an avalanche the soldiery moved along the railways, water-ways and country roads, trampling down, breaking and destroying the last nerves of poor, roadless Russia.

Afterwards—Tarnopol, Kalush, Kazan. Like a whirlwind robbery, murder, violence, incendiarism swept over Galicia, Volynia, the Podolsk and other provinces, leaving behind it everywhere a trail of blood and arousing in the minds of the Russian people, crazed with grief and weak in spirit, the monstrous thought:

" O Lord! if only the Germans would come quickly."

This was done by the soldier.

That soldier of whom a great Russian writer, with intuitive conscience and a bold heart, has said:[*]

" . . . How many hast thou killed during these days, oh

---

[*] Leonid Andreiev's article : *" To thee, Oh soldier! "*

soldier? How many orphans hast thou made? How many inconsolable mothers hast thou left? Dost thou hear the whisper on their lips, from which thou hast driven the smile of joy for evermore?

"Murderer! Murderer!

" But why speak of mothers, of orphaned children? A more terrible moment came, which none had expected—and thou didst betray Russia, thou didst cast the whole of the Motherland, which had bred thee, under the feet of the foe!

" Thou, oh soldier, whom we loved so—and whom we still love."

CHAPTER XXIII.

Officers' Organisations.

IN the early days of April the idea arose among the Headquarters' officers of organising a "Union of the Officers of the Army and the Navy." The initiators of the Union * started with the view that it was necessary "to think alike, so as to understand alike the events that were taking place, to work in the same direction," for up to the present time "the voice of the officers—of all the officers—has been heard by none. As yet we have said nothing about the great events amidst which we are living. Everyone who chooses says for us whatever he chooses. Military questions, and even the questions of our daily life and internal order, are settled for us by anyone who likes and in any way he likes." There were two objections made in principle, one being the objection to the introduction by the officers themselves into their ranks of those principles of collective self-government with which the Army had been inoculated from outside, in the form of Soviets, Committees and Congresses, and had brought disintegration into it. The second objection was the fear lest the appearance of an independent Officers' Organisation should deepen still more those differences which had arisen between the soldiers and the officers. On the basis of these views we, along with the Commander-in-Chief, at first took up an altogether negative attitude towards this proposal. But life had already broken out of its bounds and laughed at our motives. A draft declaration was published, granting the Army full freedom for forming Unions and meetings, and it would now have been an injustice to the officers to deprive them of the right of professional organisation, if only as a means of self-preservation. In practice, officers' societies had sprung up in many of the Armies, and in Kiev, Moscow, Petrograd and other towns they had done so from the earlier days of the Revolution. They all wandered in different

---

* The greatest part was played by Lieutenant-Colonels of the General Staff, Lebedev (afterwards Chief-of-Staff to Admiral Koltchak) and Pronin.

directions, groping their way, while some Unions in the large centres, under the influence of the disintegrating conditions of the rear, displayed a strong leaning towards the policy of the Soviets.

The officers of the rear frequently lived a completely different spiritual life from those of the Front. Thus, for instance, the Moscow Soviet of officers' delegates passed, in the beginning of April, a resolution to the effect that " the work of the Provisional Government should proceed . . . in the spirit of the Socialistic and political demands of the Democracy, represented by the Council of Workmen's and Soldiers' Delegates," and expressed a wish that there should be more representatives of the Socialist parties in the Provisional Government. An adulteration of the officers' views was also developing on a larger scale; the Petrograd officers' Council summoned an " All-Russia Congress of officers' delegates, Army surgeons and officers " in Petrograd for May 8th. This circumstance was the more undesirable in that the initiator of the Congress—the Executive Committee, with Lieutenant-Colonel Goushchin, of the General Staff, at its head—had already disclosed to the full its negative policy by its participation in the drafting of the declaration of soldiers' rights, by its active co-operation in the Polivanov Commission and its servility before the Council of Workmen's and Soldier's Delegates, and by its endeavours to unite with it. A proposal in this sense being made, the Council, however, replied that such a union was " as yet impossible on technical grounds."

Having discounted all these circumstances, the Supreme Commander-in-Chief gave his approval to the summoning of a Congress of officers, on condition that no pressure should be exercised either in his name or in that of the Chief-of-Staff. This scrupulous attitude somewhat complicated matters. Some of the Staffs, being out of sympathy with the idea, prevented the circulation of the appeal, while some of the High Commanders, as, for example, the Commander of the troops of the Omsk district, forbade the delegation of officers altogether. In some places also this question roused the suspicion of the soldiers and caused some complications, in consequence of which the initiators of the Congress invited the units to delegate soldiers as well as officers to be present at the sessions.

Despite all obstacles, over 300 officer delegates gathered in Moghilev, 76 per cent. being from the Front, 17 per cent. from fighting units in the rear, and 7 per cent. from the rear. On May 7th the Congress was opened with a speech by the Supreme Commander-in-Chief. On that day, for the first time, the High Command said, not in a secret meeting, not in a confidential letter, but openly, before the whole country: " Russia is perishing." General Alexeiev said: " In appeals, in general orders, in the columns of the Daily Press, we often meet with the short sentence: ' Our country is in danger.'

" We have grown too well accustomed to this phrase. We feel as if we were reading an old chronicle of bygone days, and do not ponder over the grim meaning of this curt sentence. But, gentlemen, this is, I regret to say, a serious fact. *Russia is perishing. She stands on the brink of an abyss. A few more shocks, and she will crash with all her weight into it.* The enemy has occupied one-eighth part of her territory. He cannot be bribed by the Utopian phrase: ' Peace without annexations or indemnities.' He says frankly that he will not leave our soil. He is stretching forth his greedy grip to lands where no enemy soldier has ever set foot—to the rich lands of Volynia, Podolia and Kiev—*i.e.*, to the whole right bank of our Dnieper.

" And what are we going to do ? Will the Russian Army allow this to happen ? Will we not thrust this insolent foe out of our country and let the diplomatists conclude peace afterwards, with annexations or without them ?

" Let us be frank. The fighting spirit of the Russian Army has fallen; but yesterday strong and terrible, it now stands in fatal impotence before the foe. Its former traditional loyalty to the Motherland has been replaced by a yearning for peace and rest. Instead of fortitude, the baser instincts and a thirst for self-preservation are rampant.

" At home, where is that strong authority for which the whole country is craving ? Where is that powerful authority which would force every citizen to do his duty honestly by the Motherland ? "

" We are told that it will soon appear, but as yet it does not exist.

" Where is the love of country, where is patriotism ?

" The great word ' brotherhood ' has been inscribed on our banners, but it has not been inscribed in our hearts and minds. Class enmity rages amongst us. Whole classes which have honestly fulfilled their duty to their country have fallen under suspicion, and on this foundation a deep gulf has been created between two parts of the Army—the officers and the soldiers.

" And it is at this very moment that the first Congress of officers of the Russian Army has been summoned. I am of the opinion that a more convenient, a more timely moment, could not have been chosen to attain unity in our family, to form a general united family of the corps of Russian officers, to discuss the means of breathing ardour into our hearts, *for without ardour there is no victory, without victory there is no salvation, no Russia.*

" May your work therefore be inspired with love for your Motherland and with heartfelt regard for the soldier; mark the ways for raising the moral and intellectual calibre of the soldiers, so that they may become your sincere and hearty comrades. Do away with that estrangement which has been artificially sown in our family.

" At the present moment—this is a disease common to all people would like to set all the citizens of Russia on platforms or pedestals and scrutinise how many stand behind each of them. What does it matter that the masses of the Army accepted the new order and the new Constitution sincerely, honestly and with enthusiasm?

" *We must all unite on one great object: Russia is in danger. As members of the great Army, we must save her. Let this object unite us and give us strength to work.*"

This speech, in which the leader of the Army expressed " the anxiety of his heart," served as the prologue to his retirement. The Revolutionary Democracy had already passed its sentence on General Alexeiev at its memorable session with the Commanders-in-Chief on May 4th; now, after May 7th, a bitter campaign was begun against him in the Radical Press, in which the Soviet semi-official organ *Isvestia* competed with Lenin's papers in the triviality and impropriety of its remarks. This campaign was the more significant in that the Minister of War, Kerensky, was clearly on the side of the Soviet in this matter.

As if to supplement the words of the Supreme Commander-in-Chief, I said in my speech, when touching on the internal situation in the country:

" Under pressure of the unavoidable laws of history, autocracy has fallen, and our country has passed under the rule of the people. We stand on the threshold of a new life, long and passionately awaited, for which many thousand Idealists have gone to the block, languished in the mines and pined in the *tundras.*

" But we look to the future with anxiety and perplexity.

" For there is no liberty in the Revolutionary torture-chamber.

" There is no righteousness in misrepresenting the voice of the people.

" There is no equality in the hounding down of classes.

" And there is no strength in that insane rout where all around seek to grasp all that they possibly can, at the expense of their suffering country, where thousands of greedy hands are stretched out towards power, breaking down the foundations of that country. . . . "

Then the sessions of the Congress began. Whoever was present has carried away, probably for the rest of his life, an indelible impression produced by the story of the sufferings of the officers. It could never be written, as it was told with chilling restraint by these, Captain Bouravin and Lieutenant Albov, who touched upon their most intimate and painful experiences. They had suffered till they could suffer no more; in their hearts there were neither tears nor complaints.

I looked at the boxes, where the " younger comrades " sat who had been sent to watch for " counter-Revolution." I wanted to read in their faces the impression produced by all that they had heard. And it seemed to me that I saw the blush of shame. Probably it only seemed so to me, for they soon made a stormy protest, demanded the right of voting at the Congress, and—five roubles per day " officer's allowance."

At thirteen general meetings the Congress passed a series of resolutions.

Among all the classes, castes, professions and trades which exhibited a general elemental desire to get from the weak Government all that was possible, in their own private interests, the officers were the only Corporation which never asked anything *for itself personally.*

The officers requested and demanded *authority*—over themselves and over the Army. A firm, single, national authority— " commanding, not appealing." The authority of a Government leaning on the trust of the nation, not on irresponsible organisations. Such an authority the officers were prepared wholeheartedly and unreservedly to obey, *quite irrespective of differences of political opinions.* I affirm, moreover, that all the inner social class conflict which was blazing up more and more throughout the country did not affect the officers at the Front, who were immersed in their work and in their sorrows; it did not touch them deeply; the conflict attracted the attention of the officers only when its results obviously endangered the very existence of the country, and of the Army in particular. Of course, I am speaking of the mass of the officers; individual leanings towards reaction undoubtedly existed, but they were in no respect characteristic of the Officers' Corps in 1917.

One of the finest representatives of the Officers' Class, General Markov, a thoroughly educated man, wrote to Kerensky, condemning his system of slighting the Command: " Being a soldier by nature, birth and education, I can judge and speak only of my own military profession. All other reforms and alterations in the constitution of our country interest me only as an ordinary citizen. But I know the Army; I have devoted to it the best days of my life; I have paid for its successes with the blood of those who were near to me, and have myself come out of action steeped in blood." This the Revolutionary Democracy had not understood or taken into consideration.

The Officers' Congress in Petrograd, at which about 700 delegates were gathered (May 18-26), passed off in a totally different manner. It split into two sharply-divided camps: the Officers and officials of the Rear who had given themselves to politics and a smaller number of real officers of the Line who had become delegates through a misunderstanding of the matter. The Executive Committee drew up their programme in strict agreement with the custom of the Soviet Congresses: (1) The attitude of the Congress towards the Provisional Government and the Soviet; (2) the War; (3) the Constituent Assembly; (4) the labour question; (5) the land question; and (6) the reorganisation of the Army on Democratic principles. An exaggerated importance was attached to the Congress in Petrograd, and at its opening pompous speeches were made by many members of the Government and by foreign representatives; the Congress was even greeted in the name of the Soviet by Nahamkes. The very first day revealed the irreconcilable differences between the two groups. These differences were inevitable, if only because, even on such a cardinal question as "Order No. I.," the Vice-Chairman of the Congress, Captain Brzozek, expressed the view that "its issue was dictated by historical necessity: the soldier was downtrodden, and it was imperatively necessary to free him." This declaration was greeted with prolonged applause by part of the delegates!

After a series of stormy meetings, a resolution was passed by a majority of 265 against 246, which stated that "the Revolutionary power of the country was in the hands of the organised peasants, workmen and soldiers, who form the predominating mass of the population," and that therefore the Government must be responsible to the All-Russia Soviet!

Even the resolution advocating an advance was passed by a majority of little more than two-thirds of those who cast their votes.

The attitude of the Petrograd Congress is to be explained by the declaration made on May 26th by that group, which, reflecting the real opinion of the Front, took the point of view of "all possible support to the Provisional Government." "In summoning the Congress the Executive Committee of the Petrograd

Council of Officers' Delegates did not seek for the solution of the most essential problem of the moment—the regeneration of the Army—since the question of the fighting capacity of the Army and of the measures for raising its level was not even mentioned in the programme, and was included only at our request. If we are to believe the statement—strange, to say no more—made by the Chairman, Lieutenant-Colonel Goushchin, the object of the summoning of the Congress was the desire of the Executive Committee to pass under our flag into the Council of Workmen's and Soldiers' Delegates." This declaration led to a series of serious incidents; three-quarters of the delegates left the meeting and the Congress came to an end.

I have mentioned the question of the Petrograd Officers' Council and Congress only in order to show the spirit of a certain section of the officers of the Rear, which was in frequent contact with the official and unofficial rulers, and represented, in the eyes of the latter, the " voice of the Army."

The Moghilev Congress, which attracted the unflagging attention of the Supreme Commander-in-Chief, and was much favoured by him, closed on May 22nd. At this time General Alexeiev had already been relieved of the command of the Russian Army. So deeply had this episode affected him that he was unable to attend the last meeting. I bade farewell to the Congress in the following words:

" The Supreme Commander-in-Chief, who is leaving his post, has commissioned me, gentlemen, to convey to you his sincere greetings, and to say that his heart, that of an old soldier, beats in unison with yours, that it aches with the same pain, and lives with the same hope for the regeneration of the disrupted, but ever great, Russian Army.

" Let me add a few words from myself.

" You have gathered here from the distant blood-bespattered marches of our land, and laid before us your quenchless sorrow and your soul-felt grief.

" You have unrolled before us a vivid and painful picture of the life and work of the officers amidst the raging sea of the Army.

" You, who have stood a countless number of times in the face of death! You, who have intrepidly led your men against the dense rows of the enemy's barbed wire, to the rare boom of your own guns, treacherously deprived of ammunition! You, who, hardening your hearts, but keeping up your spirits, have cast the last handful of earth into the grave of your fallen son, brother, or friend!

" Will you quail now?

" No!

" You who are weak, raise your heads. You who are strong, give of your determination, of your aspirations, of your desire to work for the happiness of your Motherland—pour them into the thinned ranks of your comrades at the Front. You are not alone. With you are all those who are honourable, all who think, all who have paused at the brink of that common sense which is now being abolished.

" The soldiers also will go with you, understanding clearly that you are leading them, not backwards, to serfdom and to spiritual poverty, but forwards, to freedom and to light.

" And then such a thunderstorm will break over the foe as will put an end both to him and to the War.

" These three years of the War I have lived one life with you, thought the same thoughts, shared with you the joy of victory and the burning pain of retreat. I have therefore the right to fling into the faces of those who have outraged our hearts, who from the very first days of the Revolution have wrought the work of Cain on the corps of officers—I have the right to fling in their faces the words: ' You lie! The Russian officer has never been either a mercenary or a Pretorian.'

" Under the old régime you were victimised, down-trodden, and deprived of all that makes life worth living. In no less a degree than yourselves, leading a life of semi-beggary, our officers of the Line have managed to carry through their wretched, laborious life like a burning torch, the thirst for achievement for the happiness of his Motherland.

" Then let my call be heard through these walls by the builders of the new life of the State:

" Take care of the officer! For from the beginning and till now he has stood, faithfully and without relief, on guard over the order of the Russian State. He can be relieved by death alone."

Printed by the Committee, the text of my speech was circulated at the Front, and I was happy to learn, from many letters and telegrams, that the words spoken in defence of the officer had touched his aching heart.

The Congress left a permanent institution at the Stavka—the " Chief Committee of the Officers' Union."* During the first three months of its existence the Committee did not succeed in

---

* The President was Colonel Novosiltsev, a member of the Fourth State Douma, a Cadet (Constitutional Democrat).

rooting itself deeply in the Army. Its activities were confined to organising branches of the Union in the Armies and in military circles, to the examination of the complaints that reached it. In exceptional cases incompetent officers were recommended for dismissal (the " black-board "); to a certain very limited degree officers expelled by the soldiers were granted assistance, and declarations were addressed to the Government and to the Press in connection with the more important events in public and military life. After the June advance the tone of these declarations became acrimonious, critical, and defiant, which seriously disturbed the Prime Minister, who persistently sought to have the Chief Committee transferred from Moghilev to Moscow, as he considered that its attitude was a danger to the Stavka.

The Committee, which was somewhat passive during the command of General Brussilov, did, indeed, take part afterwards in General Kornilov's venture. But it was not this circumstance that caused the change in its attitude. *The Committee undoubtedly reflected the general spirit with which the Command and the Russian officers were then imbued, a spirit which had become hostile to the Provisional Government.* Also, no clear idea had been formed among the officers of the political groups within the Government of the covert struggle proceeding between them, or of the protective part played by many representatives of the Liberal Democracy among them. A hostile attitude was thus created towards the Government as a whole.

Having remained hitherto perfectly loyal and in the majority of cases well-disposed, having patiently borne, much against the grain, the experiments which the Provisional Government made, deliberately or involuntarily, on the country and on the Army, these elements lived only in the hope of the regeneration of the Army, of an advance and of victory. When all these hopes crashed to the ground, then, not being united in their ideals with the second Coalitional Government, but, on the contrary, deeply distrusting it, the masses of the officers abandoned the Provisional Government, which thus lost its last reliable support.

This moment is of great historical importance, giving the key to the understanding of many later events. As a whole, deeply democratic in their personnel, views and conditions of life, *rejected by the Revolutionary Democracy* with incredible harshness and cynicism, and finding no real support in the liberal circles in close touch with the Government, the Russian officers found themselves in a state of tragic isolation. This isolation and bewilderment served more than once afterwards as a fertile soil for outside influences, foreign to the traditions of the officer caste and to its former political character—influences which led to dissension, and in the end to fratricide. For there can be no doubt that all the power, all the organisation, both of the Red and of the White Armies, rested exclusively on the personality of the former Russian officer.

And if afterwards, in the course of three years of conflict, we have witnessed the rise of two conflicting forces in the Russian public life of the anti-Bolshevist camp, we must seek for their original source not in political differences only, but also in that work of Cain towards the officers' caste, which was wrought by the Revolutionary Democracy from the first days of the Revolution.

As everyone realised that the " new order " and the Front itself are on the verge of collapse, it was obvious that officers should have attempted some organisation to meet such a contingency. But the advocates of action were lying in prison; the Chief Council of the Officers' Union, which was best suited for this task, had been broken up by Kerensky in the latter days of August. The majority of the responsible leaders of the Army were perturbed by a terrible and not unfounded fear for the fate of the Russian officers. In this respect the correspondence between General Kornilov and General Doukhonin is very characteristic. After the Bolshevist *coup d'état* on November 1 (14), 1917, General Kornilov wrote to Doukhonin from his prison in Bykhov:

" Foreseeing the further course of events, I think that it is necessary for you to take such measures as would create a favourable atmosphere, while thoroughly safeguarding Headquarters, for a struggle against the coming Anarchy."

Among these measures General Kornilov suggested " the concentration in Moghilev, or in a point near to it, under a reliable guard, of a store of rifles, cartridges, machine-guns, automatic guns and hand-grenades for distribution among the officer-volunteers, who will undoubtedly gather together in this region."

Doukhonin made a note against this point: " This might lead to excesses."

Thus the constant morbid fears of an officers' " Counter-Revolution " proved to be in vain. Events took the officers unawares. They were unorganised, bewildered; they did not think of their own safety, and finally scattered their forces.

CHAPTER XXIV

The Revolution and the Cossacks.

A PECULIAR part was played by the Cossacks in the history of the Revolution.

Built up historically, in the course of several centuries, the relations of the Cossacks with the Central Government, common to Russia, were of a dual character. The Government did all to encourage the development of Cossack colonisation on the Russian south-eastern borders, where war was unceasing. It made allowances for the peculiarities of the warlike, agricultural life of the Cossacks, and allowed them a certain degree of independence and individual forms of democratic rule, with representative organs (the Kosh, kroog, rada), an elected " Army elder " and hetmans.

" In its weakness," says Solovyov, " The State did not look too strictly on the activities of the Cossacks, so long as they were directed only against foreign lands; the State being weak, it was considered needful to give these restless forces an outlet." But the " activities " of the Cossacks were more than once directed against Moscow as well. This circumstance led to a prolonged internecine struggle, which lasted until the end of the eighteenth century, when, after a ferocious suppression of the Pougatchov Rebellion, the free Cossacks of the South-East were dealt a final blow; they gradually lost their markedly oppositionary character, and even gained the reputation of the most conservative element in the State, the pillars of the throne and the régime.

From that time onward the Government incessantly showed favour to the Cossacks by emphasising their really great merits, by solemn promises to preserve their " Cossack Liberties," [*] and

---

[*] The last Charter to the Cossacks of the Don was granted on January 24, 1906, by the Emperor Nicholas II., and contained the following words : " . . . We confirm all the rights and privileges granted to it (the Cossack Army), affirming by Our Imperial word both the indefeasibility of its present form of service, which has earned the Army of the Don historic glory and the inviolability of all its estates and lands, gained by the labours, merits and blood of its ancestors. . . ."

by the appointment of members of the Imperial family to honorary posts among the Cossacks. At the same time, the Government took all measures to prevent these " liberties " from developing to excess at the expense of that ruthless centralisation, which was a historical necessity in the beginning of the building up of the Russian State and a vast historical blunder in its later development. To the number of these measures we must refer the limitation of Cossack self-government, and, latterly, the traditional appointment to the post of Hetman of persons not belonging to the Cossack caste, and often complete strangers to the life of the Cossacks. The oldest and most numerous Cossack Army, that of the Don, has had Generals of German origin at its head more than once.

It seemed as if the Czarist Government had every reason to depend upon the Cossacks. The repeated repression of the local political labour and agrarian disturbances which broke out in Russia, the crushing of a more serious rising—the revolution of 1905-1906, in which a great part was played by the Cossack troops —all this seemed to confirm the established opinion of the Cossacks. On the other hand, sundry episodes of the " repressions," accompanied by inevitable violence, sometimes cruelty, were widely spread among the people, were exaggerated, and created a hostile attitude towards the Cossacks at the factories, in the villages, among the Liberal *intelligentcia*, and especially among those elements which are known as the Revolutionary Democracy. Throughout the whole of the underground literature —in its appeals, leaflets, and pictures—the idea of a " Cossack " became synonymous with " servant " of the Reactionary party.

This definition was greatly exaggerated. The bard of the Don Cossacks, Mitrophan Bogayevsky, says of the political character of the Cossacks: " The first and fundamental condition which prevented the Cossacks, at least in the beginning, from breaking up was the idea of the State, a lawful order, a deep-seated realisation of the necessity of a life within the bounds of law. This seeking of a lawful order runs, and has run, like a scarlet thread through all the circles of all the Cossack Armies." But such altruistic motives, by themselves, do not exhaust the question. Notwithstanding the grievous weight of universal military service, the Cossacks, especially those of the South, enjoyed a certain prosperity which excluded that important stimulus which roused against the Government and the régime both the workers' class and the peasantry of Central Russia. An extraordinarily complicated agrarian question set the caste economic interests of the Cossacks against the interests of the

The Revolution and the Cossacks

" outsider "* settlers. Thus, for instance, in the oldest and largest Cossack Army, that of the Don, the amount of land secured to an individual farm was, on the average, in *dessiateens*: for Cossacks, 19.3 to 30; for native peasants, 6.5; for immigrant peasants, 1.3. Finally, owing to historical conditions and a narrow territorial system of recruiting, the Cossack units possessed a perfectly homogeneous personnel, a great internal unity, and a discipline which was firm, though somewhat peculiar as to the mutual relations between the officers and the privates, and therefore they conceded complete obedience to their chiefs and to the Supreme Power.

With the support of all these motives, the Government made a wide use of Cossack troops for suppressing popular agitation, and thus roused against them the mute exasperation of the fermenting, discontented masses of the population.

In return for their historical " liberties," the Cossack Armies, as I have said, give all but universal military service. Its burden and the degree of relative importance of these troops among the armed forces of the Russian Empire are shown in the following table:

COMPOSITION OF THE COSSACK TROOPS IN THE AUTUMN OF 1913.

Armies.	Cavalry Regiments.	Sotnias not included in Regiments.	Infantry Battalions.
Don	60	72	—
Kouban	37	37	22
Orenburg	18	40	
Terek	12	3	
Ural	9	4	
Siberian	9	3	
Trans-Baikal	9	—	—
Semiretchensk	3	/	
Astrakhan	3	—	—
Amur	2	5	
TOTAL †	162	171	24

Partly as cavalry of the line—in divisions and corps, partly as Army corps and divisional cavalry—in regiments, sub-divisions and detached *sotnias*, the Cossack units were scattered over all the

---

* Such was the name given to the non-Cossack immigrant element in the territory.

† With artillery to correspond.

Russian fronts, from the Baltic to Persia. *Among the Cossacks, as against all the other component parts of the Army, desertion was unknown.*

At the outbreak of Revolution all the political groups, and even the representatives of the Allies, devoted great attention to the Cossacks—some building exaggerated hopes on them, others regarding them with unconcealed suspicion. The circles of the Right looked to the Cossacks for Restoration; the Liberal Bourgeoisie, for active support of law and order; while the parties of the Left feared that they were counter-Revolutionary, and therefore started a strong propaganda in the Cossack units, seeking to disintegrate them. This was to some extent assisted by the spirit of repentance which showed itself at all Cossack meetings, Congresses, " Circles " and " Radas " at which the late power was accused of systematically rousing the Cossacks against the people. The mutual relations between the Cossacks and the local agricultural population were unusually complicated, especially in the Cossack territories of European Russia.* Intermingled with the Cossack allotments were peasant lands—those of whilom settlers (the indigenous peasantry)—lands let on long lease, on which large settlements had sprung up, finally lands which had been granted by the Emperor to various persons and which had gradually passed into the hands of " outsiders." On the basis of these mutual relations dissension now arose which began to assume the character of violence and forcible seizures. With respect to the Don Army, which gave the keynote to all others, the Provisional Government considered it necessary to publish on April 7th an appeal in which, while affirming that " the rights of the Cossacks to the land, as they have grown historically, remain inviolable," also promised the " outsider " population, " whose claim to the land is also based on historical rights," that it would be satisfied, in as great a measure as possible, by the Constituent Assembly. This agrarian puzzle, which surrounded with uncertainty the most tender point of the Cossacks' hopes, was explained unequivocally, in the middle of May, by the Minister of Agriculture, Tchernov (at the All-Russia Peasant Congress), who stated that the Cossacks held large tracts of land and that now they would have to surrender a portion of their lands.

In the Cossack territories meanwhile work was in full swing in the sphere of self-determination and self-government; the

---

* In the territory of the Don the peasants formed 48 per cent. of the population and the Cossacks 46 per cent.

The Revolution and the Cossacks 243

information supplied by the Press was vague and contradictory; no one had yet heard the voice of the Cossacks as a whole. One can understand, therefore, that general attention which was concentrated on the All-Russia Cossack Congress, which gathered in Petrograd in the beginning of June.

The Cossacks paid a tribute to the Revolution and to the State, referred to their own needs (after all, the question of their holdings was the most vital one), and . smiled to the Soviet. .

The impression thus produced was indefinite; neither were the hopes of the one side fulfilled nor the fears of the other dissipated.

Meanwhile, at the initiative of the Revolutionary Democracy, a violent propaganda was set on foot for introducing the idea of doing away with the Cossacks as a separate caste. But, on the whole, this idea of self-abolition had no success. On the contrary, a growing aspiration spread among the Cossacks for maintaining their internal organisation and for the union of all the Cossack Armies.

Cossack Governments sprang up everywhere, elected Hetmans and representative institutions ("Circles" and Radas), whose authority increased in accordance with the weakening of the authority and power of the Provisional Government. Such eminent men appeared at the head of the Cossacks as Kaledin (the Don), Doutov (Orenburg), and Karaoulov (the Terek).

A triple power was formed in the Cossack territories; the Hetman with his Government, the commissary of the Provisional Government, and the Soviet.*

The Commissaries, however, after a short and unsuccessful struggle, soon subsided and exhibited no activity. Far more serious became the struggle of the Cossack authority with the local Soviets and Committees, which sought support in the unruly mob of soldiers who flooded the territories under the name of Reserve Army Battalions and Rear Army Units. This curse of the population positively terrorised the land, creating anarchy in the towns and settlements, instituting sacks, seizing lands and businesses, trampling upon all rights, all authority, and creating intolerable conditions of life. The Cossacks had nothing with which to combat this violence—all their units were at the Front. Only in the Don territory, accidentally, in the autumn of 1917, not without the deliberate connivance of the Stavka, a division was concentrated, and afterwards three divisions, with the aid of which General Kaledin attempted to restore order.

---

* In places, the Territorial Council of "outsiders."

But all the measures taken by him, as for instance the occupation by armed forces of railway junctions, of the more important mines, and of large centres, which secured normal communication and supplies for the centre and the fronts, were met not only with violent resistance on the part of the Soviets and with accusations of counter-revolutionism, but even with some suspicion on the part of the Provisional Government. At the same time the Cossacks of the Kouban and of the Terek asked the Don to send them if only a few *sotnias*, as it was " becoming impossible to breathe for *comrades*."

The friendly relations, instituted in the early days of the Revolution, between the general Russian and the Cossack Revolutionary Democracies were soon broken off finally. " Cossack Socialism " turned out to be so self-sufficing, so concentrated in its own castes and corporation limits, that it could find no place in that doctrine.

The Soviets insisted on the equalising of the holdings of the Cossacks and the peasants, while the Cossacks vigorously defended their right of property and disposal in the Cossack lands, basing it on their historical merits as conquerors, protectors, and colonisers of the former marches of Russia's territory.

The organisation of a general territorial Government failed. An internecine struggle began.

The consequences were two-fold: The first was a painful atmosphere of estrangement and hostility between the Cossacks and the " outsider " population, which later, in the swiftly changing kaleidoscope of the civil war, sometimes assumed monstrous forms of mutual extermination, as the power passed from the hands of one side into those of the other. Along with this, one or the other half of the population of the larger Cossack territories were generally deemed as participating in the building up and the economy of the land.* The second was the so-called Cossack separatism or self-determination.

The Cossacks had no reason to expect from the Revolutionary Democracy a favourable settlement of their destiny, especially in the question most vital to it—the land question. On the other hand, the Provisional Government had also assumed an ambiguous attitude in this matter, and the Government power was openly tending to its fall. The future assumed altogether indefinite outlines. Hence, independently of the general healthy aspiration towards decentralisation, there appeared among the

---

* In the principal territories—on the Don and on the Kouban—the Cossacks formed about one-half of the population.

Cossacks, who for centuries had been seeking " freedom," a tendency themselves to secure the maximum of independence, so as to place the future Constituent Assembly before an accomplished fact, or as the more outspoken Cossack leaders put it, " that there should be something from which to knock off." Hence a gradual evolution from territorial self-government to autonomy, federation, and confederation. Hence, finally—with the intrusion of individual local self-love, ambition, and interests—a permanent struggle began with every principle of an imperial tendency, a struggle which weakened both sides and greatly prolonged the civil war.* It was these circumstances, too, that gave birth to the idea of an independent Cossack army, which first arose among the Cossacks of the Kouban and was not then supported by Kaledin and the more imperialistic elements of the Don.

All that I have related refers mainly to the three Cossack bodies (the Don, the Kouban, and the Terek) which form more than sixty per cent. of Cossack-dom. But the general characteristic features belong to the other Cossack armies as well.

Along with the alterations in the composition of the Provisional Government and with the decline of its authority, changes took place in the attitude toward it of Cossack-dom, expressing themselves in the resolutions and appeals of the Council of the union of the Cossack armies, of the hetmans, circles, and Governments. If before July the Cossacks voted for all possible support to the Government and for complete obedience, later, however, *while acknowledging the authority of the Government to the very end*, it comes forward in sharp opposition to it on the questions of the organisation of the Cossack administration and *zemstvo*, of the employment of Cossacks for the repression of rebellious troops and districts and so forth. In October the Kouban rada assumes constituent powers and publishes the constitution of the " Kouban territory." It speaks of the Government in such a manner as the following: " When will the Provisional Government shake off these fumes (the Bolshevist aggression) and put an end, by resolute measures, to these scandals ? "

The Provisional Government, being already without authority and without any real power, surrendered all its positions and agreed to peace with the Cossack Governments.

It is remarkable that, even at the end of October, when, owing to the breach of communications, no correct information had yet been received on the Don about the events in Petrograd and Moscow and about the fate of the Provisional Government, and

---

* Of these phenomena I shall speak later in more detail.

when it was supposed that its fragments were functioning somewhere or other, the Cossack elders, in the person of the representatives of the South-Eastern Union, then gathering,* sought to get into touch with the Government, offering it aid against the Bolsheviks, but conditioning this aid with a whole series of economic demands: a non-interest-bearing loan of 500,000,000 roubles, the State to pay all the expenses of supporting Cossack units outside the territory of the union, the institution of a pension fund for all sufferers, and the right of the Cossacks to all " spoils of war "(?) which might be taken in the course of the coming civil war.

It is not without interest that for a long time Pourishkevitch cherished the idea of the transfer of the State Duma to the Don, as a counterpoise to the Provisional Government and for the preservation of the source of authority, in case of the fall of the latter. Kaledin's attitude towards this proposal was negative.

A characteristic indication of the attitude which the Cossacks had succeeded in retaining towards themselves in the most varied circles was that attraction to the Don which later, in the winter of 1917, led thitherward Rodzianko, Miliukov, General Alexeiev, the Bykhov prisoners, Savinkov, and even Kerensky, who came to General Kaledin, in Novotcherkassk, in the latter days of November, but was not received by him. Pourishkevitch alone did not come, and that only because he was then in prison in Petrograd, in the hands of the Bolsheviks.

And suddenly it turned out that the whole thing was a mystification, pure and simple, that at that time the Cossacks had no power left whatever.

In view of the growing disorders on the Cossack territory, the hetmans repeatedly appealed for the recall from the front of if only part of the Cossack divisions. They were awaited with enormous impatience, and the most radiant hopes were built on them. In October these hopes seemed to be on the eve of fulfilment; the Cossack divisions had started for home. Overcoming all manner of obstacles on their way, retarded at every step by the Vikzhel (All-Russia Executive Railway Committee) and the local Soviets, subjected more than once to insults, disarmament, resorting in one place to requests, in another to cunning, and in some places to armed threats, the Cossack units forced their way into their territories.

But no measures could preserve the Cossack units from the fate

---

* The Don, the Kouban, the Terex, Astrakhan, and the mountaineers of the Northern Caucasus. I shall speak of this later.

The Revolution and the Cossacks

which had befallen the Army, for the whole of the psychological atmosphere and all the factors of disruption, internal and external, were absorbed by the Cossack masses, perhaps less intensively, but on the whole in the same way. The two unsuccessful and, for the Cossacks, incomprehensible marches on Petrograd, with Krymov* and Krasnov,† introduced still greater confusion into their vague political outlook.

The return of the Cossack troops to their homeland brought complete disenchantment with it: they—at least the Cossacks of the Don, the Kouban, and the Terek‡—brought with them from the front the most genuine Bolshevism, void, of course, of any kind of ideology, but with all the phenomena of complete disintegration which we know so well. This disintegration ripened gradually, showed itself later, but at once exhibiting itself in the denial of the authority of the " elders," the negation of all power, by mutiny, violence, the persecution and surrender of the officers, but principally by complete abandonment of any struggle against the Soviet power, which falsely promised the inviolability of the Cossack rights and organisation. Bolshevism and the Cossack organisation! Such grotesque contradictions were brought to the surface daily by the reality of Russian life, on the basis of that drunken debauch into which its long-desired freedom had degenerated.

Now began the tragedy of Cossack life and the Cossack family in which an insurmountable barrier had arisen between the " elders " and the " men of the front," destroying their life and rousing the children against their fathers.

---

* The third cavalry corps, in Kornilov's advance against Kerensky.
† The third cavalry corps with Kerensky against the Bolsheviks.
‡ The Ural Cossacks, until their tragic fall in the end of 1919, knew not Bolshevism.

CHAPTER XXV

National Units.

IN the old Russian Army the national question scarcely existed. Among the soldiery the representatives of the races inhabiting Russia experienced somewhat greater hardships in the service, caused by their ignorance or imperfect knowledge of the Russian language, in which their training was carried on. It was only this ground—the technical difficulties of training—and perhaps that of general roughness and barbarism, but in no case that of racial intolerance, that often led to that friction, which made the position of the alien elements difficult, the more so that, according to the system of mixed drafting, they were generally torn from their native lands; the territorial system of filling the ranks of the Army was considered to be technically irrational and politically—not void of danger. The Little Russian question in particular did not exist *at all*. The Little Russian speech (outside the limits of official training), songs and music received full recognition and did not rouse in anyone any feeling of separateness, being accepted as Russian, as one's own. In the Army, with the exception of the Jews, all the other alien elements were absorbed fairly quickly and permanently; the community of the Army was in no way a conductor either for compulsory Russification or for national Chauvinism.

Still less were national differences to be noticed in the community of officers. Qualities and virtues—corporative, military, pertaining to comradeship or simply human, overshadowed or totally obliterated racial barriers. Personally, during my twenty-five years of service before the revolution, it never came into my head to introduce this element into my relations as commander, as colleague, or as comrade. And this was done intuitively, not as the result of certain views and convictions. The national questions which were *raised outside the Army*, in the political life of the country, interested me, agitated me, were settled by me in one or the other direction, harshly and irrecon-

National Units

cilably at times, but always without trespassing on the boundaries of military life.

The Jews occupied a somewhat different position. I shall return to this question later. But it may be said that, with respect to the old Army, this question was of popular rather than of political significance. It cannot be denied that in the Army there was a certain tendency to oppress the Jews, but it was not at all a part of any system, was not inspired from above, but sprang up in the lower strata and in virtue of complex causes, which spread far outside of the life, customs, and mutual relations of the military community.

In any case, the war overthrew all barriers, while the revolution brought with it the repeal, in legislative order, of all religious and national restrictions.

With the beginning of the revolution and the weakening of the Government, a violent centrifugal tendency arose in the borderlands of Russia, and along with it a tendency towards the nationalisation, *i.e.*, the dismemberment, of the Army. Undoubtedly, the need of such dismemberment did not at that time spring from the consciousness of the masses and had no real foundation (I do not speak of the Polish formations). The sole motives for nationalisation then lay in the seeking of the political upper strata of the newly formed groups to create a real support for their demands, and in the feeling of self-preservation which urged the military element to seek in new and prolonged formations a temporary or permanent relief from military operations. Endless national military congresses began, without the permission of the Government and of the High Command. All races suddenly began to speak; the Lithuanians, the Estonians, the Georgians, the White Russians, the Little Russians, the Mohammedans—demanding the " self-determination " proclaimed—from cultural national autonomy to full independence inclusive, and principally the immediate formation of separate bodies of troops. Finally, more serious results, undoubtedly negative as regards the integrity of the Army, were attained by the Ukrainian, Polish, and partially by the Trans-Caucasian formations. The other attempts were nipped in the bud. It was only during the last days of the existence of the Russian Army, in October, 1917, that General Shcherbatov, seeking to preserve the Roumanian front, began the classification of the Army, on a large scale, according to race—an attempt which ended in complete failure. I must add that one race only made no demand for self-determination with regard to military service—the Jewish. And whenever a proposal was made from any source —in reply to the complaints of the Jews—to organise special Jewish regiments, this proposal roused a storm of indignation among the Jews and in the circles of the Left, and was stigmatised as deliberate provocation.

The Government showed itself markedly opposed to the reorganisation of the Army according to race. In a letter to the Polish Congress (June 1st, 1917) Kerensky expressed the following view: " The great achievement of the liberation of Russia and Poland can be arrived at only under the condition that the organism of the Russian Army is not weakened, that no alterations in its organisation infringe its unity. . . . The extrusion from it of racial troops . . . would, at this difficult moment, tear its body, break its power, and spell ruin both for the revolution and for the freedom of Russia, Poland, and of the other nationalities inhabiting Russia."

The attitude of the commanding element towards the question of nationalisation was dual. The majority was altogether opposed to it; the minority regarded it with some hope that, by breaking their connection with the Council of Workmen's and Soldiers' Delegates, the newly created national units might escape the errors and infatuations of democratisation and become a healthy nucleus for fortifying the front and building up the army. General Alexeiev resolutely opposed all attempts at nationalisation, but encouraged the Polish and Tchekho-Slovak formations. General Brussilov allowed the creation of the first Ukrainian formation on his own responsibility, after requesting the Supreme Commander-in-Chief " not to repeal it and not to undermine his authority thereby."* The regiment was allowed to exist. General Ruzsky, also without permission, began the Esthonian formations,† and so forth. From the same motives, probably, which led some commanders to allow formations, but with a reverse action, the whole of the Russian revolutionary democracy, in the person of the Soviets and the army committees, rose against the nationalisation of the Army. A shower of violent resolutions poured in from all sides. Among others, the Kiev Council of Workmen's and Soldiers' Delegates, about the middle of April, characterised Ukrainisation in rude and indignant language, as simple desertion and " hide-saving," and by a majority of 264 against 4 demanded the repeal of the formation of Ukrainian regiments. It is interesting to note that as great an opponent of nationalisation was found in the Polish " Left," which had

---

* General Alexeiev ordered its disbandment, but Kerensky permitted it to remain.
† They were disbanded.

split off from the military congress of the Poles in June, because of the resolution for the formation of Polish troops.

The Government did not long adhere to its original firm decision against nationalisation. The declaration of July 2nd, along with the grant of autonomy to the Ukraine, also decided the question of nationalising the troops: " The Government considers it possible to continue its assistance to a closer national union of the Ukrainians in the ranks of the Army itself, or to the drafting into individual units of Ukrainians exclusively, in so far as such a measure does not injure the fighting capacity of the Army
and considers it possible to attract to the fulfilment of those tasks the Ukrainian soldiers themselves, who are sent by the Central Rada to the War Ministry, the General Staff, and the Stavka."

A great " migration of peoples " began.

Other Ukrainian agents journeyed along the front, organising Ukrainian *gromadas* and committees, getting resolutions passed for transfers to Ukrainian units, or concerning reluctance to go to the front under the plea that " the Ukraine was being stifled " and so forth. By October the Ukrainian committee of the Western front was already calling for armed pressure on the Government for the immediate conclusion of peace. Petlura affirmed that he had 50,000 Ukrainian troops at his disposal. Yet the commander of the Kiev military district, Colonel Oberoutchev,[*] bears witness as follows: " At the time when heroic exertions were being made to break the foe (the June advance) *I was unable to send a single soldier to reinforce the active army.* As soon as I give an order to some reserve regiment or other to send detachments to reinforce the front, a meeting would be called by a regiment which had until then lived, peaceably, without thinking of Ukrainisation, the yellow and blue Ukrainian flag would be unfurled and the cry raised: ' Let us march under the Ukrainian flag ! '

" And after that they would not move. Weeks would pass, a month, but the detachments would not stir, either under the red, or under the blue and yellow flag."

Was it possible to combat this unconcealed care for their own safety ? The answer is given by Oberoutchev again—an answer very characteristic in its lifeless party rigour:

" Of course, I could have used force to get my orders obeyed. And that force lay in my hands." But " by using force against the

---

[*] A Socialist-Revolutionary emigrant and an active worker in his party. He was appointed to this post by Kerensky, at the desire of the Kiev Council of Soldiers' Delegates.

disobedient, who are acting under the Ukrainian flag, one risks the reproach that one is struggling not against acts of anarchy, but against national freedom and the self-determination of nations. And for me, a Socialist-Revolutionary, to risk such a reproach, and in the Ukraine too, with which I had been connected all my life, was impossible. And so I decided to resign."*

And he resigned. True, it was only in October, shortly before the Bolshevist *coup d'état*, having occupied the post of commander of the troops in the most important district next the front for nearly five months.

As a development of the orders of the Government, the Stavka appointed special divisions on each front for Ukrainisation, and on the South-Western front also the 34th Army Corps, which was under the command of General Skoropadsky. To these units, which were mostly quartered in the deep reserve, the soldiers flocked from the whole front, without leave asked or given. The hopes of the optimists on the one hand and the fears of the Left circles on the other that nationalisation would create " firm units " (counter-revolutionary in the terminology of the Left) were speedily dispersed. The new Ukrainian troops were permeated with the same elements of disintegration as the regulars.

Meanwhile, among the officers and old soldiers of many famous regiments with a great historical past, now transformed into Ukrainian units, this measure roused acute pain and the recognition that the end of the Army was near.† In August, when I was in command of the South-Western front, bad news began to come to me from the 34th Army Corps. The corps seemed to be escaping from direct subordination, receiving both directions and reinforcements from the " General Secretary Petlura " directly. His commissary was attached to the Staff of the corps, over which waved the " yellow-blue flag." The former Russian officers and sergeants, left in the regiments because there was no Ukrainian command, were treated with contumely by the often ignorant Ukrainian ensigns set over them and by the soldiers. An extremely unhealthy atmosphere of mutual hostility and estrangement was gathering in these units.

I sent for General Skoropadsky and invited him to moderate the violent course of the process of Ukrainisation and, in particular, either to restore the rights of the Commanders or to release them from service in the corps. The future Hetman declared that a mistaken idea had been formed of his activity, probably because

---

* Oberoutchev. *In the Days of the Revolution.*
† Among others, my former 4th Rifle Division was subjected to Ukrainisation.

National Units

of the historical past of the Skoropadsky family,* that he was a true Russian, an officer of the Guards and was altogether free of all seeking for self-determination, that he was only obeying orders, for which he himself had no sympathy. But immediately afterwards Skoropadsky went to the Stavka, whence my Staff received directions to aid the speedy Ukrainisation of the 34th Army Corps.

The question of the Polish formations was in a somewhat different position. The Provisional Government had declared the independence of Poland, and the Poles now counted themselves " foreigners "; Polish formations had long ago existed on the South-Western front, though they were breaking up (with the exception of the Polish Lancers); having given permission to the Ukrainians, the Government could not refuse it to the Poles. Finally, the Central Powers, by creating the appearance of Polish independence, also had in view the formation of a Polish Army, which, however, ended in failure. America also formed a Polish Army on French territory.

In July, 1917, the formation of a Polish corps was assigned to the Western front, of which I was then Commander-in-Chief. At the head of the corps I put General Dovbor-Mousnitsky,† who is now in command of the Polish Army at Poznan. A strong, energetic, resolute man, who fearlessly waged war on the disintegration of the Russian troops and on the Bolshevism among them, he succeeded in a short time in creating units which, if not altogether firm, were, in any case, strikingly different from the Russian troops in their discipline and order. It was the old discipline, rejected by the Revolution—without meetings, commissaries or committees. Such units roused another attitude towards them in the Army, notwithstanding the rejection of nationalisation in principle. Being supplied with the property of the disbanded mutinous divisions and treated with complaisance by the Chief of Supplies, the corps was soon able to organise its own commissariat. By order, the ranks of the officers in the Polish corps were filled by the transfer of those who desired it, and the ranks of the soldiers —exclusively by volunteers or from reserve battalions; practically, however, the inevitable current from the front set in, caused by the same motives which influenced the Russian soldiers, devastating the thinned ranks of the Army.

In the end the Polish formations turned out to be altogether useless to us. Even at the June military congress of the Poles,

---

* The Ukrainian Hetman Skoropadsky was one of his ancestors.
† Formerly Commander of the 38th Army Corps.

fairly unanimous and unambiguous speeches were heard which defined the aims of these formations. Their synthesis was thus expressed by one of the delegates: " It is a secret for no one that the War is coming to an end, and we need the Polish Army, not for the War, not for fighting; we need it so that at the coming international conference we may be reckoned with, that there should be power at our backs."

And indeed the corps did not make its appearance at the front— it is true that it was not yet finally formed; it did not wish to interfere in the " home affairs " of the Russians (October and later —the struggle against Bolshevism) and soon assumed completely the position of " a foreign army," being taken over and supported by the French command.

But neither were the hopes of the Polish nationalists fulfilled. In the midst of the general break-down and fall of the front in the beginning of 1918 and after the irruption of the Germans into Russia, part of the corps was captured and disarmed, part of it dispersed and the remnants of the Polish troops afterwards found a hospitable asylum in the ranks of the Volunteer Army.

Personally, I cannot but say a good word for the 1st Polish Corps, to the units of which, quartered in Bykhov, we owe much in the protection of the lives of General Kornilov and the other Bykhov prisoners, in the memorable days of September to November.

Centrifugal forces were scattering the country and the Army. To class and party intolerance was added the embitterment of national dissensions, partly based on the historically-created relations between the races inhabiting Russia and the Imperial Government, and partly altogether baseless, absurd, fed by causes which had nothing in common with healthy national feeling. Latent or crushed at an earlier date, these dissensions broke out rudely at just that moment, unfortunately, when the general Russian authority was voluntarily and conscientiously taking the path of recognition of the historical rights and the national cultural self-determination of the component elements of the Russian State.

General Alexeiev's (centre) farewell.

CHAPTER XXVI.

MAY AND THE BEGINNING OF JUNE IN THE SPHERE OF MILITARY ADMINISTRATION—THE RESIGNATION OF GUTCHKOV AND GENERAL ALEXEIEV—MY DEPARTURE FROM THE STAVKA—THE ADMINISTRATION OF KERENSKY AND GENERAL BRUSSILOV

ON May 1st the Minister of War, Gutchkov, left his post. "We wished," so he explained the meaning of the " democratisation " of the Army which he tried to introduce, " to give organised forms and certain channels to follow, to that awakened spirit of independence, self-help and liberty which had swept over all. But there is a line, beyond which lies the beginning of the ruin of that living, mighty organism which is the Army." Undoubtedly that line was crossed even before the first of May.

I am not preparing to characterise Gutchkov, whose sincere patriotism I do not doubt. I am speaking only of the system. It is difficult to decide who could have borne the heavy weight of administering the Army during the first period of the Revolution; but, in any case, Gutchkov's Ministry had not the slightest grounds to seek the part of guiding the life of the Army. It did not lead the Army. On the contrary, submitting to a " parallel power " and impelled from below, the Ministry, somewhat restively, *followed the Army*, until it came right up to the line, beyond which final ruin begins.

" To restrain the Army from breaking up completely under the influence of that pressure which proceeded from the Socialists, and in particular from their citadel—the Soviet of Workmen's and Soldiers' Delegates—to gain time, to allow the diseased process to be absorbed, to help the healthy elements to gain strength, such was my aim," wrote Gutchkov to Kornilov in June, 1917. The whole question is whether the resistance to the destroying powers was resolute enough. The Army did not feel this. The officers read the orders, signed by Gutchkov, which broke up completely the foundations of military life and custom. That these orders were the result of a painful internal drama, a painful struggle and defeat—this the officers did not know, nor did it interest them. Their lack of information was so great that many of them even now, four years later, ascribe to Gutchkov the authorship of the celebrated " Order No. 1." However it may be, the officers felt themselves deceived and deserted. Their difficult position they ascribed principally to the reforms of the Minister of War, against whom a hostile feeling arose, heated still more by the grumbling of hundreds of Generals removed by him and of the ultra-monarchical section of the officers, who could not forgive Gutchkov his supposed share in the preparation of the Palace *coup d'état* and of the journey to Pskov.[*]

Thus the resignation of this Minister, even if caused " by those conditions, in which the Government power was placed in the country, and in particular the power of the Minister of the Army and the Navy with respect to the Army and the fleet," [†] had another justification as well—the want of support among the officers and the soldiery.

In a special resolution the Provisional Government condemned Gutchkov's action in " resigning responsibility for the fate of Russia," and appointed Kerensky Minister of the Army and the Navy. I do not know how the Army received this appointment in the beginning, but the Soviet received it without prejudice. Kerensky was a complete stranger to the art of war and to military life, but could have been surrounded by honest men; what was then going on in the Army was simple insanity, and this even a civilian might have understood. Gutchkov was a representative of the Bourgeoisie, a Member of the Right, and was distrusted; now, perhaps, a Socialist Minister, the favourite of the Democracy, might have succeeded in dissipating the fog in which the soldiers' consciousness was wrapped. Nevertheless, to take up such a burden called for enormous boldness or enormous self-confidence, and Kerensky emphasised this circumstance more than once when speaking to an Army audience: " At a time when many soldiers, who had studied the art of war for decades, declined the post of Minister of War, I—a civilian, accepted it." No one, however, had ever heard that the Ministry of War had been offered to a soldier that May.

The very first steps taken by the new Minister dissipated our hopes: the choice of collaborators, who were even greater opportunists than their predecessors, but void of experience in military administration and in active service; [‡] the surrounding of himself with men from " underground "—perhaps having done very great

---

[*] The proposal of abdication made to the Emperor Nicholas II.
[†] Gutchkov's official letter to the President of the Government.
[‡] Colonels: Baranovsky, Yakoubovitch, Prince Toumanov, and later Verkhovsky.

Military Administration in May and June

work in the cause of the Revolution, but without any comprehension of the life of the Army—all this introduced into the actions of the War Ministry a new party element, foreign to the military service.

A few days after his appointment Kerensky issued the Declaration of the rights of the soldier, thereby predestining the entire course of his activity.

On May 11th the Minister was passing through Moghilev to the Front. We were surprised by the circumstance that the passage was timed for 5 a.m., and that only the Chief-of-Staff was invited into the train. The Minister of War seemed to avoid meeting the Supreme Commander-in-Chief. His conversation with me was short and touched on details—the suppression of some disturbances or other that had broken out at one of the railway junctions and so forth. The most capital questions of the existence of the Army and of the coming advance, the necessity for unity in the views of the Government and the Command, the absence of which was showing itself with such marked clearness—all this, apparently, did not attract the attention of the Minister. Among other things, Kerensky passed a few cursory remarks on the inappropriateness of Generals Gourko and Dragomirov, Commanders-in-Chief of fronts, to their posts, which drew a protest from me. All this was very symptomatic and created at the Stavka a condition of tense, nervous expectation.

Kerensky was proceeding to the South-Western front, to begin his celebrated verbal campaign which was to rouse the Army to achievement. The *word* created hypnosis and self-hypnosis. Brussilov reported to the Stavka that throughout the Army the Minister of War had been received with extraordinary enthusiasm. Kerensky spoke with unusual pathos and exaltation, in stirring " revolutionary " images, often with foam on his lips, reaping the applause and delight of the mob. At times, however, the mob would turn to him the face of a wild beast, the sight of which made words to stick in the throat and caused the heart to fail. They sounded a note of menace, these moments, but fresh delight drowned their alarming meaning. And Kerensky reported to the Provisional Government that " the wave of enthusiasm in the Army is growing and widening," and that a definite change in favour of discipline and the regeneration of the Army was displaying itself. In Odessa he became even more irresistibly poetical : " In your welcome I see that great enthusiasm which has overwhelmed the country and feel that great exaltation which the world experiences but once in hundreds of years."

Let us be just.

Kerensky called on the Army to do its duty. He spoke of duty, honour, discipline, obedience, trust in its commanders; he spoke of the necessity for advancing and for victory. He spoke in the language of the established revolutionary ritual, which ought to have reached the hearts and minds of the " revolutionary people." Sometimes, even, feeling his power over his audience, he would throw at it the words, which became household words, of " rebel slaves " and " revolutionary tyrants."

In vain!

At the conflagration of the temple of Russia, he called to the fire: " Be quenched! " instead of extinguishing it with brimful pails of water.

Words could not fight against facts, nor heroic poems against the stern prose of life. The replacement of the Motherland by Liberty and Revolution did not make the aims of the conflict any clearer. The constant scoffing at the old " discipline," at the " Czar's generals," the reminders of the knout, the stick, and the " former unprivileged condition of the soldier " or of the soldier's blood " shed in vain " by someone or other—nothing of this could bridge the chasm between the two component parts of the Army. The passionate preaching of a " new, conscious, iron revolutionary discipline," *i.e.*, a discipline based on the " declaration of the rights of the soldier "—a discipline of meetings, propaganda, political agitation, absence of authority in the commanders, and so forth— this preaching was in irreconcileable opposition to the call to victory. Having received his impressions in the artificially exalted, theatrical atmosphere of meetings, surrounded both in the Ministry and in his journeyings, by an impenetrable wall of old political friends and of all manner of delegations and deputations from the Soviets and the Committees, Kerensky looked on the Army through the prism of their outlook, either unwilling or unable to sink himself in the real life of the Army and in its torments, sufferings, searchings, and crimes, and finally to attain a real standing-ground, get at vital themes and real words. These everyday questions of Army life and organisation—dry in their form and deeply dramatic in their content—never served as themes for his speeches. They contained only a glorification of the Revolution and a condemnation of certain perversions of the idea of national defence, created by that Revolution itself. The masses of the soldiery, eager for sentimental scenes, listened to the appeals of the recognised chief for self-sacrifice, and they were inflamed with the " sacred fire "; but as soon as the scene was over, both the chief and the audiences reverted to the daily occupations: the chief—

to the "democratisation" of the Army, and the masses—to "deepening the Revolution." In the same way, probably, Djerzinsky's executioners in Soviet Russia now admire, in the temple of proletarian art, the sufferings of young Werther—before proceeding to their customary occupation of hanging and shooting.

At any rate, there was much noise. So much, that Hindenburg sincerely believes even to this day that in June, 1917, the South-Western Front was commanded by Kerensky. In his book *Aus meinem Leben* the German Field-Marshal relates that Kerensky succeeded Brussilov, " who was swept away from his post by the rivers of Russian blood which he shed in Galicia and Macedonia (?) in 1916 " (the Field-Marshal has confused the theatres of war), and tells the story of Kerensky's " advance " and victories over the Austrians near Stanislavov.

* * * *

Meanwhile life at the Stavka was gradually waning. The wheels of administration were still revolving, everybody was doing something, issuing orders and giving directions. The work was purely formal, because all the plans and directions of the Stavka were upset by unavoidable and incalculable circumstances. Petrograd never took the Stavka into serious account, but at that time the attitude of the Government was somewhat hostile, and the War Ministry was conducting the work of reorganisation without ever consulting the Stavka. This position was a great burden to General Alexeiev, the more so that the attacks of his old disease became more frequent. He was extremely patient and disregarded all personal pin-pricks and all efforts at undermining his prerogatives which emanated from the Government. In his discussions with numerous Army chiefs, and organisations which took advantage of his accessibility, he was likewise patient, straightforward, and sincere. He worked incessantly, in order to preserve the remnants of the Army. Seeking to give an example of discipline, he protested but obeyed. He was not sufficiently strong and masterful by nature to compel the Provisional Government and the civilian reformers of the Army to take the demands of the Supreme Command into account; at the same time, he never did violence to his conscience in order to please the powers that be or the mob.

On May 20th, Kerensky stopped for a few hours at Moghilev on his way home from the South-Western Front. He was full of impressions, praised Brussilov, and expressed the view that the general spirit at the front and the relations between officers and men were excellent. Although in his conversation with Alexeiev Kerensky made no hint, we noticed that his entourage was somewhat uneasy, and realised that decisions in regard to certain changes had already been taken. I did not consider it necessary to acquaint the Supreme Commander-in-Chief with these rumours, and merely seized the first opportunity for postponing his intended visit to the Western Front so as not to put him into a false position.

In the night of the 22nd a telegram was received dismissing General Alexeiev and appointing General Brussilov by order of the Provisional Government. The Quartermaster-General Josephovitch woke up Alexeiev and handed him the telegram. The Supreme Commander-in-Chief was deeply moved, and tears came down his cheeks. May the members of the Provisional Government who are still alive forgive the vulgarity of the language: in a subsequent conversation with me the Supreme Commander-in-Chief inadvertently uttered the following words: " The cads! They have dismissed me like a servant without notice."

A great statesman and military leader had thus left the stage, whose virtue—one of many—was his implicit loyalty (or was it a defect?) to the Provisional Government.

On the next day Kerensky was asked—at a meeting of the Soviet—what steps he had taken in view of the Supreme Commander-in-Chief's speech at the officers' Conference (see Chapter XXIII). He replied that Alexeiev had been dismissed, and that he, Kerensky, believed that a late French politician was right in saying that " discipline of duty " should be introduced from the top." The Bolshevik Rosenfeldt (Kamenev) expressed satisfaction, because this decision fully coincided with the repeated demands of the Soviet. On the same day the Government published an official communiqué to the effect that: " In spite of the fact that General Alexeiev was naturally very tired and needed rest from his arduous labours, it was considered impossible to lose the services of this exceptionally experienced and talented leader, and General Alexeiev was therefore to remain at the disposal of the Provisional Government." The Supreme Commander-in-Chief issued the following Order of the Day as a farewell to the Armies.

" For nearly three years I have walked with you along the thorny path of the Russian Army. Your glorious deeds have filled me with joyful elation, and I was filled with sorrow in the days of our reverses. But I continued with implicit hope in Providence, in the mission of the Russian people, and in the prowess of the Russian soldier. Now that the foundations of our military power are shattered, I still preserve the same faith, as life would not be worth living without it. I reverently salute you, my comrades in arms, all those who have done their duty faithfully, all those whose hearts beat with the love of their country, all those who in the days of the popular turmoil were determined not to allow the Mother Country to be disrupted. I, the old soldier, and your late Supreme Commander-in-Chief, once more reverently salute you. Pray think kindly of me."

(Signed) GENERAL ALEXEIEV.

Towards the end of our work in common my intercourse with General Alexeiev was one of cordial friendship. In parting with me, he said: "All this structure will undoubtedly soon collapse. You will have to resume work once again. Would you then agree to work with me again?" I naturally expressed my readiness to collaborate in the future.

Brussilov's appointment signified definite elimination of the Stavka, as a decisive factor, and a change in its direction. Brussilov's unrestrained and incomprehensible opportunism, and his endeavour to gain the reputation of a revolutionary, deprived the Commanding Staffs of the Army of the moral support which the former Stavka still gave them. The new Supreme Commander-in-Chief was given a very frigid and dry reception at Moghilev. Instead of the customary enthusiastic ovation to which the "Revolutionary General" had been accustomed, whom the mob had carried shoulder high at Kamenetz-Podolsk, he found a lonely railway station and a strictly conventional parade. Faces were sulky and speeches were stereotyped. Brussilov's first steps, insignificant but characteristic episodes, had a further disheartening effect. As he was reviewing the Guard of Honour of men with the Cross of St. George, he did not greet their gallant wounded Commander, Colonel Timanovsky, or the officers, but shook hands with the men—the messenger and the orderly. They were so much perturbed by the unexpected inconvenience of such greetings on parade that they dropped their rifles. Brussilov handed to me his Order of the Day intended as a greeting to the Armies, which he had written in his own hand, and asked me to send it to Kerensky for approval. In his speech to the members of the Stavka, who had foregathered to bid farewell to General Alexeiev, Brussilov tried to make excuses. For excuses they were—his confused explanations of the sin of "deepening the Revolution" with Kerensky and "democratising" the Army with the Committees. The closing sentence of his Order, addressed to the retiring Chief, sounded, therefore, out of tune: " Your name will always remain unstained and pure as that of a man who has worked incessantly and has given himself entirely to the service of the Army. In the dark days of the past and in the present turmoil you have had the courage, resolutely and loyally, to oppose violence, to combat mendacity, flattery, subservience, to resist anarchy in the country and disruption in the ranks of its defenders."

My activities were disapproved by the Provisional Government as much as those of General Alexeiev, and I could not work with Brussilov owing to fundamental differences of opinion. I presume that during Kerensky's visit to the South-Western Front, Brussilov agreed with his suggestion of appointing General Lukomsky Chief-of-Staff. I was therefore surprised at the conversation which took place on the first day of Brussilov's arrival. He said to me: " Well, General, I thought I was going to meet a comrade-in-arms and that we were going to work together at the Stavka, but you look very surly."

" That is not quite true. I cannot stay at the Stavka any longer. I also know that General Lukomsky is to supersede me."

" What? How have they dared to appoint him without my knowledge?"

We never touched upon that subject again. I continued to work with Brussilov for about ten days pending my successor's arrival, and I must confess that work was unpleasant from the moral point of view. From the very first days of the War Brussilov and I had served together. For the first month I was Quartermaster-General on the Staff of his Eighth Army, then for two years in command of the 4th Rifle Division in that same glorious Army, and Commander of the 8th Army Corps on his front. The " Iron Division " went from victory to victory, and Brussilov particularly favoured it and constantly acknowledged its achievements. His attitude towards the Commander of the Division was correspondingly cordial. I shared with Brussilov many hardships as well as many unforgettable happy days of military triumphs. And I found it difficult to speak to him now, for he was a different man and was so recklessly, from the personal point of view—which, after all, did not matter—as well as from the point of view of the interests of the Army, throwing his reputation to the four winds. When I reported to him, every question which might be described as " un-Democratic," but was, in reality, an endeavour to maintain the reasonable standard of efficiency, was invariably negatived. Argument was useless. Brussilov sometimes interrupted me and said with strong feeling: " Do you think that I am not disgusted at having constantly to wave the Red rag? What can I do? Russia is sick, the Army is sick. It must be cured, and I know of no other remedy."

The question of my appointment interested him more than it interested me. I refused to express any definite desire and said that I would accept any appointment. Brussilov was negotiating

Kerensky addressing soldiers' meeting.

Military Administration in May and June

with Kerensky. He once said to me, "*They* are afraid that if I give you an appointment at the Front, you will begin to oust the Committees." I smiled. "No, I will not appeal to the Committees for help, but will also leave them alone." I attributed no importance to this conversation, which was conducted almost in jest; but on the same day a telegram was sent to Kerensky, of which the following was the approximate wording: "I have talked it over with Deniken. The obstacles have been removed. I request that he be appointed Commander-in-Chief of the Western Front."

In the beginning of August I proceeded to Minsk and took General Markov as Chief-of-Staff of the Front. I had no regrets in leaving the Stavka. For two months I had worked like a slave and my outlook had widened, but had I achieved anything for the preservation of the Army? Positive results were nil. There may have been some negative results; the process of disruption of the Army had been to a certain extent stayed. And that is all. One of Kerensky's assistants, afterwards High Commissar, Stankevitch, thus describes my activities: "Nearly every week telegrams were sent to Petrograd (by Deniken) containing provocative and harsh criticisms on the new methods in the Army; criticisms they were, not advice. Is it possible to advise that the Revolution should be cancelled." If that was only Stankevitch discussing Denikin it would not matter. But these views were shared by the wide circles of the Revolutionary Democracy and referred not to the individual, but to all those who "impersonated the tragedy of the Russian Army." The appreciation must therefore be answered.

Yes, the Revolution could not be cancelled, and what is more, I may state that the majority of the Russian officers, with whom I agreed, *did not wish to cancel the Revolution*. They demanded one thing only—that the Army should not be revolutionised from the top. None of us could give any other advice. And if the Commanding Staffs appeared to be "insufficiently tied to the Revolution" they should have been mercilessly dismissed and other people—were they but unskilled artisans in military matters —should have been appointed, and given full power and confidence.

Personalities do not matter. Alexeiev, Brussilov, Kornilov— represent periods and systems. Alexeiev protested. Brussilov submitted. Kornilov claimed. In dismissing these men one after another did the Provisional Government have a definite idea, or were they simply distracted to the point of convulsion and completely lost in the morass of their own internal dissensions? Would it not appear that had the order been changed in which the links had stood in that chain salvation might have ensued?

CHAPTER XXVII.

My Term as Commander-in-Chief on the Western Russian Front.

I TOOK over the Command from General Gourko. His removal had already been decided on May 5th, and an Order of the Day had been drafted at the War Ministry. Gourko, however, sent a report in which he stated that it was impossible for him to remain morally responsible for the armies under his command in the present circumstances (after the " Declaration of the Soldier's Rights " had been issued). This report afforded Kerensky an excuse for issuing on May 26th an order relieving Gourko of his post and appointing him to the command of a division. The motive was adduced that Gourko was " not up to the mark," and that " as the country was in danger, every soldier should do his duty and not be an example of weakness to others." Also that " the Commander-in-Chief enjoys the full confidence of the Government, and should apply all his energies to the task of carrying out the intentions of the Government; to decline to bear the moral responsibility was on General Gourko's part tantamount to dereliction of duty, which he should have continued to perform according to his strength and judgment." Not to speak of the fact that Gourko's dismissal had already been decided, suffice it to recall similar instances, such as the resignations of Gutchkov and Miliukov, in order to realise the hypocrisy of these excuses. And what is more—Kerensky himself, during one of the Government crises caused by the uncompromising attitude of the " Revolutionary Democracy," had threatened to resign, and had stated in writing to his would-be successor, Nekrassov, that: " Owing to the impossibility of introducing into the Government such elements as were required in the present exceptional circumstances, he could no longer bear the responsibility before the country according to his conscience and judgment, and requested therefore to be relieved of all his duties." The papers said that he had "departed from Petrograd." On October 28th, as we know, Kerensky fled, abandoning the post of Supreme Commander-in-Chief.

The old Commanding Staffs were in a difficult position. I refer not to men of definite political convictions, but of the average honest soldier. They could not follow Kerensky (the system, not the man) and destroy with their own hands the edifice which they had themselves spent their lives in building. They could not resign because the enemy was on Russian soil and they would be deserters according to their own conscience. It was a vicious circle.

Upon my arrival at Minsk I addressed two large gatherings of members of the Staff and departments of the Front, and later the Army Commanders, and expounded my fundamental views. I did not say much, but stated clearly that I accepted the Revolution without any reservations. I considered, however, that to " revolutionise " the Army was a fatal procedure, and that to introduce demagogy into the Army would mean the ruin of the Country. I declared that I would oppose it with all my might and invited my collaborators to do the same. I received a letter from General Alexeiev, who wrote: " Congratulations on your appointment. Rouse them! Make your demands calmly but persistently. I trust that the revival will come without coaxing, without red ribbons, without sonorous and empty phrases. The Army cannot continue as it is now, for Russia is being transformed into a multitude of idlers who have an exaggerated idea of their own importance (value their movements in gold). I am in heart and in thought with you, with your work and with your wishes. God help you."

The Committee of the Front impersonated at Minsk " Military Politics." On the eve of my arrival that semi-Bolshevik organisation had passed a resolution protesting against an advance and in favour of the struggle of united democracies against their Governments; this naturally helped to define my attitude towards that body. I had no direct intercourse with the Committee, which " stewed in its own juice," argued the matter of preponderant influences of the Social Democratic and Social Revolutionary factions, passed resolutions which puzzled even the Army Committees by their demagogic contents, distributed defeatist pamphlets, and incensed the men against their chiefs. According to the law, the Committees were not responsible and could not be tried. The Committee was educating in the same sense the pupils of the " school for agitators," who were afterwards to spread these doctrines along the Front. I will quote one instance showing the real meaning of these manifestations " of civic indignation and sorrow." Pupils of the school often appealed to the Chief-of-Staff and sent in "demands." On one occasion the demand for an extra pair of boots was couched in offensive terms. General Markov refused it. On the next day a resolution was published (in the paper *The Front*, No. 25) of the Conference of Pupils of the School of Agitators to the effect that they had personally tested the reluctance of Headquarters to take elective organisations into account. The pupils declared that the Committee of the Front will find in them and in those who sent them full support against "counter-revolution," and even armed assistance.

Was work in common possible in these circumstances?

The idea of the advance was finally, however, accepted by the Committee of the Front, which demanded that from itself and from Army Committees "fighting committees of contact" be established which would be entitled to partake in the drafting of plans of operations to control the Commanding Officers and Headquarters of the advancing troops, etc. I naturally refused the request, and a conflict ensued. The War Minister was very much perturbed, and sent to Minsk the Chief of his Chancery, Colonel Baronovsky, a young staff officer who prompted Kerensky in all military matters, and the Commissar Stankevitch, who remained at the Western Front for two days, was removed to the Northern Front and replaced by Kalinin. Baronovsky's friends afterwards told me that the question of my dismissal had been raised in view of "friction with the Committee of the Front." Stankevitch appeased the Committee and "fighting committees of contact" were allowed to take part in the advance, but were denied the right of control over the operations and of assisting in drawing up plans.

* * *

Of the three Army Commanders at that Front, two were entirely in the hands of the Committees. As their sectors were inactive, their presence could be temporarily tolerated. The advance was to begin on the Front of the 10th Army, commanded by General Kisselevsky, in the region of Molodetchno. I inspected the troops and the position, interviewed the Commanding Officers and addressed the troops. In the preceding chapters I have recounted impressions, facts, and episodes of the life of the Western front. I will, therefore, mention here only a few details. I saw the troops on parade. Some units had preserved the appearance and the routine of the normal pre-Revolutionary times. These, however, were exceptions, and were to be found chiefly in the Army Corps of General Dovbor-Mussnitzki, who was persistently and sternly maintaining the old discipline. Most of the units, however, were more akin to a devastated ants-nest than to an organised unit, although they had retained a semblance of discipline and drill. After the review I walked down the ranks and spoke to the soldiers. I was deeply depressed by their new mental attitude. Their speeches were nought but endless complaints, suspicions and grievances against everyone and everything. They complained of all the officers, from the Platoon Commander to the Army Corps Commander, complained of the lentil soup, of having to stand at the Front for ever, of the next regiment of the line, and of the Provisional Government for being implacably hostile to the Germans. I witnessed scenes which I shall not forget till my last hour. In one of the Army Corps I asked to be shown the worst unit. I was taken to the 703rd Suram Regiment. We drove up to a huge crowd of unarmed men who were standing, sitting, wandering about the plain behind the village. Having sold their clothes for cash or for drink, they were dressed in rags, barefooted, ragged, unkempt, and seemed to have reached the utmost limit of physical degradation. I was met by the Divisional Commander, whose lower lip trembled, and by a Regimental Commander who had the face of a condemned man. Nobody gave the order "Attention!" and none of the soldiers rose. The nearest ranks moved towards our motor cars. My first impulse was to curse the regiment and turn back. But that might have been interpreted as cowardice, so I went into the thick of the crowd. I stayed there for about an hour. Good Heavens, what was the matter with these men, with the reasonable creature of God, with the Russian field-labourer? They were like men possessed, their brain dimmed, their speech stubborn and completely lacking logic or common-sense; their shrieks were hysterical, full of abuse and foul swearing. We tried to speak, but the replies were angry and stupid. I remember that my feelings of indignation as an old soldier receded to the background and I merely felt infinitely sorry for these uncouth, illiterate Russians to whom little was given and of whom little will, therefore, be asked. One wished that the leaders of the Revolutionary Democracy had been on that plain and had seen and heard everything. One wished one could have said to them: "It is not the time to find out who is guilty, it doesn't matter whether the guilt is ours, yours, of the bourgeoisie or of autocracy. Give the people education and an 'image of man' first, and then socialise, nationalise, Communise, if the people will then follow you."

The same Suram Regiment, a few days later, gave a sound thrashing to Sokolov, the man who drafted Order No. 1, the creator of the new régime for the Army, because he demanded, in the name of the Soviet, that the regiment should do its duty and join in the advance.

After visiting the regiment, in compliance with persistent invitations from a special delegation, I went to a Conference of the 2nd Caucasian Army Corps. The members of that Conference had been elected; their discussions were more reasonable and their aims more practical. Among the various groups of delegates whom our *aides-de-camp* had joined, the argument was put forward that, as the Commander-in-Chief and all the senior Commanding Officers were present, would it not be expedient to finish them off at once? That would put an end to the advance.

To meet the senior Commanding Officer was by no means a consolation. One of the Army Corps Commanders led his troops with a firm hand, but experienced strong pressure from the Army organisations; another was afraid to visit his troops. I found the third in a state of complete collapse and in tears because someone had passed a vote of censure upon him: " And this after forty years' service! I loved the men and they loved me, but now they have dishonoured me, and I cannot serve any longer! " I had to allow him to retire. In the next room a young Divisional Commander was already in secret consultation with members of the Committee, who immediately requested me, in a most peremptory fashion, to appoint the young General to the command of the Army Corps.

The visit left me with a painful impression. Disruption was growing and my hopes were waning; and yet one had to continue the work, of which there was plenty for all of us. The Western Front lived by theory and by the experience of others. It had won no striking victories, which alone can inspire confidence in the methods of warfare, and had no real experience in breaking through the defensive line of the enemy. One was very often compelled to discuss the general plan, the plan of artillery attack, and to establish the points of initiative with those who were to carry out the general plan. We found the greatest difficulty in preparing the plans for storming a position. Owing to demoralisation, every movement of troops, every relief, trench digging, bringing batteries into position, either were not carried out at all, or else attended by delays, tremendous efforts or persuasion, and meetings. Every slightest excuse was made use of in order to avoid preparations for the advance. Owing to the technical unpreparedness of the positions, the chiefs had to perform the arduous and unnatural task of making tactical considerations subservient to the qualities of the Commanding Officers, instead of giving directions to the troops in accordance with tactical considerations. The degree of the demoralisation of different units and the condition of different sectors of a given firing line, purely accidental, had also to be taken into account. And yet the statement that our technical backwardness was one of the reasons of our collapse in 1917 should be accepted with reservations. Of course, our Army was backward, but in 1917 it was infinitely better equipped, had more guns and ammunition and wider experience of her own and of other fronts than in 1916. Our technical backwardness was a relative factor which was present at all times in the Great War before the Revolution, but was remedied in 1917, and cannot, therefore, be taken into account as a decisive feature in estimating the Russian Revolutionary Army and its work in the field.

It was the work of Sisyphus. The Commanding Officers gave their heart and soul to the work because in its success they saw the last ray of hope for the salvation of the Army and of the country. Technical difficulties could be overcome, as long as the moral could be raised.

Brussilov arrived and addressed the regiment. As a result, the officer commanding the 10th Army was relieved against my will ten days before the decisive advance. And it was not without difficulty that I secured the appointment of General Lomnovsky, the gallant Commander of the 8th Army Corps, who had arrived at the Front ten days before the action. There was an unpleasant misunderstanding about Brussilov's visit. Headquarters had mistakenly informed the troops that Kerensky was coming. This substitution provoked strong discontent among the troops. Many units declared that they were being deceived, and that unless Comrade Kerensky himself orders them to advance they would not advance. The 2nd Caucasian Division sent delegates to Petrograd to make inquiries. And efforts had to be made to appease them by promising that Comrade Kerensky was due to arrive in a few days. The War Minister had to be invited. Kerensky came reluctantly, because he was already disillusioned by the failure of his oratorical campaign on the South-Western Front. For several days he reviewed the troops, delivered speeches, was enthusiastically received and sometimes unexpectedly rebuked. He interrupted his tour, as he was invited to hurry to Petrograd on July 4th, but he returned with renewed energy and with a new up-to-date theme, making full use of the " knife with which the Revolution had been stabbed in the back " (the Petrograd rising of July 3rd-5th). Having, however, completed his tour and returned to the Stavka, he emphatically declared to Brussilov :

" I have no faith whatsoever in the success of the advance."

Kerensky was equally pessimistic in those days with regard to another matter, the future destinies of the country. He discussed in conversation with myself and two or three of his followers, the stages of the Russian Revolution, and expressed the conviction that whatever happened we should not escape the Reign of Terror. The days went by and the advance was further delayed. As early as on June 18th, I issued the following Order of the Day to the Armies of my Front:

' The Russian Army of the South-Western Front have this day defeated the enemy and broken through his lines. A decisive battle has begun on which depends the fate of the Russian people and of its liberties. Our brethren on the South-Western Front are victoriously advancing, sacrificing their lives and expecting us to render them speedy assistance. We shall not be traitors. The enemy shall soon hear the roaring of our guns. I appeal to the troops of the Western Front to make every effort and to prepare as soon as possible for an advance, otherwise we shall be cursed by the Russian people who have entrusted to us the defence of their liberty, honour, and property."

I do not know whether those who read this order, published in the papers in complete contravention of all the conditions of secrecy of operation, understood all the inner tragedy of the Russian Army. All strategy was turned topsy-turvy. The Russian Commander-in-Chief, powerless to advance his troops and thus alleviate the position of the neighbouring Front, wanted (even at the cost of exposing his intentions) to hold the German divisions which were being moved from his Front and sent to the South-Western and the Allied Front.

The Germans responded immediately by sending the following proclamation to the Front

" Russian soldiers! Your Commander-in-Chief of the Western Front is again calling on you to fight. We know of his order, and also know of the false report that our line to the South-East of Lvov has been broken. Do not believe it. In reality thousands of Russian corpses are lying before our trenches. An advance will never lead to peace. If, nevertheless, you obey the call of your commanders, who are bribed by England, then we shall continue the struggle until you are overthrown."

Finally, on July 8th, the thunder of our guns was heard. On July 9th the storming began, and three days after I was on my way from the 10th Army to Minsk, with despair in my heart, and clearly recognising that the last hope of a miracle was gone.

CHAPTER XXVIII.

The Russian Advance in the Summer of 1917—The Débâcle.

THE Russian offensive which had been planned for the month of May was being delayed. At first a simultaneous advance on all fronts had been contemplated; later, however, owing to the psychological impossibility of a forward movement on all fronts, it was decided to advance gradually. The Western Front was of secondary importance, and the Northern was intended only for demonstration. They should have moved first in order to divert the attention and the forces of the enemy from the main front—the South-Western. The first two of the above-named fronts were not, however, ready for the advance. The Supreme Command finally decided to abandon the strategical plan and to give the commanders of various fronts a free hand in starting operations as the Armies would be ready, provided these operations were not delayed too long and the enemy was not given the opportunity of carrying out re-groupings on a large scale.

Even such a strategy, simplified as it had been owing to the Revolution, might have yielded great results, considering the world-wide scope of the War; if the German Armies on the Eastern Front could not have been utterly defeated, that Front might at least have been restored to its former importance. The Central Powers might have been compelled to send to that Front large forces, war material and munitions, thus severely handicapping Hindenburg's strategy and causing him constant anxiety. The operations were finally fixed for the following dates: They were to begin on the South-Western Front on June 16th, on the Western on July 7th, on the Northern on July 8th, and on the Roumanian on July 6th. The last three dates almost coincide with the beginning of the collapse (July 6th-7th) of the South-Western Front.

As mentioned above, in June, 1917, the Revolutionary Democracy had already acquiesced in the idea that an advance was necessary, although this acquiescence was qualified. The offensive thus had the moral support of the Provisional Government, the Commanding Staffs, all the officers, the Liberal Democracy, the Defencist Coalition of the Soviet, the Commissars, of nearly all Army Committees, and of many Regimental Committees. Against the offensive the minority of the Revolutionary Democracy was ranged—the Bolsheviks, the Social-Revolutionaries of Tchernov's and of Martov's (Zederbaum) group. There was a small appendix to this minority—the Democratisation of the Army.

At the moment of writing I do not possess a complete list of the Russian Armies, but I may confidently assert that on all sectors upon which the advance had been planned we had a numerical and a technical superiority over the enemy, more especially in guns, of which we had larger quantities than ever. It fell to the lot of the South-Western Front to test the fighting capacity of the Revolutionary Army.

The group of armies under General Bohm-Ermolli (the 4th and 2nd Austrian Armies and the Southern German Armies) stood between the upper Sereth and the Carpathians (Brody-Nadvorna) on the position north of the Dniester which we had captured after Brussilov's victorious advance in the autumn of 1916. South of the Dniester stood the 3rd Austrian Army of General Kirchbach, which formed the Left Wing of the Archduke Joseph's Carpathian Front. Our best Army Corps, which were intended as shock troops, were opposed to the last three Armies mentioned above. These Austro-German troops had already been dealt many heavy blows by the Russian Armies in the summer and in the autumn of 1916. Since then, the Southern German Divisions of General Botmer, which had been hard hit, had been replaced by fresh troops from the North. Although the Austrian Armies had been to a certain extent reorganised by the German High Command and reinforced by German divisions, they did not represent a formidable force and, according to the German Headquarters, were not fit for active operations.

Since the Germans had occupied the Cherviche " Place d'armes " on the Stokhod, Hindenburg's Headquarters had given orders that no operations should be conducted, as it was hoped that the disruption of the Russian Army and of the country would follow its natural course, assisted by German propaganda. The Germans estimated the fighting capacity of our Army very low. Nevertheless, when Hindenburg realised in the beginning of June that a Russian advance was a contingency to be reckoned with, he moved six divisions from the Western-European front and sent them to reinforce the group of Armies of Bohm-Ermolli.

The Russian Advance in the Summer of 1917

The enemy was perfectly well aware of the directions in which we intended to advance. . . .

The Russian Armies of the South-Western Front, commanded by General Gutor, were to strike in the main direction of Kamenetz-Podolsk-Lvov. The Armies were to move along both banks of the Dniester: General Erdely's 11th Army in the direction of Zlochev, General Selivatchev's 7th Army towards Brjeczany, and General Kornilov's 8th Army towards Galitch. In the event of victory we would reach Lvov, break through between the fronts of Bohm-Ermolli and the Archduke Joseph, and would drive the latter's left wing to the Carpathians, cutting it off from all available natural means of communication. The remainder of our Armies on the South-Western Front were stretched along a broad front from the river Pripet to Brody for active defence and demonstration.

On June 16th the guns of the shock troops of the 7th and 11th Army opened a fire of such intensity as had never been heard before. After two days of continuous fire, which destroyed the enemy's strong position, the Russian regiments attacked. The enemy line was broken between Zvorov and Brjeczany on a front of several miles; we took two or three fortified lines. On June 19th the attack was renewed on a front of forty miles, between the Upper Strypa and the Narauvka. In this heavy and glorious battle the Russian troops took three hundred officers and eighteen thousand men prisoners in two days, twenty-nine guns, and other booty. The enemy positions were captured on many sectors, and we penetrated the enemy lines to an average depth of over two miles, driving him back to the Strypa in the direction of Zlochev.

The news of our victory spread all over Russia, evoked universal rejoicings, and raised the hopes for the revival of the former strength of the Russian Army. Kerensky reported to the Provisional Government as follows: " This day is the day of a great triumph for the Revolution. On June 18th the Russian Revolutionary Army, in very high spirits, began the advance and has proved before Russia and before the world its ardent devotion to the cause of the Revolution and its love of Country and Liberty. The Russian warriors are inaugurating a new discipline based upon feelings of a citizen's duty. . . . An end has been made to-day of all the vicious calumnies and slander about the organisation of the Russian Army, which has been rebuilt on Democratic lines. . . ." The man who wrote these words had afterwards the courage to claim that it was not he who had destroyed the Army, because he had taken over the organisation as a fatal inheritance!

After three days' respite, a violent battle was resumed on the front of the 11th Army on both sides of the railway line on the front Batkuv-Koniuchi. By that time the threatened German regiments were reinforced, and stubborn fighting ensued. The 11th Army captured several lines, but suffered heavy losses. The trenches changed hands several times after a hand-to-hand battle, and great efforts had to be made in order to break the resistance of the enemy, who had been reinforced and had recovered. This action practically signified the end of the advance of the 7th and 11th Armies. The impetus was spent and the troops began once more to sit in the trenches, the monotony of this pastime being only broken in places by local skirmishes, Austro-German counter-attacks, and intermittent gunfire. Meanwhile preparations for the advance began on June 23rd in Kornilov's Army. On June 25th his troops broke through General Kirchbach's positions west of Stanislavov and reached the line of Jesupol-Lyssetz. After a stubborn and sanguinary battle Kirchbach's troops, utterly defeated, ran and dragged along in their headlong flight the German division which had been sent to reinforce them. On the 27th General Cheremissov's right column captured Galitch, some of his troops crossed the Dniester. On the 28th the left column overcame the stubborn resistance of the Austro-Germans and captured Kalush. In the next two or three days, the 8th Army was in action on the river Lomnitza and finally established itself on the banks of the river and in front of it. In the course of this brilliant operation Kornilov's Army broke through the 3rd Austrian Army on a front of over twenty miles and captured 150 officers, 10,000 men, and about 100 guns. The capture of Lomnitza opened to Kornilov the road to Dolina-Stryi and to the communications of Botmer's Army. German Headquarters described the position of the Commander-in-Chief of the Western Front as *critical*.

General Bohm-Ermolli meanwhile was concentrating all his reserves in the direction of Zlochev, the point to which the German divisions were likewise sent which had been taken from the Western European Front. Some of the reserves had to be sent, however, across the Dniester against the 8th Russian Army. They arrived on July 2nd, reinforced the shattered ranks of the 3rd Austrian Army, and from that day positional battles began on the Lomnitza, with varying success, and occasionally stubborn fighting. The concentration of the German shock troops between the Upper Sereth and the railway line Tarnopol-Zlochev was completed on July 5th. On the next day, after strong artillery preparations, this group attacked our 11th Army, broke our front

The Russian Advance in the Summer of 1917

and moved swiftly towards Kaminetz-Podolsk, pursuing the Army Corps of the 11th Army who were fleeing in panic. The Army Headquarters, the Stavka and the Press, losing all perspective, blamed the 607th Mlynov Regiment as the chief cause of the catastrophe. The demoralised, worthless regiment had left the trenches of their own accord and opened the front. It was, of course, a very sad occurrence, but it would be naïve to describe it even as an excuse. For as early as on the 9th of July the Committees and Commissars of the 11th Army were telegraphing to the Provisional Government: " The truth and nothing but the truth about the events." " The German offensive on the front of the 11th Army, which began on July 6th, is growing into an immeasurable calamity which threatens perhaps the very existence of Revolutionary Russia. The spirit of the troops, that were prompted to advance by the heroic efforts of the minority, has undergone a decisive and fatal change. The impetus of the advance was soon spent. Most of the units are in a condition of increasing disruption. There is not a shadow of discipline or obedience; persuasion is likewise powerless and is answered by threats and sometimes by shootings. Cases have occurred when orders to advance immediately to reinforce the line were debated for hours at meetings, and reinforcements were twenty-four hours late. Some units arbitrarily leave the trenches without even waiting for the enemy to advance. . . For hundreds of miles strings of deserters—healthy, strong men who thoroughly realise their impunity—are to be seen moving along with rifles or without. The country should know the whole truth. It will shudder and will find the strength to fall with all its might upon all those whose cowardice is ruining and bartering Russia and the Revolution."

The Stavka wrote: " In spite of its enormous numerical and technical superiority, the 11th Army was retreating uninterruptedly. On the 8th of July it had already reached the Serenth, never halting at the very strong fortified position to the West of the river, which had been our starting point in the glorious advance of 1916. Bohm-Ermolli had detached some of his forces for the pursuit of the Russian troops in the direction of Tarnapol and had moved his main forces southwards between the Serenth and the Strypa, threatening to cut off the communication of the 7th Army, to throw them into the Dniester and, perhaps, cut off the retreat of the 8th Army. On July 9th the Austro-Germans had aready reached Mikulinze, a distance of one march south of Tarnapol. . . . The Armies of General Selivatchev and Cheremissov (who had succeeded General Kornilov upon the latter's appointment on July 7th to the

High Command of the South-Western Front) were in great difficulty. They could not hope to resist the enemy by manœuvring, and all that was left to them was to escape the enemy's blows by forced marches. The 7th Army was in particularly dire straits, as it was retreating under the double pressure of the Army Corps of General Botmer, who was conducting a frontal attack, and of the troops of Bohm-Ermolli, striking from the north against the denuded right flank. The 8th Army had to march over one hundred miles under pressure from the enemy.

On July 10th the Austro-Germans advanced to the line Mikulinze-Podgaitze-Stanilavov. On the 11th the Germans occupied Tarnapol, abandoned without fighting by the 1st Guards Army Corps. On the next day they broke through our position on the rivers Gniezno and Sereth, South of Trembovlia, and developed their advance in the Eastern and South-Eastern directions. On the same day, pursuing the 7th and 8th Armies, the enemy occupied the line from the Sereth to Monsaterjisko-Tlumatch.

On the 12th July, seeing that the position was desperate, the Commander-in-Chief issued orders for a retreat from the Sereth, and by the 21st the Armies of the South-Western Front, having cleared Galicia and Bukovina, reached the Russian frontier. Their retreat was marked by fires, violence, murders and plunder. A few units, however, fought the enemy stubbornly and covered the retreat of the maddened mob of deserters by sacrificing their lives. Among them were Russian officers, whose bodies covered the battlefields. The Armies were retreating in disorder; the same Armies that, only a year ago, had captured Lutsk, Brody-Stanislavov, Chernovetz in their triumphal progress . . . were retreating before the same Austro-German troops that only a year ago had been completely defeated and had strewn with fugitives the plains of Volynia, Galicia and Bukovina, leaving hundreds of thousands of prisoners in our hands. We shall never forget that in Brussilov's advance of 1916, the 7th, 8th, 9th and 11th Armies took 420,000 prisoners, 600 guns, 2,500,000 machine guns, etc. Our Allies are not likely to forget this either; they know full well that the loud echo of the Galician battle sounded on the Somme and at Goritza.

The Commissars Savinkov and Filonenko telegraphed to the Provisional Government: " There is no choice; the traitors must be executed. . . . Capital punishment must be meted out to all those who refuse to sacrifice their lives for their country. . "

In the beginning of July, after the Russian advance had ostensibly failed, it was decided at Hindenburg's Headquarters to

The Russian Advance in the Summer of 1917

undertake a new extensive operation against the Roumanian front by a simultaneous advance of the 3rd and 7th Austrian Armies across Bukovina into Moldavia and of the Right group of General Mackensen on the Lower Sereth. The objective was to seize Moldavia and Bessarabia. But on July 11th the Russian Army of General Ragosa and the Roumanian Army of General Averesco took the offensive between the rivers Susitsa and Putna against the 9th Austrian Army. The attack was successful, the enemy positions were captured, the Armies moved forward several miles, took 2,000 prisoners and over 60 guns, but the operation was not developed. Owing to the natural conditions of the theatre of war and to the direction in which the operation was undertaken, it was more akin to a demonstration in order to relieve the South-Western Front. Also the troops of the 4th Russian Army soon lost all impetus for the advance. In July and until August 4th, the troops of the Archduke Joseph and of Mackensen attacked in several directions and gained local successes, but without any appreciable result. Although the Russian divisions repeatedly disobeyed orders and occasionally left the trenches during the battle, yet the condition of the Roumanian Front was somewhat better than that of the other Front, owing to its distance from Petrograd, to the presence of disciplined Roumanian troops and to the natural conditions of the country. For these reasons we were able to keep that Front somewhat longer. This circumstance, together with the apparent weakness of the Austrian Armies, especially the 3rd and the 7th, and the complete dislocation of the communications of Bohm-Ermolli's group and of the Archduke Joseph's left wing—caused Hindenburg's Headquarters indefinitely to postpone the operation, and a period of calm ensued along the entire South-Western Front. On the Roumanian Front local actions were fought until the end of August. At the same time, German divisions began to move from the Sbrucz northwards in the direction of Riga. Hindenburg's plan was to deal the Russian Army local blows, without straining his own resources or spending large reserves, so urgently needed, on the Western-European Front. By these tactics he intended to contribute to the natural course of the collapse of the Russian front, for it was upon this collapse that the Central Powers based all their calculations in regard to operations and even in regard to the possibility of continuing the campaign in 1918.

Our efforts at advancing on other Fronts also ended in complete failure. On the 7th of July operations began on the Western Front, which I commanded. The details will be given in the next chapter. Of this operation Ludendorf wrote: " Of all the attacks directed against the former Eastern front of General Eichhorn, the attacks of July 9th, South of Smorgom, and at Krevo were particularly fierce. . . . For several days the position was extremely difficult until our reserves and our gunfire restored the front. The Russians left our trenches; they were no longer the Russians of the old days."

On the Northern Front, in the 5th Army, everything was over in one day. The Stavka wrote· " South-West of the Dvinsk our troops, after strong artillery preparation, captured the German position across the railway Dvinsk-Vilna. Subsequently, entire divisions, without pressure from the enemy, deliberately retreated to their own trenches." The Stavka noted the heroic behaviour of several units, the prowess of the officers and the tremendous losses which the latter had suffered. This fact, however unimportant from the strategical point of view, deserves to be specially noted. As a matter of fact, the 5th Army was commanded by General Danilov (afterwards a member of the Bolshevik Delegation at Brest-Litovsk. He served in 1920 in the Russian Army in the Crimea). He enjoyed exceptional prestige with the Revolutionary Democracy. According to Stankevitch, the Commissar of the Northern Front, Danilov " was the only General who had remained, in spite of the Revolution, full master in the Army and had succeeded in so dealing with the new institutions—the Commissars and the Committees—that they strengthened his authority instead of weakening it. . . . He knew how to make use of these elements, and he overcame all obstacles in a spirit of complete self-control and firmness. In the 5th Army everyone was working, learning and being educated.   . As the best and the most cultured elements of the Army were working to that end." This is a striking proof of the fact that even when the Commanding Officer becomes thoroughly familiar with Revolutionary institutions, this does not serve as a guarantee of the fighting capacity of his troops.

On July 11th Kornilov, upon his appointment to the Chief Command of the South-Western Front, sent to the Provisional Government his well-known telegram, of which he forwarded a copy to the Supreme Commander-in-Chief. In that telegram, already quoted above, Kornilov demanded the reintroduction of capital punishment, and wrote: ". . . I declare that the country is on the verge of collapse and that, although I have not been consulted, I *demand* that the offensive be stopped on all Fronts in order that the Army may be saved, preserved and re-organised on the basis of strict discipline, and in order that the lives may not be sacrificed of a few heroes who are entitled to see better days." In spite of the peculiar wording of this appeal, the idea of stopping the advance was immediately accepted by the Supreme Command, the more so that the operations had practically come to a standstill irrespective of orders as a result of the reluctance of the Russian Army to fight and to advance, as well as of the schemes of the German Headquarters.

Capital punishment and Revolutionary courts-martial were introduced at the front. Kornilov gave an order to shoot deserters and robbers and to expose their bodies with corresponding notices on the roads and in other prominent places. Special shock battalions were formed of cadets and volunteers to fight against desertion, plunder and violence. Kornilov forbade meetings at the Front and gave an order to stop them by the force of arms. These measures—which were introduced by Kornilov at his own risk and peril, his manly, straightforward utterances, and the firm tone in which, disregarding discipline, he began to address the Provisional Government, and last, but not least, his resolute action—considerably enhanced his authority with the wide circles of Liberal Democracy and with the officers. Even the Revolutionary Democracy within the Army, stunned and depressed as it was by the tragic turn of events, saw in Kornilov, for some time after the *débâcle*, the last resource and the only possible remedy in the desperate position. It may be stated that the date of July 8th, on which Kornilov took command of the South-Western Front and addressed his first demand to the Provisional Government, sealed his fate: in the eyes of many people he bacame a national hero and great hopes were centred upon him—he was expected to save the country.

During my stay at Minsk I was not very well informed of the unofficial tidings prevailing in military circles, yet I felt that the centre of moral influence had moved to Berditchev (Headquarters of the South-Western Front). Kerensky and Brussilov had somehow suddenly receded to the background. A new method of administration was put into practice: we received from Kornilov's Headquarters copies of his " demands " or notices of some strong and striking decision he had adopted, and in a few days these were repeated from Petrograd or from the Stavka, but in the shape of an order or of a regulation.

The tragedy of July undoubtedly had a sobering effect upon the men. In the first place, they were ashamed because things had happened that were so shameful and so disgraceful that even the dormant conscience and the deadened spirit of the men could not find excuses for these happenings. Several months later, in November, after fleeing from the captivity of Bykhov, I spent several days under an assumed name and in civilian clothes among the soldiers who had flooded all the railways. They were discussing the past. I never heard a single man confessing openly or cynically his participation in the treachery of July. They all tried to explain away the matter and chiefly attributed it to somebody's treason, especially, of course, the treason of the officers. None spoke of his own treachery. In the second place, the men were frightened. They felt that a kind of power, a kind of authority had arisen, and they were quietly waiting for developments. Lastly, operations had ended and nervous tension had been relieved—which caused a certain reaction, apathy and indifference. *This was the second occasion (the first took place in March) on which, had the moment been immediately and properly taken advantage of—it might have been the turning point in the history of the Russian Revolution.*

As the sounds were dying out of the last shots fired at the Front, the men who had been stunned by the disaster began to recover their senses. Kerensky was the first to return to sanity. The horror had passed away, the nerve-wrecking, maddening fear which had prompted the issue of the first stringent order. Kerensky's will-power was dominated by his fear of the Soviet, of the danger of definitely losing all prestige with the Revolutionary Democracy by resentment against Kornilov for the resolute tone of the latter's messages and by the shadow of the potential dictator. The drafts of military regulations by which it was intended to restore the power of the Commanding Officers and of the Army were drowned in red tape and in the turmoil of personal conflicts, suspicions and hatreds. The Revolutionary Democracy once again sternly opposed the new course, as it interpreted this course as an infringement upon the liberties and as a menace to its own existence. The same attitude was adopted by the Army Committees, whose powers were to be curtailed as a first step in the proposed changes. In these circles the new course was described as counter-revolutionary. The masses of the soldiery, on the other hand, soon appraised the new situation. They saw that stern words were mere words, that capital punishment was only a bogy, because there was no real force capable of mastering their arbitrariness. So fear vanished again. The hurricane did not clear the close and tense atmosphere. New clouds were overhanging and peals of a new deafening thunder were to be heard in the distance.

General Kornilov's arrival at Petrograd.

General Kornilov in the trenches.

CHAPTER XXIX.

THE CONFERENCE AT THE STAVKA OF MINISTERS AND COMMANDERS-IN-CHIEF ON JULY 16TH.

UPON my return from the Front to Minsk I was summoned to the Stavka at Moghilev, where a Conference was to be held on July 16th. Kerensky suggested that Brussilov should invite, of his own accord, the prominent military chiefs, in order to discuss the actual condition of the Front, the consequences on the July disaster, and to determine the course of future military policy. It transpired that General Gourko, who had been invited by Brussilov, had not been admitted to the Conference by Kerensky. A telegram was sent to Kornilov from the Stavka saying that, in view of the difficult position of the South-Western Front, his attendance was impossible, and that he was requested to present in writing his views on the questions under discussion. It should be noted that, at that time, on July 14th and 15th, the 11th Army was in full retreat from the Sereth to the Zbrucz, and that everyone was anxious to hear whether the 7th Army had succeeded in crossing the Lower Sereth and the 8th the line of Zalestchiki, thus avoiding the blows of the German Armies that were trying to cut their retreat.

So sad was the plight of the country and the Army that I decided to disclose to the Conference the full truth on the condition of the Army in all its hideous nakedness, and in disregard of all conventionalities. I reported myself to the Supreme Commander-in-Chief. Brussilov surprised me. He said: " I have come to the conclusion that this is the limit and we must put the question squarely. All these Commissars, Committees and Democratisations are driving the Army and Russia to ruin. I have decided categorically to demand that they should cease to disorganise the Army. I hope that you will back me? " I answered that this was in full accord with my intentions and that the object of my visit was to put the question squarely of the future destinies of the

Army. I must confess that Brussilov's words reconciled me with him and I therefore decided to eliminate from my speech all the bitter things which I had intended to say against the Supreme Command.

We waited about an hour and a half for the Conference to meet. We afterwards learnt that a small incident had occurred. The Prime Minister had not been met at the station either by Brussilov or by his Chief-of-Staff (General Lukomsky), who had been detained by urgent military business. Kerensky waited for some time and grew nervous. He finally sent his *aide-de-camp* to Brussilov with the order to come to the station at once and to report. The incident was not commented upon, but all those who have been in touch with politics know that the actors on that stage are mere men, with all their weaknesses, and that the game is often continued behind the curtain.

The Conference was attended by the Prime Minister Kerensky, the Foreign Minister Terestchenko, the Supreme C.-in-C. Brussilov, his Chief-of-Staff General Lukomsky, Generals Alexeiev and Russky, the C.-in-C. of the Northern Front General Klembovsky, by myself as C.-in-C. of the Western Front, and by my Chief-of-Staff General Markov, Admiral Maximov, Generals Velitchko and Romanovsky, the Commissar of the Western Front Savinkov, and two or three young men of Kerensky's suite.

General Brussilov addressed the Conference in a short speech, which struck me as being very vague and commonplace. In fact, he said nothing at all. I had hoped that Brussilov would keep his word and would sum up the situation and draw conclusions. I was mistaken. Brussilov did not speak again. I opened the discussion. I said:

" It is with deep emotion and in full consciousness of a grave responsibility that I am delivering my report to the Conference. I beg to be excused if I speak as openly and frankly as I have always done. I was outspoken with the old Autocracy, and intend to be just as outspoken with the new—the Revolutionary Autocracy.

" When I took Command of the Front, I found the Armies in a state of complete disruption. This seemed the more strange that neither in the reports received at the Stavka or in those I received upon taking over the Command had the situation been described in such gloomy colours. The explanation is obvious: as long as the Army Corps were not conducting active operations, excesses were comparatively few; but no sooner was the order given for doing the duty of a soldier, for taking up positions or for the advance, than the instinct of self-preservation asserted itself and the picture of disruption was unveiled. Some ten divisions refused to take up positions. All Commanding Officers of all grades had to work very hard, to argue, to persuade. . . . In order to be able to carry out the slightest measure of any importance, it became imperative to reduce the numbers of mutinous troops. A whole month was thus lost, although some divisions obeyed orders. Disruption was rampant in the 2nd Caucasian Corps and in the 169th Infantry Division. Several units had lost human appearance, not only morally but physically. I shall never forget the hour which I spent in the 703rd Suram Regiment. There were up to ten private stills in each regiment; drunkenness, cardplaying, rioting, plunder and even murder. I took a drastic step. I sent the 2nd Caucasian Corps (except the 51st Infantry Division and the 169th Infantry Division) to the rear and ordered them to be disbanded. Before the operation had developed, I thus lost about 30,000 bayonets without firing a shot. The 28th and 29th Infantry Divisions, which were considered the best, were sent to occupy the sector of the Caucasians. What happened? The 29th Division, after a forced march to its destination, returned on the next day almost in its entirety (two and a half regiments). The 28th Division sent one regiment to the trenches, and that regiment passed a resolution against advancing. Every possible measure was taken in order to raise the spirit of the troops. The Supreme Commander-in-Chief visited the Front. From his conversations with the members of Committee and with the men elected from two Army Corps he gathered the impression that 'the soldiers were all right, but the Commanding Officers had lost heart.' That is not so. The Commanding Officers did all they could in extremely difficult and painful surroundings, but the Supreme Commander-in-Chief is unaware of the fact that the meeting of the 1st Siberian Corps, where his speech was most enthusiastically received, continued after his departure. New speakers came forward and appealed to the men not to listen to the ' old Bourgeois ' (forgive me, that is so. . . . Brussilov interjected: " I do not mind ") and they heaped vile abuse upon his head. These appeals were also enthusiastically greeted. The War Minister, who visited the troops and by his fiery eloquence incited them to deeds of valour, was enthusiastically received by the 28th Division. Upon his return to the train he was met by a regimental deputation which announced that half an hour after the Minister had gone the regiment, as well as another one, had decided not to advance. The picture was particularly moving and evoked great enthusiasm when, in the 29th Division, the Commanding Officer of the Poti Infantry Regiment knelt to receive the Red Banner. The men swore—there were three speakers and passionate cheering—to die for the country. On the first day of the advance the regiment did not reach our trenches, but turned round in a disgraceful manner and retreated six miles behind the battlefield.

" The Commissars and the Committee were among the factors which were meant to give moral support to the troops, but practically contributed to their demoralisation. Among the Commissars there may have been favourable exceptions of men who did a certain amount of good without interfering with other people's business. But the institution itself cannot fail to contribute to the disruption of the Army because it implies a dual power, friction and interference uncalled for and criminal. I am compelled to describe the Commissars of the Western Front. One of them, for all I know, may be a good and honest man, but he is an Utopian and not only ignorant of Army life, but of life in general. He has a great idea of his own importance. In demanding that the Chief-of-Staff should obey his orders, he declares that he is entitled to dismiss Commanding Officers, including the General Officer commanding the Army. In explaining to the troops the extent of his authority, he thus describes it: ' As the fronts are subordinate to the War Minister, I am the War Minister for the Western Front.' Another Commissar, who knows about as much of Army life as the first one, is a Social Democrat standing somewhere on the verge between Bolshevism and Menchevism. He is the noted reporter of the Military Section of the All-Russian Congress of Soviets who has expressed the view that the Army has not been sufficiently disorganised by the ' Declaration ' and demanded further ' Democratisation.' He claimed the right for the men to veto appointments of Commanding Officers, insisted upon part 2 of Paragraph 14 of the Declaration which empowered the Commanding Officers to use arms against cowards and traitors being cancelled, and upon freedom of speech being granted not only off parade, but on duty. The 3rd Commissar, who was not a Russian, and who appeared to treat the Russian soldier with contempt, in addressing the regiment used such foul language as had never fallen from the Commanding Officers under the Czar's régime. Curiously enough the conscious and free Revolutionary warriors accept such treatment as their due and obey him. That Commissar, according to the Commanding Officers, is undoubtedly useful.

" The Committees are another disintegrating force. I do not deny that some of the Committees have done excellent work, and have done their best to fulfil their duty. In particular some of their members have been exceedingly useful, and have rendered their country the supreme service of dying the death of heroes. But I affirm that the good they have done will not compensate for the tremendous mischief done to the Army by the introduction of all these new authorities, by friction, by interference, and by discrediting the commands. I might quote hundreds of resolutions bearing that stamp, but will confine myself merely to the most blatant cases. The struggle for seizing power in the Army is carried on openly and systematically. The Chairman of the Committee of the Front has published in his paper an article advocating that governmental powers be granted to the Committee. The Army Committee of the 3rd Army has passed the resolution, which to my intense surprise was endorsed by the Commanding Officer, requesting ' that the Army Committees be invested with the plenary powers of the War Minister and of the Central Committee of the Soviets which would entitle them to act in the name of that Committee.' When the famous ' Declaration ' was discussed opinions varied in the Committee of the Front in regard to Paragraph 14. Some members wanted the second part to be eliminated; others demanded that a proviso be added empowering the members of the Committee of the Front to take the same measures including armed force against the same persons, and even against the Commanding Officers themselves. Is that not the limit? In the report of the All-Russian Congress a demand is formulated for the Soldiers' Committees to be allowed to cancel appointments of Commanding Officers, and to partake in the administration of the Army. You must not think that this is merely theory. Far from it. The Committees endeavour to get hold of everything, to interfere with purely military questions, with the routine and the administration. And this is being done in an atmosphere of complete anarchy caused by wholesale insubordination.

" Moral preparations for the advance were proceeding apace. On June 8th the Committee of the Front passed a resolution against the advance, but changed its mind on the 18th. The Committee of the 2nd Army decided against the offensive on June 1st, but cancelled its decision on June 20th. In the Minsk Soviet 123 votes against 79 decided against the advance. All the Committees of the 169th Infantry Division passed a vote of censure on the Provisional Government, and described the offensive as " treason to the Revolution." The campaign against the authorities manifested itself in a series of dismissal of Senior Commanders, in which the Committees almost invariably participated. Shortly before the opening of the operations an Army Corps Commander, the Chief-of-Staff, and a Divisional Commander of the most important sector occupied by the shock troops, had to resign, and the same fate was shared by about 60 Commanding Officers, from Army Corps Commander to Regimental Commander. It is impossible to estimate the amount of harm done by the Committee. They have no proper discipline of their own. If the majority passes a reasonable resolution, that does not suffice. It is put into practice by individual members of the Committee. Taking advantage of their position as members of Army Committees, the Bolsheviks have more than once spread mutiny and rebellion with impunity. As a result, authority is undermined instead of being strengthened, because so many different individuals and institutions are supposed to exercise that authority. And the Commander in the Field, who is being discredited, dismissed, controlled and watched from all sides, is nevertheless expected to lead the troops into action with a strong hand. Such was the moral preparation. The troops have not yet been deployed. But the South-Western Front required immediate assistance. The enemy had already removed from my Front to the South-West three or four divisions. I decided to attack with the troops which presented at least a semblance of loyalty. In three days our guns had smashed the enemy trenches and wrought havoc among them, had inflicted heavy losses among the Germans, and had opened the way for our infantry. The first line had been almost entirely broken, and our men had already visited the enemy batteries. That breach of the Front promised to develop into a great victory, for which we had been hoping for so long.

I now revert to descriptions of the battle. ' The units of the 28th Infantry Division took up their positions only four hours before the attack; of the 109th Regiment only two and a half companies, with four machine-guns and 30 officers, reached the appointed line; only one-half of the 110th came up. Two battalions of the 111th Regiment, who had occupied the defiles, refused to advance; men of the 112th Regiment retired to the rear in batches. Units of the 28th Division were met by a strong artillery fire, machine-gun and rifle fire, and remained behind their barbed wire, as they were incapable of advancing. Only a few shock troops and volunteers of the Volga Regiment, with a company of officers, succeeded in capturing the first line, but the fire was so strong that they failed to keep the position, and towards the afternoon units of the 29th Division returned to their original lines after suffering heavy losses, especially in officers. On the sector of the 51st Division the attack began at five minutes past seven. The 202nd Gori Regiment and the 204th

The Conference at the Stavka 287

Ardagan-Michailovsky Regiment, as well as two companies of the Sukhum Regiment, with a shock company of the Poti Regiment, made a dash across two lines of trenches, bayoneted the enemy, and began to storm the third line at half-past seven. The break was so rapid and so unexpected that the enemy failed to establish a barrage. The 201st Poti Regiment, which was following the advance troops, approached our first line of trenches, but refused to go any further, so that our troops who had broken through were not reinforced in time. The units of the 134th Division, which followed, could not carry out their orders because the men of the Poti Regiment had crowded in the trenches, while the enemy had opened a very strong gun fire. These units, therefore, partly dispersed and partly lay in our trenches. Seeing that no reinforcements were forthcoming from the rear and from the flanks, the men of the Gori and Ardagan Regiments lost heart, and some of the companies, in which all the officers had been killed, began to retire. They were followed by the remainder of the troops without, however, any pressure from the Germans, who did not put their batteries and machine-guns into action until the retreat had begun. . . . The units of the 29th Division were late in going into position, because the men advanced reluctantly, as their mood had changed. A quarter of an hour before the appointed time the 114th Regiment on the right flank refused to advance, and the Erivan Regiment had to be drawn up from the Army Corps Reserves. For some unknown reason the 113th and 116th Regiments also failed to move. . After this failure desertion began to grow, and at dawn became general. The men were tired, nervous; they had lost the habit of fighting, and were unaccustomed to the roar of the guns owing to long months of inactivity, of fraternisation, and of meetings. They left the trenches *en masse*, they abandoned the machine-guns and retired to the rear. . . . *The Headquarters of the 20th Army Corps sent the following report of the battle:* ' *The cowardice and lack of discipline in certain units reached such a pitch that the Commanding Officers were compelled to ask our artillery to cease firing, because the fire of our own guns caused a panic among our soldiers.*'

" I will quote another description of the battle made by an Army Corps Commander who took command on the eve of battle, and whose impressions are therefore totally unbiassed: ' . . . Everything was ready for the advance: the plan had been worked out in detail; we had a powerful and efficient artillery; the weather was favourable because it did not allow the Germans to take advantage of their superiority in aircraft; we had superior numbers, our Reserves were drawn up in time, we had plenty of ammunition, and the sector was well chosen for the advance, because we were in a position to conceal strong artillery forces in the close neighbourhood of our trenches. The undulations of ground also afforded many hidden approaches to the Front; the distance between ourselves and the enemy was small, and there were no natural obstacles between us which would have had to have been forced under fire. Finally, the troops had been prepared by the Committees, the Commanding Officers and the War Minister, Kerensky, and their efforts induced the troops to take the first, the most arduous steps. We attained considerable success without suffering appreciable losses. Three fortified lines had been broken through and occupied, and there remained only separate defensive positions. The fighting might soon have reached the phase of bayonet fighting; the enemy artillery was silenced, over 1,400 Germans, many machine-guns and other booty had been captured. Also, our guns had inflicted heavy casualties in killed and wounded upon the enemy, and it may be confidently stated that the forces that were opposing our Corps had been temporarily knocked out. Along the entire front of our Corps only three or four enemy batteries and occasionally three or four machine-guns were firing, and there were isolated rifle shots. But—night came. Immediately I began to receive anxious reports from officers commanding sectors at the Front to the effect that the men were abandoning the unattacked Front Line *en masse*, entire companies deserting. It was stated in some of the reports that the firing line in places was only occupied by the Commanding Officer, his staff, and a few men. The operations ended in an irretrievable and hopeless failure. In one day we had lived through the joy of victory, which had been won in spite of the low spirits of the men, as well as the horror of seeing the fruits of victory deliberately cast away by the soldiery. And yet the country needed that victory for its very life. I realised that we, the Commanding Officers, are powerless to alter the elemental psychology of the men, and I wept long and bitterly.'

" This inglorious operation, however, resulted in serious losses, which it is now difficult to estimate, as crowds of fugitives returned daily. Over 20,000 wounded men have already passed through sorting stations in the rear. I will refrain at present from drawing any conclusion, but the percentage of various kinds of wounds is symptomatic: 10 per cent. heavily wounded, 30 per cent. finger and wrist wounds, 40 per cent. light wounds from which bandages were not removed at the dressing stations (many

The Conference at the Stavka

wounds were probably simulated), and 20 per cent. bruised and sick. Such was the end of the operation. I have never yet gone into battle with such superiority in numbers and technical means. Never had the conditions been more full of such brilliant promise. On a front of about 14 miles I had 184 battalions against 29 enemy battalions; 900 guns against 300 German: 138 of my battalions came into action against 17 German battalions of the 1st line. All that was wasted. Reports from various Commanders indicate that the temper of the troops immediately after the operation was just as indefinite as before. Three days ago I summoned the Army Commanders and addressed to them the question: 'Could their Armies resist a strong enemy attack, provided reserves were forthcoming?' The answer was in the negative. 'Could the Armies resist an organised German offensive in their present condition, numerical and technical?' Two of the Army Commanders gave indefinite replies, and the Commanding Officer of the 10th Army answered in the affirmative. They all said: 'We have no infantry.' I will go further, and I will say:

"*We have no Army. It is necessary immediately, and at all costs to create that Army.* The new Government regulations, which are supposed to raise the spirit of the Army, have not yet penetrated into its depths, and the impression they have produced cannot yet be defined. One thing is certain—that repression alone cannot drag the Army out of the morass into which it has fallen. It is repeated every day that the Bolsheviks have caused the disruption of the Army, but I disagree. It is not so. The Army has been disrupted by others, and the Bolsheviks are like worms which have bred in the wounds of the Army. The Army has been disrupted by the regulations of the last four months, and it is the bitter irony of fate that this has been done by men who, however honest and idealistic, are unaware of the historical laws governing the existence of the Army, of its life and routine. At first this was done under pressure from the Soviet, which was primarily an Anarchist institution. Later it developed into a fatal, mistaken policy. Soon after the War Minister had taken up his duties he said to me: 'The process of revolutionising the country and the Army has been completed. Now we must proceed with creative work. . . .' I ventured to reply: 'The process is completed, but it is too late.'"

General Brussilov here interrupted me, and asked me to curtail my Report, as the Conference would otherwise be too protracted. I realised that the length of the Report was not what mattered, but it was its risky substance, and I replied: "I consider that this question is of paramount importance, and request that I be allowed to complete my statement, otherwise I shall have to cease speaking." A silence ensued, which I intrepreted as a permission to continue.

I then proceeded: " The Declaration of the Soldiers' Rights has been issued. Every one of the Commanding Officers has stated that it would bring about the ruin of the Army. The late Supreme C.-in-C., General Alexeiev, telegraphed that the Declaration was the last nail which was being driven into the coffin prepared for the Russian Army. The present Supreme C.-in-C., when in command of the South-Western Front, declared here, at Moghilev, at the Conference of Commanders-in-Chief, that the Army may yet be saved and may advance, but on one condition—if the Declaration is not issued. Our advice, however, was unheeded. Paragraph 3 of the Declaration authorises free and open expressions of political, religious, social, and other views. The Army was thus flooded by politics. When the men of the 2nd Caucasian Grenadier Division were disbanded they were quite sincerely puzzled. ' What is the reason? We were allowed to speak whenever and whatever we wished, and now we are being disbanded. . . .' You must not think that such a broad interpretation of the ' Liberties ' is confined to the illiterate masses. When the 169th Infantry Division was morally disrupted, and all the Committees of that Division passed a vote of censure upon the Provisional Government and categorically refused to advance, I disbanded the Division. But there arose an unexpected complication: the Commissars came to the conclusion that no crime had been committed, because the spoken and the written word were unrestricted. The only thing that could be incriminated was direct disobedience of Army orders. . . . Paragraph 6 stipulates that all literature should be delivered to the addressees, and the Army was flooded with criminal Bolshevik and Defeatist literature. The stuff upon which our Army was fed—and apparently at the expense of Government funds and of the people's treasure —can be gauged from the report of the Moscow Military Bureau, which alone supplied to the Front the following publications:

From March 24th to May 1st—
    7,972 copies of the *Pravda*
    2,000 ,, ,, *Soldiers' Pravda*
    30,375 ,, ,, *Social Democrat*

From May 1st to June 11th—
    61,522 copies of the *Soldiers' Pravda*
    32,711 ,, ,, *Social Democrat*
    6,999 ,, ,, *Pravda*

and so on. The same kind of literature was sent to the villages by the soldiers.

" Paragraph 14 stipulates that no soldier can be punished without a trial. Of course, this liberty applied only to the men, because the officers continued to suffer the heaviest penalty of dismissal. What was the result? The Central Military Justice Administration, without reference to the Stavka and in view of the impending Democratisation of the Courts, suggested that the latter should suspend their activities, except for cases of special importance, such, for example, as treason. The Commanding Officers were deprived of disciplinary powers. Disciplinary Courts were partly inactive, partly were boycotted. Justice completely disappeared from the Army. This boycott of Disciplinary Court and reports on the reluctance of certain units to elect juries are symptomatic. The legislator may come across the same phenomenon in respect of the new Revolutionary Military Courts, in which juries may also have to be replaced by appointed judges. As a result of a series of legislative measures, authority and discipline have been eliminated, the officers are dishonoured, distrusted, and openly scorned. Generals in High Command, not excluding Commanders-in-Chief, are being dismissed like domestic servants. In one of his speeches at the Northern Front the War Minister inadvertently uttered the following significant words: ' It lies within my power to dismiss the entire personnel of the High Command in twenty-four hours, and the Army would not object.' In the speeches addressed to the Western Front it was said that ' in the Czarist Army we were driven into battle with whips and machine-guns . that Czarist Commanders led us to slaughter, but now every drop of our blood is precious. . . .' I, the Commander-in-Chief, stood by the platform erected for the War Minister, and I was heart-broken. My conscience whispered to me: ' That is a lie. My " Iron " Rifles, only eight battalions and then twelve, took over 60,000 prisoners and 43 guns. . . . I have never driven them into battle with machine-guns. I have never led my troops to slaughter at Mezolaborch, Lutovisko, Lutsk, Chartoriisk.' To the late Commander-in-Chief of the South-Western Front these names are indeed familiar. . . .

" Everything may be forgiven and we can stand a great deal if it is necessary for victory, if the troops can regain their spirit and can be induced to advance. . . . I will venture to draw a comparison. Sokolov and other Petrograd delegates came to our front, to the 703rd Suram Regiment. He came with the noble object of combating dark ignorance and moral decrepitude, which were particularly apparent in that regiment. He was mercilessly flogged. We were, of course, revolted against that crowd of savage scoundrels, and everyone was perturbed. All kinds of committees passed votes of censure. The War Minister condemned the behaviour of the Suram Regiment in fiery speeches and Army orders, and sent a telegram of sympathy to Sokolov.

" And here is another story. I well remember January, 1915, near Lutovisko. There was a heavy frost. Colonel Noskov, the gallant one-armed hero, up to the waist in snow, was leading his regiment to the attack under a heavy fire against the steep and impregnable slopes of Height 804. . Death spared him then. And now two companies came, asked for General Noskov, surrounded him, killed him and went away. I ask the War Minister, did he condemn these foul murderers with the whole might of his fiery eloquence, of his wrath and of his power, and did he send a telegram of sympathy to the hapless family of the fallen hero?

" When we were deprived of power and authority, when the term ' Commanding Officer ' was sterilised, we have once again been insulted by a telegram from the Stavka to the effect that: ' Commanding Officers who will now hesitate to apply armed force will be dismissed and tried.' No, gentlemen, you will not intimidate those who are ready to lose their lives in the service of their country.

" The senior Commanding Officers may now be divided into three categories: some of them disregarding the hardships of life and service with a broken heart, are doing their duty devotedly to the end; others have lost heart and are following the tide; the third are curiously brandishing the Red Flag, and mindful of the traditions of the Tartar captivity, are crawling before new gods of the Revolution as they crawled before the Czars. It causes me infinite pain to mention the question of the Officers. . . . It is a nightmare, and I will be brief. When Sokolov became familiar with the Army, he said: ' I could not imagine that your officers could be such martyrs. I take off my hat to them.' Yes, in the darkest days of Czarist autocracy, the police and the gendarmerie never subjected the would-be criminal to such moral torture and derision as the officers have to endure at present from the illiterate masses, led by the scum of the Revolution. Officers who are giving their lives for the country. They are insulted at every turn. They are beaten. Yes, beaten. But they will not come and complain to you. They are ashamed, dreadfully ashamed. Alone, in their dug-outs, many of them are silently weeping over their dismal fate. No wonder many officers consider that the best solution is to be killed in action. Listen to the subdued and placid tragedy of the following words which occur in a Field Report: ' In vain did the officers marching in front try to lead the men into action. At that a moment a white flag was raised on Redoubt No. 3. Fifteen officers and a small batch of soldiers then went forward. Their fate is unknown—they did not return.' (38th Corps). May these heroes rest in peace and their blood be upon the heads of their conscious and unconscious executioners.

" The Army is falling to pieces. Heroic measures are needed for its salvation: (1) The Provisional Government should recognise its mistakes and its guilt, as it has not understood and estimated the noble and sincere impulse of the officers who had greeted the news of the Revolution with joy, and had sacrificed innumerable lives for their country. (2) Petrograd, entirely detached from the Army, and ignorant of its life and of the historical foundations of its existence, should cease to enact military regulations. Full power must be given to the Supreme Commander-in-Chief, who should be responsible only to the Provisional Government. (3) Politics must disappear from the Army. (4) The ' Declaration ' must be rescinded in its fundamentals. Commissars and Committees must be abolished, and the functions of the latter must gradually be altered. (5) Commanding Officers must be restored to power. Discipline and the outward form of order and good conduct must likewise be restored. (6) Appointments to prominent posts must be made not only according to the standard of youth and strength, but also of experience in the field and in administration. (7) Special law-abiding units of all arms must be placed at the disposal of Commanding Officers as a bulwark against mutiny, and against the horrors of possible demobilisation. (8) Military Revolutionary Courts must be established and capital punishment introduced in the rear for the troops and for civilians guilty of the same crimes.

" If you ask me whether these measures are likely to produce good results, I will answer frankly: Yes, but not at once. It is easy to destroy the Army, but time is needed for its reconstruction. The measures I suggest would at least lay the foundations for the creation of a strong Army. In spite of the disruption of the Army, we must continue the struggle, however arduous it may be, and we must even be prepared to retreat into the depths of the country. Our Allies should not count upon immediate relief through our advance. Even in retreating and remaining on the defensive, we are drawing upon us enormous enemy forces, which, were they relieved, would be sent to the Western Front and would crush the Allies and then turn against us. Upon this new Calvary the

Russian people and the Russian Army may yet shed rivers of blood and endure privations and misfortunes. But at the end of the Calvary a bright future is in store.

" There is another way. The way of treason. It would give a respite to our martyred country. But the curse of treachery cannot give us happiness. At the end of that path there is political, moral and economic slavery. The destinies of the country are in the hands of the Army. I now appeal to the Provisional Government represented here by two Ministers:

" You must lead Russia towards truth and enlightenment under the banner of Liberty, but you must give us a real chance of leading the troops in the name of that same Liberty under our old banners. You need have no fear. The name of the autocrat has been removed from these banners as well as from our hearts. It is no longer there. But there is a Mother Country; there is a sea of blood; and there is the glory of our former victories. You have trampled that banner into the dust. The time has now come. Raise the banners and bow to them if your conscience is still within you."

* * * *

I had finished. Kerensky rose, shook hands with me, and said: " Thank you, General, for your outspoken and sincere speech."

In the evidence which Kerensky subsequently gave to the High Commission for the investigation of Kornilov's movement, the Prime Minister explained this gesture by the fact that he approved, not of the contents of my speech, but of my courage, and that he wished to emphasise his respect for every independent opinion, albeit entirely divergent from the views of the Provisional Government. In substance, according to Kerensky, " General Deniken had for the first time drawn a plan for the Revanche—that music of the future military reaction." There is in these words a deep misinterpretation. We had not forgotten the Galician retreat of 1915 or its causes, but, at the same time, we could not forgive Kalush and Tarnopol in 1917. It was our duty, our right, and our moral obligation not to wish for either of these contingencies. I was followed by General Klembovsky. I had left the Assembly, and only heard the end of his speech. He described the condition of his Front in terms almost identical to mine, with great restraint, and came to a conclusion that could only have been prompted by deep despair: he suggested that power should be vested at the Front in a kind of peculiar triumvirate consisting of the Commander-in-Chief, a Commissar, and an elected soldier. . . .

The Conference at the Stavka

General Alexeiev was unwell, spoke briefly, described the condition of the rear, of the reserves and garrison troops, and endorsed the suggestions I had made.

General Ruzsky, who had been undergoing a protracted cure in the Caucasus, and was therefore out of touch with the Army, analysed the situation such as it appeared to him from the speeches that had been made. He quoted a series of historical comparisons between the old Army and the new Revolutionary one with such emphasis and bluntness that Kerensky, in replying, accused Ruzsky of advocating the return to Czarist autocracy. The new men were unable to understand the passionate grief of an old soldier for the Army. Kerensky was probably unaware of the fact that Ruzsky had been repudiated, and also passionately accused by the Reactionary circles of the opposite crime, for the part which he had played in the Emperor's abdication.

A telegram was read from General Kornilov, urging that capital punishment should be introduced in the rear, chiefly in order to cope with the licentious bands of Reservists; that disciplinary powers should be vested in the Commanding Officers; that the competence of the Army Committees should be restricted and their responsibilities fixed; that meetings should be prohibited as well as anti-national propaganda, and visits to the Front prohibited to various delegations and agitators. All this was practically implied in my programme, but under another shape, and was described as " military reaction." But Kornilov had other suggestions. He advocated that Commissars should be introduced into the Army Corps and given the right to confirm the verdicts of the Military Revolutionary Tribunals, as well as to effect a " cleansing " of the commanding staffs. This last proposal impressed Kerensky by its " breadth and depth of vision "—greater than those which emanated from the " old wiseacres," whom he considered intoxicated " with the wine of hate. . . ." There was an obvious misunderstanding, because Kornilov's " cleansing " was not intended against the men of solid military traditions (mistakenly identified with Monarchist Reaction), but against the hirelings of the Revolution—unprincipled men, deprived of will-power and of the capacity of taking the responsibility upon their own shoulders.

Savinkov, the Commissar of the South-Western Front, also spoke, expressing his own views only. He agreed with the general description of the Front which we had given, and pointed out that it is not the fault of the Revolutionary Democracy that the soldiery of the old régime is still distrustful of their Commanding Officers; that all is not well with the latter from the military and political points of view, and that the main object of the new Revolutionary institutions was to restore normal relations between these two elements of the Army.

Kerensky made the closing speech of the Conference. He tried to justify himself—spoke of the elemental character of the inevitable " Democratisation " of the Army. He blamed us for seeing in the Revolution, and in its influence upon the Russian soldier, the only cause of the *débâcle* of July, and he severely condemned the old régime. Finally, he gave us no definite directions for future work. The members of the Conference dispersed with a heavy feeling of mutual misunderstanding. I was also discouraged, but at the bottom of my heart I was pleased to think—alas! I was mistaken—that our voices had been heeded. My hopes were confirmed by a letter from Kornilov which I received soon after his appointment to the Supreme Command:

" I have read the Report you made at the Stavka on July 16th with deep and sincere satisfaction. I would sign such a Report with both hands; I take off my hat to you, and I am lost in admiration before your firmness and courage. I firmly believe that, with the help of the Almighty, we will succeed in accomplishing the task of reconstructing our beloved Army and of restoring its fighting power."

Fate has, indeed, cruelly derided our hopes!

CHAPTER XXX.

General Kornilov.

TWO days after the Moghilev Conference General Brussilov was relieved of the Supreme Command. The attempt to give the leadership of the Russian Armies to a person who had not only given proof of the most complete loyalty to the Provisional Government, but had evinced sympathy with its reforms, had failed. A leader had been superseded, who, on assuming the Supreme Command, gave utterance to the following:

" I am the leader of the Revolutionary Army, appointed to this responsible post by the people in revolution and the Provisional Government, in agreement with the Petrograd Soviet of Workmen's and Soldiers' Delegates. I was the first to go over to the people, serve the people. I will continue to serve them, will never desert them."[*]

Kerensky, in his evidence before the Commission of Inquiry, explained Brussilov's dismissal by the catastrophal condition of the Front, by the possible development of the German offensive, the absence of a firm hand at the front, and of a definite plan; by Brussilov's inability to evaluate and forestall the complications of the military situation, and lastly, by his lack of influence over both officers and men.

Be it as it may, General Brussilov's retirement from the pages of military history can in no wise be regarded as a simple episode of an administrative character. *It marks a clear recognition by the Government of the wreck of its entire military policy.*

On July 19th, by an Order of the Provisional Government, **Lavr** Georgievich Kornilov, General of Infantry, was appointed to the post of Supreme Commander-in-Chief.

In Chapter VII. I spoke of my meeting with Kornilov, then Commander-in-Chief of the Petrograd district. The whole meaning of his occupation of this post lay in the chance of bringing

---
[*] 9th July—Reply to the greeting of the Moghilev Soviet.

the Petrograd garrison to a sense of duty and subordination. This Kornilov failed to accomplish. A fighting General who carried fighting men with him by his courage, coolness, and contempt of

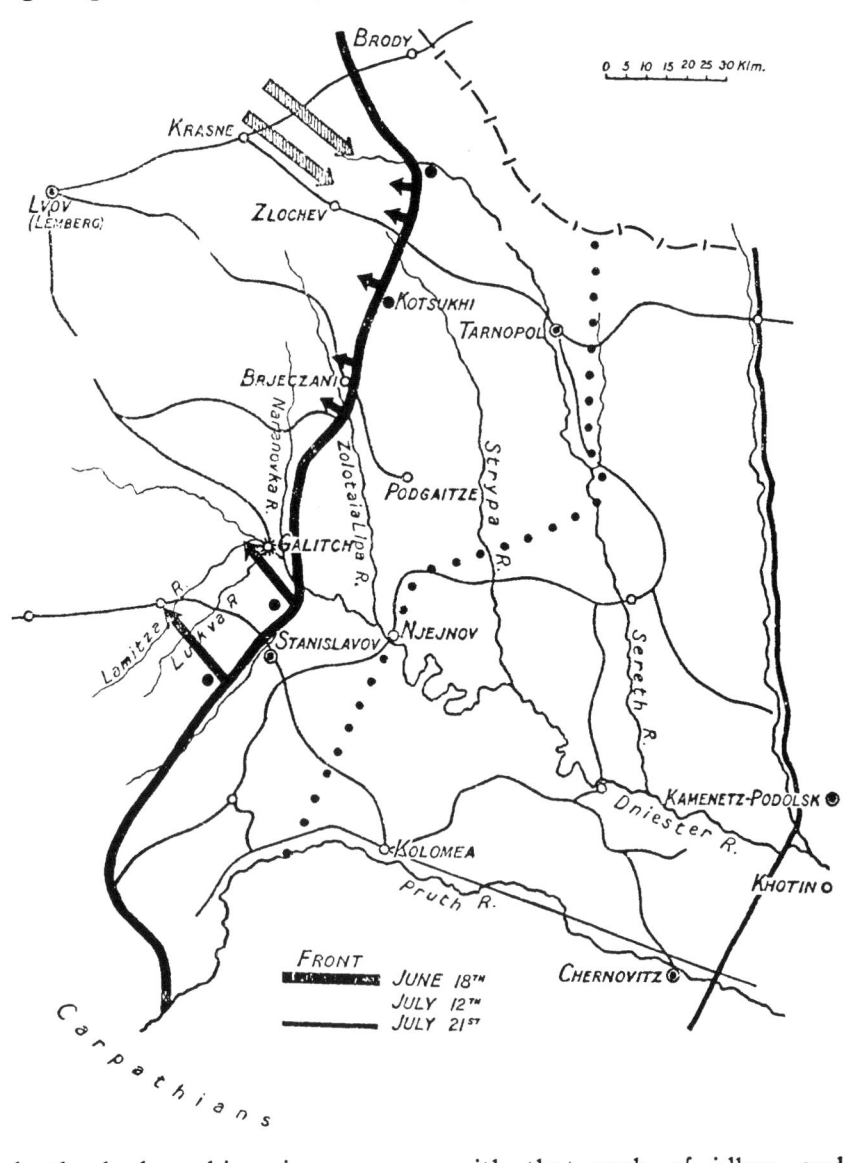

death, had nothing in common with that mob of idlers and hucksters into which the Petrograd garrison had been transformed. His sombre figure, his dry speech, only at times softened by sincere feeling, and above all, its tenour so far removed from the bewildering slogans of the Revolution, so simple in its profession of a soldier's faith—could neither fire nor inspire the Petrograd soldiery. Inexperienced in political chicanery, by profession alien to those methods of political warfare which had been developed by the joint efforts of the bureaucracy, party sectarianism, and the revolutionary underworld, Kornilov, as Commander-in-Chief of the Petrograd district, could neither influence the Government nor impress the Soviet, which, without any cause, distrusted him from the very beginning. Kornilov would have managed to suppress

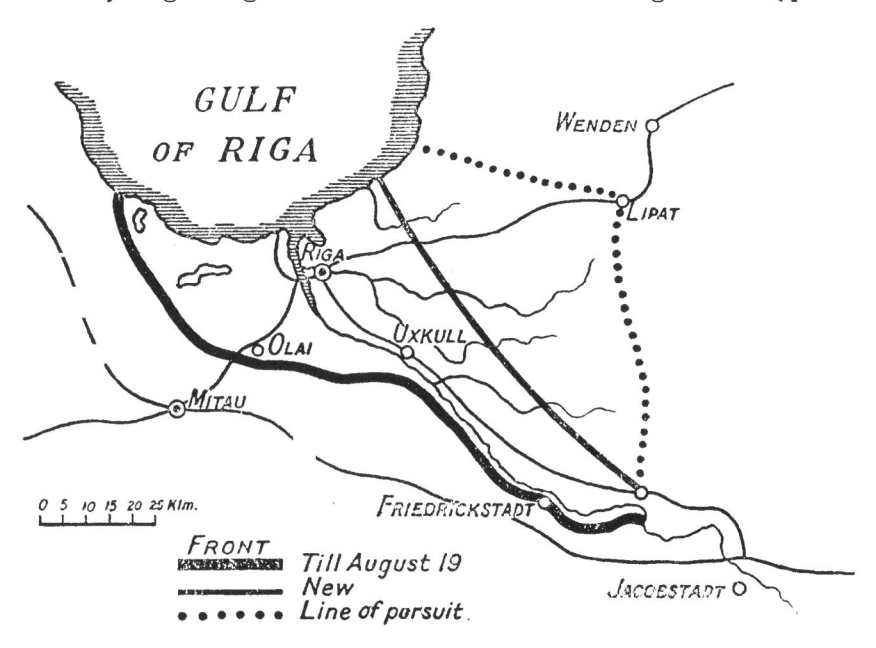

the Petrograd praetorians, even if he had perished in doing so, but he could not attract them to himself.

He felt that the Petrograd atmosphere did not suit him, and when on April 21st, the Executive Committee of the Soviet, after the first Bolshevist attacks, passed a resolution that no military unit could leave barracks in arms without the permission of the Committee, it was totally impossible for Kornilov to remain at a post which gave no rights and imposed enormous responsibilities.

There was yet another reason: the Commander-in-Chief of the Petrograd district was subordinated, not to the Stavka, but to the Minister of War, Gutchkov had left that post on April 30th, and Kornilov did not wish to remain under Kerensky, the vice-president of the Petrograd Soviet.

The position of the Petrograd garrison and command was so

incongruous that this painful problem had to be solved by artificial measures. On Kornilov's initiative, and with General Alexeiev's full approval, the Stavka, in conjunction with the Headquarters of the Petrograd District, drew up a scheme for the organisation of the Petrograd Front, covering the approaches to the capital through Finland and the Finnish Gulf. This Front was to include the troops in Finland and Kronstadt, on the coast, of the Reval fortified region and the Petrograd garrison, the depôt ballations of which it was proposed to expand into active regiments and form into brigades; the inclusion of the Baltic Fleet was likewise probable. Such an organisation—logical from a strategical point of view, especially in connection with the information received of the reinforcement of the German Front on the line of advance on Petrograd—gave the Commander-in-Chief the legal right to alter the dispositions to relieve the troops at the front and behind, etc. I do not know whether this would have really made it possible to free Petrograd from the garrison which had become a veritable scourge to the Capital, the Provisional Government, and even (in September) to the non-Bolshevist sections of the Soviet. The Government most thoughtlessly bound itself by a promise, given in its first declaration, that " the troops which had taken part in the revolutionary movement should not be either disarmed or moved from Petrograd."

This plan, however, naturally failed on Kornilov's departure, as his successors, appointed one after another by Kerensky, were of such an indefinite political character, and so deficient in military experience, that it was impossible to place them at the head of so large a military force.

At the end of April, just before his retirement, Gutchkov wished to make Kornilov Commander-in-Chief of the Northern Front, a post which had become vacant after General Ruzsky's dismissal. General Alexeiev and I were at the Conference with Thomas and the French military representatives, when I was called up to the telegraph instrument to talk with the Minister of War. As General Alexeiev remained at the meeting, and Gutchkov was ill in bed, the negotiations, in which I acted as an intermediary, were exceedingly difficult to carry on, both technically and because, in view of the indirect transmission, it was necessary to speak somewhat guardedly. Gutchkov insisted, Alexeiev refused. No less than six times did I transmit their replies, which were at first reserved and then more heated.

Gutchkov spoke of the difficulty of managing the Northern Front, which was the most unruly, and of the need of a firm hand there. He said that it was desirable to retain Kornilov in the immediate vicinity of Petrograd, in view of future political possibilities. Alexeiev refused flatly. He said nothing about " political possibilities," basing his refusal on the grounds of Kornilov's inadequate service qualifications for command, and the awkwardness of passing over Senior Commanders more experienced and acquainted with the Front, such as General Abram Dragomirov, for instance. Nevertheless, when the next day an official telegram arrived from the Ministry in connection with Kornilov's appointment, Alexeiev replied that he was uncompromisingly against it, and that if the appointment were made in spite of this, he would immediately send in his resignation.

Never had the Supreme Commander-in-Chief been so inflexible in his communications with Petrograd. Some persons, including Kornilov himself (as he confessed to me afterwards), involuntarily gained the impression that the question was a somewhat wider basis one than that of the appointment of the Commander-in-Chief . . . that the fear of a future dictator played a certain part. However, this supposition is flatly contradicted by placing this episode in conjunction with the fact that the Petrograd Front was created for Kornilov—a fact that was of no less importance and fraught with possibilities.

In the beginning of May Kornilov took over the 8th Army on the South-Western Front. General Dragomirov was appointed Commander-in-Chief of the Northern Front.

This is the second event which gives the key to the understanding of the subsequent relations between Alexeiev and Kornilov.

According to Kornilov, the 8th Army was in a state of complete disintegration when he assumed command. "For two months," says he, " I had to visit the units nearly every day and personally explain to the soldiers the necessity for discipline, encourage the officers, and urge upon the troops the necessity of an advance. . Here I became convinced that firm language from the Commander and definite action were necessary in order to arrest the disintegration of our Army. I understood that such language was expected both by the officers and the men, the more reasonable of whom were already tired of the complete anarchy. . . ."

Under what conditions Kornilov made his rounds we have already shown in Chapter XXIII. I hardly think that he managed to arouse the mass of soldiers to consciousness. The Kalush of June 28th and the Kalush of July 8th show the 8th Army equally as heroes and as beasts. The officers and a small part of the real soldiers, however, were more than ever under the spell of Kornilov's personality. Its power increased among the non-

Socialistic sections of the Russian public likewise. When, after the rout of July 6th, General Gutor—who had been appointed to the highly responsible post of Commander-in-Chief of the South-Western Front, merely not to resist the democratisation of the Army—yielded to despair and collapsed, there was no one to replace him except Kornilov (on the night of July 8th). . . . The spectre of the " General on a White Horse " was already looming in sight and disturbing the spiritual peace of many.

Brussilov was strongly opposed to this appointment. Kerensky hesitated for a moment. The position, however, was catastrophical. Kornilov was bold, courageous, stern, resolute and independent, and would never hesitate to show initiative or to undertake any responsibility if circumstances required it. Kerensky was of the opinion* that Kornilov's downright qualities, though dangerous in case of success, would be only too useful in case of a panic-stricken retreat. And " when the Moor has done his work, let the Moor go. . . . " So Kerensky insisted on Kornilov's appointment as Commander-in-Chief of the South-Western Front.

On the third day after taking over his duties, Kornilov wired to the Provisional Government: " I declare that if the Government does not confirm the measures proposed by me, and deprives me of the only means of saving the Army and of using it for its real purpose of defending the Motherland and liberty, then I, General Kornilov, will of my own accord lay down my authority as Commander-in-Chief. . . . "

A series of political telegrams from Kornilov produced a profound impression on the country, and inspired some with fear, some with hate, and others with hope. Kerensky hesitated, but what about the support of the Commissars and Committees? The tranquilisation and reduction to order of the South-Western Front attained, among other means, by Kornilov's bold, resolute struggle against the Army Bolsheviks? The oppressive isolation felt by the Minister of War after the conference of July 16th? The uselessness of retaining Brussilov as Supreme Commander-in-Chief and the hopelessness of placing at the head of the Army Generals of the new type, as shown by the experiment of appointing Brussilov and Gutor? Savinkov's persistent advice? Such were the reasons which forced Kerensky—who fully recognised the inevitability of the coming collision with the man who repudiated his military policy with every fibre of his soul—to decide on the appointment of Kornilov to the post of Supreme Commander-

---

*See his evidence before the Commission of Inquiry.

in-Chief. There is not the slightest doubt that Kerensky did this in a fit of despair. Probably it was the same feeling of fatality that induced him to appoint Savinkov acting Minister of War.

The collisions occurred sooner than might have been expected. On receiving the order for his appointment, Kornilov at once sent the Provisional Government a telegram " reporting " 'that he could accept command and " lead the nation to victory and to the prospect of a just and honourable peace only on the following conditions:

" (1) Responsibility to his own conscience and to the whole nation.

" (2) Complete non-interference with his orders relating to military operations and, therefore, with the appointment of the Higher Command.

" (3) The application of the measures recently introduced at the Front to all places in the rear where drafts for the Army were quartered.

" (4) Acceptance of his proposals telegraphed to the Conference at the Stavka on July 16th."

When in due course I read this telegram in the newspapers, I was not a little surprised at the first condition, which established a highly original form of suzerainty on the part of the Supreme Command until the convocation of the Constituent Assembly. I waited impatiently for the official reply. There was none. As it turned out, on receiving Kornilov's ultimatum, the Council of the Government hotly debated the matter, and Kerensky demanded that the prestige of the High Command should be upheld by the immediate removal of the new Supreme Commander-in-Chief. The Government did not agree to this, and Kerensky, ignoring the other points mentioned in the telegram, replied only to the second, by recognising the right of the Supreme Commander-in Chief to select his own direct assistants.

Diverging from the established procedure of appointments, the Government, simultaneously with Kornilov's appointment and without his knowledge, issued an order appointing General Cheremissov Commander-in-Chief of the South-Western Front. Kornilov regarded this as a complete violation of his rights, and sent another ultimatum, declaring that he could continue to hold Supreme Command only on condition of Cheremissov's immediate removal. He declined to go to Moghilev before this question was settled. Cheremissov, on his part, was very " nervy," and threatened to " bomb his way " into Front Headquarters and to establish his rights as Commander-in-Chief.

This complicated matters still further, and Kornilov reported by wire* to Petrograd that, in his opinion, it would be more regular to dismiss Cheremissov. " For the purpose of strengthening discipline in the Army, we decided to take severe measures with the soldiers; the same measures must likewise apply to the higher military commanders."

The Revolution had upset all mutual relations and the very essence of discipline. As a soldier, I was bound to see in all this the undermining of the authority of the Provisional Government (if such existed), and I could not but recognise that it was both the right and the duty of the Government to make everyone respect its authority.

As a chronicler, however, I must add that the military leaders had no other means of stopping this disintegration of the Army, proceeding from above. And had the Government actually possessed the power, and in full panoply of right and might had been able to assert itself, there would have been no ultimatums either from the Soviet or from the military leaders. Furthermore, there would have been no need for the events of the 27th of August, and those of the 25th of October would have been impossible.

The matter finally resolved itself into the arrival of Commissar Filonenko at Front Headquarters. He informed Kornilov that all his recommendations had been accepted by the Government, in principle, while Cheremissov was placed at the disposal of the Provisional Government. General Balnev was hastily, at random, selected to command the South-Western Front, and Kornilov assumed the Supreme Command on the 27th of July.

The spectre of the " General on the White Horse " became more and more clearly visible. And the eyes of many, suffering at the sight of the madness and the shame now engulfing Russia, were again and again turned to this spectre. Honest and dishonest, sincere and insincere, politicans, soldiers and adventurers, all turned to it. And all with one voice cried out, " Save Us ! "

He, the stern and straightforward soldier, deeply patriotic, untried in politics, knowing little of men, hypnotised both by truth and flattery, and by the general longing expectation of someone's coming, moved by a fervent desire for deeds of sacrifice—he truly believed in the predestined nature of his appointment. He lived and fought with this belief, and died for it on the banks of the Kuban.

---

* Conversation by telegraph with Colonel Bazanovsky.

Kornilov became a sign and rallying point. To some, of counter-Revolution; to others, of the salvation of their native land.

Around this point a struggle for influence and power was commenced by people who, unaided, without him could not have attained to such power.

A characteristic episode had already taken place on the 8th of July, at Kamenets-Podolsk. Here, in Kornilov's entourage, there occurred the first conflict between Savinkov and Zavoiko, the former being the most prominent Russian Revolutionary, leader of the Terrorist fighting group of the Social-Revolutionary Party, organiser of the most notorious political assassinations—those of Plehve, Minister of the Interior, of the Grand Duke Serge, etc. Strong-willed and cruel by nature, completely lacking in the controlling influences of " conventional morality," despising both the Provisional Government and Kerensky, supporting the Provisional Government from motives of expediency, as he understood it, ready at any moment to sweep them aside—he saw in Kornilov merely a weapon in the fight for Revolutionary power, in which *he* must have a dominant interest. Zavoiko was one of those peculiar personages who afterwards clustered closely round Kornilov and played such a prominent part in the August days. He was not very well known even to Kornilov. The latter stated, in his evidence before the Supreme Commission of Inquiry, that he became acquainted with Zavoiko in April, 1917; that Zavoiko had been " marechal de noblesse " of the Haisin district of Podolia, had been employed on the Nobel oilfields in Baku, and, by his own statements, had been employed in prospecting for minerals in Turkestan and Western Siberia. He arrived in Czernowitz, enrolled as a volunteer in the Daghestan Mounted Regiment, and was retained at Army Headquarters as personal aide to Kornilov. That is all that is known of Zavoiko's past.

Kornilov's first telegram to the Provisional Government was edited by Zavoiko, who " gave it the form of an ultimatum with a concealed threat, in case of non-compliance with the demands presented to the Provisional Government, to proclaim a military dictatorship on the South-Western Front."*

I discovered all this subsequently. During all these events I continued working at Minsk, completely engrossed now, not by the offensive, but by the organisation of any sort of skeleton defence of the half-collapsed Front. There was no information,

---

* Savinkov: *The Kornilov Affair*. Savinkov's expostulations prevailed. Kornilov even consented to remove Zavoiko from the limits of the Front, but soon recalled him.

no rumours even, of what was going on at the head of affairs. Only an increased tension was noticeable in all official relations.

Quite unexpectedly, in the end of July the Stavka offered me the post of Commander-in-Chief of the South-Western Front. I communicated by wire with General Lukomsky, the Chief-of-Staff of the Supreme Commander-in-Chief, and told him that I should obey orders and go wherever I was sent, but would like to know the reason for this exchange. If the reasons were political I should ask to be left at my old post. Lukomsky assured me that what Kornilov had in view was only the military importance of the South-Western Front and the proposed strategical operations in that quarter. I accepted the post.

I parted from my assistants with regret, and, having transferred my friend, General Markov, to the new front, left for my new place of service together with him. On my way I stopped at Moghilev. The Stavka was in a very optimistic mood; everyone was animated and hopeful, but there were no signs of any "underground" conspiratory working. It should be mentioned that in this respect the military were so naively inexperienced, that when they really began to "conspire" their work took such *obvious* forms that the deaf could not help hearing, nor the blind seeing, what was going on.

On the day of our arrival Kornilov held a Council of the Chiefs of Departments of the Stavka, at which the so-called "Kornilov programme" for the restoration of the Army was discussed. I was invited to attend. I shall not repeat all the fundamental propositions, which have already been mentioned both by me and in Kornilov's telegrams—such demands, for instance, as the introduction of Revolutionary courts-martial and capital punishment in the rear, the restoration of disciplinary authority to Commanders and raising their prestige, the limitation of the activity of the Committees and their responsibility, etc. I remember that side by side with clear and irrefutable propositions —the draft memorandum drawn up by the Departments of the Stavka—there were bureaucratic lucubrations hardly applicable in actual life. For instance, with the object of making disciplinary authority more palatable to Revolutionary Democracy, the authors of the memorandum had drawn up a curiously detailed list of disciplinary misdemeanour with a corresponding scale of penalties. And this was meant for the seething whirlpool of life, where all relations were trampled underfoot, all standards violated, where every fresh day brought forward an endless variety of departures from the regulations!

At any rate, the Supreme Command was finding the proper path, and apparently Kornilov's personality was a guarantee that the Government would be obliged to follow that path. Undoubtedly a long struggle with the Soviets, Committees, and soldiery was still to be waged, but, at least, the definiteness of the policy gave moral support and a tangible basis for this heavy task in the future. On the other hand, the support given to Kornilov's measures by Savinkov's War Ministry gave reason to hope that Kerensky's vacillations and indecision would finally be overcome. The attitude to this question of the Provisional Government as a whole was of no practical importance, and could not even be officially expressed. At that time it seemed as if Kerensky had, in some degree, freed himself from the yoke of the Soviet, but, just as formerly all the most important questions of State had been settled by him apart from the Government, in conjunction with the leading Soviet circles, now, in August, the direction of State affairs passed into the hands of a triumvirate composed of Kerensky, Nekrassov, and Tereschenko, leaving both the Socialist and Liberal groups of the Government out of the running.

After the meeting was over Kornilov asked me to stay, and, when all had left, said to me, almost in a whisper: " It is necessary to struggle, otherwise the country will perish. N. came to see me at the Front. He is nursing his scheme of a *coup d'état* and of placing the Grand-Duke Dmitri on the throne. He is organising something or other, and has suggested collaboration. I told him flatly that I would take no part in any Romanov adventures. The Government itself understands that it can do nothing. They have offered my joining in the Government. . No, thank you! These gentlemen are far too much entangled with the Soviets, and cannot decide on anything. I have told them that if authority is given me I shall carry on a decisive struggle. We must lead Russia to a Constituent Assembly, and then let them do what they like. I shall stand aside and not interfere in any way. Now, General, may I rely on your support?"

" To the fullest extent."

This was my second meeting and my second conversation with Kornilov. We embraced heartily and parted . . . only to meet again in the Bykhov Prison.

CHAPTER XXXI.

My Service as Commander-in-Chief of the South-Western Front—The Moscow Conference—The Fall of Riga.

I WAS touched by General Alexeiev's letter:
" My thoughts are with you in your new appointment. I consider that you have been sent to perform a superhuman task. Much has been said, but apparently little has been done there. Nothing has been done even after the 16th July by Russia's chief babbler. The authority of the Commanders is being steadily curtailed. Should you want my help in anything I am ready to go to Berdichev, to go to the Front, to one Command or another. . . . God preserve you!"

Here was a man, indeed, whom neither an exalted position nor misfortunes could change. He was full of his modest, disinterested work for the good of his native land.

A new front, new men. The South-Western Front, shaken by the events in July, was gradually recovering. Not, however, in the sense of real convalescence, as the optimists thought, but of a return approximately to its condition prior to the offensive. There were the same strained relations between officers and men, the same slip-shod service, the desertion, and open unwillingness to fight, which was only less actively expressed owing to the lull in operations; finally there was the same Bolshevist propaganda, only more active, and not infrequently disguised under the form of Committee "fractions" and preparations for the Constituent Assembly. I have a document referring to the 2nd Army of the Western Front. It is highly characteristic as an indication of the unparalleled toleration and, indeed, encouragement of the disintegration of the Army on the part of the representatives of the Government and Commanders, under the guise of liberty and conscious voting at the elections. Here is a copy of the telegram sent to all the senior officers of the 2nd Army:

The Army Commander, in agreement with the Commissar, and at the request of the Army fraction of the Bolshevist Social-Democrats, has permitted the organisation, from the 15th to 18th October, of preparatory courses for instructors of the aforesaid fraction for the elections to the Constituent Assembly, one representative of the Bolshevist organisation of each separate unit being sent to the said courses. No. 1644.

SUVOROV.*

The same toleration had been exercised in many cases previously, and was founded on the exact meaning of the regulations for Army Committees and of the " Declaration of Soldiers' Rights."

Carried away by the struggle against counter-revolution, the Revolutionary institutions had paid no attention to such facts as public meetings with extreme Bolshevist watchwords being held at the very place where the Front Headquarters were situated, or that the local paper, *Svobodnaia Mysl*,† most undisguisedly threatened the officers with a St. Bartholomew's Eve.

The front was *holding out*. That is all that could be said of the situation. At times there would be disturbances ending tragically, such as the brutal murder of Generals Girshfeld, Hirschfeld, and Stefanovich, Commissar Linde. The preliminary arrangements and the concentration of the troops for the coming partial offensive were made, but there was no possibility of launching the actual attack until the " Kornilov programme " had been put into practice and the results known.

I waited very impatiently.

The Revolutionary organisations (the Commissariat and Committee) of the South-Western Front were in a position; they had not yet seized power, but some of it had already been yielded to them voluntarily by a series of Commanders-in-Chief—Brussilov, Gutor, Baluev. Therefore, my coming at once roused their antagonism. The Committee of the Western Front lost no time in sending a scathing report on me to Berdichev on the basis of which the next issue of the Committee's organ published an impressive warning to the " enemies of democracy." As usual, I totally omitted to invoke the aid of the Commissariat, and sent a message to the Committee saying that I could have nothing to do with it unless it kept rigidly within the limits of the law.

The Commissar of the Front was a certain Gobechio. I saw him once only, on my arrival. In a few days he got transferred to the Caucasus, and his post was taken by Iordansky.‡ As soon as

---

* Chief of Staff of the Army.
† Free Thought. (Transl. note).
‡ Former Editor of the *Souvremenny Mir* (Contemporary World), and Social-Democrat of the *Yedinstvo* Group. In 1921 he edited the Bolshevist newspaper in Helsingfors.

he arrived he issued an " order to the troops at the Front." Afterwards he was unable to understand that two persons could not command the Front at one and the same time. Iordansky and his assistants, Kostitsin and Grigorier—a literary man, zoologist, and doctor respectively—were probably rather prominent men in their own profession, but utterly ignorant of military life.

The Committee of the Front was no better and no worse than others.* It took the " Defencist " point of view, and even supported the repressive measures taken by Kornilov in July, but at that time the Committee was not in the least degree a *military* institution organically connected—for good or evil—with the true Army life. It was merely a mixed party organ. Divided into " fractions " of all the Socialist parties, the Committee positively revelled in politics, and introduced them at the Front likewise. The Committee carried on propaganda on a large scale, convened congresses of representatives in order to have them converted by Socialist fractions, including such as were openly antagonistic to the policy of the Government. I made an attempt to stop this work in view of the impending strategical operations and the difficult period of transition, but met with determined opposition on the part of Commissar Iordansky. At the same time, the Committee was perpetually interfering in all questions of military authority, spreading sedition and distrust to the commanders.

* *

Meanwhile, both in Petrograd and Moghilev, events were taking their course, and we could grasp their meaning only in so far as they were reflected by newspaper reports, rumours and gossip.

There was still no " programme." The Moscow State Conference† raised great hopes, but it met without making any changes in either State or military policy. On the contrary, it even outwardly emphasises the irreconcilable enmity between the Revolutionary Democracy and the Liberal Bourgeoisie, between the Commanders and the soldiers' representatives.

If the Moscow Conference yielded no positive results, nevertheless, it fully exposed the mood of the opponents, the leaders and the rulers. All unanimously recognised that the country was in deadly peril. Everyone understood that the social relations had suffered an upheaval, that all branches of the nation's economy had been uprooted. Each party reproached the other with supporting the selfish interests of their class. This, however, was not the most

---

* Undoubtedly better than the Committee of the Western Front.
† Held on August 14th, 1917.

important matter, for, strange as it may seem, the primary causes of social class war, even the agrarian and labour questions, merely led to disagreement, without rousing any irreconcilable dissentions. Even when the Plekhanov, the old leader of the Social-Democrats, amid universal approval, turned to the Right demanding sacrifice, and to the Left demanding moderation, it seemed as if the chasm between the two opposing social camps was not so very great.

All the attention of the Conference was taken up by other questions, those of *authority and of the Army*.

Miliukov enumerated all the sins of the Government, vanquished by the Soviets, its " capitulation " to the ideology of the Socialist parties and Zimmerwaldists, capitulation in the Army, in foreign policy, to the Utopian demands of the working classes, to the extreme demands of nationalities.

" The usurpation of the authority of the State by Central and Local Committees and Soviets," said General Kaledin distinctly, "must be stopped at once and decisively."

Maklakov smoothed the way for his attack: " I demand nothing, but I cannot help drawing attention to the alarm felt by the social conscience when it sees that the ' Defeatists ' of yesterday have been invited to join the Government." Shulgin (Right) is agitated. He says: " I want your (the Provisional Government's) authority to be really strong, really unlimited. I want this, though I know that a strong Government easily turns to despotism, which is more likely to crush me than you, the friends of that Government."

On the Left, Jehkheidze sings the praises of the Soviets: " It is only owing to the Revolutionary organisations that the creative spirit of the Revolution has been preserved, for the salvation of the country from the disintegration of authority and from anarchy. " " There is no power higher than that of the Provisional Governments," says Tzeretelli, " because the source of this power the sovereign people has, through all the organs at its disposal, directly delegated this power to the Provisional Government." Of course, in so far as that Government submits to the will of the Soviets ? . . . And over all one hears the dominating voice of the President of the Congress, who is seeking for " heavenly words " in order to " express his shuddering horror " at coming events, " and at the same time brandishing a wooden sword and threatening his hidden enemies thus: ' Be it known to everyone who has once tried to offer armed resistance to the authority of the people that the attempt will be smothered in blood and iron. Let those beware who think that the time has come for them to overthrow the Revolutionary Government with the help of bayonets.' "

The contradiction was still more striking in military matters. In a dry but powerful speech, the Supreme Commander-in-Chief drew a picture of the destruction of the Army, involving the whole country in its ruin, and with great reserve explained the gist of his programme. General Alexeiev related, with genuine bitterness, the sad story of the sins, sufferings and gallantry of the former Army.

" Weak in technical resources and morally strong in spirit and discipline," he related how the Army had lived to see the bright days of the Revolution, and how later on, " when it was thought to be a danger to the conquests of the Revolution, it was inoculated with deadly poison." Kaledin, the Don Cossack Attaman, representing thirteen Cossack Armies and unhampered by any official position, spoke sharply and distinctly : " The Army must keep out of politics. There must be no political meetings with their party struggles and disputes. All the (Army) Soviets and Committees must be abolished. The Declaration of Soldiers' Rights must be revised. Discipline must be raised both at the Front and in the rear. The disciplinary authority of the Commanders must be restored. All power to the leaders of the Army ! "

Kuchin, the representative of the Army and Front Committees, rose to reply to these trite military axioms. " The Committees were a manifestation of the instinct of self-defence. They had to be formed as organs for the protection of the privates, as hitherto there had been nothing but oppression . . . the Committees had brought light and knowledge to the soldiers. . . . Then came the second period—one of decay and disorganisation . ' rearguard consciousness ' made its appearance, but failed to digest all the mass of questions which the Revolutions had raised in the minds of the soldiery. . ." Now the speaker did not deny the necessity for repressive measures, but they " must be compatible with the definite work of Army organisations. . . ." How this was to be done had been shown by the united front of Revolutionary Democracy, namely, the Army must be animated, not by the desire of victory over the enemy, but by " a repudiation of Imperialistic aims, and a desire for the speedy attainment of universal peace on Democratic principles. The commanders should possess complete independence in the conduct of military operations, and have a decisive voice in questions of discipline and service training." The object of the organisations, on the other hand, was to introduce their policy wholesale among troops, and " the Commissars must be the introducers of (this) single Revolutionary policy of the Provisional Government, the Army Committees must direct the social and political life of the soldiers. The restoration of the disciplinary authority of the commanders is not to be thought of," etc.

What is the Government going to do? Will it find enough strength and boldness to burst the fetters placed on it by the Bolshevistic Soviet? *

Kornilov said firmly, repeating his words twice: " I do not doubt for a moment that the (my) measures will be carried out without delay."

And if not—was it to be War?

He also said: " It is impossible to admit that the determination to carry out these measures should in every case be aroused merely by the pressure of defeats and loss of territory If the rout at Tarnopol and the loss of Galicia and Bukovina did indeed result in restoration of discipline at the Front, it cannot be admitted that order in the rear should be restored at the cost of the loss of Riga, and that order on the railways should be restored by the cession of Moldavia and Bessarabia to the enemy."

On the 20th Riga fell.

Both strategically and tactically the Front of the lower Dvina was in complete preparedness. Taking into consideration the strength of the defensive positions, the forces were also sufficient. The officers in command were General Parsky, Army Commander, and General Boldyrev, Corps Commander; both experienced Generals, and certainly not inclined to counter-Revolution in the opinion of the Democrats.†

Finally, from deserters' reports, our Headquarters knew not only the direction but even the day and the hour of the contem plated attack.

Nevertheless, on the 19th August the Germans (Von Hutier's 8th Army), after heavy artillery preparation, occupied the Uxküll bridgehead in the face of feeble opposition on our part, and crossed the Dvina. On 20th August the Germans assumed the offensive also along the Mitau road; towards evening of the same day the enemy's Uxküll group, having pierced our lines on the Egel, began deploying in a northerly direction, threatening the

* In August the balance of forces in the Soviet altered rapidly in favour of the Bolsheviks, giving them a majority.

† General Parsky now occupies an important post in the Soviet Army, while General Boldyrev was subsequently Commander-in-Chief of the Anti-Bolshevist " Front of the Constituent Assembly " on the Volga.

retreat of the Russian troops towards Wenden. The 12th Army, abandoning Riga, retired some 60-70 versts, losing touch with the enemy, and on the 25th occupied the so-called Wenden position. The Army lost in prisoners alone some 9,000 men, besides 81 guns, 200 machine-guns, etc. A further advance did not enter into the German plans, and they commenced to establish themselves on the extensive terrain of the right bank of the Dvina, immediately sending off two divisions to the Western Front.

We lost the rich industrial town of Riga, with all its military structures and supplies; more important still, we lost a safe defensive line, the abandonment of which placed both the Dvina Front and the way to Petrograd under a constant threat.

The fall of Riga made a great impression in the country. Quite unexpectedly, however, it called forth from the Revolutionary Democracy, not repentance, not patriotic fervour, but, instead, a still greater bitterness towards the leaders and officers. The Stavka in one *communiqué*[*] inserted the following sentence: " The disorganised masses of the soldiery are flocking in uncontrollable masses along the Pskov high road and the road to Bieder-Limburg." This statement, undoubtedly true, and neither mentioning nor relating to the causes of the above, raised a storm amongst the Revolutionary Democracy. The Commissars and Committees of the Northern Front sent a series of telegrams refuting the " provocative attacks of the Stavka " and assuring that " there was no shame in this reverse "; that " the troops honestly obey all demands of their leaders . . . there have been no cases of flight or treachery on the part of the troops."

The Commissar for the Front, Stankevitch, while demurring against there being no shame in such a causeless and inglorious retreat, pointed out, amongst other things, a series of errors and delinquencies on the part of the Commanders. It is extremely possible that there were errors, both personal and of leadership, as well as purely objective deficiencies, caused by mutual mistrust, slackening of obedience, and the *débâcle* of the technical services. At the same time, it is undoubtedly a fact that the troops of the Northern Front, and especially the 12th Army, were the most disorganised of all, and, logically, could not offer the necessary resistance. Even the apologist of the 12th Army, Commissar Voitinsky, who always considerably exaggerated the fighting value of these troops, telegraphed on the 22nd to the Petrograd Soviet: " The troops show want of confidence in their powers, absence of training for battle, and, consequently,

---

[*] 21st August.

insufficient steadiness in open warfare. . . . Many units fight bravely, as in the early days; others show signs of weariness and panic."

Actually, the debauched Northern Front had lost all power of resistance. The troops rolled back to the limit of pursuit by the German advanced detachments, and only moved forward subsequently on losing touch with Hutier's main body, which had no intention of passing beyond a definite line.

Meanwhile, all the papers of the Left commenced a fierce campaign against the Stavka and the Commands. The word " treachery " was heard. . . . Tchernov's *Delo Naroda*, a Defeatist paper, complained: " A torturing fear creeps into the mind: are not the mistakes of the commanders, the deficiencies in artillery, and the incapacity of the leaders being unloaded on to the soldiers—courageous, heroic, perishing in thousands." The *Izvestia* announced also the motives for the " provocation "· " The Stavka, by putting forth the bogy of menacing events, is trying to terrorise the Provisional Government and make it adopt a series of measures, directly and indirectly aimed at the Revolutionary Democracy and their organisations. . "

In conjunction with all these events, the feeling against the Supreme Commander-in-Chief, General Kornilov, was increasing in the Soviets, and rumours of his approaching dismissal appeared in the Press. In answer to these, a series of angry resolutions addressed to the Government, and supporting Kornilov, made their appearance.* The resolution of the Council of the Union of Cossack Troops contained even the following passage: " The supersession of Kornilov will inevitably imbue the Cossacks with the fatal impression of the futility of further Cossack sacrifices "; and, further, that the Council " declines all responsibility for the Cossack troops at and behind the Front should Kornilov be removed."

Such was, then, the situation. Instead of pacification, passions burned fiercer, contradictions increased, the atmosphere of mutual mistrust and morbid suspicion was thickened.

* * * * *

I still postponed my tour of the troops, not abandoning hope of a satisfactory issue to the struggle and of the publication of the " Kornilov programme."†

---

* From the Chief Committee of the Union of Officers, the Military League, the Council of the Union of Cossack Troops, the Union of the Knights of St. George, the Conference of Public Men, etc.

† Until August 27th, *i.e.*, until the rupture with Kornilov, Kerensky could not bring himself to sign the draft laws embodying the " programme."

What could I bring the men? A deep, painful feeling, words appealing to "common-sense and conscience," concealing my helplessness, and like the voice of one crying in the wilderness? All had been and gone, leaving bitter memories behind. It will always be so: thoughts, ideas, words, moral persuasion will never cease to rouse men to deeds of merit; but what if overgrown, virgin soil must be torn up with an iron plough? .

What should I say to the officers, sorrowfully and patiently awaiting the end of the regular and merciless lingering death of the Army? For I could only say to them: If the Government does not radically alter its policy the end of the Army has come.

On the 7th August orders were received to move the Caucasian Native ("Wild") Division from under my command northwards; on the 12th the same order was received for the 3rd Cavalry Corps, then in Reserve, and later for the Kornilov "shock" Regiment. As always, their destination was not indicated. The direction prescribed, on the other hand, equally pointed to the Northern Front, at that time greatly threatened, and to Petrograd. I recommended General Krymov, commanding the 3rd Cavalry Corps, for the command of the 11th Army. The Stavka agreed, but demanded his immediate departure for Moghilev on a special mission. On his way there Krymov reported to me. Apparently he had not yet received definite instructions—at any rate, he spoke of none; however, neither he nor I doubted that the mission was in connection with the expected change in military policy. Krymov was at this time cheerful and confident, and had faith in the future; as formerly, he considered that only a crushing blow to the Soviets could save the situation.

Following on this, official information was received of the formation of the Detached Petrograd Army, and the appointment of an officer of the General Staff to be Quartermaster-General of this Army was desired.

Finally, about the 20th, the situation became somewhat clearer. An officer reported to me at Berdichev, and handed me a personal letter from Kornilov, wherein the latter suggested I should hear this officer's verbal report. He stated as follows:

" According to reliable information, a rising of the Bolsheviks will take place at the end of August. By this time the 3rd Cavalry Corps,* commanded by Krymov, would reach Petrograd,

---

* The 3rd Cavalry Corps was summoned to Petrograd by the Provisional Government

General Kornilov's welcome in Moscow.

would crush the rising, and simultaneously put an end to the Soviets."

Simultaneously, Petrograd would be proclaimed in a state of war, and the laws resulting from the "Kornilov programme" would be published. The Supreme Commander-in-Chief requested me to despatch to the Stavka a score or more of reliable officers—officially "for trench mortar instruction"; actually they would be sent to Petrograd, and incorporated in the Officers' Detachment.

In the course of the conversation he communicated the news from the Stavka, painting all in glowing colours. He told me, among other things, of rumours concerning new appointments to the Kiev, Odessa and Moscow commands, and of the proposed new Government, mentioning some existing ministers, and some names entirely unknown to me. The part played in this matter by the Provisional Government, in particular by Kerensky, was not clear. Had he decided on an abrupt change of military policy, would he resign, or would he be swept away by developments impossible of prediction by pure logic, or the most prophetic common sense?

In this volume I described the entire course of events during August in that sequence and in that light, in which these tragic days were experienced on the South-Western Front, not giving them the perspective of the stage and the actors acquired subsequently.

The seconding of the officers—with all precautions to prevent either them or their superiors being placed in a false position—was commenced, but it is hardly likely that it could have been accomplished by the 27th. Not one Army Commander was supplied by me with the information I had received; in fact, not one of the senior officers at the front knew anything of the events brewing.

It was clear that the history of the Russian Revolution had entered on a new phase. What would the future bring? General Markov and I spent many hours discussing this subject. He—nervous, hot-headed and impetuous—constantly wavered between the extremes of hope and fear. I also felt much the same; and both of us quite clearly saw and felt the *fatal inevitability* of a crisis. The Soviets—Bolshevists or semi-Bolshevists, no matter which—would unfailingly bring Russia to her doom. A conflict was unavoidable. But *over there*, was there an actual chance, or was everything being done in heroic desperation?

---

* From the report of the inquiry it is seen that Savinkov, in charge of the Ministry of War, and the head of Kerensky's secretariat, Colonel Baranovsky, despatched to the Stavka, themselves admitted the possibility of simultaneous action by the Soviet of Workmen's and Soldiers' Delegates and the Bolsheviks, the former under the influence of the publication of the "Kornilov programme," and the necessity for ruthlessly suppressing this. (Protocol Appendix XIII. to Kornilov's deposition.)

CHAPTER XXXII.

General Kornilov's Movement and its Repercussion on the South-West Front.

ON August 27th I was thunderstruck by receiving from the Stavka news of the dismissal of General Kornilov from the post of Supreme Commander-in-Chief.

A telegram, unnumbered, and signed " Kerensky," requested General Kornilov to transfer the Supreme Command temporarily to General Lukomsky, and, without awaiting the latter's arrival to proceed to Petrograd. Such an order was quite illegal, and not binding, as the Supreme Commander-in-Chief was in no way under the orders either of the War Minister or of the Minister-President, certainly not of Comrade Kerensky.

General Lukomsky, Chief-of-Staff, answered the Minister-President in Telegram No. 640, which I give below. Its contents were transmitted to us, the Commanders-in-Chief by Telegram No. 6412. which I have not preserved. Its tenor, however, is clear from the deposition of Kornilov, in which he says: " I ordered that my decision (not to surrender my command, and first to elucidate the situation), and that of General Lukomsky, be communicated to the Commanders-in-Chief on all fronts."

Lukomsky's telegram, No. 640, ran as follows:

All persons in touch with military affairs were perfectly aware that, in view of the existing state of affairs, when the actual direction of internal policy was in the hands of irresponsible public organisations, having an enormously deleterious effect on the Army, it would be impossible to resurrect the latter; on the contrary, the Army, properly speaking, would cease to exist in two or three months. Russia would then be obliged to conclude a shameful separate peace, whose consequences to the country would be terrible. The Government took half measures, which, changing nothing, merely prolonged the agony, and, in saving the Revolution, did not save Russia. At the same time, the preservation of the benefits of the Revolution depended solely on the salvation of Russia, for which purpose the first step must be the establishment of a really strong Government and the reform of the home Front. General Kornilov drew up a series of demands, the execution of which has been delayed. In these circumstances, General Kornilov, actuated by no motives of personal gain or aggrandisement, and supported by the clearly-expressed will of the entire right-thinking sections of the Army and the Civil community, who demanded the speedy establishment of a strong Government for the saving of their native land, and of the benefits of the Revolution, considered more severe measures requisite which would secure the re-establishment of order in the country.

The arrival of Savinkov and Lvov, who in your name made General Kornilov similar proposals,* only brought General Kornilov to a speedy decision. In accordance with your suggestions, he issued his final orders, which it is now too late to repeal.

Your telegram of to-day shows that you have now altered your previous decision, communicated in your name by Savinkov and Lvov. Conscience demands from me, desiring only the good of the Motherland, to declare to you absolutely that it is now impossible to stop what was commenced with your approval; this will lead but to civil war, the final dissolution of the Army, and a shameful separate peace, as a consequence of which the conquests of the Revolution will certainly not be secured to us.

In the interests of the salvation of Russia you must work with General Kornilov, and not dismiss him. The dismissal of General Kornilov will bring upon Russia as yet unheard-of horrors. Personally, I decline to accept any responsibility for the Army, even though it be for a short period, and do not consider it possible to take over the command from General Kornilov, as this would occasion an outburst in the Army which would cause Russia to perish.

LUKOMSKY.

All the hopes which had been entertained of the salvation of the country and the regeneration of the Army by peaceful means had now failed. I had no illusions as to the consequences of such a conflict between General Kornilov and Kerensky, and had no hopes of a favourable termination if only General Krymov's Corps did not manage to save the situation. At the same time, not for one moment did I consider it possible to identify myself with the Provisional Government, which I considered criminally incapable, and therefore immediately despatched the following telegram :

I am a soldier and am not accustomed to play hide and seek. On the 16th of July, in a conference with members of the Provisional Government, I stated that, by a series of military reforms, they had destroyed and debauched the Army, and had trampled our battle honours in the mud. My retention as Commander-in-Chief I explained as being a confession by the Provisional Government of their deadly sins before the Motherland, and of their wish to remedy the evil they had wrought. To-day I receive information that General Kornilov, who had put forward certain demands capable yet of saving the country and the Army,† has been removed from the Supreme Command. Seeing herein a return to the planned destruction of the Army, having as its consequence the downfall of our country, I feel it my duty to inform the Provisional Government that I cannot follow their lead in this.

145   DENIKIN.

---

* As we shall see later, Savinkov stated in his evidence that he " suggested no political combinations in the name of the Minister-President."

† The " Kornilov programme " is meant here.

Simultaneously Markov sent a telegram to the Government stating his concurrence in the views expressed by me.*

At the same time I ordered the Stavka to be asked in what way I could assist General Kornilov. He knew that, besides moral support, I had no actual resources at my disposal, and, therefore, thanking me for this support, demanded no more.

I ordered copies of my telegrams to be sent to all Commanders-in-Chief, the Army Commanders of the South-Western Front, and the Inspector-General of Lines of Communication. I also ordered the adoption of measures which would isolate the Front against the penetration of any news of events, without the knowledge of the Staff, until the conflict had been decided. I received similar instructions from the Stavka. I think it hardly necessary to state that the entire Staff warmly supported Kornilov, and all impatiently awaited news from Moghilev, still hoping for a favourable termination.

Absolutely no measures for the detention of any persons were taken: this would have been of no use, and did not enter into our plans.

Meanwhile, the Revolutionary Democracy at the Front were in great agitation. The members of the Front Committee on this night left their quarters and lodged in private houses on the outskirts of the town. The assistants of the Commissar were at the time away on duty, and Iordansky himself in Zhitomir. An invitation from Markov to him to come to Berdichev had no result, either that night or on the 28th. Iordansky expected a " treacherous ambush."

Night fell, a long, sleepless night, full of anxious waiting and oppressive thoughts. Never had the future of the country seemed so dark, never had our powerlessness been so galling and oppres-

---

* The Commanders-in-Chief of the other Fronts sent the Provisional Government telegrams of a completely loyal nature on August 28th. Their tenor is seen from the following extracts: " Northern Front—General Klembovsky: Consider change in Supreme Command extremely dangerous when the threat of an external enemy to the integrity of our native land and our freedom demands the speedy adoption of measures for the strengthening of the discipline and fighting value of our Army." " Western Front—General Baluev: The present situation of Russia demands the immediate adoption of exceptional measures, and the retention of General Kornilov at the head of the Army is an imperative necessity, no matter what the political situation." " Roumanian Front—General Scherbachev: The dismissal of General Kornilov will infallibly have a fatal effect on the Army and the defence of the Motherland. I appeal to your patriotism in the name of the salvation of our native land." All the Commanders-in-Chief mentioned the necessity for the introduction of the measures demanded by Kornilov.

sive. A historic tragedy, played out far from us, lay like a thundercloud over Russia. And we waited, waited.

I shall never forget that night. Those hours still live in mental pictures. Successive telegrams by direct wire: Agreement apparently possible. No hopes of a peaceful issue. Supreme Command offered to Klembovsky. Klembovsky likely to refuse. One after another copies of telegrams to the Provisional Government from all Army Commanders of my Front, from General Oelssner and several other Senior Officers, voicing their adherence to the opinion expressed in my telegram. A touching fulfilment of their *civic duty* in an atmosphere saturated with hate and suspicion. Their *soldier's oath* they could no longer keep. Finally, the voice of despair from the Stavka. For that is the only name for the General Orders issued by Kornilov on the night of the 28th

The telegram of the Minister-President, No. 4163* in its entire first part is a downright lie: it was not I who sent Vv. N. Lvov, a member of the State Duma, to the Provisional Government. He came to me as a messenger from the Minister-President. My witness to this is Alexei Aladyin, member of the State Duma.

The great provocation, placing the Motherland on the turn of fate, is thus accomplished.

People of Russia. Our great Motherland is dying. Her end is near.

Forced to speak openly, I, General Kornilov, declare that the Provisional Government, under pressure from the Bolshevik majority in the Soviets, is acting in complete accordance with the plans of the German General Staff and simultaneously with the landing of enemy troops near Riga, is killing the Army, and convulsing the country internally.

The solemn certainty of the doom of our country drives me in these terrible times to call upon all Russians to save their dying native land. All in whose breasts a Russian heart still beats, all who believe in God, go into the Churches, pray Our Lord for the greatest miracle, the salvation of our dear country.

I, General Kornilov, son of a peasant Cossack, announce to all and everyone that I personally desire nothing save the preservation of our great Russia, and vow to lead the people, through victory over our enemies, to a Constituent Assembly, when they themselves will settle their fate and select the form of our new national life.

I cannot betray Russia into the hands of her ancient enemy—the German race!—and make the Russian people German slaves. And I prefer to die honourably on the field of battle, that I may not see the shame and degradation of our Russian land.

People of Russia, in your hands lies the life of your native land!

This order was despatched to the Army Commanders for their information. The next day one telegram from Kerensky was

---

* This telegram was not received at Headquarters. Kerensky gives the episode with Lvov thus: " On August 26th General Kornilov sent to me Vv. N. Lvov, member of the State Duma, with a demand that the Provisional Government should cede all its military and civil authority, leaving him to form a Government for the country in accordance with his own personal views."

received at the Commissariat, and from then all our communications with the outside world were interrupted.*

Well, the die was cast. A gulf had opened between the Government and the Stavka, to bridge which was now impossible.

On the following day, the 28th, the Revolutionary institutions, seeing that absolutely nothing threatened them, exhibited a feverish activity. Iordansky assumed the "military authority," made a series of unnecessary arrests in Zhitomir among the senior officials of the Chief Board of Supplies, and issued, under his signature and in his own name, that of the Revolutionary organisations and that of the Commissary of the Province, an appeal, telling, in much detail and in the usual language of proclamations, how General Denikin was planning "to restore the old régime and deprive the Russian people of Land and Freedom."

At the same time similar energetic work was being carried on in Berdichev under the guidance of the Frontal Committee. Meetings of all the organisations went on incessantly, along with the "education" of the typical rear units of the garrison. Here the accusation brought forward by the Committee was different: "The counter-Revolutionary attempt of the Commander-in-Chief, General Denikin, to overthrow the Provisional Government and restore Nicholas II. to the throne." Proclamations to this effect were circulated in numbers among the units, pasted on walls, and scattered from motor-cars careering through the town. The nervous tension increased, the streets were full of noise. The members of the Committee became more and more peremptory and exigent in their relations with Markov. Information was received of disorders which had arisen on the Lyssaya Gora (Bald Hill). The Staff sent officers thither to clear up the matter and determine the possibility of pacification. One of them—a Tchekh officer, Lieutenant Kletsando—who was to have spoken with the Austrian prisoners, was attacked by Russian soldiers, one of whom he wounded slightly. This circumstance increased the disturbance still more.

From my window I watched the crowds of soldiers gathering on the Lyssaya Gora, then forming in column, holding a prolonged meeting, which lasted about two hours, and apparently coming to no conclusion. Finally the column, which consisted of a troop of orderlies (formerly field military police), a reserve

---

* On the morning of the 29th a telegram from the Quartermaster-General at the Stavka somehow reached us, in which again hopes of a peaceful settlement were held out.

sotnia, and sundry other armed units, marched on the town with a number of red flags and headed by two armoured cars. On the appearance of an armoured car, which threatened to open fire, the Orenburg Cossack *sotnia,* which was on guard next the Staff quarters and the house of the Commander-in-Chief, scattered and galloped away. We found ourselves completely in the power of the Revolutionary Democracy.

" Revolutionary sentries" were posted round the house. The Vice-President of the Committee, Koltchinsky, led four armed " comrades " into the house for the purpose of arresting General Markov, but then began to hesitate, and confined himself to leaving in the reception-room of the Chief-of-Staff two " experts " from the Frontal Committee to control his work. The following wireless was sent to the Government: " General Denikin and all his staff have been subjected to personal detention at his Stavka. In the interests of the defence the guidance of the activity of the troops has been left in their hands, but is strictly controlled by the delegates of the Committee."

Now began a series of long, endless, wearisome hours. They will never be forgotten. Nor can words express the depth of the pain which now enveloped our hearts.

At 4 p.m. on the 29th Markov asked me into the reception-room, where Assistant-Commissary Kostitsin came with ten to fifteen armed Committee members and read me an " order from the Commissary of the South-Western Front, Iordansky," according to which I, Markov, and Quartermaster-General Orlov were to be subjected to preliminary arrest for an attempt at an armed rising against the Provisional Government. As a man of letters Iordansky seemed to have become ashamed of the arguments about " land," " freedom," and " Nicholas II.," designed exclusively for inflaming the passions of the mob.

I replied that a Commander-in-Chief could be removed from his post only by the Supreme Commander-in-Chief or by the Provisional Government; that Commissary Iordansky was acting altogether illegally, but that I was obliged to submit to force.

Motor-cars drove up, accompanied by armoured cars, and Markov and I took our seats. Then came the long waiting for Orlov, who was handing over the files; then the tormenting curiosity of the passers-by. Then we drove on to Lyssaya Gora. The car wandered about for a long time, halting at one building after another, until at last we drove up to the guard-house; we passed through a crowd of about a hundred men who were awaiting our arrival, and were greeted with looks full of hatred and with coarse abuse. We were taken into separate cells;

Kostitsin very civilly offered to send me any of my things I might require, but I brusquely declined any services from him; the door was slammed to, the key turned noisily in the lock, and I was alone.

In a few days the Stavka was liquidated. Kornilov, Loukomsky, Romanovsky, and others were taken off to the Bykhov Prison.

The Revolutionary Democracy was celebrating its victory.

Yet at that very time the Government was opening wide the doors of the prisons in Petrograd and liberating many influential Bolsheviks—to enable them to continue, publicly and openly, their work of destroying the Russian Empire.

On September 1 the Provisional Government arrested General Kornilov; on September 4 the Provisional Government liberated Bronstein Trotsky. These two dates should be memorable for Russia.

* * * *

Cell No. 1. The floor is some seven feet square. The window is closed with an iron grating. The door has a small peep-hole in it. The cell is furnished with a sleeping bench, a table, and a stool. The air is close—an evil-smelling place lies next door. On the other side is cell No. 2, with Markov in it; he walks up and down with large, nervous strides. Somehow or other I still remember that he makes three steps along his cell, while I manage, on a curve, to make five. The prison is full of vague sounds. The strained ear begins to distinguish them, and gradually to make out the course of prison life, and even its moods. The guards—I guess them to be soldiers of the prison guard company—are rough and revengeful men.

It is early morning. Someone's voice is booming. Whence? Outside of the window, clinging to the grating, hang two soldiers. They look at me with cruel, savage eyes, and hysterically utter terrible curses. They throw in something abominable through the open window. There is no escape from their gaze. I turn to the door—there another pair of eyes, full of hatred, peers through the peep-hole; thence choice abuse pours in also. I lie down on the sleeping-bench and cover my head with my cloak. I lie for hours. The whole day, one after another, the " public accusers " replace each other at the window and at the door—the guards allow all to come freely. And into the narrow, close kennel pours, in an unceasing torrent, a foul stream of words, shouts, and curses, born of immense ignorance, blind hate, and bottomless coarseness. One's whole soul seems to be drenched with that abuse, and there is no deliverance, no escape from this moral torture chamber.

What is it all about? " Wanted to open the Front " " sold himself to the Germans "—the sum, too, was mentioned— " for twenty thousand roubles " . . . " wanted to deprive us of land and freedom." This was not their own, this was borrowed from the Committee. But Commander-in-Chief, General, gentleman—this, indeed, was their own! " You have drunk our blood, ordered us about, kept us stewing in prison; now we are free and you can sit behind the bars yourself. You pampered yourself, drove about in motor-cars; now you can try what lying on a wooden bench is, you ——. You have not much time left. We shan't wait till you run away—we will strangle you with our own hands." These warriors of the rear scarcely knew me at all. But all that had been gathering for years, for centuries, in their exasperated hearts against the power they did not love, against the inequality of classes, because of personal grievances and of their shattered lives—for which someone or other was to blame— all this now came to the surface in the form of unmitigated cruelty. And the higher the standing of him who was reckoned the enemy of the people, and the deeper his fall, the more violent was the hostility of the mob and the greater the satisfaction of seeing him in its hands. Meanwhile, behind the wings of the popular stage stood the managers, who inflamed both the wrath and the delight of the populace; who did not believe in the villainy of the actors, but permitted them even to perish for the sake of greater realism in the performance and to the greater glory of their sectarian dogmatism. These motives of party policy, however, were called " tactical considerations."

I lay, covered head and all by my cloak and, under a shower of oaths, tried to see things clearly:

" What have I done to deserve this ? "

I went through the stages of my life. . . My father was a stern soldier with a most kindly heart. Up to thirty years of age he had been a peasant serf and was drafted into the Army, where, after twenty-two years of hard service in the ranks, under the severe discipline of the times of Nicholas I, he was promoted to the rank of 2nd Lieutenant. He retired with the rank of Major. My childhood was hard and joyless, amidst the poverty of a pension of 45 roubles a month. Then my father died. Life became still harder. My mother's pension was 25 roubles a month. My youth was passed in study and in working for my daily bread. I became a volunteer in the Army, messing in barracks with the privates. Then came my officer's commission, then the Staff College. The unfairness of my promotion, my complaint to the Emperor against the all-powerful Minister of War, and my return to the 2nd Artillery Brigade. My conflict with a moribund group of old adherents of serfdom; their accusation of demagogy. The General Staff. My practice command of a company in the 183rd Pultussk Regiment. Here I put an end to the system of striking the soldiers and made an unsuccessful experiment in " conscious discipline." Yes, Mr. Kerensky, I did this also in my younger days. I privately abolished disciplinary punishment—"watch one another, restrain the weak-spirited—after all, you are decent men —show that you can do your duty without the stick." I finished my command: during the year the behaviour of the company had not been above the average, it drilled poorly and lazily. After my departure the old Sergeant-Major, Stsepoura, gathered the company together, raised his fist significantly in the air and said distinctly, separating his words:

" Now it is not Captain Denikin whom you will have. Do you understand ? "

" Yes, Sergeant-Major."

It was said, afterwards, that the company soon showed improvement.

Then came the war in Manchuria; active service; hopes for the regeneration of the Army. Then an open struggle, in a stifled Press, with the higher command of the Army, against stagnation, ignorance, privileges and licence—a struggle for the welfare of the officer and the soldier. The times were stern—all my service, all my military career was at stake. Then came my command of a regiment, constant care for the improvement of the condition of the soldiers, after my Pultussk experience—strict service demands, but also respect for the human dignity of the soldier. At that time we seemed to understand one another and were not strangers. Then came war again, the " Iron " Division, nearer relations with the rifleman and work with him in common. The staff was always near the positions, so as to share mud, want of space, and dangers with the men. Then a long, laborious path, full of glorious battles, in which a common life, common sufferings and common fame brought us still closer together, and created a mutual faith and a touching proximity.

No, I have never been an enemy to the soldier.

I threw off my cloak, and, jumping from the wooden bed, went up to the window, where the figure of a soldier clung to the grating, belching forth curses.

" You lie, soldier! It is not your own words that you are speaking. If you are not a coward, hiding in the rear, if you have been in action, you have seen how your officers could die. You have seen that they. "

His hands loosened their grip and the figure disappeared. I think it was simply because of my stern address, which, despite the impotence of a prisoner, produced its usual effect.

Fresh faces appeared at the window and at the peep-hole in the door.

It was not always, however, that we met with insolence alone. Sometimes, through the assumed rudeness of our gaolers we could see a feeling of awkwardness, confusion and even commiseration. But of these feelings they were ashamed. On the first cold night, when we had none of our things, a guard brought Markov, who had forgotten his overcoat, a soldier's overcoat, but half an hour later—whether he had grown ashamed of his good action, or whether his comrades had shamed him—he took it back. In Markov's cursory notes we find: " We are looked after by two Austrian prisoners. . . . Besides them, we have as our caterer a soldier, formerly of the Finland Rifles (a Russian), a very kind and thoughtful man. During our first days he, too, had a hard time of it—his comrades gave him no peace; now, however, matters are all right; they have quieted down. His care for our food is simply touching, while the news he brings is delightful in its simplicity. Yesterday, he told me that he would miss us when we are taken away.

" I soothed him by saying that our places would soon be filled by new generals—that all had not yet been destroyed."

My heart is heavy. My feelings seem to be split in two : I hate and despise the savage, cruel, senseless mob, but still I feel the old pity for the soldier: an ignorant, illiterate man, who has been led astray, and is capable both of abominable crimes and of lofty sacrifices!

Soon the duty of guarding us was given to the cadets of the 2nd Zhitomir School of 2nd Lieutenants. Our condition became much easier from the moral point of view. They not only watched over the prisoners, but also guarded them from the mob. And the mob, more than once, on various occasions, gathered near the guard-room and roared wildly, threatening to lynch us. In such cases the company on guard gathered hastily in a house nearly opposite us and the cadets on guard made ready their machine-guns. I recall that, calmly and clearly realising my danger, when the mob was especially stormy, I planned out my method of self-defence: a heavy water-bottle stood upon my table; with it I might hit the first man to break into my cell; his blood would infuriate and intoxicate the " comrades," and they would kill me at once, without torturing me.

With the exception, however, of such unpleasant moments, our life in prison went on in a measured, methodical way; it was quiet and restful; after the strain of our campaigning, and in comparison with the moral suffering we had undergone, the physical inconveniences of the prison régime were mere trifles. Our life was varied by little incidents. Sometimes a Bolshevist cadet standing at the door would tell the sentry loudly, so that his words might be heard in the cell, that at their last meeting the comrades of Lyssaya Gora, having lost all patience, had finally decided to lynch us, and added that this was what we deserved. Another time, Markov, passing along the corridor, saw a cadet sentry leaning on his rifle, with the tears streaming from his eyes—he felt sorry for us. What a strange, unusual exhibition of sentiment in our savage days.

For a fortnight I did not leave my cell for exercise, not wishing to be an object of curiosity for the " comrades," who surrounded the square before the guard-room and examined the arrested generals as if they were beasts in a menagerie. I had no communication with my neighbours, but much time for meditation and thought.

And every day as I open my window I hear from the house opposite a high, tenor voice—whether of friend or foe I know not —singing:

" This is the last day that I ramble with you, my friends."

CHAPTER XXXIII.

In Berdichev Gaol—The Transfer of the " Berdichev Group "
of Prisoners to Bykhov

BESIDES Markov and me, whose share in events has been depicted in the preceding chapters, the following were cast into prison:

3. General Erdeli, Commander of the Special Army.

4. Lieutenant-General Varnovsky, Commander of the 1st Army.

5. Lieutenant-General Selivatchev, Commander of the 7th Army.

6. Lieutenant-General Elsner, Chief of Supplies to the South-Western Front.

The guilt of these men lay in their expression of solidarity with my telegram No. 145, and of the last, moreover, in his fulfilment of my orders for the isolation of the frontal region wtih respect to Kiev and Zhitomir.

7 and 8. General Elsner's assistants—General Parsky and General Sergievsky—men who had absolutely no connection with events.

9. Major-General Orlov, Quartermaster-General of the Staff of the Front—a wounded man with a withered arm, timid, and merely carrying out the orders of the Chief-of-Staff.

10. Lieutenant Kletsando, of the Tchekh troops, who had wounded a soldier of Lyssaya Gora on August 28th.

11. Captain Prince Krapotkin, a man over sixty years of age, a Volunteer, and the Commandant of the Commander-in-Chief's train. He was not initiated into events at all.

General Selivatchev, General Parsky and General Sergievsky were soon released. Prince Krapotkin was informed on September 6th that his actions had not been criminal, but was set free only on September 23rd, when it appeared that we were not to be tried at Berdichev. For a charge of rebellion to hold good against us an association of eight men at the very least had to be discovered. Our antagonists were much interested in this figure, being desirous of observing the rules of decorum. . There was another prisoner, however, kept in reserve and separate from us, at the Commandant's office, and even afterwards transferred to Bykhov—a military official named Boudilovitch—a youth weak in body, but strong in spirit, who on one occasion dared to tell a wrathful mob that it was not worth the little finger of those whom it was maltreating.* No other crime was imputed to him.

On the second or third day of my imprisonment I read in a newspaper, which had accidentally or purposely found its way into my cell, an order from the Provisional Government to the Senate, dated August 29th, which ran as follows:

" Lieutenant-General Denikin, Commander-in-Chief of the Armies of the South-Western Front, to be removed from the post of Commander-in-Chief and brought to trial for rebellion.— Signed: Minister-President A. Kerensky and B. Savinkov—in charge of the War Ministry."

On the same date similar orders were issued concerning Generals Kornilov, Lukomsky, Markov and Kisliakov. Later an order was issued for the removal of General Romanovsky.

On the second or the third day of my arrest the guard-room was visited, for our examination, by a Committee of Investigation, under the superintendence of the Chief Field Prosecutor of the Front, General Batog, and under the presidency of Assistant Commissar Kostitsin, consisting of:

Lieutenant-Colonel Shestoperov, in charge of the Juridical Section of the Commissariat; Lieutenant-Colonel Frank, of the Kiev Military Court; 2nd Lieut. Oudaltsov and Junior Sergeant of Artillery Levenberg, members of the Committee of the Front.

My evidence, in view of the facts of the case, was very short, and consisted of the following statements: (1) None of the persons arrested with me had taken part in any active proceedings against the Government; (2) all orders given to and through the Staff during my last days, in connection with General Kornilov's venture, proceeded from me; (3) I considered, and still consider, that the activity of the Provisional Government is criminal and ruinous for Russia, but that nevertheless I had not instituted a rebellion against it, but having sent my telegram No. 145, I had left it to the Provisional Government to take such action towards me as it might see fit.

---

* He went through the Kouban campaigns with the Volunteer Army and served in it to the day of his death, from spotted typhus, in 1920.

In Berdichev Gaol

Later the Chief Military Prosecutor, Shablovsky, having acquainted himself with the material of the investigation and with the circumstances which had arisen around it in Berdichev, was horrified at the " uncautious formulation " of my evidence.

By September 1st Iordansky was already reporting to the War Ministry that the Committee of Investigation had discovered documents establishing the existence of a conspiracy which had long been preparing. . . . At the same time, Iordansky, man of letters, inquired of the Government whether, in the matter of the direction of the cases of the Generals arrested, he could act within the limits of the law, *in conformity with local circumstances*, or whether he was bound to be guided by any *political considerations* of the Central Authority. In reply he was informed that he must act reckoning with the law alone and *taking into consideration local circumstances*.*

In view of this explanation, Iordansky decided to commit us for trial by a Revolutionary Court-Martial, to which end a Court was formed of members of one of the Divisions formerly subordinated to me at the Front, while Captain Pavlov, member of the Executive Committee of the South-Western Front, was marked down for public prosecutor.

Thus the interests of competency, impartiality and fair play were observed.

Iordansky was so anxious to obtain a speedy verdict for myself and for the Generals imprisoned with me that on September 3rd he proposed that the Commission, without waiting for the elucidation of the circumstances, should present the cases to the Revolutionary Court-Martial in groups, as the guilt of one or other of the accused was established.

We were much depressed by our complete ignorance of what was taking place in the outer world.

On rare occasions Kostitsin acquainted us with the more important current events, but in the Commissar's comments on the events only depressed us still more. It was clear, however, that the Government was breaking up altogether, that Bolshevism was raising its head higher and higher, and that the country must inevitably perish.

About September 8th or 10th, when the investigation was over, our prison surroundings underwent, to some extent, a change. Newspapers began to appear in our cells almost daily; at first secretly, afterwards, from September 22nd, officially. At the same time, after the relief of one of the Companies of Guards, we

---

* Official communication.

decided to try an experiment: during our exercise in the corridor I approached Markov and started talking with him; the sentries did not interfere. From that time we began talking with one another every day; sometimes the sentries demanded that we should stop, and then we were silent at once, but more frequently they did not interfere. In the second half of September visitors also were allowed; the curiosity of the " comrades " of Lyssaya Gora was now apparently satisfied; fewer of them gathered about the square, and I used to go out to walk every day, was able to see all the prisoners and exchange a few words with them now and again. Now, at least, we knew what was doing in the world, while the possibility of meeting one another removed the depression caused by isolation.

From the papers we learned that the investigation of the Kornilov case was committed to the Supreme Investigation Committee, presided over by the Chief Military and Naval Prosecutor, Shablovsky.*

About September 9th, in the evening, a great noise and the furious shouts of a large crowd were heard near the prison. In a little while four strangers entered my cell—confused and much agitated by something or other. They said they were the President and members of the Supreme Committee of Investigation for the Kornilov case.†

Shablovsky, in a still somewhat broken voice, began to explain that the purpose of their arrival was to take us off to Bykhov, and that, judging by the temper which had developed in Berdichev, and by the fury of the mob which now surrounded the prison, they could see that there were no guarantees for justice here, but only savage revenge. He added that the Committee had no doubt as to the inadmissibility of any segregation of our cases, and as to the necessity of a common trial for all the participators in the Kornilov venture, but that the Commissariat and the Committees were using all means against this. The Committee, therefore, asked me whether I would not wish to supplement my evidence by any facts which might yet more clearly establish the connection between our case and Kornilov's. In view of the impossibility of holding the examination amidst the roar of the crowd which had gathered, they decided to postpone it to the following day.

The Committee departed; soon after the crowd dispersed.

---

* The members of the Commission were: Col. Raupach and Col. Oukraintsev, military jurists; Kolokolov, examining magistrate; and Lieber and Krochmal, members of the Executive Committee of the Soviet of Workmen's and Soldiers' delegates.

† Shablovsky, Kolokolov, Raupach and Oukraintsev.

What more could I tell them? Only, perhaps, something of the advice which Kornilov had given me at Moghilev, and through a messenger. But this was done as a matter of exceptional confidence on the part of the Supreme Commander-in-Chief, which I could in no case permit myself to break. Therefore, the few details which I added next day to my original evidence did not console the commission and did not, apparently, satisfy the volunteer, a member of the Committee of the Front, who was present at the examination.

Nevertheless, we waited with impatience for our liberation from the Berdichev chamber of torture. But our hopes were clouded more and more. The newspaper of the Committee of the Front methodically fomented the passions of the garrison; it was reported that at all the meetings of all the Committees resolutions were passed against letting us out of Berdichev; the Committee members were agitating mightily among the rear units of the garrison, and meetings were held which passed off in a spirit of great exaltation.

The aim of the Shablovsky Commission was not attained. As it turned out in the beginning of September, to Shablovsky's demand that a separate trial of the " Berdichev group " should not be allowed, Iordansky replied that " to say nothing of the transfer of the generals to any place whatsoever, even the least postponement of their trial would threaten Russia with incalculable calamities—complications at the front, and a new civil war in the rear," and that both on political and on tactical grounds it was necessary to have us tried in Berdichev, in the shortest possible time, and by Revolutionary Court-Martial." *

The Committee of the Front and the Kiev Soviet of Workmen's and Soldiers' Delegates would not agree to our transfer, despite all the arguments and persuasions brought forward at their meeting by Shablovsky and the members of his Commission. On the way back, at Moghilev, a consultation took place on this question between Kerensky, Shablovsky, Iordansky and Batog. All, excepting Shablovsky, came to the altogether unequivocal conclusion that the front was shaken, that the soldiery was restless and demanding a victim, and that it was necessary to enable the tense atmosphere to discharge itself, even at the cost of injustice.
Shablovsky rose and declared that he would not permit such a cynical attitude toward law and justice.

I remember that this tale perplexed me. It is not worth while disputing about points of view. But if the Minister-President is

---

* Shablovsky's interview in the " Retch."

convinced that in the matter of protecting the State it is admissible to let oneself be guided by expediency, in what way, then, was Kornilov to blame?

On September 14th a debate took place in Petrograd, in the last " court of appeal "—in the military section of the Executive Committee of the Council of Workmen's and Soldiers' Delegates —between Shablovsky and the representative of the Committee of the South-Western Front, fully supported by Iordansky. The last two declared that if the Revolutionary Court-Martial was not held on the spot, in Berdichev, in the course of the next five days the lynching of the prisoners was to be feared. However, the Central Committee agreed with Shablovsky's arguments, and sent its resolution to that effect to Berdichev.

So an organised lynching was prevented. But the Revolutionary institutions of Berdichev had at their service another method for liquidating the " Berdichev group," an easy and irresponsible one—the method of popular wrath. . , .

A rumour spread that we were to be taken away on the 23rd, then it was stated that our departure would take place on the 27th at 5 p.m. from the passenger station.

To take the prisoners away without making the fact public was in no way difficult: in a motor-car, on foot in a column of cadets, or, again, in a railway carriage—a narrow gauge-line came close up to the guard-house and joined on to the broad gauge-line outside the town and the railway station.* But such a method of transferring us did not agree with the intentions of the Commissariat and the Committees.

General Doukhonin inquired from the Stavka, of the Staff of the Front, whether there were any reliable units in Berdichev, and offered to send a detachment to assist in our move. The Staff of the Front declined assistance. The Commander-in-Chief, General Volodchenko, had left on the eve, the 26th, for the Front

Much talk and an unhealthy atmosphere of expectation and curiosity were being artificially created around this question. . . .

Kerensky sent a telegram to the Commissariat: " I am sure of the prudence of the garrison, which may elect, from among its numbers, two representatives to accompany."

In the morning the Commissariat began visiting all the units in the garrison, to obtain their consent to our transfer.

The Committee had appointed a meeting of the whole garrison for 2 p.m., *i.e.*, three hours before our departure, and in the field,

---

* On that same morning we had been taken without any escort, with only one guard accompanying us, to the bath, about two-thirds of a mile from the guard-house, without attracting any attention.

moreover, immediately beside our prison. This mass meeting did indeed take place; at it the representatives of the Commissaria and of the Committee of the Front announced the orders for our transfer to Bykhov, thoughtfully announced the hour of our departure and appealed to the garrison . . . to be prudent; the meeting continued for a long time and, of course, did not disperse. By 5 o'clock an excited crowd of thousands of men had surrounded the guard-room, and its dull murmur made its way into the building

Among the officers of the Cadet Battalion of the 2nd Zhitomir School of 2nd Lieutenants, which was on guard this day, was Captain Betling, wounded in many battles, who before the War had served in the 17th Archangelogorod Infantry Regiment, which I commanded.* Betling asked the superior officer of the School to replace by his half-company the detachment appointed to accompany the prisoners to the railway station. We all dressed and came out into the corridor. We waited. An hour, two hours passed. . . .

The meeting continued. Numerous speakers called for an immediate lynching. . . . The soldier who had been wounded by Lieutenant Kletsando was shouting hysterically and demanding his head. . . . Standing in the porch of the guard-room, Assistant Commissaries Kostitsin and Grigoriev were trying persuasion with the mob. That dear Betling, too, spoke several times, hotly and passionately. We could not hear his words.

At last, pale and agitated, Betling and Kostitsin came up to me.

" How will you decide? The crowd has promised not to touch anyone, only it demands that you should be taken to the station on foot. But we cannot answer for anything."

I replied

" Let us go."

I took off my cap and crossed myself:

" Lord, bless us ! "

* *

The crowd raged. We, the seven of us, surrounded by a group of cadets, headed by Betling, who marched by my side with drawn sword, entered the narrow passage through this living human sea, which pressed on us from all sides. In front were

---

* This gallant officer was afterwards one of the first Volunteers, was wounded again in Kornilov's first Kouban campaign in 1918, and died in the spring of 1919 of spotted typhus.

Kostitsin and the delegates (twelve to fifteen) chosen by the garrison to escort us. Night was coming on, and in its eerie gloom, with the rays of the searchlight on the armoured car cutting through it now and then, moved the raving mob, growing and rolling on like a flaming avalanche. The air was full of a deafening roar, hysterical shouts, and mephitic curses. At times they were covered by Betling's loud, anxious voice

" Comrades, you have given your word! . . . Comrades, you have given your word! "

The cadets, those splendid youths, crushed together on all sides, push aside with their bodies the pressing crowd, which disorders their thin ranks. Passing the pools left by yesterday's rain, the soldiers fill their hands with mud and pelt us with it. Our faces, eyes, ears, are covered with its fetid, viscid slime. Stones come flying at us. Poor, crippled General Orlov has his face severely bruised; Erdeli and I, as well, were struck—in the back and on the head.

On our way we exchanged monosyllabic remarks. I turned to Markov:

" What, my dear Professor, is this the end? "

" Apparently. "

The mob would not let us come up to the station by the straight path. We were taken by a roundabout way, some three miles altogether, through the main streets of the town. The crowd is growing. The balconies of the Berdichev houses are full of curious spectators; the women wave their handkerchiefs. Gay, guttural voices come from above:

" Long live freedom! "

The railway station is flooded with light. There we find a new, vast crowd of several thousand people. And all this has merged in the general sea which rages and roars. With enormous difficulty we are brought through it under a hail of curses and of glances full of hatred. The railway carriage. An officer—Elsner's son—sobbing hysterically and addressing impotent threats to the mob, and his soldier servant, lovingly soothing him, as he takes away his revolver; two women, dumb with horror—Kletsando's wife and sister, who had thought to see him off. . . .

We wait for an hour, for another. The train is not allowed to leave—a prisoner's car is demanded. There were none at the station. The mob threatens to do for the Commissaries. Kostitsin is slightly buffeted. A goods car is brought, all defiled with horse-dung—what a trifle! We enter it without the assistance of a platform; poor Orlov is lifted in with difficulty; hundreds of hands are stretched towards us through the firm and steady ranks of the cadets. . It is already 10 p.m. The engine gives a jerk. The crowd booms out still louder. Two shots are heard. The train starts.

The noise dies away, the lights grow dimmer. Farewell Berdichev!

Kerensky shed a tear of delight over the self-abnegation of " our saviours "—as he called—not the cadets, but the Commissaries and the Committee members.

" What irony of fate! General Denikin, arrested as Kornilov's accomplice, was saved from the rage of the frenzied soldiers by the members of the Executive Committee of the South-Western Front and by the Commissaries of the Provisional Government."

" I remember with what agitation I and the never-to-be-forgotten Doukhonin read the account of how a handful of these brave men escorted the arrested generals through a crowd of thousands of soldiers who were thirsting for their blood. . . ."*
Why slander the dead? Certainly, Doukhonin was no less anxious for the fate of the prisoners than for the fate of their revolutionary escort. . . .

That Roman citizen, Pontius Pilate, smiled mockingly through the gloom of the ages. . . ,

---

* The Kornilov case.

CHAPTER XXXIV.

SOME CONCLUSIONS AS TO THE FIRST PERIOD OF THE REVOLUTION.

HISTORY will not soon give us a picture of the Revolution in a broad, impartial light. Those prospects which are now opening out to our view are sufficient only to enable us to grasp certain particular phenomena in it and, perhaps, to reject the prejudices and misconceptions which have sprung up around them.

The Revolution was inevitable. It is called a Revolution of the whole people. This is correct only in so far as the Revolution was the Result of the discontent of literally all classes of the population with the old power. But upon the question of its achievements opinions were divided, and deep breaches were bound to appear between classes on the very next day after the downfall of the old Power.

The Revolution was many-faced. For the peasants—the ownership of the land; for the workmen—the ownership of profits; for the Liberal Bourgeoisie—changed political conditions of life in the land and moderate social reforms; for the Revolutionary Democracy—power and the maximum of social achievement; for the Army—absence of authority and the cessation of the War.

With the downfall of the power of the Czar, there was left in the country, until the summoning of a Constituent Assembly, no lawful power, no power that had a juridical basis. This is perfectly natural and follows from the very nature of a Revolution. But whether through genuine misconception or deliberately perverting the truth, men have fabricated theories, known to be false, about the " general popular origin of the Provisional Government " or about the " full powers of the Soviet of Workmen's and Soldiers' Delegates," as an organ supposed to represent the " whole of the Russian Democracy." What an elastic conscience one must have, if, while professing democratic principles and protesting violently against the slightest deviation from orthodox conditions of the lawfulness of elections, one can still ascribe full powers, as

The First Period of the Revolution

the organ of democracy, to the Petrograd Soviet or to the Congress of Soviets, the election of which is of an extraordinary simplified and one-sided character. It was not without reason that for a long time the Petrograd Soviet hesitated to publish lists of its members. As to the supreme Power, to say nothing of its "popular origin" from a "private meeting of the State Duma," the technique of its construction was so imperfect that repeated crises might have put an end to its very existence and to every trace of its continuity. Finally, a really "popular" Government could not have remained isolated, left by all to the will of a group of usurpers of authority. That same Government which, in the days of March, so easily obtained general recognition. Recognition, yes, but not practical support.

After March 3rd, and up to the Constituent Assembly, *every* supreme authority bore the marks of self-assumed power, and *no* power could satisfy all classes of the population, in view of the irreconciliableness of their interests and the intemperance of their desires.

Neither of the ruling powers (the Provisional Government and the Soviet) enjoyed the due support of the *majority*. For this majority (80 per cent.) said, through its representatives in the Consituent Assembly of 1918: " We peasants make no difference between parties; parties fight for power, while our peasant business is the land alone." But even if, forestalling the will of the Constituent Assembly, the Provisional Government had satisfied these desires of the majority in full, it could not have reckoned on this majority's immediate submission to the general interests of the State, nor on its *active* support: engaged in the redistribution of the land, which also had a strong attraction for the elements at the Front, the peasantry would scarcely have given the State, voluntarily, the forces and the means for putting it in order, *i.e.* plenty of corn and plenty of soldiers—brave, faithful and obedient to the law. Even then the Government would have been faced with insoluble problems: an Army which did not fight, an unproductive industry, a transport system which was being broken down and . the civil war of parties.

Let us, therefore, set aside the popular and democratic origin of the Provisional authority. Let it be self-assumed, as it has been in the history of all revolutions and of all peoples. But the very fact of the wide recognition of the Provisional Government gave it a vast advantage over all the other forces which disputed its authority. It was necessary, however, that this power should become so strong, so absolute in its nature, so autocratic, as, having crushed all opposition by force, perhaps by arms, to have led the country to a Constituent Assembly, elected in surroundings which did not admit of the falsification of the popular vote, and to have protected this Assembly.

We are apt to abuse the words " elemental force," as an excuse for many phenomena of the Revolution. That " molten element " which swept Kerensky away with the greatest ease, has it not fallen into the iron grip of Lenin-Bronstein and, for more than three years, been unable to escape from Bolshevist duress?

If such a power, harsh, but inspired by reason and by a true desire for popular rule, had assumed authority and, having crushed the *licence* into which *freedom* had been transmuted, had led this authority to a Constituent Assembly, the Russian people would have blessed, not condemned it. In such a position will every provisional authority find itself which accepts the heritage of Bolshevism; and Russia will judge it, not by the juridical marks of its origin, but by its works.

Why is the overthrow of the incompetent authority of the old Government to be an achievement, to the memory of which the Provisional Government proposed erecting a monument in the Capital, while the attempt to overthrow the incompetent authority of Kerensky, made by Kornilov, after exhausting all lawful means and after provocation on the part of the Minister-President, is to be counted rebellion?

But the need for a powerful authority is far from being exhausted by the period preceding the Constituent Assembly. Did not the Assembly of 1918 call in vain on the country, not for submission, but simply for protection from physical outrage on the part of the turbulent sailor horde? Yet not a hand was raised in its defence. Let us grant that *that* Assembly, born in an atmosphere of mutiny and violence, did not express the will of the Russian people and that the future Assembly will reflect that will more perfectly. I think, however, that even those who have the most exalted faith in the infallibility of the democratic principle do not close their eyes to the unbounded possibilities of the future which will be the heritage of such a physical and psychological transformation in the people as is unknown to history and has never yet been investigated by anyone.

Who knows whether it may not be necessary to confirm the democratic principle, the authority itself of the Constituent Assembly, and its commands, by iron and fresh bloodshed. . . .

Be that as it may, the *outward* recognition of the Provisional Government took place. It would be difficult and useless to separate, in the work of the Government, that which proceeded from its free will and sincere convictions from what bears the stamp of the forcible influence of the Soviet. If Tzeretelli was entitled to declare that " there has never yet been a case when, in important questions, the Provisional Government has not been ready to come to an agreement," so have we the right to identify their work and their responsibility.

All this activity, *volens nolens*, bore the character of destruction, not creation. The Government repealed, abolished, disbanded, permitted. . In this lay the centre of gravity of its work. I picture to myself the Russia of that period as a very old house, in need of capital reconstruction. In the absence of means and while waiting for the building season (the Constituent Assembly), the builders began extracting the decayed girders, some of which they did not replace at all, others they replaced with light, temporary props, and others again they reinforced with new baulks without fastenings—the latter means turning out to be the worst. And the house crashed down. The causes of such a method of building were first: the absence of a complete and symmetrical plan among the Russian political parties, the whole energy, mental and will tension of which were directed mainly towards the destruction of the former order. For we cannot give the name of practical plans to the abstract outlines of the party programmes; they are rather lawful or unlawful diplomas for the right of building. Secondly—that the new ruling classes did not possess the most elementary technical knowledge of the art of ruling, as the result of a systematic, age-long setting them aside from these functions. Thirdly—the non-forestalling of the will of the Constituent Assembly, which, in any case, called for heroic measures for its summoning, and therewith no less heroic measures for securing real freedom of election. Fourthly—the odiousness of all that bore the stamp of the old order, even though it were sound at bottom. Fifthly—the self-conceit of the political parties, each of which individually represented the " will of the whole people " and was distinguished by extreme irreconcilableness towards its antagonists.

I might probably continue this list for a long time, but I shall pause on one fact which has a significance which is far from being confined to the past. The Revolution was expected, it was prepared, but *no one*, not a single one of the political groups *had prepared itself for it*. And the Revolution came by night, finding everyone, like the foolish virgins in the Gospel, with lamps unlit. One cannot explain and excuse everything by elemental forces alone. No one had troubled to construct beforehand a general plan of the canals and sluices necessary to prevent the inundation from becoming a flood. Not one of the leading parties possessed a programme for the interregnum in the life of the country, a programme which, in its character and scale, could not correspond with normal plans of construction, either in the system of administration or in the sphere of economic and social relations. It would scarcely be an exaggeration to say that the only assets in the possession of the progressive and Socialist blocks on March 27th, 1917, were: for the former—the choice for the post of Minister-President of Prince Lvov, for the latter—the Soviets and Order No. 1. After this began the convulsive, unsystematic vacillation of the Government and of the Soviet.

It is to be regretted that this difference, which constitutes a marked distinction between two periods—the provisional and the constructive—two systems, two programmes, has not yet become sufficiently clear in public consciousness.

The whole period of the active struggle with Bolshevism passed under the sign of the mingling of these two systems, of divergent views and of incapacity to construct a provisional form of authority. It would seem that now, too, the anti-Bolshevist forces, while increasing the divergence of their views and building plans for the future, are not preparing for the process of assuming the power after the downfall of Bolshevism, and will again approach the task with naked hands and wavering mind. Only now the process will be immeasurably more difficult. For the second excuse—after " elemental forces "—for the failure of the Revolution, or rather of its leading men—" the heritage of the Czarist régime "—has paled very much on the background of the sanguinary Bolshevist mist which has enveloped the land of Russia.

* * *

The new power (the Provisional Government) was faced by a question of the first importance—the War. On its decision rested the fate of the country. The decision in favour of continuing the alliance and the War rested on ethical motives, which at that time did not rouse any doubts, and on practical motives, which were in some degree disputable. Now, even the former have been shaken, since both the Allies and the enemy have treated the fate of Russia with cruel, cynical egotism. Nevertheless, I have no doubt of the correctness of the decision then taken to continue the War. Many suppositions might be made as to the possibilities of a separate peace—whether that of Brest-Litovsk or one less grievous for the State and for our national self-love. But it is to be thought that such a peace in the spring of 1917 would have led either to the dismemberment of Russia and her economic *débâcle* (a general peace at the expense of Russia), or to the complete victory of the Central Powers over our Allies, which would have produced incomparably deeper convulsions in their countries than those which the German people are now experiencing. Both in the one case and in the other, no objective data would be present for any change for the better in the political, social and economic conditions of Russian life and any turning of the Russian Revolution into other channels. Only, besides Bolshevism, Russia would have added to her liabilities the hatred of the defeated for many years.

Having decided to fight, it was necessary to preserve the Army by admitting a certain conservatism into it. Such a conservatism serves as a guarantee for the stability of the Army and of that authority which seeks support in it. If the participation of the Army in historical cataclysms cannot be avoided, neither can it be turned into an arena for political struggle, creating, instead of the principle of service—*pretorians or opritchniks*, whether of the Czar, of the Revolutionary Democracy, or of any party is a matter of indifference.

The Army was broken up.

On those principles which the Revolutionary Democracy took as a basis for the existence of the Army, the latter could neither build nor live. It was no mere chance that all the later attempts at armed conflict with Bolshevism began with the organisation of an Army on the normal principles of military administration, to which the Soviet command as well sought to pass gradually. No elemental circumstances, no errors on the part of military dictatorships and of the powers co-operating with or opposing them which led to the failure of the struggle (of this some truths will be spoken later) are able to cast this undeniable fact into the shade. Nor is it a mere chance that the leading circles of the Revolutionary Democracy could create no armed forces, except that pitiful parody on them—the " National Army " on the so-called " front of the Constituent Assembly." It was just this circumstance that led the Russian Socialist emigrants to the theory of non-resistance, of the negation of armed struggle, to the concentration of all their hopes on the inner degeneration of Bolshevism and its overthrow by some immaterial " forces of the people themselves," which, however, could not express themselves otherwise than by blood and iron : " the great, bloodless " Revolution is drowned in blood from its beginning to its end.

To refuse to consider that vast question—the re-creation of a National Army on firm principles—is not to solve it.

What then ? On the day that Bolshevism falls will peace and good-will immediately show forth in a land corrupted by a slavery worse than that of the Tartar yoke, saturated with dissension, revenge, hatred, and . . . an enormous quantity of arms? Or, from that day forward, will the self-interested desires of many foreign Governments disappear, or will they grow stronger when the menace of the moral infection of the Soviet has vanished? Finally, even should the whole of old Europe, morally regenerated, beat out its swords into ploughshares, is it impossible for a new Tchingiz-Khan to come out of the depths of that Asia which has accounts age-long and huge beyond measure, against Europe?

The Army will be regenerated. Of that there can be no doubt.

Shaken in its historical foundations and traditions, like the heroes of the Russian legends, it will stand for no short time at the cross-roads, gazing anxiously into the misty distances, still wrapped in the gloom before the dawn, and listening intently to the vague sounds of the voices calling to it. And among the delusive calls it will seek, straining its hearing to the utmost, for the real voice — the voice of its own people.

Printed in Great Britain
by Amazon